Lost Letters of Medieval Life

[illegible] ... si vacat ... [illegible] ... nostres ... fideles ... [illegible]

Comes extreme comiti de alta marcha salutem. Assuetudine [illegible] id quod ab ... cessat ... [illegible] ... que colentes rudes reddit longa ... desidie ... temporibus amonet ... frequenter torneamenta ... quod inter nos ... tornetur de illo loco ... affidatum. Ad quod ut veniatis ... [illegible] ... ad castellum ... et in vallo ... [illegible] ... consideravimus ... [illegible]

Comes comiti salutem. ... [illegible] ... Quia ... [illegible] ... post ... et ... [illegible] ... nostrorum gesta recolentes ... [illegible] ... hostibus in bello ... debuerunt ... [illegible] ... ad honorem ... [illegible]

Comes baroni salutem. Ad vos ... [illegible] ... de mera ... libertate ... Vos rogamus ... [illegible] ... nobis ... [illegible] ... defendenda ... debeatis ... [illegible]

Comiti baro salutem. ... [illegible] ... fide ... [illegible] ... nos ... [illegible] ... comitiones ... [illegible] ... negociis ... [illegible] ... scribere.

Baro baroni salutem. Bona communicata ... [illegible] ... in loco ... [illegible] ... et piscium abundanciam ... [illegible] ... nobis duos ... [illegible] ... et duos ... [illegible] ... que ... placet ... [illegible] ... destinassem.

Baro baroni salutem. A quodam milite socio nostro didicimus quod ... [illegible] ... reclamandum ... [illegible] ... nobis ... [illegible] ... filius vestro ... [illegible] ... filium ... nobis ... [illegible] ... volare ...

Lost Letters of Medieval Life

English Society, 1200–1250

EDITED AND TRANSLATED BY

Martha Carlin and David Crouch

PENN

University of Pennsylvania Press

Philadelphia

THE MIDDLE AGES SERIES
Ruth Mazo Karras, Series Editor
Edward Peters, Founding Editor
A complete list of books in the series is available from the publisher.

Published by
University of Pennsylvania Press
Philadelphia, Pennsylvania 19104-4112
www.upenn.edu/pennpress

Printed in the United States of America on acid-free paper

10 9 8 7 6 5 4 3 2 1

Library of Congress Cataloging-in-Publication Data

Lost letters of medieval life : English society, 1200-1250 / edited and translated by Martha Carlin and David Crouch.
    p. cm. (The Middle Ages series)
    Includes bibliographical references and indexes.
    ISBN: 978-0-8122-4459-5 (hardcover : alk. paper)
    1. England—Civilization—1066-1485—Sources.   2. Letter writing—Early works to 1800.
3. England—Social life and customs—1066-1485—Sources.   I. Carlin, Martha.   II. David
Crouch. III. Series: The Middle Ages series.
DA170 .L67   2013
942.03′4
                                                                              2012023969

Frontispiece: Bodleian Library, Oxford, Fairfax MS 27, fol. 4v. The four texts that begin with a "C" are DOCUMENTS 65–68; the two texts that begin with a "B" are DOCUMENT 61 and the beginning of DOCUMENT 62.

CONTENTS

CHAPTER 2. WAR AND POLITICS   99

War   99

Politics   124

CHAPTER 4. FAMILY AND COMMUNITY   219

News, Gossip, and Family   219

Student Life   245

ILLUSTRATIONS

PREFACE

In 1847 the English antiquary Thomas Hudson Turner published a brief note about a manuscript that recently had come to his notice, and which contained a collection of model business correspondence.[1] Turner included tantalizing transcriptions of three letters, all in Latin, between an earl and the merchants who supplied him with wine, cloth, and furs. However, other than saying that the collection dated from the reign of Henry III (1216–72), he provided no detailed description of its contents and no means of identifying the manuscript itself. But such as it was, this was the first printed notice of the work that provides the bulk of the documents in this collection.

Intrigued by Turner's extracts from the business correspondence, of which few examples survive from thirteenth-century England, Martha Carlin searched for the manuscript and located it at last in the British Library, where it formed one section (Article 5, folios 88–133) of a larger volume, Additional MS 8167 (hereafter Add. 8167). Turner's letters proved to be drawn from a formulary, a collection of model correspondence designed for the instruction of business students.

Although Turner's article of 1847 seems to have escaped later scholarly notice, a number of scholars since his day have also noted the existence of the formulary material in Add. 8167. In 1879 Georg Waitz printed a description of urban trades and crafts that occurs on folios 88r–90v but did not discuss the other contents of Article 5 or of the manuscript more generally. Waitz also mistakenly identified the manuscript as dating from the fourteenth century.[2] Charles Homer Haskins printed one of the student letters in the collection in 1898.[3] In 1935 Noël Denholm-Young discussed the model manorial account in Add. 8167,[4] and shortly afterward H. G. Richardson described Article 5 in some detail and identified it as containing the earliest English formulary.[5] In 1947 and again in 1971, Dorothea Oschinsky briefly discussed the formulary's material on estate accounting.[6] More recently, Martin Camargo examined the significance of Add. 8167 in the history of *dictamen* (the art of letter-writing) in England,[7] and Christopher Woolgar mentioned the model diet account in Add. 8167 in his study of medieval household accounts.[8] Each of these scholars, however, focused on individual elements of the formulary; none of them remarked on the extraordinary range of the documents themselves or their significance as a collection.

As our study of the documents expanded we discovered that, despite Richardson's belief that Add. 8167 was the oldest English formulary, several other collections (discussed below) were even earlier. A particularly rich and important one is in the Bodleian Library, where it forms part of Fairfax MS 27 (hereafter Fairfax 27). As we planned out the project that has become this book, it was clear that the letters in Fairfax 27 form a significant complement to the material in Add. 8167. This book therefore is a selection of letters and other documents drawn from these two early thirteenth-century formularies. They allow us to rediscover a lost medieval world through the model documents they preserve, which represent whole classes of genuine letters and other material that have not survived to the present day because they were discarded as of no lasting importance. Luckily, we can infer their existence and character from these surviving exemplars. It has to be said that the selection of material was the easy part. One reason why this is the first serious study of these documents is they are by no means easy to read. Many of them were ineptly drafted, and clumsily transcribed and altered by the medieval copyists, a not unusual feature in what were classroom products.[9] Recovering their sense was frequently a frustrating task, but the importance of the material meant that it was a worthwhile and necessary endeavor.

NOTES

1 Thomas Hudson Turner, "Original Documents," *Archaeological Journal*, 4 (1847), 142–44.

2 Georg Waitz, *Neues Archiv*, 4 (1879), 339–43. Martha Carlin has printed a corrected transcription and a translation of this text in "Shops and Shopping in the Early Thirteenth Century: Three Texts," in *Money, Markets and Trade in Late Medieval Europe: Essays in Honour of John H. A. Munro*, ed. Lawrin Armstrong, Ivana Elbl, and Martin M. Elbl (Leiden: Brill, 2007), 491–537.

3 Charles Homer Haskins, "The Life of Medieval Students as Illustrated by Their Letters," *American Historical Review*, 3, no. 2 (January 1898), 210, n. 2; rpt. in idem, *Studies in Mediaeval Culture* (New York: Oxford University Press, 1929), 10. This letter is DOCUMENT 81 in our collection.

4 See Noël Denholm-Young, "Robert Carpenter and the Provisions of Westminster," *English Historical Review*, 50 (1935), 22–35, rpt. in idem, *Collected Papers on Mediaeval Subjects* (Oxford: Basil Blackwell, 1946), 96–110; and again in idem, *Collected Papers* (Cardiff: University of Wales Press, 1969), 173–86. See also idem, *Seignorial Adminstration in England* (London: Oxford University Press, 1937), 121–22.

5   Henry Gerald Richardson, "An Oxford Teacher of the Fifteenth Century," *Bulletin of the John Rylands Library*, 23, no. 2 (1939), 447–50. See also Henry Gerald Richardson, "The Oxford Law School Under John," *Law Quarterly Review*, 57 (1941), 319–38; and Henry Gerald Richardson and George Osborne Sayles, "Early Coronation Records [Part I]," *Bulletin of the Institute of Historical Research*, 13 (1935–36), 134–38.

6   Dorothea Oschinsky, "Medieval Treatises on Estate Accounting," *Economic History Review*, 17, no. 1 (1947), 54, 58; eadem, *Walter of Henley and Other Treatises on Estate Management and Accounting* (Oxford: Clarendon, 1971), 16, 226, 235.

7   Martin Camargo, "The English Manuscripts of Bernard of Meung's 'Flores Dictaminum,'" *Viator*, 12 (1981), 197–219 (especially 204–8).

8   Christopher M. Woolgar, ed., *Household Accounts from Medieval England*, vol. 1, British Academy, Records of Social and Economic History, new ser., 17–18 (Oxford: Oxford University Press, for the British Academy, 1992–93), 16 and n. 21. Two further scholars who have cited Add. 8167 may not in fact have seen the manuscript themselves, since their descriptions of it are incorrect. Margaret Wade Labarge commented briefly on the model household accounts, but erroneously reported that the manuscript contains versions in both French and Latin. *A Baronial Household of the Thirteenth Century* (London: Eyre and Spottiswoode, 1965; rpt. New York: Barnes and Noble, 1966), 189 and n. 1. D. Vance Smith's characterization of Add. 8167 as a "Household miscellany and household formulary" in the bibliography of his book *Arts of Possession: The Medieval Household Imaginary* (Minneapolis: University of Minnesota Press, 2003), 275, is similarly incorrect.

9   Suzanne Tuczek, in *Die Kampanische Briefsammlung* (Paris Lat. 11867). *Monumenta Germaniae Historica: Briefe des Späteren Mittelalters* (Hanover: Hahnsche Buchhandlung, 2010), edits a fourteenth-century English formulary that exhibits a similar level of inept draftsmanship.

ABBREVIATIONS

Add. 8167	British Library, London, Additional MS 8167.
BL	British Library, London.
Calendar of Patent Rolls	*Calendar of the Patent Rolls Preserved in the Public Record Office: Henry III*. 6 vols. London: H. M. Stationery Office, 1901–13.
CCCC 297	Corpus Christi College Library, Cambridge, MS 297.
Close Rolls	*Close Rolls of the Reign of Henry III*, 14 vols. (London: H. M. Stationery Office, 1902–38).
Complete Peerage	George Edward Cokayne, *The Complete Peerage of England, Scotland, Ireland and Great Britain*, new ed., ed. Vicary Gibbs, 13 vols. in 14 (London: St. Catherine Press, 1910–59).
Councils and Synods	Frederic Maurice Powicke and Christopher R. Cheney, eds., *Councils and Synods, with Other Documents Relating to the English Church*, 2, *A.D. 1205–1313*, 2 vols. (Oxford: Clarendon, 1964).
CUL	Cambridge University Library.
Curia Regis Rolls	*Curia Regis Rolls Preserved in the Public Record Office*, 20 vols. (London: H. M. Stationery Office, 1922–2007).
Domesday Book	Abraham Farley et al., eds., *Domesday Book seu Liber Censualis Willelmi primi regis Angliae*, 4 vols. (London: Record Commission, 1783–1816).
EHR	*English Historical Review*.
Fairfax 27	Bodleian Library, Oxford, Fairfax MS 27.
Fœdera	Thomas Rymer, *Fœdera conventiones litteræ et acta publica*, ed. Adam Clarke and Frederick Holbrooke, 4 vols. in 7 (London: Record Commission, 1816–69).

Fol., fols.

Folio, folios. A folio is a leaf of a book. The front of the leaf is called the "recto" side (e.g., fol. 1r), and the back of the leaf is called the "verso" side (e.g., fol. 1v). Some manuscripts are paginated rather than foliated; that is, the numeration occurs on each page rather than each leaf (e.g., "pp. 1–5").

Gonville & Caius 205/111

Gonville and Caius College, Cambridge, MS 205/111.

Handbook of Dates

Christopher R. Cheney, ed., *A Handbook of Dates for Students of British History*, new ed., revised by Michael Jones, Royal Historical Society Guides and Handbooks, No. 4 (Cambridge: Cambridge University Press, 2000)

MS, MSS

Manuscript, manuscripts.

Oxford DNB

Henry Colin Gray Matthew and Brian Howard Harrison, eds., *Oxford Dictionary of National Biography* (Oxford: Oxford University Press, 2004 (printed ed.), 2004– (online ed.).

Pipe Rolls

Publications of the Pipe Roll Society (1884–)

Rotuli litterarum patentium

Thomas Duffus Hardy, ed., *Rotuli litterarum patentium in Turri londinensi asservati*, vol. 1, part 1 (London: Record Commission, 1835).

Shirley, ed., *Letters*

Walter W. Shirley, ed., *Royal and Other Historical Letters Illustrative of the Reign of Henry III. from the Originals in the Public Record Office*, 2 vols., Rolls Series, 27 (London: Longman, 1862–66). Shirley's numerical references to documents in the class now known as Ancient Correspondence in The National Archives (TNA) are obsolete. For this volume, the current corresponding TNA references have been obtained from Patricia Barnes, *PRO Lists and Indexes,* No. XV: *List of Ancient Correspondence of the Chancery and Exchequer*, revised ed. (New York: Kraus Reprint, 1968), and its two-volume index: *Lists and Indexes, Supplementary Series,* No. 15, *Index to Ancient Correspondence of the Chancery and Exchequer* (New York: Kraus Reprint, 1969).

Stubbs, *Select Charters*	William Stubbs, *Select Charters and Other Illustrations of English Constitutional History*, ed. Henry William Carless Davis (9th ed., Oxford: Oxford University Press, 1913).
TNA, PRO	The National Archives, Public Record Office, London.
Walters MS W. 15	Walters Art Museum, Baltimore, Maryland, MS W. 15

A NOTE ON MONEY

In medieval Europe, gold coins were rarely minted in the Latin West until the 1250s.[1] The principal coin was the silver penny; higher denominations, such as shillings, marks, and pounds, were used for reckoning and accounting purposes only, and were not minted as coin. In the first half of the thirteenth century the principal denominations used in money-reckoning were based on multiples of twelve and twenty (dozens and scores), and were as follows:

The largest denomination was the pound (in Latin, *libra*; abbreviated *li.* in medieval texts; £ in modern usage).

One pound contained twenty shillings (in Latin, *solidi*; abbreviated *s.*).

One shilling contained twelve pennies or pence (in Latin, *denarii*; abbreviated *d.*).

Thus, £1 = 20*s.* = 240*d.*

Other common divisions of the pound were:

The mark (in Latin, *marca*; abbreviated *m.*), which in England and Scotland was two-thirds of a pound (13*s.* 4*d.*, or 160*d.*).[2]

Half a mark, which in England and Scotland was one-third of a pound (6*s.* 8*d.*, or 80*d.*).

A penny could be divided into:

2 halfpennies (in Latin, *oboli*; abbreviated *ob.*).

4 farthings (quarter-pennies; in Latin, *quadrantes*; abbreviated *q.* or *qua.*).

Thus, 1*d.* = 2 *ob.* = 4*q.*

In England, in the first half of the thirteenth century, the silver penny, also known as the sterling, was the only coin produced by the mints, apart from a small number of struck halfpennies and farthings that were issued in 1222.[3] The penny depicted the king's head on the obverse and a cross on the reverse, each encircled by an inscription, in a design introduced in 1180 under Henry II. This design was used unaltered until 1247, which is why the bearded image and name of the king on the penny in Figure 1 are actually those of Henry II,

Figure 1. Short cross penny of John or Henry III, struck at London *c.* 1216. Fitzwilliam Museum, Cambridge, CM. 1286–2001. Short cross penny, class 6c2, London mint, moneyer Rauf; weight: 1.46 grams. The obverse (king holding scepter) is inscribed hENRICVS REX. The reverse (short cross) is inscribed with the name of the moneyer and the mint location: + RAVF.ON.LVNDE. The London moneyer "Rauf" (Ralph) is named as Radulf de Frowic in a list of mint officials in 1218. He was a member of a prominent London family associated with the mint in the thirteenth and fourteenth centuries. For this information we are grateful to Martin Allen.

even though it was issued under his son John (1199–1216) or his grandson Henry III (1216–72).

Under John and Henry III a pound of money in English pennies weighed almost a pound, and the coins were made from silver purer than the modern sterling standard of 0.925.[4] An ironic result of the consistently high bullion content was that the coinage began to suffer from coin-clippers, who pared away the rim to steal the silver, thus reducing the value of the coin. In 1205 King John had to call in short-weight coins and make weights available for the weighing of coin. By the mid-1240s coin-clipping had once more become rife. According to contemporary chronicler Matthew Paris, there was great public unhappiness over the state of the coinage, which "was clipped round almost to the inner part of the ring, and the border which bore the letters was either entirely destroyed or enormously defaced." In response, in 1247 Henry III changed the design of the penny, substituting a long cross in place of the earlier short cross. The long cross extended to the edge of the coin, to reveal if the coin had been clipped. The new Long Cross coinage was introduced in November 1247, and the design remained in use until 1279.[5] For the money supply, see DOCUMENT 3.

Figure 2. Weighing coin to ensure that it is of full weight. From the Joseph window of Chartres Cathedral (*c.* 1210).

NOTES

1   On gold coinage in the Latin West, see Peter Spufford, *Money and Its Use in Medieval Europe* (Cambridge: Cambridge University Press, 1988), 50–53, 167–70, 176–78, 180–86.

2   On the origins of the units of pounds, shillings, and pence, and the value of the mark, see Spufford, *Money and Its Use*, 33–34, 223–24.

3   Martin Allen, "The English Currency and the Commercialization of England Before the Black Death," in *Medieval Money Matters*, ed. Diana Wood (Oxford: Oxbow Books, 2004), 34–35. Cf. the UK Detector Finds Database (ref. no. 335), at http://www.ukdfd.co.uk/ukdfddata/showrecords.php?product = 335&cat = 152 [seen August 1, 2007]. According to R. J. Eaglen, struck halfpennies "are known, but very rare, from the ninth and tenth centuries," and also from the reign of Henry I, for which he reports eleven examples. R. J. Eaglen, "The Evolution of Coinage in Thirteenth Century England," in *Thirteenth Century England IV: Proceedings of the Newcastle Upon Tyne Conference 1991*, ed. P. R. Coss and S. D. Lloyd (Woodbridge, Suffolk: Boydell, 2002), 19. Three additional struck halfpennies of Henry I have since been recorded, for a total of fourteen (pers. comm., Martin Allen).

4   Martin Allen, *Mints and Money in Medieval England* (Cambridge: Cambridge University Press, 2012), 142–47 (weight standards), 159–61 (standards of fineness). We are very grateful to Dr. Allen for these references. Allen's work supersedes previous over-precise assessments that from 1158 to 1279 the English penny was stabilized at a weight of 1.46 grams and a fineness of 0.925. See, e.g., Spufford, *Money and Its Use*, 402.

5   Eaglen, "Evolution of Coinage," 17–18; *Matthew Paris's English History*, trans. J. A. Giles, vol. 2 (London: H. G. Bohn, 1852–54), 262–65 (*sub anno* 1248). For Matthew Paris's account of this episode in his *Historia Minor*, with his sketch of one of the new Long Cross pennies, see *Matthæi Parisiensis . . . Historia Anglorum, sive, ut vulgo dicitur, Historia Minor*, ed. Sir Frederic Madden, vol. 3, Rolls Series, 44 (London, 1866–69), 27–28.

Introduction

THE LOST LETTERS

This is a book about everyday life in early thirteenth-century England, as revealed in the correspondence of people from all classes of society, from peasants and shopkeepers to bishops and earls. While examples of the letters of wealthy and powerful people of this period have long been known, not only has the correspondence of ordinary people not survived, it has been generally assumed by historians that it never existed in the first place. In fact, numerous examples of such correspondence were hiding in plain sight. They can be found in the handbooks of form letters and other model documents, known as formularies, which for centuries were used to teach the art of letter-writing and keeping accounts. The writing-masters (*dictatores*) and their students who produced these formularies compiled examples of all the kinds of correspondence—formal and informal, official and personal, secular and ecclesiastical—that a man or woman of means, or a man with professional training, might expect to encounter, either on his (or her) own behalf or on behalf of employers or clients. Tucked among the sample letters from popes to bishops and model writs from kings to sheriffs in these formularies are examples of a much more casual, ephemeral kind of correspondence. These are the low-level letters that evidently were widely exchanged, but which the original correspondents generally did not preserve because they were not of lasting importance. Some genuine examples of such letters have survived because they were sent or received by someone of standing (such as Ralph de Neville, bishop of Chichester and chancellor to Henry III) whose correspondence later came into the royal archives and was preserved there. Most original correspondence, however, especially that of ordinary people, has long since disappeared without a trace, but contemporary formularies preserve examples of these lost letters. Two such English formularies, both dating from the second quarter of the thirteenth century, are especially rich in documents of this kind, and it is from their collections that the letters and other materials in this volume are drawn.

The documents edited here reflect the affairs and concerns of every class of society, from kings to peasants. They record the duties, entertainments, opportunities, challenges, difficulties, evils, dangers, and expenses of daily life, both public and private. They speak of politics, national and local, secular and ecclesiastical, and they constantly speak about money: the cost of war, credit, a royal wedding, farm equipment, timber, merchandise, hospitality, and justice. The documents also reveal something of the intellectual and psychological landscape of the period in their use of language and metaphor, their rhetorical constructions and lines of argument, their idealistic assertions and social sensitivities, and their use of proverbial expressions and quotations from the Bible and the Latin classics. As a result, the letters and other texts included in this volume comprise a virtual encyclopedia of English life in the first half of the thirteenth century.

Although these texts were intended to serve as general models, and therefore can have a generic or fictitious character, they are designed to reflect actual conditions. Some of the documents seem to have been adopted with little or no change from genuine originals; others, while perhaps inspired by genuine correspondence, evidently were revised to a greater or lesser extent to enable them to serve as generic models; still others appear to be wholly fictitious. All of the documents, however, even the "fictitious" ones, were expected to represent plausible circumstances and to serve real epistolary or administrative needs, and thus can shed important light on many aspects of life in early thirteenth-century England.

The documents in this volume have been chosen to represent as many facets as possible of daily life among all levels of society, and they reveal a wide range of activities, relationships, practices, and procedures that are otherwise recorded poorly or not at all for this period. They relate, for example, many details about the logistics of life in the noble household, such as how great lords shopped by letter and ordered goods on credit, how they communicated with distant agents and officers, and how they summoned their followers to a tournament or to war. The letters also shed light on many facets of domestic life and neighborhood relations, such as how absent husbands wrote to wives, and how the wives responded; how a scarcity of iron could drive a farmer to beg his neighbor for the loan of a plow; how a tenant might send word to his lord about the malfeasance of the local bailiff; and how neighbors could warn one another of the approach of rapacious royal provisioning agents or report the behavior of an unfaithful wife. Most strikingly, they reveal, in the constant requests for credit or cash, the financial difficulties that beset rich as well as poor in an age without banks. The wealthy and powerful could demand loans from clients and credit from merchants to tide them through a temporary cash-flow crisis. Those who lacked lands to mortgage or goods to pledge, however, had to beg friends and patrons for emergency loans or gifts to enable them to take advantage of economic opportunities, or to save themselves from the dire threat of impending forfeitures, lawsuits, and imprisonment.

It was a world in which naked power often reigned supreme, regardless of law, justice, or pious ideals; a world in which wealth and connections, rather than merit or fairness, determined outcomes. Those with means may often have provided assistance to needy suppliants from a sense of aristocratic *largesse*, Christian obligation, or neighborly or family duty, but such acts of charity also served their own political interests by reinforcing local hierarchies of patronage, power, and dependence.

The picture of life in early thirteenth-century England that these letters present is, in its overall character, a very familiar one. What is new here is the level of detail they offer—of background, of nuance and new voices. The formularies in fact represent a rich genre of primary sources that social and economic historians have heretofore largely ignored. We have attempted in this volume to remedy that situation.

EARLY FORMULARIES

By the thirteenth century the history of the formulary—a handbook of model documents—already stretched back many centuries to the days of the Roman Empire. The idea that there should be set forms for legal documents survived the fall of Rome. In the Latin West, examples of formularies clearly designed for teaching scribes their trade survive from the post-Roman kingdoms of the Franks, which included modern France and Germany, and from the Visigothic kingdom in what is now Spain. These early formularies reveal that there was a broad geographical spread of ideas about how to construct documents and the phrases (*formulae*) to use in them, which extended from the Rhine to the Ebro.[1]

Around 1100 the dominant region in producing formularies was northern Italy. Two influential works of the 1080s (the *Dictaminum radii* and *Ars dictandi*) derive from the author Alberic of Monte Cassino. Even more influential was the tract of Adalbert Samaritanus (*Praecepta dictaminis*), produced around 1115 at Bologna, and most influential of all was the work of one Master Bernard, sometimes called "of Bologna," though he has been actually located working at Faenza, east of Bologna in the Romagna, late in the 1130s and early 1140s. His *Liber artis omnigenum dictaminum* ("Book of technique for all sorts of correspondence") has been hailed as the first modern formulary, with its concentration on mannered prose, hierarchical addresses, and prologues (or *exordia*) to fit any need. Bernard's tract was intended to provide guidelines for stylish business correspondence to suit any likely addressee and circumstance.

His text provided a mix of practical instruction and sample business documents, an arrangement repeated in western formularies throughout the succeeding centuries.[2]

The center of the production of formularies moved to France in the mid-twelfth century. There Bernard of Bologna's works had a major impact, perhaps first taking root in the region of the upper Loire valley, where the most influential of all later western formularies (in terms of survival of manuscripts) appeared.[3] This was the *Flores dictaminum* of Bernard of Meung, which was published in its final form in the year 1187. Within a year or so of its appearance, the Cistercian Italian monk Transmundus (who had been a prominent notary at the papal curia) published his *Introductiones de arte dictandi* in Burgundy, which neatly stitched together the Italian and French notarial traditions. These two works established the western pattern of formulary, which matched instruction with numerous examples of model documents. In the case of the *Flores*, these were often copies of genuine documents (correspondence, settlements, charters, and testaments).[4] For the most part, however, the sample documents were more generic, featuring anonymous salutations and imaginary situations.[5]

The influence of Bernard of Bologna and Bernard of Meung stretched across the Channel into England. Peter de Blois, archdeacon of Wells, was acquainted with the senior Bernard's work in 1181. A late twelfth-century version (now lost) of the *Flores dictaminum* was copied in Oxford in the 1240s. Around 1250 that copy was bound into the volume represented by British Library, Additional MS 8167, which also contains the English formulary that is the principal subject of this book.[6]

In England, the compilation of basic formularies seems to have begun before the end of the twelfth century, though no full native example survives. A fragment of an English letter collection is known from the survival of a part of one of its folios, which was used about 1200 to create a seal tag for a document now in the Lancashire Record Office. Since one of the three sample letters that it preserves can be closely dated to 1188, it was thus a formulary with a very short shelf life, perhaps no more really than a clerk's notepad. All three of the texts that it contains relate to northern England, and it seems likely that it was assembled by a clerk from a stock of discarded ephemera in order to create a collection of models on which to base future correspondence.[7]

The earliest known English formulary is in a manuscript now in the Walters Art Museum in Baltimore (MS W. 15), which dates from 1202–9, and contains model documents relating to church administration. More general in its concerns is a small parchment roll containing a collection of outgoing business correspondence compiled either by Abbot David of Bristol or by a clerk in his employ early in the 1220s.[8] But since it also includes a sample letter drawn from a dictaminal treatise, the educational intention of the collection is clear, even though it is very much a "homemade" product. Roughly contemporary is a rather more specialized sort of tract, a formulary intended to instruct a papal judge delegate in the proper form of documents to be issued in the course of an ecclesiastical case. Like Abbot David's roll, it was a private production based on genuine original documents and assembled in a monastic scriptorium in Canterbury (either St. Augustine's or Christ Church). It has been suggested that the inspiration for the production of this specialized collection was a decretal (legal pronouncement) of Pope Innocent III in 1215 that ordered that the process carried out before a judge delegate be thoroughly documented.[9]

The model letters in this book are drawn from two formularies: British Library, Additional MS 8167, fols. 88r–135v, and Bodleian Library, Fairfax MS 27, fols. 1r–6v. Both are distinctively English in type, and both are associated with Oxford. They are principally collections of letters with some brief instructions on aspects of letter-writing, deriving from the same practical journeyman tradition as the Lancashire fragment and Abbot David's roll. Both were copied and edited from earlier collections, evidently to meet a need for examples of business correspondence and financial accounts. It seems likely that they were generated by and for business students working under masters in Oxford, though not within the university. The needs of such men in regard to dictaminal practice were shared by lords, merchants, and other men of affairs. In the later fourteenth century Francesco di Marco Datini, a wealthy merchant of Prato, wrote to his notary's son, asking to borrow a book containing forms of address to persons of rank and office, from emperors and popes down to nuns, advocates, and doctors, "so that when I must address a letter to one of these, I may not have to take thought."[10]

BRITISH LIBRARY, ADDITIONAL MS 8167

This volume of 203 parchment folios was written, apparently in Oxford, in the first half of the thirteenth century, and was acquired by a monk of Westminster Abbey around 1250.[11] In 1830 it was presented to the British Museum by Henry Petrie, Esq.[12] The volume is made up of sixteen sections (articles), of which Article 5 (folios 88r–135v) contains an untitled and anonymous formulary—that is, a collection of form documents. This particular formulary, which is especially full and interesting, contains some 218 model documents and a number of other materials, or about 249 texts in all. Among its wide variety of model texts are letters, legal documents, and specimen financial accounts, together with instructions on how to write letters and keep accounts, all of English provenance.[13] Article 5 is written in several professional hands. The headings and instructions are rubricated (highlighted in red ink), and each new text begins with a large capital letter in red or blue ink, ornamented with decorative scrollwork. Of the one hundred documents in the present volume, eighty-one are taken from Article 5 of Add. 8167.

The formulary in Article 5 of Add. 8167 was probably designed both for the instruction of students and for the use of laypeople and clerics of all ranks, especially people of property and the professional administrators, agents, lawyers, clerks, and scriveners who handled their affairs and their correspondence. It was probably written in Oxford about 1248–50, making it one of the earliest known English "dictaminal" collections (so called from the Latin *dictamen* or *ars dictaminis*, the art of letter-writing).[14] The model manorial and household accounts included in the collection are the earliest known specimen financial accounts from medieval England.[15]

The various sections of the volume were assembled and bound together by about 1250, when the volume was obtained for Westminster abbey by one of its monks, William of Hasele or Haseley. Notes on a flyleaf (fol. 2r) record his acquisition of the volume and mention a dispute during the abbacy of Richard of Crokele in 1250, as well as national events of 1258 and Crokele's death at Winchester in 1258, on the feast of St. Kenelm the Martyr.[16] It is the reference to the dispute in 1250 that provides the date by which the volume was bound and acquired by Hasele.

The date of the formulary's compilation can otherwise only be inferred from internal evidence. Here there are some difficulties. Much of its content seems to date from the 1220s–30s, and some of it from the beginning of the century. These materials were evidently drawn from earlier collections, and edited or revised to suit the unknown compiler's purpose. This can sometimes be seen by the names of the supposed authors of some of the formulary's letters. DOCUMENT 24, for instance, was issued in the name of R(anulf), Earl of Chester (died 1232), to tenants who owed him military service, and indeed may have been ultimately modeled on a summons issued by the earl himself in 1213. Sometimes there is a datable reference to a contemporary event. DOCUMENTS 34–36, for example, all concern a national debate about the heavy taxation levied by King Henry III for the marriage of his sister to the German emperor in 1235.

The process of editing and updating the contents of the formulary can be seen especially clearly in DOCUMENT 1. Unusually for the documents in this formulary, it includes a date: the thirtieth year since Henry III's coronation (i.e., October 28, 1245–October 27, 1246). However, a much earlier version of DOCUMENT 1 exists in another Oxford formulary, Walters MS W. 15, which dates the text to "the year in which H. bishop of Lincoln died" (*anno in quo .H. lincolniensis episcopus obijt*).[17] Since the Walters formulary itself dates from 1202–9, Bishop H. was probably Hugh of Avalon, Bishop of Lincoln, who died on November 16, 1200. This indicates that the compiler of our formulary deliberately revised the dating clause from 1200 to 1245–6 to update his text, and that Article 5 thus was probably written in 1246 or later.

Evidence from another document also suggests that Article 5 was compiled in the later 1240s. DOCUMENT 64 is a missive about a tournament that was to be staged at Blyth, in Nottinghamshire, and it names one of the participants as the real-life baron "E." (Edmund) de Lacy. Edmund was born *c.* 1230. He was proclaimed of age at eighteen in May 1248,[18] and DOCUMENT 64 is likely to have been written after Edmund had come of age—that is, in 1248 or later. Since Add. 8167 was acquired by Westminster Abbey about 1250, the formulary itself must therefore have been a recent product drawn up between the summer of 1248 and 1250.

BODLEIAN LIBRARY, FAIRFAX MS 27

Another early formulary occupies the first six folios of a manuscript in the Bodleian Library, Fairfax MS 27. This formulary, like that in Add. 8167, is bound into a larger volume. Originally, however, it was a small booklet of only six parchment leaves, written rather densely in one crabbed hand of the 1220s or 1230s, and containing sixty-two documents: a brief dictaminal treatise on forms of address, followed by some sixty-one model letters, both ecclesiastical and secular. The dictaminal treatise is decorated with an elaborate opening initial, and each of the sixty-one letters that follow has a simple opening initial in red. On folios 1r–4r the top line of each page is also ornamented with elaborated ascenders, and an occasional wavy line in red ink is used to fill in blank lines at the end of some texts. The final folio (fol. 6) is now mutilated, the parchment sliced diagonally from the top right to the bottom left, cutting away portions of the texts on both sides of the leaf. The pattern of soiling and wear on folios 1v and 6v indicate that the booklet was for some time in a simple parchment wrapper, and got worn and bent about, making it look very much like a working text. This is an impression supported by several marginal annotations in fourteenth- and fifteenth-century hands. Nineteen of the one hundred documents in the present volume are taken from the formulary in Fairfax 27.

The texts of the formulary in Fairfax 27 seem to be contemporary with its handwriting. Several historical figures are mentioned, including Pope "Gregory" (Gregory IX, 1227–41) and King "Henry" (Henry III, 1216–72). One of its letters (DOCUMENT 30) refers to "Llywelyn" as a Welsh prince fighting the barons of the Welsh March (frontier). He is evidently Llywelyn the Great of Gwynedd (d. 1240), who conducted episodes of warfare against the Marchers and Henry III, the latest being in 1234. Since DOCUMENT 30 is addressed to an earl of Chester, it presumably dates from before 1237, when the earldom became extinct. The indications are therefore that this formulary was compiled in the years on either side of 1230.

At some time in the fifteenth century the formulary was bound together with a number of fourteenth-century Latin and Anglo-Norman treatises to make a volume of 95 folios. Internal evidence suggests that this volume may possibly have belonged to the Augustinian priory of Bolton in Craven, Yorkshire, and the formulary, too, may have belonged to the priory before its inclusion in the bound volume.[19]

None of the texts in Fairfax 27 overlaps with those in Add. 8167, but at least one of the model letters in Fairfax 27 (fol. 2r) can also be found in a later formulary in Corpus Christi College, Cambridge (MS 297, fol. 96r), which has much material in common with Add. 8167.[20] It is thus possible that the formularies in both Add. 8167 and Fairfax 27 share at least one common source. The two formularies certainly resemble one another very much in their general character and mixture of model letters, including letters to and from lords, clerics, knights, county and manorial officers, husbands and wives, students, and neighbors. Together, the documents in these formularies witness not only the developing legal, administrative, and record-keeping procedures of the period, but also, to an extraordinary degree, its social, economic, and political history.

OTHER RELATED FORMULARIES

At least three other formularies have links to Add. 8167. The first of these, now Walters Art Museum MS. W. 15, consists of sixty-one model documents copied into a gospel book, filling the last five pages (fols. 79v–81v) of a quire at the end of the Gospel of St. Matthew. This formulary may have been written in Oxford and dates from *c.* 1202–9.[21] H. G. Richardson noted that seventeen of the model texts in Walters MS. W. 15 can also be found in Add. 8167,[22] showing that the latter drew on exemplars that in some cases were nearly half a century old. We have included one of these shared texts in the present volume as DOCUMENT 1.

The remaining two formularies that are related to Article 5 in Add. 8167 both date from the second half of the thirteenth century and are in Cambridge. The first of these, Gonville and Caius College, MS 205/111, was compiled between 1261 and 1268 by an estate bailiff called Robert Carpenter II of "Hareslade" (Haslett, near Shorwell), on the Isle of Wight.[23] Carpenter's formulary incorporated some of the same texts as those in Add. 8167.[24] A third version of the formulary is in Corpus Christi College, Cambridge (hereafter CCCC), MS 297, and dates from a generation later.[25] Internal evidence makes it clear that neither of the Cambridge manuscripts was copied from Add. 8167, but from some other exemplar or exemplars. As a result, their texts often provide different and sometimes better readings than can be found in Add. 8167, and make it clear that the latter was not the archetype manuscript but was itself based on one or more earlier exemplars. As noted above, CCCC 297 also shares at least one text with the formulary in Fairfax 27.

ENGLAND, 1199–1250

The letters and other documents discussed in this volume derive from the reign of John (1199–1216) and from the first half of the reign of Henry III (1216–1272). John, the youngest son of Henry II (1154–89) and Eleanor of Aquitaine (died 1203), became king upon the death of his brother, Richard the Lionheart (1189–99). John's reign was a turbulent one. Some of the problems he faced were inherited from his predecessors, notably the ongoing war with King Philip Augustus of France, which led to the collapse of John's rule in Normandy and Anjou in 1204–6. His reign was dominated by continual attempts to recover his ancestral possessions in France, which finally ended with the defeat of his powerful ally and nephew, the Emperor Otto IV, at Bouvines in 1214. Other problems were caused by John himself. His personality was an unpleasant one: he trusted no-one and did not inspire confidence in his barons; he was obsessive about accumulating money and not too particular about how he did it. John was not a bloody tyrant; the murders ascribed to him (his nephew Arthur in 1202 and that of the Briouze family in 1210) can plausibly be explained away as the results of a jail break or jail fever. He was, however, unable to control his barons, and eventually they turned on him with an agenda for reform. Enshrined in Magna Carta (1215), this agenda had a long political life, and its concerns liberally populate the letter collections of the 1230s and 1240s. The last months of John's reign were a period of warfare combating rebel barons who were allied with an invading French army headed by Louis, the son of King Philip Augustus, who captured London and claimed the crown. After John's sudden death on October 19, 1216, the war continued to be fought on behalf of his nine-year-old heir, Henry III, by Earl William Marshal of Pembroke, who successfully defeated the rebels and expelled Louis and the French from England in 1217.[26]

Henry III's reign was one of the longest in English history and not without crises. He became king at the age of nine upon the death of his father, King John. Until 1227, Henry was a minor in tutelage to a variety of guardians, though he emerges as a power in his own right after 1223. The rule of England was initially in the hands of Earl William Marshal of Pembroke, described as "protector" or "regent," until his resignation just before his death in May 1219. Effective power then passed into the hands of Hubert de Burgh, who had served as chamberlain and justiciar (chief minister) of King John. Hubert as justiciar of Henry III had to deal with a number of turbulent and powerful magnates during his period of power, not least William Marshal's son and namesake, who married the king's sister, Eleanor, and died in 1231. He also had to confront risings by the count of Aumale in 1221 and Faulkes de Breauté in 1224, as well as the rivalry of the formidable and manipulative Angevin bishop of Winchester, Peter des Roches. Hubert himself fell from power as a result of a conspiracy of the des Roches party in 1232.[27]

Henry III's personal rule was a long catalogue of failures resulting from his overblown ambition in France and the Empire, his mismanagement of an over-powerful and politically assertive aristocracy, and his ill-judged favoritism toward his relatives. He had long lost the confidence of his nobility by the time of the first major crisis of his personal rule, the Marshal rebellion of 1233–34, which was triggered by the triumph of Bishop Peter des Roches's faction at court over Hubert de Burgh, and Peter's subsequent confrontation with Earl Richard Marshal of Pembroke. This was complicated by the rising military power of the princely house of Gwynedd in Wales, which under Llywelyn ab Iorwerth (*c.* 1197–1240) and Dafydd ap Llywelyn (1240–1246) was beginning to construct a powerful and semi-autonomous Welsh state.[28] Llywelyn's support enabled Earl Richard Marshal to defy the king and caused royal power to retreat in the marches. Documents 30–33 concern the military vulnerability of the Welsh Marches and the turbulence of the Welsh.

King Henry was unfortunate in the legacy of his father's reign. The imposition of Magna Carta by the barons on King John in 1215, and then on the young King Henry, inaugurated a period in which an articulate and powerful aristocracy united to pursue its own agenda for good government against the king. In essence the government of England was in the hands of the aristocracy between 1216 and 1227, and it was to this period that the solemn reissues of Magna Carta in 1217 and 1225 under Henry III's seal were made, as a reassurance that aristocratic concerns were being heeded by the government. Documents 37 and 38 echo the perpetual concern of the barons and knights of

England that the liberties recognized in Magna Carta should be respected, and their fear that the king wished to undermine them.

In 1227 Henry III experienced for the first time the aristocracy's ability to confront him and demand reform, when his own brother, the earl of Cornwall, rallied eight of the greatest earls and their baronial retinues to his side at Stamford and made armed representations to the king over his treatment and the recent cancellation of the concessions in Magna Carta over forest jurisdiction. The barons delicately suggested that the root of the problem was the bad advice the king was getting from the justiciar, Hubert de Burgh. This confrontation was settled by compromise, but the Marshal rebellion of 1233–34 showed quite how far things could go. In 1235, the impending marriage of Henry's sister Isabel to Emperor Frederick II required the king to raise the huge sum of £20,000 for Isabel's dowry. This was far beyond the king's capacity to pay, and it triggered an unprecedented request for taxation to meet the sum. The king had to go to the aristocracy to seek consent, and there was a long debate before the aid was granted (echoed in DOCUMENTS 34–36). Eventually, the king's political and fiscal bankruptcy led to further drastic showdowns with the nobility: an aristocratic coup in 1258 and the Baronial Rebellion of 1264–65.[29]

The aristocracy in Henry III's reign appears indeed to have been more powerful and less compliant to the king's will than it had been in the previous century. In part this was due to King John's catastrophic loss of Normandy and his other possessions in northern France in 1204 to the French king, Philip Augustus. The higher aristocracy had lost its lands in Normandy, and the new generation was less than keen to fund expensive campaigns to regain them. However, Henry III made several attempts to recover Poitou, and armies and fleets were summoned to mount attacks in France (see DOCUMENTS 24, 25, 26, and 29). The magnates were the ultimate source of troops. They were ordered to report to ports for embarkation with their retinues to meet their feudal obligations. DOCUMENTS 24 and 25 demonstrate that the size of retinues depended on the king's need and the willingness of knights to answer the summons from their lords, and that in the end, the size of the army that appeared had more to do with the money available than traditional service.[30]

Another major, though distant, actor in English affairs was the pope, Innocent III (1198–1216). He had involved himself deeply in the politics of John's reign, and a succession of papal legates acted as Rome's vicegerents in England from 1214 until 1221. England became very important for the papacy as a source of wealth from the tribute that Innocent III imposed on King John and his successors and from taxation of the clergy (see DOCUMENT 55), and as a potential ally in the perpetual tension between Rome and Emperor Frederick

II's kingdom of Sicily. The pope's schemes for the overthrow of the Hohen-staufen dynasty ensnared Henry III into accepting Sicily for his younger son, Edmund, in 1254. It was the financial impossibility of meeting the pope's demands that led to the collapse of Henry III's personal rule and the baronial coup of 1258.[31] Within England, the Church did not come into any major collision with the monarchy during Henry III's reign comparable to that experienced during the reigns or Henry II or John. The Church did, however, mount resistance to the heavy burden of taxation that Henry's government wished to levy on it (see DOCUMENT 36).

OXFORD, C. 1200–1250

Higher studies at the schools of the town of Oxford can be traced back to masters teaching there in the first half of the twelfth century, but until the 1180s there was nothing much to distinguish Oxford from other towns with such schools, such as Northampton.[32] The rise of the Oxford schools happened gradually, and appears to have owed something to their masters' focus on canon law at a time when the tensions between king and Church were being resolved in favor of the autonomy of church courts. The town had by then a substantial clerical population, with a major collegiate church (St. George) within the castle, two large monasteries (St. Frideswide's priory and Oseney abbey) just outside its walls, and eight parish churches within. The prominent cleric, Gerald of Wales, gave a public reading of his *Topography of Ireland* to the masters of the Oxford schools in the late 1180s, and by his own account they were present in some numbers, even if none was eminent enough for Gerald to name.[33] We do at least know of two Frisian students who came to Oxford around 1190 to study Roman and canon law, copying texts they found there. It is in this decade that we begin to learn also of the masters who were leading these schools, and all the ones known are identifiable as canonists.

Around 1200 the schools of Oxford began to diversify rapidly away from law. In part this was due to a period of hostilities between the kings of England and France, which may have made the study of theology and other subjects in the greater and more famous schools of Paris difficult for English students. The teaching of theology had already begun at Oxford by the mid-1190s, when the influential and well-connected scholar Alexander Neckam was running a school there. His contemporary in the town was Edmund Rich, who taught the liberal arts before turning to theology, and who seems to have made quite an impact on his fellow masters in Oxford.[34] He was later archbishop of Canterbury (1234–40) and was canonized. The schools at Oxford fell into decay following the interdict imposed on England by Pope Innocent III in 1208. In 1209 this was compounded by a dispute between the masters and the civic authorities of Oxford, who had arrested and hanged for complicity two students who had shared a house with another who had murdered his mistress. The masters left Oxford in a body, and the dispute between them and the town was pursued in the papal curia, which in 1214 produced a settlement before the papal legate in England, Guala Bicchieri. This document established the immunities of the schools in the town, and made it once more attractive to masters. The settlement instituted a chancellor, appointed by the diocesan bishop, to preside over the students of all the schools and to conduct relations with the town. With that act the foundation of a corporate university of masters and scholars was laid.

The formularies that are the subject of this book were not, however, a product of the university's masters or students. Rather, they were handbooks designed to assist students taking a business course at private schools, where they studied *dictamen* (the art of letter-writing) and learned to cast accounts. These formularies were the product of such schools, whether written by or for their students. We know very little of the way in which these students were taught. Dictaminal practice was not one of the principal subjects in which the university came to specialize; these were theology, Roman law, and liberal arts. On the other hand, it was allied to the study of both law and grammar, and was undoubtedly a practical subject with an immediate use to men who wanted employment as clerks and estate officers. We do not know if it was taught to separate groups or was an additional vocational course offered to students principally engaged in other studies. It is not known whether there were masters taking on pupils in *dictamen* alone. There are some indications that it was taught alongside other subjects. The great Robert Grosseteste (bishop of Lincoln, 1235–53) taught theology in the Oxford schools from the mid-1220s to 1235, but he was also the author of a practical treatise on estate management.[35] It is therefore possible that he took pupils in both subjects.

The formularies in Add. 8167 and Fairfax 27 include examples of model correspondence between students and their parents. One can only imagine that the solicitations for money and assurances of good conduct proffered by the students in these letters provoked a good deal of mirth in the schoolroom. In one such letter (DOCUMENT 82), for example, a student reports to his mother that he is safe and happy at Oxford, apart from his lack of clothes, food, and money.

LITERACY IN EARLY THIRTEENTH-CENTURY ENGLAND

The model letters in the formularies from people of all ranks of society force us to re-reassess completely the literacy of this period. In 1978 Ralph V. Turner argued that Latin literacy became widespread among the knightly class of twelfth- and thirteenth-century England,[36] and Michael Clanchy's ground-breaking study of medieval literacy, *From Memory to Written Record*,[37] suggested that there was an explosion of literacy in the course of the twelfth century. His argument was that when the king's government began demanding information from his local officers, these men had to acquire the functional skills of literacy to know what was required and communicate it. It therefore became necessary for knights to learn to read if they had any ambition to have a career in administration. The royal administration's appetite for information increased throughout the century, and the law courts began to generate more and more records.

The formularies that are the subject of this book, however, also include examples of routine correspondence between men of property and their wives (DOCUMENTS 75–77 and 100), their household officers (DOCUMENTS 15, 69, and 74), their manorial officers (DOCUMENTS 51–53 and 98–99), the merchants and craftsmen with whom they dealt (DOCUMENTS 2–6, 8, and 97), and even peasants (DOCUMENT 49), as well as numerous exchanges between friends and neighbors (e.g., DOCUMENTS 9–12, 16, 26–28, 33, 57, 61–62, 70, and 90–92). While many people would have had assistance in handling their correspondence (for example, in the early fourteenth-century household of Lord and Lady Eresby, one of the duties of their chaplain was "to assist in writing letters and other things, as needed"),[38] these formularies suggest that the extent of literacy was probably much broader than Clanchy's functional outlook implies. They give us grounds to believe that casual correspondence was widespread and that literacy was well established in every social class in England by the early thirteenth century, and probably by the late twelfth,[39] which would also explain the otherwise unaccountable phenomenon of peasant seals appearing in the decades before 1200.[40]

To Clanchy, literacy in the twelfth and thirteenth centuries was an administrative tool. The world of letters circulating for social purposes that we present here does not fit in his model. He dismisses the idea of the letter as an indicator of lay literacy, seeing letters as part of a purely clerical literary culture, written to impress a small circle.[41] This argument can be countered in several ways, however. For example, there was a culture of lively political communication that is overlooked by Clanchy. John Gillingham sees King Richard and his council as industrious in circularizing newsletters to the political community in England in order to mold its opinion on vital issues.[42] They would do so only if they knew they had an audience eager for news in that medium. It is possible to discern as early as the 1130s circles of letter-writing among male and female aristocrats in England and France, where letters were exchanged for family and personal reasons.[43] Recently, Martin Aurell had suggested that literacy among the lay aristocracy of this period went well beyond the functional, and was fully engaged with Latin liturgy and theology as well as vernacular poetry.[44] The letters collected here would also suggest that literacy was already, by the thirteenth century, integral to the lives of people of all conditions, and used as much for social as for administrative purposes.

LANGUAGE AND STRUCTURE OF THE LETTERS

In an age highly conscious of status, language was a ubiquitous tool for claiming, disputing, acknowledging, and confirming inequalities in rank and authority.[45] Both in speech and in writing people of different ranks were addressed in distinctly different ways, and these are clearly reflected in the letters and in the brief instructions on letter-writing in this collection. Distinctive features of medieval discourse that appear in these model letters include the convention that important or senior people (including one's parents) were listed first in salutations. For example, in a salutation such as "To his dearest friend A., B. sends greetings" (DOCUMENT 47), A. is the more important or senior person, or is being placed first by an equal out of politeness or respect. A superior writing to an inferior or junior person, or an equal wishing to disparage an equal, would name himself first in the salutation, as in "A. to B., greetings" (DOCUMENT 85). Important or senior people also were often addressed by honorific titles, and commonly referred to themselves, and were addressed by others, in the plural (*nos, vos*), as a sign of their elevated rank. Poor and ordinary people, however, or juniors writing to seniors (including children writing to parents), referred to themselves and were addressed in the singular (*ego, tu*). For example, in DOCUMENT 47, an earl writes to his agent ("*clienti*," perhaps a moneylender) to demand 100 shillings with which to purchase a horse. Throughout this letter the earl refers to himself in the plural and addresses his agent in the singular, using such phrases as, "*pro amore nostro et fide quam nobis debes .C. solidos facias nos habere ad unum equum emendum*" ("for our love and the faith you owe us, let us have 100s. to buy a horse"). In DOCUMENT 13, a man who has been ordered by his lord to find the latter a horse reports back, addressing the earl in the plural and referring to himself in the singular. Another convention widely reflected in this collection was that an important person might employ the formal plural form of address to someone of inferior rank rather than the familiar singular, as a sign of politeness and respect. For example, in DOCUMENTS 2, 5, and 6 an earl addresses a vintner, draper, and skinner, to whom he owes money and from whom he wishes to order goods on credit, as *vos*, not *tu*.[46] However, a polite inferior did not presume to respond to a superior as if to an equal, even if so addressed. The model replies of the vintner and skinner (Documents 3, 4, and 8) respectfully address the earl in the plural, while referring to themselves, modestly, in the singular. Similarly, a writer of standing might address someone of equal rank in the plural, while referring to himself in the singular, as a sign of respect and modesty, especially (as in Documents 10 and 91) if he were seeking a favor. The same usage can be seen in Document 76 in the case of a wife writing to her husband.

Medieval English observed a similar protocol by having both a formal or "polite" second-person singular pronoun (*you*) and an informal or familiar one (*thou* in the nominative case, *thee* in all other cases). This distinction is absent, however, in modern English, which has dropped the familiar *thou/thee* and uses "you" for both formal and informal address. Because such distinctions are blurred in modern English, in the letters edited here they are often clearer in the original Latin than in the translations.

Certain expressions or phrases that, at first glance, can seem unusual or idiosyncratic in these letters, perhaps even suggesting that many were composed by a single author, in fact were stock terms used in other formal correspondence of this period in England. Such phrases include:

> *Karissimo amico* ("To my dearest friend")
> *salutem et se totum* ("[X sends] greetings and his entire self")
> *peto* (or *rogo*) *attencius* ("I seek [*or* ask] earnestly")
> *si placet* ("if it please you")
> *sciatis pro vero* ("you should know for a fact")
> *tantum faciatis ut* ("may you act in such a way that")
> *omni occasione et dilacione postpositis* ("with every argument and
>   delay having been set aside")

Good analogues to some of the model letters in this volume, and to the expressions and phrases listed above, can be found among the early thirteenth-century letters preserved in the class known as Ancient Correspondence (SC 1/–) in The National Archives (TNA; formerly the Public Record Office, PRO). For example, a letter sent about March 2, 1220, by William Marshal II, earl of Pembroke, to Henry III, opens with the salutation "*Karissimo domino suo*" ("To his dearest lord") and offers "*salutem, et se totum*" ("greetings, and his entire self"). Other phrases used in Marshal's letter include: "*Et ideo vobis attencius supplico si placet*" ("And on that account I beseech you earnestly, if it please you"), and "*Scientes pro vero*" ("Knowing for a fact").[47] A letter sent in 1225 by Roger Bigod, kt, to Ralph de Neville, bishop of Chichester, includes in the salutation the phrase "*salutem, et se totum*."[48] A letter sent, perhaps before midsummer 1218, by William, earl of Warenne, to Hubert de Burgh, justiciar of England, in which the earl asks his friend to obtain the repayment of part of the money that the earl had lent to the Crown, includes such phrases as "*Rogo vos et attentius deprecor, sicut dominum et amicum carissimum*" ("I ask you, and I pray you earnestly, as my lord and dearest friend"), "*Tantum igitur, si placet, inde faciatis ut*" ("Therefore, if it please you, may you act in such a way that"), "*attentius rogo, ut . . . tantum faciatis*" ("I ask earnestly, that . . . you may act only in such a way"), and "*pro certo sciatis*" ("you should know for a fact").[49] A few years later (between 1222 and 1224) Ralph de Neville, at that time bishop-elect of Chichester, wrote to his officer G. Savage to send money at once, "*omni dilatione et excusatione postpositis*" ("with every delay and excuse having been set aside").[50]

As in their modern equivalents, most medieval letters opened and closed with standard salutations ("A. to B., greetings") and valedictions ("farewell"). Many routine letters were written in a plain, matter-of-fact style, while official correspondence, both secular and ecclesiastical, contained much formulaic text. Diplomatic, ecclesiastical, scholarly, and student letters, by contrast, were often written in elaborate style to negotiate, edify, entertain, or impress. Their authors drew heavily on proverbial expressions and on classical and biblical tags and allusions; in the letters edited here, the classical author who is quoted most frequently is Ovid (see Documents 84, 85, 86, and 93).

Formal letters were written to follow a set structure that had been established since the late eleventh century. There were four or five main parts to a formal letter, beginning with the *salutatio* (salutation or greeting), of the kinds described above, carefully graded according to the respective ranks of the sender and recipient and often filled with elaborate courtesies. This was followed by the *exordium* (introduction), which typically quoted a proverbial expression or scriptural quotation that would set the theme and tone of the letter. Then came the *narratio* (the main narrative), which set forth the argument that formed the central purpose of the letter. This generally led to a *petitio* (petition), the request that was the actual purpose of many letters. Then came a *conclusio* (conclusion), which drew upon the major premise of the *exordium* and the minor premise of the *narratio* and finished with additional expressions of courtesy, at the very end of which was a brief valediction (farewell).[51] Examples of instructions for the drafting of formal letters can be found in this volume in Documents 7 and 15.

EDITORIAL PRINCIPLES

In selecting the one hundred documents for this volume (eighty-one from Add. 8167 and nineteen from Fairfax 27) from the more than three hundred texts in the two formularies, our primary intent was quite different from that of the original authors and compilers. Their purpose was to provide model texts for the use of students and others who needed to master the arts of writing letters and casting accounts in Latin. Our purpose was to choose materials from among those exemplars that would represent as many facets as possible of daily life among all levels of society.

All texts are given in the original Latin, as well as in English translation. The Latin texts were transcribed by Martha Carlin from Add. 8167 and by David Crouch from Fairfax 27. Unless otherwise noted, all translations and commentaries are the work of Martha Carlin and David Crouch. The Latin texts are given *verbatim* and *litteratim*, but for the sake of clarity we have modernized the punctuation, capitalization, and the use of "u" and "v." The original texts are heavily abbreviated, and for clarity's sake we have also silently expanded most of these abbreviations. Occasionally the proper expansion of an abbreviation is unclear; in such cases we have indicated the unexpanded abbreviation by the use of an apostrophe ('). Contemporary annotations and emendations to the manuscript are identified in the text or notes.

To assist the reader we have tried to identify and clarify any grammatical slips, missing words, and spellings that might be confusing. (We have not, however, attempted to identify or rectify all minor slips or spellings that might be irregular but not especially confusing.) Whenever possible we have also identified quotations from classical and biblical sources.

NOTES

1   For these texts, see three studies by Alice Rio: "Freedom and Unfreedom in Early Medieval Francia: The Evidence of Legal Formulae," *Past and Present*, 193 (2006), 12–16; *The Formularies of Angers and Marculf: Two Merovingian Legal Handbooks* (Liverpool: Liverpool University Press, 2008); and *Legal Practice and the Written Word in the Early Middle Ages: Frankish Formulae, c. 500–1000* (Cambridge: Cambridge University Press, 2009), 192–94. For a tenth-century formulary deriving from the abbey of Ripoll in Catalonia, and the Visigothic tradition, see Michel Zimmermann, *Ecrire et lire en Catalogne: ixe–xiie siècle*, 2 vols. (Madrid: Casa de Velázquez, Madrid, 2003), 1:253–57.

2   For this and the succeeding paragraph, see Franz Josef Worstbrock, Monika Klaes, and Jutta Lütten, eds., *Repertorium der Artes Dictandi des Mittelalters*, vol. 1, *von den Anfängen bis um 1200* (Münich: Wilhelm Fink Verlag, 1992). For the early dominance of the late eleventh-century treatise of Alberic of Montecassino, see Franz Josef Worstbrock, "Die Anfänge der mittelalterlichen Ars dictandi," *Frühmittelalterliche Studien*, 23 (1989), 1–42. For Master Bemard of Bologna, see Anne-Marie Turcan-Verkerk, "Le *Liber artis omnigenum dictaminum* de Maître Bernard (vers 1145): Etats successifs et problèmes d'attribution," *Revue d'Histoire des Textes*, nouv. sér. 5 (2010), 99–158 (première partie); 6 (2011), 261–328 (deuxième partie). For a general discussion of medieval European letter-writing treatises from the eleventh century on, see

also Malcolm Richardson, "The *Ars dictaminis,* the Formulary, and Medieval Epistolary Practice," in *Letter-Writing Manuals and Instruction, from Antiquity to the Present: Historical and Bibliographic Studies,* ed. Carol Poster and Linda C. Mitchell (Columbia: University of South Carolina Press, 2007), 52–66.

3   Turcan-Verkerk, in "Le *Liber Artis Omnigenum Dictaminum,* 2ème partie," 271–73, considers the arguments for the transmission of Bernard's influence through Tours or Champagne.

4   For a published version of such a collection from a copy of the *Flores Dictaminum,* see Lucien Auvray, "Documents Orléanais du xiie et du xiiie siècle: extraits du formulaire de Bernard de Meung," *Mémoires de la Société archéologique et historique de l'Orléanais,* 23 (1892), 393–413.

5   See Léopold Delisle, *Notice sur une Summa Dictaminis jadis conservée à Beauvais* (Paris: Imprimerie nationale, 1898), 171–205.

6   Bernard of Meung's *Flores Dictaminum* is on fols. 169r–178r. On this text, see Worstbrock et al., eds., *Repertorium der Artes Dictandi des Mittelalters,* vol. 1, 50; and Martin Camargo, "The English Manuscripts of Bernard of Meung's 'Flores Dictaminum,'" *Viator,* 12 (1981), 204–8.

7   Nicholas Vincent, "William Marshal, King Henry II and the Honour of Châteauroux," *Archives,* 25 (2000), 14–15.

8   BL, Cotton Roll iv 28, edited by Rosalind Hill in *Ecclesiastical Letter Books of the Thirteenth Century* (Oxford: privately printed, 1936), 218–41.

9   BL, Cotton MS Julius D ii, fols. 143v–147v, edited in Jane E. Sayers, "A Judge Delegate Formulary from Canterbury," in eadem, *Law and Records in Medieval England: Studies on the Medieval Papacy, Monasteries and Records* (London: Variorum, 1988), 201–11.

10   Iris Origo, *The Merchant of Prato* (London: Jonathan Cape, 1957; rpt. New York: Penguin, 1992), 336.

11   The monk, William de Hasele (or Haseley), subsequently became sub-prior of Westminster. He compiled a book of the customs of Westminster Abbey (now BL, Cotton MS Otho C. xi), edited by Edward Maunde Thompson in *Customary of the Benedictine Monastery of St. Peter, Westminster,* Henry Bradshaw Society, 28 (1904), 1–247. See the entry on "Haseley, William de," in the *Oxford DNB.* We are grateful to Barbara Harvey for this reference.

12   A handwritten note in the British Library's catalogue of Egerton MSS notes the presentation by Petrie of Add. MSS 8166 and 8167.

13   For a full description of Add. 8167, including Article 5 (fols. 88r–135v), see the British Library's *Catalogue of Additional Manuscripts,* which is available online. This information is summarized by Martin Camargo in "English Manuscripts of Bernard of Meung's 'Flores Dictaminum,'" 204–8.

14   According to Martin Camargo, the brief dictaminal treatises and collections of model documents and precedents in Article 5 of Add. 8167 "represent the earliest extant specimen of what came to be the standard course on *dictamen* at Oxford." Camargo, "English Manuscripts of Bernard of Meung's 'Flores Dictaminum,'" 205. For further information about the manuscript and its contents, see the detailed description in the British Library's catalogue of Additional Manuscripts, which is available both in print and online.

15   Christopher M. Woolgar, ed., *Household Accounts from Medieval England,* 2 vols., British Academy, Records of Social and Economic History, new ser., 17–18 (Oxford:

Oxford University Press, for the British Academy, 1992–93), 1: 16. According to Woolgar, only about a dozen English household accounts survive from before 1250. Ibid., 1:10.

16 E. H. Pearce, *The Monks of Westminster. Being a Register of the Brethren of the Convent from the Time of the Confessor to the Dissolution, with Lists of the Obedientiaries and an Introduction* (Cambridge: Cambridge University Press, 1916), 49–50.

17 Walters MS W. 15, fol. 81r.

18 *Complete Peerage*, vol. 7, 680–81.

19 See [Bodleian Library], *A Summary Catalogue of Western Manuscripts in the Bodleian Library at Oxford*, 7 vols. in 9 (Oxford: Clarendon, 1895–1953), vol. 2, part 2, pp. 785–86, no. 3907.

20 Noted by H. G. Richardson, who printed a composite version of this letter, based on both manuscripts, in Herbert Edward Salter, William Abel Pantin, and Henry Gerald Richardson, eds., *Formularies Which Bear on the History of Oxford, c. 1204–1420*, 2 vols., Oxford Historical Society (1942), 2:348–49. The Cambridge manuscript is discussed below.

21 According to the museum's unpublished description of this manuscript, MS W. 15 is a glossed gospel book dating from the first quarter of the thirteenth century, with a contemporary binding of oak boards covered with deerskin. The text of the formulary has been dated to *c.* 1202–9. It is copied onto folios 79v–81v at the end of Quire 9, the last quire of the Gospel of Matthew. The formulary's script and ink match the main contents of the book, and its ruling utilizes the same ruling as the Gospel of Matthew. The Gospel of Mark begins with a new quire on folio 82r. See Jane E. Sayers, *Papal Judges Delegate in the Province of Canterbury, 1198–1254: A Study in Ecclesiastical Jurisdiction and Administration* (London: Oxford University Press, 1971), 47–54; and F. Donald Logan, "An Early Thirteenth-Century Papal Judge-Delegate Formulary of English Origin," *Studia Gratiana*, 14, Collectanea Stephan Kuttner, vol. 4 (Bologna, 1967), 73–87.

22 Salter, Pantin, and Richardson, eds., *Formularies Which Bear on the History of Oxford*, vol. 2, 344, n. 4; for transcriptions of eleven documents from the Walters MS, see vol. 2, 273–77.

23 For the suggested date of 1261 × 68, see Pamela R. Robinson, *Catalogue of Dated and Datable Manuscripts c. 737–1600 in Cambridge Libraries*, 2 vols. (Cambridge, 1988), 1: p. 75, no. 241, and 2: pl. 115.

24 See Noël Denholm-Young, "Robert Carpenter and the Provisions of Westminster"; idem, *Seignorial Adminstration*, 121–22; Cecil Anthony Francis Meekings, "More About Robert Carpenter of Hareslade," *English Historical Review*, 72 (1957), 260–69; Silvio Brendler, "Hareslade: A Note on Robert Carpenter's Place of Abode," *Notes and Queries* (March 2002), 12–13; and Oschinsky, *Walter of Henley*, 39, 228–9, 237–39. Sometime after 1283 Carpenter's eldest son, Robert Carpenter III (b. 1258), compiled his own formulary and included within it a copy of his father's text; his version is now Cambridge University Library, MS Mm. I. 27. For its date, see Robinson, *Catalogue of Dated and Datable Manuscripts*, vol. 1, p. 75, no. 241. M. R. James described the elder Carpenter's formulary and noted its correspondence with the younger Carpenter's formulary, in *A Descriptive Catalogue of the Manuscripts in the Library of Gonville and Caius College, Cambridge*, 2 vols. (Cambridge: Cambridge University Press, 1907–8), 1:238–42.

25 Henry Gerald Richardson, "An Oxford Teacher of the Fifteenth Century," *Bulletin of the John Rylands Library*, 23, no. 2 (1939), 447–50. See also Richardson, "The Oxford

Law School Under John," *Law Quarterly Review*, 57 (1941), 319–38; Richardson and George Osborne Sayles, "Early Coronation Records [Part I]," *Bulletin of the Institute of Historical Research*, 13 (1935–36), 134–38; and Montague Rhodes James, *A Descriptive Catalogue of the Manuscripts in the Library of Corpus Christi College, Cambridge*, 2 vols. (Cambridge: Cambridge University Press, 1912), 2:76–79.

26 See W. Lewis Warren, *King John*, 2nd ed. (London: Methuen, 1978); David Crouch, *William Marshal: Knighthood, War and Chivalry, 1147–1219*, 2nd ed. (London: Longman, 2002).

27 See David A. Carpenter, *The Minority of Henry III* (London: Methuen, 1990); Nicholas Vincent, *Peter des Roches* (Cambridge: Cambridge University Press, 1996).

28 For the rise and statist ambition of Gwynedd and the idea of a "prince of Wales," see David Stephenson, *The Governance of Gwynedd* (Cardiff: University of Wales Press, 1984); Huw Pryce, ed., *The Acts of the Welsh Rulers, 1120–1283* (Cardiff: University of Wales Press, 2005), 21–34, 344–480.

29 For the outbreak of the Baronial Rebellion and the issues that lay behind it, see David A. Carpenter, "What Happened in 1258?" in *War and Government in the Middle Ages: Essays in Honour of J. O. Prestwich*, ed. John Gillingham and James C. Holt (Woodbridge, Suffolk: Boydell, 1984), 106–19; John Maddicott, *Simon de Montfort* (Cambridge: Cambridge University Press, 1994), 151ff.

30 For the shape of the thirteenth-century aristocracy, see John Malcolm William Bean, *From Lord to Patron: Lordship in Late Medieval England* (Manchester: Manchester University Press, 1989); Peter R. Coss, *The Origins of the English Gentry* (Cambridge: Cambridge University Press, 2003); David Crouch, *The English Aristocracy, 1070–1272: A Social Transformation* (New Haven: Yale University Press, 2011).

31 See Clifford Hugh Lawrence, ed., *The English Church and the Papacy in the Middle Ages* (London: Burns & Oates, 1965); Jane E. Sayers, *Papal Government and England During the Pontificate of Honorius III, 1216–1227* (Cambridge: Cambridge University Press, 1983).

32 This section summarizes material in Richard W. Southern, "From Schools to University," in *The History of the University of Oxford*, vol. 1, *The Early Oxford Schools*, ed. Jeremy I. Catto (Oxford: Oxford University Press, 1984), 1–36.

33 Gerald of Wales, *De rebus a se gestis*, in *Opera*, ed. John Sherren Brewer, Rolls Series, 21 (London: Longman, 1861), vol. 1, 73.

34 For Edmund Rich at Oxford, see Clifford Hugh Lawrence, *St. Edmund of Abingdon* (Oxford: Oxford University Press, 1960), 110–24.

35 For Grosseteste's early career, see Richard W. Southern, *Robert Grosseteste* (Oxford: Oxford University Press, 1986), 70–82. For his "Rules," intended for the instruction of a countess, see Dorothea Oschinsky, *Walter of Henley and Other Treatises on Estate Management and Accounting* (Oxford: Clarendon, 1971), 191–99, 387–415.

36 Ralph V. Turner, "The *Miles Literatus* in Twelfth- and Thirteenth-Century England: How Rare a Phenomenon?" *American Historical Review*, 83 (1978), 928–65; rpt. in idem, *Judges, Administrators and the Common Law in Angevin England* (London: Hambledon, 1994), 119–36.

37 Michael T. Clanchy, *From Memory to Written Record: England, 1066–1307*, 2nd ed. (Oxford: Blackwell, 1993). But see also the important study by Martin Aurell, *Le Chevalier lettré: savoir et conduite de l'aristocratie aux XXIIe et XIIIe siècles* (Paris: Fayard, 2011), which offers an entirely different perspective on lay literacy.

38 *Sire Hugh de Byford chapelain e aumoner le seigneur e eidera descrire lettres e altres choses quant mestier serra, e en absence del garderober countrerollera les despens del*

hostiel, e abreuira les despens del hostiel mon seigneur quant il va hors del hostiel et de ceo acountera a garderober deuant seneschal del hostiel. TNA: PRO, C 47/3/33 (household ordinances of Lord and Lady Eresby), dated January 5, "year 12" (*lan xij*). For differing ideas of its date, James Conway Davies, *The Baronial Opposition to Edward II: Its Character and Policy* (Cambridge: Cambridge University Press, 1918), 56 (1318), and Thomas Frederick Tout, *Chapters in the Administrative History of Mediaeval England: The Wardrobe, the Chamber and the Small Seals*, vol. 2 (Manchester: Manchester University Press, and London: Longman, 1920–33), 182–83 (1284). Christopher Woolgar dated these ordinances to 12 Edward II (1318) or 12 Edward III (1339) in *Household Accounts*, vol. 2, 702–3.

39 On the growth of literacy in England in the late twelfth and early thirteenth centuries from the manorial perspective, see also Mark Bailey, trans. and ed., *The English Manor c. 1200–c. 1500* (Manchester: Manchester University Press, 2002), 19–20, 22–24.

40 F. M. Stenton identified some twenty-nine charters bearing seals of free peasants (both men and women) in Lincolnshire dating from *c.* 1160 to *c.* 1200 in *The Free Peasantry of the Northern Danelaw* (Oxford: Clarendon, 1969; originally published in the *Bulletin de la Société Royale des Lettres de Lund*, 1925–26). The twenty-nine sealed charters are nos. 12, 21, 25, 30, 31, 50–54, 105, 109, 117, 118, 121, 130, 136, 142, 168, 169, 172, 173, 181, 183, 190, 191, 209, 228, and 239. Stenton also lists (28–136, passim) dozens of additional charters with peasant seals from Lincolnshire, Leicestershire, Nottinghamshire, and Derbyshire dating from the first half of the thirteenth century. P. D. A. Harvey noted that "by the end of the twelfth century the use of seals had spread far beyond the humblest knights . . . those who had seals in 1200 may already have included villeins as well as townsmen and the smallest freeholders." Paul D. A. Harvey, "Personal Seals in Thirteenth-Century England," in *Church and Chronicle in the Middle Ages: Essays Presented to John Taylor*, ed. Ian Wood and Graham A. Loud (London: Hambledon, 1991), 119. Hilary Jenkinson published a photograph of an agreement dated 1217 $\times$ 32 between Ranulf, earl of Chester and Lincoln, and the "men" (tenant smallholders) of Frieston and Butterwick, Lincolnshire, to which are appended the fifty-six seals of the latter, in *A Guide to Seals in the Public Record Office* (London: H. M. Stationery Office, 1968), p. 7 and Plate II. This agreement (TNA, PRO, DK 27/270) is also discussed in Harvey, "Personal Seals in Thirteenth-Century England," 120; and in Paul D. A. Harvey and Andrew McGuinness, *A Guide to British Medieval Seals* (London: British Library and Public Record Office, 1996), 77. T. A. Heslop republished the Lincolnshire agreement (which he dated simply to "*c.* 1225"), and also published an example of a peasant seal of *c.* 1200 in Durham, in a picture essay on peasant seals in Edmund King's *Medieval England, 1066–1485* (Oxford: Phaidon, 1988), 214–15. Cf. Clanchy, *From Memory to Written Record*, 50–51.

41 Clanchy, *From Memory to Written Record*, 89–90: at p. 90, "the spoken word of messengers sufficed for conveying the ordinary business of the day."

42 John Gillingham, "Royal Newsletters, Forgeries and English Historians: Some Links Between Court and History in the Reign of Richard I," in *La Cour Plantagenêt (1154–1204)*, ed. Martin Aurell (Poitiers: Centre d'Etudes Supérieures de Civilisation Médiévale, 2000), 171–86. For a private newsletter from the Angevin court circulated around Thomas Becket's circle in 1169, see *Materials for the History of Thomas Becket*, ed. James Craigie Robertson and Joseph Brigstocke Sheppard, Rolls Series, 67 (London: Longman, 1872–85), vol. 7, *Epistolae*, no. 476.

43 David Crouch, "Between Three Realms: The Acts of Waleran II, Count of Meulan and Worcester," in *Records, Administrations and Aristocratic Society in the Anglo-Norman Realm*, ed. David Crook and Nicholas Vincent (Woodbridge, Suffolk: Boydell, 2009), 75–90.

44 Aurell, *Le Chevalier lettré.*

45 On petitionary language and the evidence of formularies in early medieval France, see Geoffrey Koziol, *Begging Pardon and Favor: Ritual and Political Order in Early Medieval France* (Ithaca, N.Y.: Cornell University Press, 1992), Chap. 1.

46 In DOCUMENT 6, the earl also slips once into the informal singular in referring to himself, when he begs his draper to accommodate "me" (rather than "us") with cloth. In DOCUMENT 97 a knight, addressing the carpenter whom he wishes to hire, occasionally shifts from the familiar *tu* into the respectful *vos*, and he speaks of himself using the informal "I" as well as the formal "we." This may represent careless drafting by the author of this letter, but possibly it was an intentional phrasing designed to gratify the carpenter.

47 TNA: PRO, SC 1/4/74.

48 TNA: PRO, SC 1/6/46.

49 Shirley, ed., *Letters*, vol. 1, 15–16 (this letter is now TNA: PRO, SC 1/1/214).

50 TNA: PRO, SC 1/6/6.

51 For brief overviews of the structure of formal letters, see Charles Homer Haskins, "The Life of Medieval Students as Illustrated by Their Letters," *American Historical Review*, 3, no. 2 (1898), 204–5; and Transmundus, *Introductiones dictandi*, ed. and trans. Anne Dalzell, Studies and Texts, 123 (Toronto: Pontifical Institute of Medieval Studies, 1995), 19–20. See also Giles Constable, "The Structure of Medieval Society According to the *Dictatores* of the Twelfth Century," in *Law, Church, and Society: Essays in Honor of Stephan Kuttner*, ed. Kenneth Pennington and Robert Somerville (Philadelphia: University of Pennsylvania Press, 1977), 253–67.

Lost Letters of Medieval Life

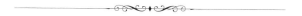

England and Wales in the early thirteenth century.

CHAPTER 1

─ ⚬⚭⚬⚬ ─

Money

CREDIT, DEBT, AND COMMERCE

──────── 1 ────────

Legal Agreement for Pledging a Rural Estate[1]

Hec est convencio pignorancie

Hec est convencio facta inter A. et B., scilicet, quod predictus A. invadiavit dicto B. x acras terre, cum capitali mesuagio et cum omnibus pertin-
enciis, infra villam cum firma rusticorum, pro x. marcis. Set predictus
A. excepit[2] et reservavit[3] ad opus suum forisfacturam [rusticorum],[4] et
presencias ad natalem, et precaturas temporum augusti, stagnum et
molendinum, quibus predictis [exceptis],[5] prenominatus[6] [B.][7] habebit
omnia que pertinent ad predictam in omnibus locis et aisiamentis ad
comodum suum faciendum donec predictus A. reddiderit predicto B. x.
marcas argenti vel equivalenciam.[8] Hanc terram invadiavit predicto B.
anno tricesimo[9] a coronacione[10] Regis Henrici tercii.

This is an agreement for a pledge

This is the agreement made between A. and B., namely, that the said A.
has pledged to the said B. ten acres of land, with a capital messuage and
all its appurtenances, within the vill [of—], together with the farm of its
villeins, for ten marks. But the aforesaid A. has excluded and reserved to
his own use the forfeits of [the villeins] and the presents at Christmas,[11]
and the August boon-works, the pond and the mill. Apart from those
said exceptions, the aforesaid [B.] shall have all things that appertain to
the said land in all places and easements, to put to his own profit, until
the said A. shall pay to the said B. ten marks of silver or the equivalent.

He has pledged this land to the said B. in the thirtieth year since the coronation of King Henry III [October 28, 1245 × October 27, 1246].[12]

This document provides a small snapshot of life on an English manor in the first half of the thirteenth century. The lord of the manor in an unnamed vill[13] is evidently in need of cash. To get it, he has pledged a "capital messuage" (a building plot containing a high-status dwelling) and its appurtenances, together with additional specified economic assets. That is, the lord has pledged the manor house (which he may or may not have used as a personal residence) and all other buildings and other things attached to it, together with ten acres (4.05 ha.) of land, the "farm" of his villeins (i.e., the cash rent and other obligations, such as weekly labor-services, due from his unfree tenants),[14] and any easements (rights of access) that belonged to the property. He has, however, excluded from the pledge and reserved to his own use some valuable perquisites (entitlements) that are part of this estate.[15] These are the forfeits (fines or fees) paid by the servile tenants (serfs or villeins) to the lord's manorial court;[16] the "presents" at Christmas, which in fact were not voluntary gifts, but annual rents in kind, such as eggs, hens, and loaves of bread, that tenants were required to render to their lord;[17] the seasonal ("boon") works, such as reaping or carting, which were due from the villeins and sometimes also from free tenants at harvest-time in August; and the use and profits of the pond (probably the millpond, which might double as a fishpond)[18] and the mill, which servile tenants were required to use, for a fee, for grinding their grain.[19]

The fact that the lord of this manor has reserved the labor-services that were due from his villeins at harvest-time implies that his demesne (home farm) consisted of more than the ten acres pledged here, and that he needed the villeins' labor to bring in the harvest or perform other seasonal tasks. This reservation, together with that of the fines paid by the lord's villeins to his manor court and of the "presents" that they owed to him at Christmas, suggests that the manor was a populous and prosperous one, with enough tenants to make the lord's court and mill profitable, and to provide valuable labor-services at harvest-time and "gifts" at Christmas.

To redeem this pledge, the lord would have to pay ten marks (£6 13s. 4d.) in silver or the equivalent value in grain or some other commodity. That sum probably included a percentage of concealed interest, meaning that he would have received a loan of less than ten marks in cash.[20] Although the term of the loan is not specified, the lord evidently does not expect to be able to redeem his property in less than half a year, or he would not have reserved perquisites that would require a period of at least five months (August-Christmas) to yield their value.

The reference to a pond suggests that the mill mentioned in this document was probably a watermill. The windmill, a recent invention, occurs in other documents in this volume (see CHAPTER 5). For other accounts of life on the manor, see DOCUMENTS 20–21, 49–53, 90, 93 and 98–99.

The date attached to this document is of great significance in dating the formulary in Add. 8167 (see INTRODUCTION, pp. 6–8). The dating of legal documents was by no means universal in practice or consistent in form at this time. In early thirteenth-century England, the routine keeping of written records was a comparatively recent development, and many documents were not dated at all. When the date was included, it might be given as the year A.D., expressed in Latin as *anno domini* ("in the year of the Lord") or as *anno gracie* ("in the year of grace"). However, there was widespread disagreement about when the year began. The historian Gervase of Canterbury, a Benedictine monk (d. 1210), noted that "the solar year, according to Roman tradition and the custom of the church, begins on 1 January," but that three other Christian holy days were commonly used as well for beginning the new year. "Some people," he wrote, "begin the year at the Annunciation [March 25], some at the Passion [Easter], some at the Circumcision [January 1], . . . but most, whom I shall follow, begin the year of grace at Christmas. For it is our custom to count men's years and age not from conception but from birth."[21] In France during the reign of Philip Augustus (1180–1223), the royal chancery adopted Easter as the start of the new year, but in England the practice shifted from beginning the new year at Christmas to beginning it on March 25, the feast of the Annunciation (also known as Lady Day).[22]

Such inconsistencies could cause much confusion, and in England, beginning in the reign of Richard I "the Lionheart" (1189–99), when a document was dated, it became common to avoid or to supplement the A.D. date by citing the regnal year of the sovereign. During the reigns of Richard I and of his brother John (1199–1216) and John's son Henry III (1216–72), regnal years were dated (as here in DOCUMENT 1) from the day of the king's coronation; later sovereigns' regnal years were dated from the day of their accession.[23] Other dating systems were also in use, however, either in conjunction with the regnal date or in place of it. For example, some letters issued by prelates were dated from their assumption of office (e.g., "in the fourth year of our pontificate"), while other documents were dated by reference to important events (e.g., the captivity of Arthur, duke of Brittany, discussed below). There were also multiple systems in use for identifying the precise day on which a document was dated. Some documents, then as now, simply named the day and month (e.g., "the third day of June"), while others identified them by reference to a saint's-day (e.g., "Tuesday before the feast of St Michael the Archangel") or by the usage of the ancient Roman calendar (e.g., "the calends of August").

Examples of the variety of dating systems that were in use in early thirteenth-century England can be seen in contemporary formularies. In the formulary in Walters MS W. 15 (*c.* 1202–9), a brief instruction on dating clauses gives three different examples: "in the year from the incarnation of the Lord, 1199; or thus, in the fourth year from the coronation of King John; or, in the second year from the captivity of Arthur."[24] In Add. 8167, one model agreement (*convencio*) also gives three different forms for dates: "This was done in the year of the Lord 1220; or, in the ninth year since the return of King R[ichard] to England; or thus, in the fourth year since the coronation of King J[ohn]."[25] Another gives the year since the king's coronation, followed by the day and month according to the ancient Roman calendar: "in the fourth year since the coronation of King [Henry] III, on the fourth day before the calends of August" (i.e., July 29, 1220).[26]

Such a variety of dating systems helped to make the drafting and interpretation of important documents a demanding task, one requiring a collection of reference works and training manuals such as the formularies represented in this volume.

NOTES

1 Add. 8167, fols. 94v–95r, collated with an earlier version of the text in Walters Art Museum, Baltimore, MS W. 15 (hereafter Walters MS W. 15), fol. 81r, and a later version in CCCC 297, p. 298 (fol. 149v). For Walters MS W. 15 and CCCC 297, see INTRODUCTION, pp. 8–9.

2 Add. 8167, fol. 95r.

3 *servavit* in Add. 8167; *reservavit* in Walters MS W. 15 and CCCC 297.

4 *iustic'* ("of justice") in Add. 8167; *rusticorum* ("of the villeins") in Walters MS W. 15 and CCCC 297.

5 *exceptis* is missing in Add. 8167, but is supplied in both Walters MS W. 15 and CCCC 297.

6 *prenoiatus* in Add. 8167.

7 Add. 8167 incorrectly gives *A.* here; both Walters MS W. 15 and CCCC 297 give *B.*

8 Corrected in MS from *equivalencciam.*

9 Corrected in MS from *trisesimo.*

10 *carnacione* (fleshiness or corpulency) in MS. The same error occurs in another model agreement (*convencio*) on fol. 94r, which is discussed below.

11 *presencias ad natalem*; the later version of this text in CCCC 297 uses the expanded phrase *presencias sive exennia ad natale[m]* ("presents or gifts at Christmas").

12 *Handbook of Dates*, 33.

13 The vill (often a village or town) was the basic unit of local civil administration. See Mark Bailey, trans. and ed., *The English Manor c. 1200–c. 1500* (Manchester: Manchester University Press, 2002), 7, n. 15.

14 On free and servile tenures and status, see Bailey, trans. and ed., *English Manor*, 28–37.

15 On English law regarding the pledging of land, see Paul Brand, "Aspects of the Law of Debt, 1189–1307," in *Credit and Debt in Medieval England c. 1180–c. 1350*, ed. Phillipp R. Schofield and Nicholas J. Mayhew (Oxford: Oxbow Books, 2002), 19, 30–31. On peasant rents and services generally, see Henry Stanley Bennett, *Life on the English Manor* (Cambridge: Cambridge University Press, 1937), Chap. 5.

16 For a useful overview of manor courts, including the income that they could yield, see Bailey, trans. and ed., *English Manor*, 167–78; see also Bennett, *Life on the English Manor*, Chap. 8, especially 198–204, 217–19.

17 The lord then often used these "presents" to form the substance of the Christmas dinner that he hosted for his tenants. George C. Homans, *English Villages of the Thirteenth Century* (Cambridge, Mass.: Harvard University Press, 1941; rpt. New York: Norton, 1975), 357.

18 In the later version of this pledge in CCCC 297, the last item reserved by the pledger to his own use was the *stangnum molendini* (that is, the millpond, not the pond and the mill).

19 Bailey, trans. and ed., *English Manor*, 31–32; Richard Holt, *The Mills of Medieval England* (Oxford: Basil Blackwell, 1988), 36–53; Bennett, *Life on the English Manor*, 129–35. On the use of mills for fulling cloth, see Eleanora Carus-Wilson, "An Industrial Revolution of the Thirteenth Century," *Economic History Review*, 11, no. 1 (1941); rpt. with a postscript in eadem, *Medieval Merchant Venturers: Collected Studies*, 2nd ed. (London: Methuen, 1967), 183–210.

20 On concealed interest in loans of this kind, see DOCUMENT 14.

21 Quoted in Robert Bartlett, *England Under the Norman and Angevin Kings, 1075–1225* (Oxford: Clarendon, 2000), 640.

22 Bartlett, *England Under the Norman and Angevin Kings*, 640–41.

23 *Handbook of Dates*, 21.

24 *Anno ab incarnatione domini millesimo centesimo nonagesimo nono; vel sic, Anno iiij a coronacione regis Johannis; vel anno secundo a captivitate arturi.* Walters MS W. 15, fol. 81r; printed in Herbert Edward Salter, William Abel Pantin, and Henry Gerald Richardson, eds., *Formularies Which Bear on the History of Oxford, c. 1204–1420*, Oxford Historical Society, vol. 2 (1942), 277. Arthur, duke of Brittany, was the posthumous son (b. 1187) of King John's elder brother Geoffrey, and thus a dangerous rival to John. Captured in Mirebeau on August 1, 1202, he was imprisoned by John, first at Falaise and subsequently at Rouen, where he was allegedly murdered by John himself on April 3, 1203. See *Oxford DNB*, s.n. "Arthur, duke of Brittany." The casual reference in the Walters document to a date in the second year since Arthur's captivity suggests that Arthur may in fact have lived—or at least was thought to be still alive—well beyond the latter date.

25 *Anno domini mᵒ ccᵒ xxᵒ vel anno nono secundo a reversione regis R[icardi]. Anglie vel sic anno quarto a c[oro]nacione .I[ohannis]. regis facta fuit.* Add. 8167, fol. 94r. Here, as in DOCUMENT 1, the MS incorrectly gives *carnacione* (abbreviated as "cᵃnac[i]o[n]e") instead of *coronacione*. Richard I was crowned for a second time on April 17, 1194, after his return from captivity.

26 *anno quarto a coronacione Regis [Henrici] tercii quarto kalendarum augusti.* Add. 8167, fol. 95r. In this agreement, the word *coronacione* is correctly given. The two agreements on fols. 94r and 95r are not among the documents included in the present volume.

2

An Earl Orders Wine from His Vintner[1]

Comes mandat creditori[2] suo ut mittat sibi vinum.

A. comes Glovernie dilecto sibi A. vinetario de C., salutem et dileccionem. Quoniam quicquid vobis de vino credito[3] multociens debuimus ad diem vestrum semper plenarie persolvemus, et nichil est in reragio,[4] audacius in hoc stanti negocio confugimus, attencius rogantes quatinus v. dolea vini, scilicet duo gasconiensis et tria andegavensis,[5] quodlibet ad precium xx. solidorum, usque ad pasca floridum nobis acomodetis. Scituri quod denarios vestros ad diem nominatum omni occasione[6] et dilacione remota persolvemus. Tantum ergo faciatis[7] ut vobis ad gratiarum teneamur acciones. Valete.

An earl sends word to his [vintner] to send him some wine

A., earl of Gloucester, to his beloved A., vintner of C., greetings and love. Since whatever we have owed you for wine bought on credit on many occasions we have always paid in full on your day, and nothing is in arrears, the more confidently in this present business we have turned to you, asking earnestly that you accommodate us with five tuns[8] of wine, namely, two of Gascon and three of Angevin, at a price of 20*s.* each, until Palm Sunday. You will know that we shall pay your money on the day named without any argument or delay; therefore, may you act in such a manner that we shall be bound to you in gratitude. Farewell.

The earl's tone in this letter is distinctly friendly. Instead of commanding, he is making a polite request, although there is a clear assumption that the addressee will comply with it. The earl addresses his vintner (wine-merchant) as "beloved" and sends him not only greetings, but also "love." These terms do not signify personal affection, but rather confidence in the addressee's loyalty and trustworthiness, while at the same time acknowledging that the addressee is not in the writer's employ or under his direct control.

This letter is ostensibly written by "A., Earl of Gloucester," and indeed in the early thirteenth century there was an earl of Gloucester with this initial, Amaury de Montfort. In May 1200, under an arrangement with King John, Amaury exchanged his county of Évreux in Normandy for the earldom of Gloucester (to which his mother had been co-heiress); he died without heirs between Michaelmas 1210 and November 1213.[9] Earl Amaury was married to

Millicent (or Maud), daughter of the Norman baron Hugh de Gournai.[10] He seems to have passed much of his adult life in Normandy, and until 1200 was probably in England only infrequently.[11] However, possible evidence of his subsequent presence there comes from seven surviving charters and references to three others that no longer survive, which were issued by Earl Amaury concerning his English estates. The places of issue are not given, but the names of the witnesses and the contents of the charters suggest English venues. The first of these charters probably dates from before 1205, another from Michaelmas 1210, and a third pre-dates the latter; the rest are undated.[12] In addition, by 1216 Earl Amaury's widow had married an English baron, William de Cantilupe II (d. 1251).[13] It therefore seems likely that Earl Amaury spent at least some time in England after 1200, and perhaps was living there at the time of his death.

The association of DOCUMENT 2 with Earl Amaury must therefore be regarded as possible, though far from certain. It may at least be based on a genuine letter by an earl or other lord, if not by Amaury himself. Eight additional letters from Add. 8167 in the current volume (DOCUMENTS 3, 4, 5, 6, 8, 15, 24, and 47) are also connected with earls, two of them (in DOCUMENTS 5 and 15) named as earls of Gloucester, and it is conceivable that this group of letters derives from genuine examples of the correspondence of one or more of the earls of Gloucester in the first half of the thirteenth century. The likely date of the letter above, in the decade or so after 1204 (see below), certainly would fit with Amaury de Montfort's earldom.

However, since these comital letters also exemplify a nicely representative set of requests and responses, it is equally possible that some or even all of them are fictitious and were composed for teaching purposes. If so, DOCUMENTS 2, 5, and 15 may have been attributed to the earl of Gloucester because he was the only earl to have substantial estates in the vicinity of Oxford and was therefore a natural magnate for the unknown Oxford compiler of this formulary to name.

In the letter above, the earl explains that he has often bought wine from the vintner on credit and has always paid up in full and on time. Now he wants to order five pounds' worth of imported French wine on credit, with no down payment, and to pay the full sum on Palm Sunday. The earl's letter to his vintner offers a glimpse into the consumer's side of the wine trade, which was one of the most important sectors of medieval commerce.

In thirteenth-century France the autumn vintage was shipped as quickly as possible, ideally within weeks of pressing, but bad weather, bureaucratic delays, and uncertain shipping conditions could prevent some shipments from being sent to England until the following spring. The grapes were typically pressed in September, and the wine was ready for export in October. The ships carrying the new vintage arrived at the English ports—principally Bristol, Southampton, London, Hull, and Sandwich—between October and January. Wine that failed to reach its French port in time for the sailing of the autumn wine fleet, or which reached the port but remained unsold, was allowed to settle and was then drawn off the lees, or "racked." A second fleet, carrying this "racked" wine, came to England in the spring, preferably in time for Easter (when demand and prices were high), but in some cases as late as May or even June.[14]

The earl of Gloucester in this model letter wishes to defer paying for the wine until Palm Sunday, which means that the letter could have been dated at any time between October and March. Since Palm Sunday is the Sunday before Easter, and Easter falls each year between March 22 and April 25,[15] the earl is thus asking for credit of anywhere between one and five months for this order.

There was some grape cultivation in thirteenth-century England, but the climate was not generally favorable enough to produce either a large harvest or good wine.[16] As a result, most wine drunk in England was imported, primarily from France. Even imported wine, however, could be of poor quality, and all wines were subject to deterioration during transport and storage. Peter of Blois, a French-born cleric who in 1174 or 1175 joined the household of the archbishop of Canterbury and became a familiar figure at the court of Henry II (1154–89), wrote bitingly of the dreadful wine—sour, thick, greasy, stale, and tasting of pitch from the cask—that was served to the royal household and the king's guests. "I have sometimes seen even great lords," he reported, "served with wine so muddy that a man must needs close his eyes, and clench his teeth, wry-mouthed and shuddering, and filtering the stuff rather than drinking."[17]

The wines in this model letter come from Anjou (the county around the city of Angers) in northwestern France, and from Gascony in the southwest, with its famous port of Bordeaux at the mouth of the Garonne, which opened, via the Gironde, into the Bay of Biscay (map 2). Both Gascony (which formed part of the duchy of Aquitaine) and Anjou had become part of the English royal patrimony in France in 1154, when Henry, count of Anjou and husband of Eleanor, duchess of Aquitaine, became king of England.

During the reigns of Henry II (1154–89) and his son Richard I (1189–99) the wines of Anjou were shipped downstream on the Loire for export from the Breton port of Nantes, which should have given them a competitive edge in the cost of shipping to England. However, Angevin wines occupied only a secondary rank in the English market during this period. Instead, the English

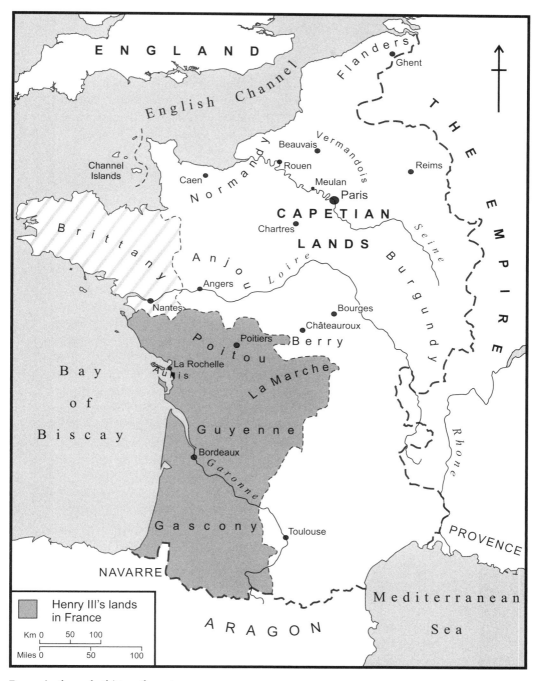

France in the early thirteenth century.

market was dominated by wines from Poitou (the county around Poitiers) and Aunis, which together occupied the region between the Sèvre and the Gironde in the center of western France. These wines were shipped from the port of La Rochelle in the northern part of the Bay of Biscay. The wines of Gascony, the most distant of all, are poorly recorded in England before the second decade of the thirteenth century. Although Gascon as well as Poitevin wines are mentioned in London in the 1170s, King John's regulations for the price of wines, made in 1199, list only French wines from the Seine valley (exported via Rouen in Normandy), from Anjou, and from Poitou. These were taxed, respectively, at 25s., 24s., and 20s. per barrel, suggesting their relative values. No major shipments of Gascon wines to England are recorded before 1213–14.[18]

In 1204 Richard's brother and successor King John (1199–1216) lost Anjou and the rest of the English territories in northwestern France to the French king Philip Augustus, and in 1224 Poitou and La Rochelle likewise fell. Gascony, however, remained under English control until the mid-fifteenth century, and from the reign of Henry III Gascon wines dominated the English market.[19] These developments suggest that this model letter may have been based on one written in the reign of King John in the decade or so following the loss of Anjou in 1204, when some wine from the French king's dominions was still being shipped to England but Gascon wine was beginning to dominate the English market.[20] This dating would fit well with the identification of the earl of Gloucester here as Amaury de Montfort.

An early thirteenth-century date for this letter is also suggested by the price of the wines. The wines in DOCUMENTS 2–3 are priced at 20s. per tun, but by 1250–51 the typical price had evidently risen by 50 percent, to 30s. per tun.[21] Between 1261 and 1268 Robert Carpenter II compiled a book of texts on estate management that included material derived from another copy of the formulary in Add. 8167, and Carpenter's version of the vintner's response to this request (DOCUMENT 3) gives the price of the wine as 40s. (£2) per tun.[22]

NOTES

1   Add. 8167, fol. 97r–v.
2   Although the heading here says that the earl is writing to his "creditor," in the body of the letter the earl notes explicitly that his account with the vinter is *not* in arrears.
3   Corrected in MS from *creditorio*.
4   Fol. 97v.
5   *andegavense* in MS.
6   *o^iccasione* in MS.
7   *facientes* in MS.
8   A tun was a measure of capacity for wine and other liquids. It generally contained 252 gallons (*c.* 954 liters), but sometimes contained 208, 240, or 250 gallons. Ronald

E. Zupko, *A Dictionary of English Weights and Measures, from Anglo-Saxon Times to the Nineteenth Century* (Madison: University of Wisconsin Press, 1968), 175.

9   Amaury or Amauri, the fourth earl of Gloucester was the son of Mabel, eldest daughter and co-heiress of William, the second earl. Edmund Boleslaw Fryde, Diana E. Greenway, S. Porter, and Ian Roy, eds., *Handbook of British Chronology*, Royal Historical Society, Guides and Handbooks 2, 3rd ed. (London, 1986), 463.

10 *Oxford DNB*, s.nn. "Cantilupe [Cantelupe], William (II) de (d. 1251)," and "Cantilupe, Thomas de [St Thomas of Hereford] (c. 1220–1282)."

11 Robert B. Patterson, ed., *Earldom of Gloucester Charters: The Charters and Scribes of the Earls and Countesses of Gloucester to A.D. 1217* (Oxford: Clarendon, 1973), 5–8 and nos. 79–80.

12 Patterson, ed., *Earldom of Gloucester Charters*, nos. 41 (probably before 1205), 53, 94 (before September 29, 1210), 94 n. (September 29, 1210), 153, 154, 176, 214, 215, 235.

13 Her new husband, like his father William de Cantilupe I, was named by Roger of Wendover as one of King John's "evil counsellors," but their son Thomas became bishop of Hereford and was canonized in 1320. *Oxford DNB*, s.nn. "Cantilupe [Cantelupe], William (II) de (d. 1251)" and "Cantilupe, Thomas de [St Thomas of Hereford] (c. 1220–1282)."

14 Yves Renouard, "The Wine Trade of Gascony in the Middle Ages," in *Essays in French Economic History*, ed. Rondo Cameron (Homewood, Ill.: Richard D. Irwin, for the American Economic Association, 1970), 64–90, especially 73–80. The latter article was originally published as "Le Grand commerce des vins de Gascogne au Moyen Age," *Revue historique*, 221 (1959), 261–304. There is a brief summary of Renouard in Margaret Wade Labarge, *A Baronial Household of the Thirteenth Century* (London: Eyre and Spottiswoode, 1965; rpt. New York: Barnes and Noble, 1966), 106–7. See also Rosalind Kent Berlow, "Wine and Winemaking," in *Dictionary of the Middle Ages*, ed. Joseph R. Strayer, vol. 12 (New York: Charles Scribner's Sons, 1982–89), 648–54. Some shipments of Gascon wines also reached the ports of Great Yarmouth, King's Lynn, Newcastle, and Chester. See Renouard, "Wine Trade of Gascony," 74 and n. 4.

15 *Handbook of Dates*, 83–155.

16 Labarge, *Baronial Household*, 104; James A. Galloway, "Driven by Drink? Ale Consumption and the Agrarian Economy of the London Region, c. 1300–1400," in *Food and Eating in Medieval Europe*, ed. Martha Carlin and Joel T. Rosenthal (London: Hambledon, 1998), 88.

17 Translated by George Gordon Coulton in *Medieval Panorama: The English Scene from Conquest to Reformation* (Cambridge: Cambridge University Press, 1938; rpt. New York: Meridian Books, 1955), 233. For the Latin text, see Lena Wahlgren, *The Letter Collections of Peter of Blois: Studies in the Manuscript Tradition*, Studia Graeca et Latina Gothoburgensia, 58 ([Göteborg, Sweden:] Acta Universitatis Gothoburgensis, 1993), ep. 14 B, 159–60. Wahlgren's Introduction (9–18) gives an overview of Peter of Blois's career. A member of the household of three successive archbishops of Canterbury (Richard, Baldwin, and Hubert Walter), he also became archdeacon of Wells and, *c.* 1202, of London; he died c. 1211–12.

18 Renouard, "Wine Trade of Gascony," 68–67; see also Labarge, *Baronial Household*, 105–12. For an amusing contemporary French discussion of white wines, see Henri d'Andeli's poem *La Bataille des vins*, which depicts King Philip Augustus (1180–1223) as summoning all the good white wines to his court, where they dispute about

which is the best. *Les Dits d'Henri d'Andeli*, ed. Alain Corbellari, Classiques français du Moyen Âge, 146 (Paris: Champion, 2003).

19 Renouard, "Wine Trade of Gascony," 72–88.

20 Alan David Francis, *The Wine Trade* (London: Adam & Charles Black, 1972; rpt. New York: Harper and Row, 1973), 7; Anne Crawford, *A History of the Vintners' Company* (London: Constable, 1977), 15.

21 An account of 207 tuns of "wine of France" (*vini Franciae*) seized and purchased on the king's behalf at London and Sandwich between the feasts of All Saints and Easter in 35 Henry III (November 1, 1250–April 16, 1251), valued them at 20s. the tun for wine taken by "prise" (a royal perquisite) but 30s. the tun for wine acquired by purchase. Shirley, ed., *Letters*, vol. 2, 95–98 (this letter is now TNA: PRO, SC 1/11/36). For prise, see DOCUMENT 19. For the capacity of the tun, see note 8, above.

22 Gonville & Caius 205/111, p. 279. On Robert Carpenter and his formulary, see INTRODUCTION, p. 9.

3

How the Vintner Should Respond if the Earl Has a Good Credit Rating[1]

Responsio ad literas predictas

Dileccio domino suo et amico W. Comiti de .S., suus A. vinetarius salutem. Literas[2] vestras nuper accepi petitorias quatinus v. dolea vini gasconiensis[3] et tria andegavensis,[4] quodlibet ad precium xx. solidorum, usque ad pasca floridum vobis acomodarem. Quoniam quicquid michi debuistis optime persolvistis, precibus vestris ad presens adquiesco et v. dolea ut petistis vobis acomodo, de vobis confidens quod ad diem nominatum iuxta consuetudinem vestram michi debitum meum persolvetis.[5]

Response to the aforesaid letter

To his beloved lord and friend, W., earl of S., A. his vintner sends greetings. I have lately received your letter asking that I accommodate you with five tuns of Gascon wine and three of Angevin, at a price of 20s. each, until Palm Sunday (*Pasca Floridum*). Since whatever you have owed me you have paid in the best manner, I agree to your present request and shall accommodate you with the five tuns as you requested, trusting in you that on the day named, according to your custom, you will pay your debt to me in full.

A shortage of cash, at all levels of society, is a frequent theme in this collection of model letters (see, e.g., DOCUMENTS 2–6, 9–14, 86–88, and 99). The letters make it clear that people of all classes, including, as here, great lords, often had cash-flow problems and depended heavily on credit.

It is very difficult to estimate the amount of coin in circulation. Martin Allen has argued that in 1180 there was probably less than £100,000 circulating in coin in England—perhaps as little as £15,000–£60,000 (representing about 3.6 million–14.4 million pennies). Over the next thirty years the money supply evidently increased sharply, so that around 1210 there may have been between £100,000 and £300,000 in circulation (about 24 million–72 million pennies). A further increase in the money supply in the succeeding decades produced a total of about £460,000–£490,000 (about 110.4 million to 117.6 million pennies) in circulation on the eve of the recoinage of 1247.[6]

Midpoint figures from Allen's calculations would represent an increase in the money supply from some £55,000 (13.2 million pennies) in 1180 to around £200,000 (48 million pennies) in 1210, and then to about £475,000 (114 million pennies) in 1247. J. L. Bolton has argued that much of this increase in the money supply dated from the mid-1230s and later. The mints at London and Canterbury, for example, which together probably were producing about four million coins a year in the 1220s, struck an average of around ten million coins each year from 1234 to 1247. The new Long Cross penny was introduced in the spring of 1248, and the two mints produced seventy million coins in 1248–50.[7]

Despite this considerable increase in mint production, shortages of cash persisted. The lack of ready money could plague even the king himself. On May 11, 1249, for example, Henry III wrote to his treasurer from Marlborough, where he was planning to celebrate the great religious festival of Pentecost (Whitsunday, which in 1249 fell on May 23), to send him five hundred marks in cash "without delay" (*sine dilatione*), since "we need to have money on hand daily to pay for the expenses of our household, because we have found the countryside on every side destitute of cash."[8]

This model letter, though clearly written in response to Document 2, is nevertheless addressed to "W., Earl of S.," instead of to "A., Earl of Gloucester." The most likely explanation for this discrepancy is that both model letters are simply fictitious. However, the details given in these documents are quite plausible, and it is possible that they were based on genuine correspondence. See Document 2 for a discussion of the possible attribution of other letters in this collection to Amaury de Montfort.

NOTES

1   Add. 8167, fol. 97v.
2   *litera* in MS.
3   *gasconensi* in MS.

4   *andegavense* in MS.

5   Corrected in MS from *persolvistis*.

6   These estimates are drawn from Martin Allen, *Mints and Money in Medieval* England (Cambridge: Cambridge University Press, 2012), 318–26 and 344, Table 10.12. We are deeply grateful to Dr. Allen for providing us with extracts from his book prior to its publication, and for much helpful information on coinage. For the recoinage and the introduction of the Long Cross penny in November 1247, see above, "A Note on Money."

7   For the Long Cross penny, see p. xxiv, "A Note on Money." The years 1248–50 were exceptional. See Peter Spufford, *Money and Its Use in Medieval Europe* (Cambridge: Cambridge University Press, 1988), 196–97, 202–4; and James L. Bolton, "Inflation, Economics and Politics in Thirteenth-Century England," in *Thirteenth Century England IV: Proceedings of the Newcastle Upon Tyne Conference 1991*, ed. Peter R. Coss and Simon D. Lloyd (Woodbridge, Suffolk: Boydell, 1992), 6.

8   *oportet nos singulis diebus habere pecuniam ad manum solvendam pro expensis hospitii nostri, eo quod invenimus patriam undique pecunia destitutam.* Shirley, ed., *Letters*, vol. 2, 54 (this letter is now TNA: PRO, SC 1/2/93).

--------------------------------- 4 ---------------------------------

How the Vintner Should Respond if the Earl Does Not Repay His Debts[1]

Si non solvit bene quod debuit tunc dicat sic

[Tamen][2] de libertate vestra confidens, presumens preces vestras ad effectum mancipare, vobis v. dolea vini petita acomodo, rogans attencius quatinus de antiquo debito, quod super est in reragio, pariter cum hoc novo debito ad dictum diem michi persolvatis. Valete.

If he has not paid well what he has owed, then let him say thus

[Nevertheless,] trusting in your generosity, being so bold as to put your wishes in effect, I shall accommodate you with the five tuns of wine you requested, beseeching you earnestly that you pay me in full your old debt, which is in arrears, equally with this new debt, on the said day. Farewell.

The problem of what to do when a wealthy and powerful customer failed to pay for a previous order but nevertheless demanded further goods must have been a frequent one for medieval merchants. Buying and selling on credit was, as we have seen, a standard way of doing business, and in the small world of elite medieval shoppers and vendors, it was impossible to hide behind corporate anonymity.

This fragment of a model letter, which is designed to serve as a negative variant to the positive version in Document 3, represents the uneasy middle ground for the merchant between a confident offer of credit and a firm refusal. Here the vintner retains the deferential language of the "happy to oblige!" letter in Document 3, while at the same time reminding the earl that his previous bill is overdue and must be settled along with the present one. His appeal to the earl's "generosity" (*liberalitate*) as a goad to payment is shrewd, since for persons of high standing open-handed largesse was one of the key virtues, while a reputation for close-fistedness was extremely damaging.[3] The vintner here is letting the earl know, by implication, that if he fails to pay his bills this time he risks losing both his commercial credit rating and his social reputation.

A fuller and slightly testier version of this response is given in the formulary compiled by Robert Carpenter II between 1261 and 1268.[4] In this version, the vintner's correspondent is simply "A." rather than an earl. The writer is instructed to repeat the text of the previous letter of acceptance (Document 3) as far as the word "*acomodarem*," and then to say: "Although sometimes you have not fully paid me what you have owed to me, nevertheless (*tamen*), trusting in your loyalty and generosity, I have put your wishes into effect."[5]

Carpenter's formulary also includes two unequivocally negative responses to the same request for wine on credit. In both of these the writer is also instructed to repeat the letter of acceptance as far as the word "*acomodarem*." Then, to reject the request outright, the writer was to say: "since I have often advanced you wine [on credit], hoping to receive some measure of appreciation (*honorem*), or at least full payment, on the appointed day, but in fact I have received no appreciation, unless only by happenstance (*improuissione*), and no full payment, but rather only in part and less than fully, and often with quarrels; on that account, at present I neither wish nor dare to advance you anything."[6] To excuse himself from fulfilling the request, however, the writer was simply to say: "I do not have wine with which I can satisfy you, on which account at present I cannot fulfill your request."[7]

The replies in Documents 3 and 4, together with those in Carpenter's formulary, make it clear that these collections of model letters, and the exemplars from which they were copied, were intended for the use of merchants and other tradespeople as well as their wealthy customers. As such, they provide an important glimpse into the otherwise largely unrecorded business correspondence of early thirteenth-century England.

NOTES

1   Add. 8167, fol. 97v.

2   *Tantum* in Add. 8167, but a fuller version of this text in Gonville & Caius 205/111, pp. 279–80, gives *Tamen*, which is a better fit for the context. See below.

3   See, e.g., David Crouch, *The Birth of Nobility: Constructing Aristocracy in England and France, 900–1300* (London: Longman, 2005), 68–71.

4   On Robert Carpenter and his formulary, see INTRODUCTION, p. 9.

5   *Litteras vestras etcetera ut prius. usque ad hoc verbum. acomodarem. et tunc dicetur sic. Quamvis igitur quod michi debuistis; aliquando plenarie non persoluistis. tamen de fidelitate et libertate vestra confidens. preces vestras effectui.* Gonville & Caius 205/111, pp. 279–80.

6   *A. B. salutem. litteras vestras etcetera ut prius usque ad hoc uerbum. acomodarem. Inde sic. Quoniam vobis multociens vini acomodauj. sperans aliquantum honorem. uel saltem plenariam solucionem ad diem prefixum suscipere. set nullam honorem in re; nisj tantum inprouissione. nec solucionem integre; immo partim. et minus plenarie cum rixis sepissime recepj. unde ad presens nec volo nec audeo; vobis aliquid comodare. valete.* Gonville & Caius 205/111, p. 280.

7   *A. B. salutem. litteras vestras etcetera usque acomodarem. Inde sic. Ego vero nullum tale vinum habeo. vnde vobis satisfacere possum. quapro[p]ter peticionem vestram; ad presens adimplere non possum. valete.* Gonville & Caius 205/111, p. 280.

5

An Earl Orders Cloth from His Draper, to Whom He Owes Money[1]

Comes mandat pannario creditori suo

B. comes Glovernie dilecto sibi A. pannario London' salutem et dileccionis affectum. Quamvis merita nostra non exigant (*vel non precesserint*),[2] tamen de libertate vestra confidimus (*ad vos in hoc instanti negocio confugimus*), rogans attencius quatinus xx. ulnas de scarleta rubea et totidem de perso et totidem de minueto, ad racionabile forum (*vel precium*) prout sustinere poteritis, usque ad clausum pasca, absque pignore si vobis placuerit, michi acomodetis (*vel, super x. anulos aureos et x. ciphos argenteos quos vobis transmittimus*). Sciatis enim pro vero quod ad diem prefixum, omni occasione remota, vobis bene persolvemus. Tantum ergo faciatis ut vobis tanquam familiari et creditori nostro grates et honores cum denariis vestris referamus. Valete.

An earl sends word to his draper, to whom he owes money

B., earl of Gloucester, to his beloved A., draper of London, greetings and love. Although our merits are not compelling (*or, have not been outstanding*), nevertheless we have relied on your generosity (*we have turned to you in this present business*), asking anxiously that you accommodate me with twenty ells of red scarlet, and the same of perse (dark blue) [scarlet], and the same of shorn (*minueto*) [scarlet],[3] at the most reasonable cost (*or price*) that you can manage, until the Sunday after Easter, without a pledge, if you please (*or, upon the ten gold rings and ten silver cups that we send you*). For you know for a fact that we shall pay you well on the appointed day, without any delay. Therefore, may you act in such a manner that we shall return our thanks and respect to you, as our friend as much as our creditor, along with your money. Farewell.

This letter provides another example of how magnates could, as a matter of course, order costly goods by letter, in Latin, from merchants with whom they had accounts. The earl here, who (as in DOCUMENT 2 and elsewhere) may have been a genuine earl or a fictitious one,[4] acknowledges that his credit record has not been outstanding; in fact, according to the heading of this letter, his account is in arrears. Nevertheless, he asks his London draper to send him sixty ells (68.58 meters) of scarlet, a luxurious woolen broadcloth.[5] The letter includes several instances of variant phrasing, which are shown italicized above, in parentheses. In one, the earl asks to receive these goods on credit; in an alternate version, he secures his credit by sending a pledge of ten gold rings and ten silver cups. This sounds extravagant, but the scarlets that the earl is ordering here represent some of the most expensive textiles available in the medieval world: fine woolens, densely woven, dyed in rich colors, and fulled and shorn so as to shrink the cloth by as much as half, to felt the texture of the weave into invisibility, and to shear away the fuzzy nap. The finished cloth had a satiny softness and sheen but was strong and heavy enough to last for a lifetime and more.

Medieval scarlets came in a variety of colors, all of them based on a dyestuff made of the dessicated eggs of pregnant shield lice or scale insects of the Coccidae family (especially *Kermococcus vermilio*), which infested Mediterranean oak trees. This dyestuff, known as "grain" (*granum*) due to its granular appearance, produced the brilliant red hue that the word "scarlet" signifies today. Grain was also used in conjunction with other dyes to produce a range of deep colors, from black, purple, and murrey (mulberry), to brown, perse (dark blue), grays, and greens.[6]

In the early thirteenth century, scarlets were produced in eastern England, especially at Lincoln, but the center of the industry was in Flanders.[7] In a contemporary Arthurian romance, Heinrich von dem Türlin's *Diu Crône* ("The Crown," *c.* 1210 × *c.* 1240), King Arthur and Queen Ginover (Guinevere) host a grand Christmas celebration at Tintagel in Cornwall, and among the gifts they receive are scarlet bedspreads "that glowed like fire" from the Flemish city of Ghent. Later in the poem there is a description of an elderly

Figure 3. A draper's assistant measures out some cloth. From the St. James the Greater window of Chartres Cathedral (*c.* 1220–25).

nobleman who wears a stunning *kleit* (robe or garment) of red scarlet (*einem rôten scharlât*), also from Ghent: "[It] was more costly than any other in the world. It was colored by the purest dye and always looked like a flaming fire: there were no signs of fading. It was soft to the touch, for the thread was smooth, fine, tightly woven, and made from choice, gleaming wool. *Burre*[8] would have been worthless here because it would not have enhanced, but greatly dulled, the bright luster of the fabric. Nothing marred its beauty; it was faultless. The color was midway between light and dark. It was made by Adanz in Ghent."[9]

Medieval English broadcloths such as scarlets were measured in clothyards of 37 inches (0.9144 meters).[10] A single scarlet cloth, which in England measured 24 clothyards by 1.75 clothyards (22.555 m × 1.64465 m) in its finished state, required about 90 pounds (40.82 kg) of the finest English wool.[11] Since an entire fleece of this fine, short-stapled, curly wool weighed only 1 to 2.5 lb. (0.45 to 1.13 kg), each cloth contained the equivalent of the clip from thirty-six to ninety sheep. A scarlet cloth fully dyed in grain also required 20 to 36 lb. (9.1 to 16.3 kg) of dyestuff.[12]

King John (1199–1216) paid 8*s.* per clothyard (0.9144 m) for scarlets, and in 1265 his daughter Eleanor de Montfort, countess of Leicester, paid 7*s.* per ell (1.143 m).[13] The sixty ells of cloth that the earl has ordered here thus would have had a retail value of about £21 to £29 4*s.* 0*d.* In the 1220s in southern England a typical daily wage for women was 1*d.* Male laborers earned 1¹/₂*d.* to 2*d.*, and skilled craftsmen earned 2*d.* to 4*d.*[14] At £21, therefore, sixty ells of scarlet would have cost the equivalent of 1,260 to 2,520 days' wages for a skilled craftsman, 2,520 to 3,360 for a laborer, or 5,040 for a woman. At £29 4*s.* 0*d.*, the cloth would have represented 1,752 to 3,504 days' wages for a skilled craftsman, 3,504 to 4,672 for a laborer, and 7,008 for a woman.

A suit of clothing for a man or woman was known as a "robe." Many robes consisted of two or three garments: a tunic or *cote* (undergown) and super-tunic or *surcote* (overgown), perhaps with a matching hood or other item. More elaborate robes included additional pieces, such as a waistcoat (*corsettus*) or a cloak.[15] A robe for a craftsman took five linear ells (225 inches, or 5.715 m) of broadcloth.[16] Men and women of higher rank, including senior servants in great households who received "livery" robes as part of their wages, often wore longer, fuller garments. For example, the household accounts for 1265 of Eleanor, countess of Leicester, recorded that the robe of Robin Picard, one of her messengers, took six ells (6.858 m) of russet cloth.[17] For her nephew Edmund, son of Richard of Cornwall, the countess bought cloth for two robes, one containing 6¹/₂ ells (7.4295 m), and the other, a summer robe (*roba aestiva*) that included a waistcoat (*corsetto*) and a cloak (*clochia*), containing nine ells (10.287 m).[18] A generation later, in 1284–85, most of the livery robes and hoods issued by Bogo de Clare, a wealthy clerical pluralist, took seven ells (8.001 m) of fabric each.[19]

A cloth of twenty ells would have measured 22.86 meters in length, just over the statutory length of 22.555 meters (24 clothyards) for a broadcloth. This suggests that the three cloths ordered by the earl in lengths of twenty ells apiece probably represented three whole cloths, each of which could have provided the fabric for three robes of 6¹/₂ ells each. An entire finished broad-cloth measured 37.095 square meters in area and weighed 64 lb. avoirdupois (about 29.03 kg), or 782.575 grams per square meter.[20] A robe made from one-third of such a cloth would have contained about 12.36 square meters of fabric and weighed about 21.33 lb. (about 9.67 kg), exclusive of linings and trimmings. All robes, however, would have been lined; cool-weather clothing was generally lined and trimmed with fleece or fur (see DOCUMENTS 6 and 8).[21] The elderly nobleman's scarlet *kleit* in *Diu Crône*, for example, was lined with beaver and bordered in front with sable.[22] A scarlet robe with a fabric-lined *cote* and a fur-lined *surcote*, cloak, and hood thus may have weighed as much as a contemporary suit of armor.[23]

NOTES

1   Add. 8167, fol. 97v.

2   The phrases shown here italicized and in parentheses represent variant phrasings included in the text (see discussion below). An earl uses a similar phrase in DOCUMENT 67.

3   For the translation of *minueto* here as "shorn," see Martha Carlin, "Shops and Shopping in the Early Thirteenth Century: Three Texts," in *Money, Markets and Trade in Late Medieval Europe: Essays in Honour of John H. A. Munro*, ed. Lawrin Armstrong, Ivana Elbl, and Martin M. Elbl (Leiden: Brill, 2007), 524, n. 78, which discusses similar uses of the word in another document in this formulary, a description of urban trades and crafts (fols. 88r–90v).

4   There was no earl of Gloucester whose name began with "B," though it is possible that in this letter, as in others in this collection, the initials used in the salutation have been reversed or scrambled. See the discussion under DOCUMENT 2 of the possible attribution of this and other letters to the Earl Amaury de Montfort (recognized 1200; died 1210 × 13).

5   The ell measured 45 inches (114.3 cm).

6   On medieval scarlets, see John Munro, "The Anti-Red Shift—to the Dark Side: Colour Changes in Flemish Luxury Woollens, 1300–1550," in *Medieval Clothing and Textiles*, vol. 3, ed. Robin Netherton and Gale R. Owen-Crocker (Woodbridge, Suffolk: Boydell, 2007), 56–66; available online at http://www.chass.utoronto.ca/~munro5/MedCloth04chapfourC.pdf [seen November 1, 2007]; and idem, "Medieval Woollens: Textiles, Textile Technology and Industrial Organisation, c. 800–1500," in *The Cambridge History of Western Textiles*, ed. David Jenkins, vol. 1 (Cambridge: Cambridge University Press, 2003), 194–217.

7   On English production of scarlets, see Eleanora M. Carus-Wilson, "The English Cloth Industry in the Late Twelfth and Early Thirteenth Centuries," *Economic History Review*, 14 (1944), 32–33, 37 n. 5, rpt. in eadem, *Medieval Merchant Venturers*, 212–13, 218 n. 4; and Patrick Chorley, "English Cloth Exports During the Thirteenth and Early Fourteenth Centuries: The Continental Evidence," *Historical Research*, 61, no. 144 (February 1988), 4.

8   The meaning of this word is unknown; the context suggests something lustrous or sparkling used to give a sheen to the fabric.

9   *The Crown: A Tale of Sir Gawein and King Arthur's Court by Heinrich von dem Türlin*, trans. J. W. Thomas (Lincoln: University of Nebraska Press, 1989), xii and lines 505–8 (Christmas), 6832–57 (scarlet *kleit*). For the original text, see *Diu Crône von Heinrich von dem Türlin*, ed. Gottlob Heinrich Friedrich Scholl (Stuttgart, 1852). For other literary references to scarlets, see Raymond van Uytven, "Cloth in Medieval Literature of Western Europe," in *Cloth and Clothing in Medieval Europe: Essays in Memory of Professor E. M. Carus-Wilson*, ed. Negley Boyd Harte and Kenneth G. Ponting, Pasold Studies in Textile History, 2 (London: Heinemann Educational Books, The Pasold Research Fund, 1983), 151–83.

10   Pers. comm. from John Munro (August 26, 2008). We are grateful to Professor Munro for this and for additional information on the correct dimensions and weights of English broadcloths, as discussed below.

11   Munro, "Anti-Red Shift," 63 (wools used); idem, "Industrial Change in the Fifteenth- and Sixteenth-Century Low Countries: The Arrival of Spanish Merino

Wools and the Expansion of the '*Nouvelles Draperies*,'" Working Paper No. 18 (unpub.; dated July 17, 2002), 9, n. 23 (finished size of English broadcloth, and weight of the cloth before [90 lb.] and after [64 lb., or 29.03 kg] fulling and shearing), available online at http://www.chass.utoronto.ca/ecipa/archive/UT-ECIPA-MUNRO-02–03.pdf [seen October 31, 2007]. These figures all derive from fifteenth-century sources.

12 Munro, "Medieval Woollens," 187 (fleece weight), 214–16 (scarlets and kermes). On the dimensions of woolen cloths before and after fulling, see p. 205. On the respective costs of labor, wool, and dyestuff in a finished scarlet cloth, see p. 216. On medieval fleece weights, see also M. J. Stephenson, "Wool Yields in the Medieval Economy," *Economic History Review*, 2nd ser., 41, no. 3 (1988), 368–91.

13 Carus-Wilson, "English Cloth Industry," 37, n. 5, in original article, or 218, n. 4, in reprint (King John); Thomas Hudson Turner, ed., *Manners and Household Expenses of England in the Thirteenth and Fifteenth Centuries*, Roxburghe Club Publications, no. 57 (London, 1841), "Rotulus Hospitii Comitissæ Leicestri;ae, A.D. 1265," 25 (Eleanor de Montfort).

14 Howard M. Colvin, ed., *Building Accounts of King Henry III* (Oxford: Clarendon, 1971), 8–12 (the above wage-rates are given by Colvin for the years 1220–27).

15 Labarge, *Baronial Household*, 130–31, 139–41; Frédérique Lachaud, "Liveries of Robes in England, c. 1200–1330," *English Historical Review*, 111, no. 441 (April 1996), 279–98, especially 288–89; eadem, "An Aristocratic Wardrobe of the Late Thirteenth Century: The Confiscation of the Goods of Osbert de Spaldington in 1298," *Historical Research*, 67, no. 162 (February 1994), 91–100, especially 96–97.

16 Regulations for the weavers and fullers of Marlborough at the end of the twelfth century prohibited them from having anything "pertaining to the making of cloth worth a penny except 5 ells a year to clothe themselves." Carus-Wilson, "English Coth Industry," 49 in original article, or 237 in reprint.

17 Turner, ed., *Manners and Household Expenses*, 74. Robin Picard probably is to be identified with the messenger "Picardus" mentioned on pp. 56–57; cf. Labarge, *Baronial Household*, 69. For livery robes, see also DOCUMENTS 6 and 77.

18 Turner, ed., *Manners and Household Expenses*, 25, 74. In the fifteenth century a robe took about seven linear meters of cloth (7.66 yards, or 6.12 ells). Munro, "Medieval Woollens," 216.

19 Montague Spencer Giuseppi, "The Wardrobe and Household Accounts of Bogo de Clare, A.D. 1284–6," *Archaeologia*, 70 (1918–20), 36–38.

20 For this information we are grateful to John Munro. One pound avoirdupois = 0.453592 kg.

21 Elspeth M. Veale, *The English Fur Trade in the Later Middle Ages*, 2nd ed., London Record Society, 38 (2003), 2–9.

22 *The Crown*, trans. Thomas, and *Diu Crône*, ed. Scholl, lines 6858–69.

23 According to Robert Bartlett, the mail coat or hauberk probably weighed about 25–30 lb. (11.4–13.6 kg). *England Under the Norman and Angevin Kings*, 253.

6

An Earl Orders Furs from His Skinner, to Whom He Owes Money[1]

Comes mandat creditori suo pellipario

C.[2] comes dilecto[3] sibi .H. pellipario salutem, et amoris integritatem. Penulis et fururis ad hoc instans pasca quamplurimum indigeo, set denarios ad illas comparandas non habeo. Quare vos imploro, quatinus xx. penulas de griso et totidem ex variis, de agnelino minuto et crispo, de propria selda vestra michi acomodetis vel aliunde ad credenciam. Habere faciatis de propriis [?vel][4] ratum habentes de alienis manibus capientes,[5] et denarios vestros ad diem prenominatum, omni occasione remota, de manibus meis vel R. senescalli mei recipietis. Valete.

An earl sends word to his skinner, to whom he owes money

Earl C. to his beloved skinner H., greetings and complete love. I am sorely lacking in fur panels and linings at this present Easter, but I do not have the money to pay for them. So I implore you that you accommodate me with 20 panels of gris, and the same of vair [and] of lambskin with fine and curly [fleece], from your own seld or from elsewhere, on credit (*ad credenciam*). Arrange to supply [them] from your own stock (*de propriis*), [or], having this authorization (*ratum habentes*), obtain [them] from the hands of others, and you will receive your money on the aforesaid day, without any dispute, from my own hands or those of R., my steward. Farewell.

Earl "C." is probably fictitious, but the circumstances with which he is challenged may reflect the trials of a genuine debtor-earl.[6] He writes here a rather obsequious letter to his skinner, to whom he owes money. After sending the skinner not only greetings but also "complete love," the earl explains that he needs furs for Easter but that he does not have the money to pay for them, and begs the skinner to supply these furs on credit.

The fur panels that the earl orders consist of vair and gris, which were the choicest imported squirrel skins, and the cheaper lambskin, probably a domestic product. Vair and gris came from the coldest parts of northern and central Europe, especially from Scandinavia and Russia, but also from Poland and Bulgaria. Vair ("variegated") was the whole skin of the red squirrel in wintertime, when it had a gray back and a white belly; gris ("gray") was the gray

Figure 4. A rich man washes before dining. He wears a fur-lined cloak, and another hangs above on a pole. From the Dives and Lazarus window in the ambulatory of Bourges Cathedral (*c.* 1210–15).

winter back alone; miniver ("small vair") was the white belly alone, with a little gray surrounding it.[7] The contrasting colors of the fur and the patchwork seaming required by the use of such small skins produced a checkerboard or similar geometric effect (Fig. 4).

The squirrel skins ordered by the earl in the letter above probably would have been used to line the finest garments of the earl and his family, and the lambskins for lining their more ordinary clothing. Gerald of Wales (*c.* 1146–1220 × 23) wrote, as evidence of his own charity and humility, that when, during a famine, he heard poor people crying at his door for alms, he sold all his cloaks and hoods and pelisses lined with vair and miniver and cony, gave the money to the poor, and after that wore only lambskin.[8] Lambskins were also used in magnate households for lining livery robes, the suits of uniform clothing issued to many officers, servants, and professional men as part of their wage or retainer.[9] Around 1226–32, for example, Simon de Senliz, steward to Ralph de Neville, bishop of Chichester and chancellor of England, wrote to Neville about stocking his London house with supplies for the winter, and reported that he had procured enough lambskin linings to meet the winter needs of the chancellor's household.[10]

Fine furs were extremely expensive, but even lambskin was costly. King John paid 6s. to 7s. each for lambskin linings, about 20s. for linings containing ten *tiers* of northern squirrel, and 100s. for a lining for ermine.[11] In 1265 Eleanor, countess of Leicester, paid 9s. in September for one panel (*penula*) of white lambskin to line a cloak. She also owed 18s. for a lining (*furura*) of miniver purchased in Easter week for her daughter Eleanor, and 27s. for a miniver hood for her brother, Richard of Cornwall, together with one and a half linings of miniver for his son Edmund, which had been purchased in London in early May.[12]

As is clear from the letter above and from other sources, such as the stained-glass window in Figure 5, furs were generally sold already made up into linings or panels (*furrure* or *penule*). Each panel was composed of multiple rows (*tiers*) of furs stitched together, and the cost of a panel depended on the number of its *tiers*.[13] The panels were then shaped as needed to line individual garments. The linings and trimmings of a single gown often required hundreds of skins; the number of skins used to line a complete robe could run into the thousands.[14] The sixty fur panels ordered by the earl of Gloucester in this letter correspond neatly to the sixty ells of scarlet cloth ordered by the earl in DOCUMENT 5. This suggests that a standard size for fur panels in England at this time may have been one clothyard (37 inches) in width by one ell (45 inches) in length. If so, this would have made it easy for a customer buying cloth by the ell to order the appropriate number of fur panels with which to line it.

In the letter above, the earl's urgent wish to put on a fine sartorial display despite his lack of funds reflects the practice of celebrating Easter by the wearing of new clothes. It also reflects the earl's desire to maintain his aristocratic state by dressing well rather than trying to get the last ounce of wear out of his clothing, which was considered beneath the dignity of a person of rank. In Guillaume de Lorris's allegorical poem the *Romance of the Rose*, Covetousness is sneeringly described as wearing torn, patched, out-of-date clothing, and refusing to replace it until it is thoroughly worn out.[15] The celebrated French preacher Jacques de Vitry (d. 1240) told the story of a miserly knight who, after dining at a nobleman's court, ordered his cloak to be brought. When his

Figure 5. A skinner and his assistant display fur linings from a chest to customers. From the St. James the Greater window of Chartres Cathedral (*c.* 1220–25).

servant could not find it quickly among the other cloaks, the knight snapped, "Son of a whore, fetch my cloak at once! Can't you recognize it?" Goaded, the servant retorted for everyone to hear, "I have known it well for seven years, sir, but I could not find it!" at which all the other knights began to laugh.[16]

The "seld" mentioned in the letter above was a covered bazaar, a new feature of English towns in this period. Selds emerged at the end of the twelfth century in cities where property values in prime commercial streets were so high that many retail traders could not afford their own shop. Instead, they rented space in a seld and sold goods there from stalls, benches, or chests (Figure 5). The selds were typically located behind the street frontages in upscale commercial streets, and they enabled traders to enjoy a prime location at an affordable rent.[17]

NOTES

1   Add. 8167, fols. 97v–98r.
2   Fol. 98r commences here.

3   *dilecco* in MS.

4   Word supplied to preserve the sense of the passage.

5   In CCCC 297, p. 255, this passage reads: *de propria selda, id est soude vestra michi acomodetis, vel aliunde ad credenciam habere faciatis. de propriis ratum habentes. de alienis manu capientes.*

6   See DOCUMENT 2 for a discussion of the possibility that this and other letters may be connected with Amaury de Montfort, fourth earl of Gloucester (recognized 1200; died 1210 × 13). In a later version of this letter in CCCC 297, pp. 254–55, the sender is named simply as *miles* ("a knight").

7   On fur panels and linings, squirrel skins and lambskins, see Veale, *English Fur Trade*, 17–20, 216–19, 221, 223–29.

8   *The Autobiography of Gerald of Wales*, ed. and trans. Harold Edgeworth Butler (London: Cape, 1937; rpt. Woodbridge, Suffolk: Boydell, 2005), 128. Gerald, also known as Gerald of Barry, a priest who had been born into the Norman aristocracy of south Wales, aspired unsuccessfully to become bishop and archbishop of St David's. See *Oxford DNB*, s.n. "Gerald of Wales"; and Martin Aurell, *The Plantagenet Empire, 1154–1224*, trans. David Crouch (Harlow, Essex: Pearson Longman, 2007), 1.

9   For livery robes, see also DOCUMENTS 5 and 77.

10   *Procuravi . . . quod vos fururas agnorum habetis ad sufficientiam, ut credo, contra hyemem ad opus familie vestre.* TNA: PRO, SC 1/6/149.

11   Veale, *English Fur Trade*, 18.

12   Turner, ed., *Manners and Household Expenses*, 18, 26, 73.

13   Cf. the ordinances of the Skinners' Company of London for 1327 and 1365, in Henry Thomas Riley, ed., *Memorials of London and London Life in the XIIIth, XIVth, and XVth Centuries* (London: Longman, 1868), 153–54, 328–30.

14   Veale, *English Fur Trade*, 19–21.

15   Guillaume de Lorris and Jean de Meun, *The Romance of the Rose*, trans. Harry W. Robbins, ed. Charles W. Dunn (New York: E. P. Dutton, 1962), Chap. 2, lines 47–69. These lines come from the earlier part of the poem, begun by Guillaume de Lorris about 1237.

16   Jacques de Vitry, *The Exempla, or Illustrative Stories from the Sermones Vulgares of Jacques de Vitry*, ed. Thomas Frederick Crane (London: Folk Lore Society, 1890; rpt. New York: Burt Franklin, 1971), no. 181, pp. 77, 207.

17   On selds, see Derek Keene, "Shops and Shopping in Medieval London," in *Medieval Art, Architecture and Archaeology in London*, ed. Lindy Grant (British Archaeological Association Conference Transactions for the Year 1984, 1990), 38–43; David M. Palliser, T. R. Slater, and E. Patricia Dennison, "The Topography of Towns, 600–1300," in *The Cambridge Urban History of Britain*, vol. 1, *600–1540*, ed. David M. Palliser (Cambridge: Cambridge University Press, 2000), 184–85; Derek Keene, "London from the Post-Roman Period to 1300," in *The Cambridge Urban History of Britain*, vol. 1, 201; and D. Clark, "The Shop Within? An Analysis of the Architectural Evidence for Medieval Shops," *Architectural History*, 43 (2000), 83–84, n. 6.

7

The Manner in Which One Should Write a Positive or Negative Response to a Request[1]

In literis responsalibus ad peticionem notandam quod aud[2] comodat aud expresse negat aud se excusat. In literis autem talibus visi tres partes ad minus sunt. Primo, debet salutare respondens; secundo, ostendere quid petitum sit; tercio, qualiter velit parere vel qualiter debeat negare vel excusare; quarto, si placet, poterit concludere. Item qui vult[3] parere[4] petitis, potest ostendere per "vero," vel per "aud" suam impotenciam excusare. Inde per "quare" vel per "quapropter" potest procedere ad excusacionem.

In letters of response to a request, note that either one agrees or expressly denies or excuses oneself. Moreover, in such letters there are at least three parts. Firstly, the respondent should send greetings; secondly, he should describe what is sought; thirdly, he should [describe] in what way he wishes to agree, or for what reason he must refuse or excuse [himself]; fourthly, if he pleases, he can conclude. Item, he who wishes to agree to requests can show [this] by *vero* ("truly") or excuse his inability [to agree] by *aud* ("or"). Then, by *quare* ("wherefore") or *quapropter* ("on which account") he can proceed to his excuse.

The short set of instructions above is one of several brief dictaminal texts (texts on the art of letter-writing) contained in this formulary.[5] It specifies the three- or four-part structure to be followed in replying to letters of request, and the formulas to be used for introducing the response itself. As in formal letters generally, a reply to a letter of request was to open with a salutation (greeting). The salutation always reflected the rank or occupation of the addressee, and the latter's status relative to that of the sender. Next, the reply was to recite what had been sought in the original request. This made it clear, without obfuscation or ambiguity, what obligation the sender was willing to undertake or was rejecting. Thirdly, the sender was to say in what way he wished to agree to the request, or for what reason he had to refuse or excuse himself from agreeing to it. If he wished to agree to the request, he was to introduce his response with "truly" (*vero*). If he wished to excuse himself or deny the request, however, he was to introduce this rejection by using "or" (*aud*), followed by "wherefore" (*quare*) or "on which account" (*quapropter*) to introduce his reason or excuse. Finally, if he wished, he could end the letter with a formal conclusion, which would have included courtesies similar to those in the salutation.[6]

In the manuscript, DOCUMENT 7 is followed by DOCUMENTS 8 and 85, which exemplify the instructions it contains.

NOTES

1 Add. 8167, fol. 98r.
2 Here and below, *aud* is used for *aut* ("or").
3 *wlt* in MS.
4 Corrected in MS from *paretre*.
5 See also the instructions for writing salutations and addressing letters to creditors at the beginning of this formulary (fol. 88r), published by Carlin in "Shops and Shopping," 518–19, 523; and the discussion of orders and refusals in DOCUMENT 15.
6 For discussions of dictaminal literature and the language and structure of formal letters, see the INTRODUCTION, pp. 15–17 above.

8

Letter of Refusal from a Skinner Ruined by a Fire[1]

Dilecto amico, et cetera, literas vestras nuper accepi, in quibus me petistis ut ego vobis penulas et fururas perquirerem, quod libenter fecissem, set ignis nuper superveniens[2] totam pecuniam meam redegit in cinerem. Unde vobis mittere non potui quod non habui, nec creditores inveni qui aliquid michi crederent post incendium, dubitaverunt enim perdere totum quod michi acomodarent. Precor igitur ne moleste feratis quod petita vobis non misi, cum sciatis causam inpedimenti. Valete.

To my beloved friend, etc. I have lately received your letter in which you requested that I purchase for you fur panels and linings (*penulas et fururas*), which I would freely have done, had not a recent fire reduced all my wealth to ashes. So I could not send you that which I did not have, nor have I found creditors who would lend me anything after the fire, for they feared to lose everything that they might lend me. I pray, therefore, that you do not take it amiss that I have not sent what you requested, since you know the cause of the impediment. Farewell.

This graceful letter of refusal, which in the manuscript follows the instructions in DOCUMENT 7 on how to write such letters, reads in fact as if it were written in direct response to DOCUMENT 6. It is possible that it, too (like the other letters discussed in DOCUMENT 2), may ultimately derive from correspondence associated with Amaury de Montfort, fourth earl of Gloucester, and thus its exemplar would date from between the latter's accession to the earldom in 1200 and his death in 1210 × 1213. If so, then it is tempting to speculate that the fire that destroyed the skinner's shop may have been the great London fire of July 1212 (see below).

The skinner here describes two major hazards of medieval urban life and commerce. One was that a merchant who had lost his stock or other assets would be unable to obtain credit, which would effectively prevent him from doing business. The other great hazard was fire. In an age of timber buildings, thatched roofs, and open hearths, fires were an ever-present danger, and at a time of rapid urban development many densely built-up towns and cities suffered major conflagrations.[3] London, for example, suffered disastrous fires in 1077, 1087, and 1133,[4] and an idealized description of the city written about 1173 by William FitzStephen claimed that its only two "plagues" were "the immoderate drinking of fools and the frequency of fires."[5] After another catastrophic fire struck London in July 1212, the mayor ordained new building and craft regulations. These prohibited the use of reeds, rushes, straw, and stubble for roofing and required that all who had roofs already thatched with reeds or rushes were to plaster them over within a week. The new regulations also ordered the demolition of all wooden houses in the city's central thoroughfare, Cheap, which posed a threat to the stone houses there. Brewhouses, bakehouses, and public cookshops, all of which used their ovens and hearths at night, when the streets were largely empty and a fire might escape notice until it was too late to contain, were singled out for special regulation. Bakers and brewers were ordered to use wood instead of reeds, straw, or stubble in baking and brewing at night, and all bakehouses and brewhouses, together with the cluster of public cookshops on the Thames, which sold hot take-away food, were ordered to be whitewashed and plastered inside and out. The cookshops were also to have their internal partitions removed. As an aid to fire-fighting, each alderman, who had charge of the city's wards, was ordered to provide a crook (a long pole with a hooked top) with a cord, evidently for tearing down burning buildings, and every householder was to keep a wooden or stone vessel filled with water outside his house.[6] These regulations were evidently effective, since there were no major fires in London between 1212 and the Great Fire of 1666.

The skinner in the letter above reports that all his assets have been destroyed by the fire, suggesting that his dwelling adjoined or occupied the same building as his shop and stockroom. This was a common arrangement in medieval towns. Building plots were usually long and narrow, with a narrow end facing the street. In the twelfth century, to exploit the commercial front-age, many streets were lined with small wooden shops, behind which lay timber or (for the wealthy) stone houses. However, evidence from London suggests that around 1180–1220 the technology for constructing multi-story timber-framed buildings was redeveloped for the first time in Britain since the Roman period.[7] As a result, in the course of the thirteenth century many valu-able commercial frontages were built up with two- or three-story buildings. The ground floors were used for shops and workshops and the upper stories as dwellings.[8]

The skinner's model letter thus provides a window not only onto the haz-ards of commercial and urban life in early thirteenth-century England, but also onto technological and topographical developments of the period.

NOTES

1 Add. 8167, fol. 98r.
2 Corrected in MS. from *superveniens nuper*.
3 Palliser, Slater, and Dennison, "Topography of Towns, 600–1300," 181–84.
4 Christopher N. L. Brooke, assisted by Gillian Keir, *London, 800–1216: The Shaping of a City* (London: Secker and Warburg, 1975), 31, 33, 212n., 284.
5 Brooke and Keir, *London, 800–1216*, 116. For a detailed comparison of the five prin-cipal manuscripts of FitzStephen's description of London, see Hannes Kleineke, "William FitzStephen's 'Description of London': A New Edition" (M.A. dissertation, Royal Holloway and Bedford New College, University of London, 1994). We are grateful to Dr. Kleineke for providing Martha Carlin with a copy of his dissertation. The line concerning London's two "plagues" ("*Sole pestes Londonie sunt immodica stultorum potatio et frequens incendium*") can be found on p. 30 and Appendix C., p. xviii, of Kleineke's edition. On one of these manuscripts and its owner, see also Kleineke, "Carleton's Book: William FitzStephen's 'Description of London' in a Late Fourteenth-Century Common-Place Book," *Historical Research*, 74 (2001), 117–26.
6 Helena M. Chew and William Kellaway, eds., *London Assize of Nuisance, 1301–1431: A Calendar*, London Record Society, 10 (1973), ix–xi; Henry Thomas Riley, ed., *Liber Custumarum*, in *Munimenta Gildhallae Londoniensis: Liber Albus, Liber Custumarum, et Liber Horn*, vol. 2, part 1, Rolls Series, 12 (London: Longman, 1859–62), 86–88. On London's public cookhouses in 1212, see Martha Carlin, "Fast Food and Urban Living Standards in Medieval England," in *Food and Eating in Medieval Europe*, ed. Martha Carlin and Joel T. Rosenthal (London: Hambledon, 1998), 29–30.
7 Palliser, Slater, and Dennison, "Topography of Towns, 600–1300," in *Cambridge Urban History of Britain*, 1, ed. Palliser, 183–84.
8 For example, between 1248 and 1265 the prioress of Clerkenwell sold a piece of property in London consisting of a row of three shops with houses above (*domos . . . una cum tribus sopis que coniuncte sunt sub dictis domibus*). William Owen Hassall, ed., *Cartulary of St Mary Clerkenwell*, Camden 3rd Ser., 71 (London: Royal Historical Society, 1949), no. 362. Cf. Derek Keene, "Issues of Water in Medieval London to c. 1300," *Urban History*, 28, no. 2 (2001), 172.

9
A Friend Requests Five Marks to Buy Wool[1]

He [sic] sunt litere petitorie aliquid et grates referende de accionibus precollatis

Karissimo amico suo A., B. si placet salutem. Pro beneficiis michi a vobis multociens collatis, et adhuc si placet conferendis libertatem[2] vestram multiplici et uberima gratiarum accione, prosequen, rogo ergo attencius cuius[3] munus est liberale, ut[4] beneficium[5] aliis conferetis et[6] diu possitis conferre et diu vestros sustinere. Veruntamen adurget me necessitas non dum tardo loco [sic] januam vestre pietatis pulsare. Igitur attencius, rogo et precor vestram munificenciam ut divine pietatis intuitu, et precum mearum interventu, .v. marcas ad presens michi acomodetis. Sciatis enim pro vero quod ego afforui duas pisas lane, et non habeo denarios quos pro lana taxata possim dare. Quare tantum faciatis ne arras[7] meas datas admittam pro defectu nummorum. Valete.

This is a letter requesting something, and bearing thanks for earlier favors

To his dearest friend A., B., if it please, sends greetings. For all the many past—and, if it please, future—favors conferred on me by you, following your generosity with manifold and copious giving of thanks, I entreat, therefore, earnestly, of one whose performance of duty is [so] liberal, that you confer your assistance upon others, that you may long be able to confer it, and may long be able to sustain your dependents. However, necessity forces me all too soon to knock on the door of your charity. Therefore, I anxiously ask and pray your munificence that, through the prompting of holy charity and the interposition of my prayers, you will lend me five marks right away. For you know for a fact that I made a bargain for two weys of wool, and I do not have the money to pay for that wool. Therefore, I hope that you will act in such a way that I will not lose my down payment for lack of cash. Farewell.

Wool was the premier export commodity of medieval England. In 1297, the barons sitting in Parliament in 1297 declared that wool represented "half the value of the whole land."[8] Throughout Europe, woolen textiles were in widespread use for outer clothing of all kinds, as well as for blankets, hangings, and coverings of all kinds. English wool was in high demand both at home and abroad because of its excellent quality, and it was bought and sold not only by specialist wool-merchants but by a very broad spectrum of buyers and sellers.[9]

The sender of this letter is in desperate need of five marks (£3 6s. 8d.) with which to pay for a large quantity of wool that he has contracted to buy, but for which he does not have the cash. In the hope of obtaining a quick loan he has turned in this emergency to a friend who has been very generous in the past. While this letter may have been fictitious, composed simply to illustrate one type of letter of request, it closely echoes genuine letters of the period both in subject and in language. For example, in a letter written about 1218, William, earl of Warenne, asks his "dearest lord and friend" (*dominum et amicum carissimum*) Hubert de Burgh, justiciar of England, to obtain the repayment of part of the money that the earl had lent to the Crown, because the earl has large debts himself that are about to come due, including £100 that must be paid to the earl of Arundel by the feast of St John the Baptist (June 24). He is writing to Hubert de Burgh, to whom he is also in debt, because the latter was one of the pledges for Warenne's loan to the Crown, because of de Burgh's generosity in the past, and because Warenne cannot obtain loans from either Jews or Christians and has no one else to whom he can turn.[10]

The sender of DOCUMENT 9 secured his deal to buy the wool by putting down a binder or deposit in the form of earnest money (*arras meas datas*). Often this was merely a symbolic sum in the form of a single penny known as "Godsilver" or "God's penny." For example, in May 1265, when Eleanor de Montfort's clerk and tailor bought goods on credit for her from four London merchants, they gave the vendors a penny apiece, "for Godsilver" (*pro argento Dei*), as pledge of payment.[11] Here, however, the sender has clearly put down a more substantial sum, which he will lose if he cannot come up with the remaining five marks.

The two weys of wool that he has contracted to buy would have made one sack, generally weighing 364 lb. (165.108 kg).[12] At a cost of five marks (66s. 8d., or 800d.), this would have come to just under 2.2d. per pound or about 2s. 6³/₄d. per stone (14 lb.), but the cost would in fact have been higher because of the unknown but significant amount of the earnest money. If the sender put down one mark in earnest money, that would have brought the price of his sack of wool to just over 3s. per stone. Because English wool prices hovered around 2s. per stone between 1200 and 1227, but jumped to around 3s. per stone between 1232 and 1246, DOCUMENT 9 probably dates from the latter period.[13]

The loan of £3 6s. 8d. (800d.) that the sender of this letter is requesting represented a very large sum. In the 1220s in southern England a master craftsman might earn £3 13s. 0d. (876d.) in a full year's work, while a male laborer might earn £2 2s. 7d. (511d.), and a woman laborer only £1 4s. 4d.(292d.).[14]

NOTES

1 Add. 8167, fols. 98v–99r.
2 Fol. 99r commences here.
3 *eius* in MS.
4 *et* in MS.
5 *bnficium* in MS.
6 *ut* in MS.
7 Corrected in MS from *arram.*
8 Quoted in Michael M. Postan, *Medieval Trade and Finance* (Cambridge: Cambridge University Press, 1973), 342.
9 On England's wool trade with Flanders in the twelfth and thirteenth centuries, see Terrence H. Lloyd, *The English Wool Trade in the Middle Ages* (Cambridge: Cambridge University Press, 1977), Chap. 1. On buyers of wool at English fairs, see Ellen Wedemeyer Moore, *The Fairs of Medieval England: An Introductory Study* (Toronto: Pontifical Institute of Mediaeval Studies, 1985), 48–50 and Chap. 2. For the career of a German immigrant, Dietrich (Terricus) of Cologne (d. 1247), who established himself in Stamford and London as a merchant dealing, inter alia, in wool, cloth, and wine, see Natalie Fryde, "How to Get On in England in the Thirteenth Century? Dietrich of Cologne, Burgess of Stamford," in *England and Europe in the Reign of Henry III (1216–1272)*, ed. Bjorn K. U. Weiler, with Ifor W. Rowlands (Aldershot, Hampshire: Ashgate, 2002), 207–13.
10 *Sciatis autem quod nullum in praesenti necessitate refugium habeo nisi ad vos; quia si a Judaeis vel a Christianis succursum haberem, nullam inde querelam vobis exponerem.* Shirley, ed., *Letters*, vol. 1, 15–16 (this letter is now TNA: PRO, SC 1/1/214). For the Crown's debt to Warenne, see *Rotuli litterarum clausarum*, vol. 1, *1204–1224*, ed. Thomas Duffus Hardy (London: Record Commission, 1833), 349. For a discussion of Jewish moneylending in England, see DOCUMENTS 12 and 13.
11 Turner, ed., *Manners and Household Expenses*, 25. See also Moore, *Fairs of Medieval England*, 117.
12 On the weight of a sack of wool, most commonly containing two weys or 26 stone of 14 lb. each, see Zupko, *Dictionary of English Weights and Measures*, 149.
13 On wool prices in the first half of the thirteenth century, expressed in shillings per stone of 14 lb., see Terrence H. Lloyd, *The Movement of Wool Prices in Medieval England, Economic History Review Supplements*, 6 (1973), Table 1 (p. 38). Table 1 provides no price data for the years 1228–31. The annual mean price rose in 1247 to 3.39s. per stone, and then fell sharply in 1248 to 2.67s. and in 1249 to 2.42s. per stone.
14 For these wage-rates, see DOCUMENT 12.

10

A Friend Requests a Loan to Buy Wool and Cloth at the Fair[1]

C. mandat D. ut comodat sibi denarios ad nundinas

Karissimo[2] amico suo .A. B. salutem. Profecturus ad nundinas non habeo monetam ad merces emendas necessessarias [*sic*]. Quapropter vestre dileccioni supplices preces effundo, petens attencius quatinus, pro amore meo et servicio mei, acomodetis michi aliquos denarios unde possim lanam et telam emere. Habeo enim duo sterlingos quibus adpresens [*sic*] magis indigeo. Quare tantum faciatis, ut indigencia mea in hac parte relevetur.[3] Valete.

C. sends word to D. to lend him cash for the fair

To his dearest friend A., B. sends greetings. I am about to go to the fair, but I don't have the money to buy the things I need. On which account, I pour out prayers [and] supplications to your love, seeking earnestly that, for the sake of my love and service, you lend me some cash with which to buy wool and cloth. For at present I have no more than two pennies (*sterlingos*). So may you act in such a way that my need in this matter might be relieved. Farewell.

This letter, like DOCUMENTS 44, 45 and 46, is evidently written by a man of standing to someone who owes him "love and service." Like DOCUMENT 9, it touches on two key economic factors of early thirteenth-century England: the widespread shortage of cash (on which see DOCUMENT 3) and the commercial primacy of wool and woolen cloth (discussed in DOCUMENT 9). It also addresses the importance in this period of the annual English cloth fairs in their trade.

In the first half of the thirteenth century, a large number of annual trade fairs served as wholesale markets for the sale of wool and cloth and other goods in England. Five fairs were especially important: at Stamford (mid-Lent to Easter), St. Ives (eight days at Easter), Boston (June 24–July 2), Winchester (August 31–September 16), and Northampton (beginning November 1). There were also major fairs at Lynn (now King's Lynn, July 13–27); at Bury St. Edmunds (late November); and from 1245, at Westminster (mid-October). With the exception of St. Edward's fair at Westminster, which was not founded until 1245, these fairs were at their zenith of prosperity between 1180 and 1220.[4]

A useful impression of the kinds of cloth sold at these fairs comes from a description of urban trades and crafts in England at the beginning of the formulary in Add. 8167. A draper, according to this account, should sell a wide range of woolen cloths, either in his seld (his stall in an urban bazaar) or at fairs. Among these cloths were English broadcloths, scarlets, russets of Leicester or Oxford, burels of London or Beauvais, haberget of Stamford, and gray cloth (*grisetum*) of Totnes or Cornwall.[5] In addition, the fairs offered English wool; textiles from Flanders, Brabant, France, and northern Italy; Scandinavian furs; wines, primarily from southern Europe; spices from the Orient; horses; hunting-birds; cattle; non-precious metals; and other goods.[6]

Not only merchants, but also wealthy prelates and aristocrats and the royal household, made bulk purchases at the fairs. In 1226 × 32, for example, Simon de Senliz, steward of Ralph de Neville, bishop of Chichester and chancellor to Henry III, wrote to Neville for instructions on what sort of cloth and what quantity he should buy at the fair of St. Ives for winter and summer; presumably this cloth was to be used for winter and summer livery robes for Neville's staff, as well as for Neville himself.[7] Henry III made extensive purchases of woolen cloth at the major fairs and, like the sender of the letter above, he was at times unable to come up with the cash to pay for them. In June 1256, for example, Roger de Ros and Hugh of the Tower (*de Turri*), the keepers of his Great Wardrobe, went on a shopping expedition to Boston fair, but the king had no ready money to send with them. Instead, he ordered the sheriffs of the northern counties to levy 700 marks (£466 13*s.* 4*d.*) from judicial fines that were due to the Crown and to send the cash to Roger and Hugh at Boston fair. The sheriffs, however, failed to deliver the full amount, and in November the king ordered that they deliver the missing sums to Roger and Hugh at Stamford fair so that they could make his purchases there.[8]

The English fairs continued to play an important role in the cloth trade until the 1280s or so. In the later thirteenth century, however, the pattern of large-scale vending changed as merchants from all parts of the country increasingly sold products directly to major customers year-round without resorting to the annual fairs. The rise of London in particular as the country's pre-eminent center for the supply of domestic and imported goods of all kinds, including luxury textiles, resulted in the shift of royal and aristocratic bulk purchasing of such goods from the fairs to the capital.[9]

NOTES

1   Add. 8167, fol. 101r–v. On the discrepancy in initials between heading and text, see DOCUMENT 33, n. 1.
2   Fol. 101v commences here.
3   Corrected in margin of MS (in a different hand) from *reveletur*.
4   Moore, *Fairs of Medieval England*, 9–23; Kay Staniland, "Provision and the Great Wardrobe in the Mid-Thirteenth Century," *Textile History*, 22, no. 2 (Autumn 1991), 239–52, especially 240–45. The dates given above for the fairs generally follow Staniland (p. 241) rather than the vaguer information in Moore (pp. 10–11). The dates of Northampton fair are unclear; Moore simply gives "November," and Staniland gives November 1. It was known as All Saints' fair, and in the twelfth century was held on All Saints' Day (November 1). Moore, *Fairs of Medieval England*, 21, 25. For a

detailed examination of St Giles' fair in Winchester, see Derek Keene, *Winchester Studies,* vol. 2 *Survey of Medieval Winchester* (Oxford: Clarendon, 1985), 1113–23.

5   Carlin, "Shops and Shopping," 498–500, 519, 524. On selds, see Document 6, p. 51. On broadcloths and scarlets, see Document 5.

6   Moore, *Fairs of Medieval England,* 50–62; Staniland, "Provision and the Great Wardrobe," 241–51.

7   TNA: PRO, SC 1/6/141. On liveries of robes, see Documents 5, 6, and 77.

8   *Calendar of Patent Rolls, 1247–58,* 483. On Roger de Ros and Hugh of the Tower, see also Staniland, "Provision and the Great Wardrobe," 240–41; and Thomas Frederick Tout, *Chapters in the Administrative History of Mediaeval England: The Wardrobe, the Chamber and the Small Seals* (Manchester: Manchester University Press, and London: Longman, 1920–33), vol. 1, 273–78, 310, 312; vol. 4, 356–67; vol. 6, 33–34.

9   Moore, *Fairs of Medieval England,* 204–22; Richard Britnell, "The Economy of British Towns, 600–1300," in *Cambridge Urban History of Britain,* vol. 1, *600–1540,* ed. Palliser, 109. See also Derek Keene, "Wardrobes in the City: Houses of Consumption, Finance and Power," in *Thirteenth Century England,* vol. 7, *Proceedings of the Durham Conference, 1997,* ed. Michael Prestwich, Richard Britnell, and Robin Frame (Woodbridge, Suffolk: Boydell, 1999), 61–79.

11

A Man Sends Pledges That His Neighbor Can Use to Secure a Loan[1]

Vicinus vicino salutem. Non minus vestre comoditati quam proprie, deum testor, insisterem si denarios haberem quos vobis acomodarem. Set cum in denariis vestre voluntati satisfacere non valeam, vadia vobis transmitto que pro voto vestro poteritis obligare pro denariis quibus indigetis, ne vestrum negocium pro defectu mei retardetur. De die impignoracionis et aquitancionis[2] michi monstrare faciatis ut per me possunt redimi, si vobis ad hoc facultas non extiterit.

A neighbor to a neighbor, greetings. Not less mindful of your advantage than my own, as God is my witness, I would insist, if I had the cash, on lending it to you. But since I cannot fulfill your wish in cash, I send you pledges that you will be able to put up as your surety for the cash that you lack, so that your affairs will not be impeded by my default. Let me know the day of the pledging and the due-date, so that they (i.e., the pledges) can be redeemed by me if it should not be in your power to do so.

The lack of ready money that here has entangled the financial affairs of a pair of neighbors is echoed in many other documents in this volume (see Document 3) and clearly affected the ordinary functioning of the local economy.

In the case above, the sender wishes to assist his neighbor in the latter's request for a loan, but does not have the cash on hand with which to do so. In its place he offers unspecified valuables (perhaps jewelry or plate) that the neighbor can use as security for obtaining a loan elsewhere, most likely from pawnbrokers such as those discussed in DOCUMENT 14.

The sender here is careful always to use the respectful plural (*vos*) in addressing his neighbor, while referring to himself in the modest singular (*ego*). This suggests that he is inferior in rank to the neighbor, but he is not the neighbor's dependent or in his employ, or he would have addressed him as his lord rather than as his neighbor. The sender's polite request at the conclusion of the letter—that the neighbor should let him know when the loan will fall due, so that he can redeem his pledges if the neighbor is unable to do so—suggests that he thinks that the neighbor is unlikely to redeem the pledges himself. Since the pledges were probably worth much more than the anticipated loan (see DOCUMENT 14), it thus was in the sender's interest to redeem them rather than to allow them to be forfeited for non-payment.

While the exceptional generosity offered by the sender here might have been sheer wishful thinking on the part of the actual author of this letter, the inclusion of model letters such as this in formularies was not mere fancifulness, but reflected actual conditions of the period. People of wealth routinely received petitions such as that described above, and it clearly was very useful to have a variety of form letters at hand—both favorable, as here and in DOCUMENT 92, and unfavorable, as in DOCUMENT 14—with which to respond to them.

NOTES

1 Fairfax 27, fol. 6r.
2 Corrected in MS from *quitancionis*.

THE JEWS

12

A Friend Begs for Money to Repay a Loan[1]

Peticio ad comodandos denarios

> Karissimo amico A. B. suus per omnia[2] salutem. De dileccione vestra quam plurimum confisus, dileccioni vestre preces humilimas et huberimas [*sic*] effundo, petens attencius quatinus pro amore meo acomodes michi duas marcas argenti ad redimenda vadia mea que sunt in

iudaismo.³ Sciturus quod ea amisurus sum nisi ea redimero in proxima dominica, sic enim convenit inter me et Judeum cui⁴ ea pignoravi⁵ (*vel sic: qui ea inpignorare accepit*).⁶ Ideo tantum faciatis, ne pro duabus marcis precium admittam quatuor marcarum. Valete.

Request for a cash loan

To his dearest friend A., B., his [friend] in all things, greetings. Trusting fully in your love, I pour out to your love the humblest and richest prayers, anxiously beseeching that, for my love, you lend me two marks in cash to redeem my pledges, which are in the Jewry. You will know that I shall forfeit them unless I redeem them next Sunday, for so it was agreed between me and the Jew to whom I pledged them (*or thus: who received them as a pledge*). Therefore, I hope that you will act in such a way that, for [want of] two marks, I do not lose [pledges] worth four marks. Farewell.

Here a man writes to a friend to beg for an emergency cash loan so that he can redeem pledges (*vadia*) that he has pawned to a Jewish pawnbroker for two marks (£1 6s. 8d.). If he fails to repay this sum, which is about to fall due, he will lose his pledges, which are worth four marks (£2 13s. 4d.).⁷

The writer of this letter employs a flowery and very humble style, as befits one who is asking for a substantial favor and has nothing but gratitude to offer in return. He evidently comes from a genteel background, since he has friends of means and since he could offer a moneylender pledges worth four marks (£2 13s. 4d., or 640d.) as collateral for the loan. These pledges represented a substantial sum. A typical wage for a male laborer who was hired by the day or week was 1½d. to 2d. per day (1d. per day for a woman), while a skilled craftsman earned 2d. to 4d. per day. However, each year there were fifty-two Sundays and three to four weeks of religious holidays when work was forbidden. Wage-workers hired by the day or week thus would have lost at least seventy-three days' wages per annum (fifty-two Sundays plus 3.5 weeks of six days each). A master craftsman who earned an average of 3d. per day and who worked every day allowable would thus have earned a maximum wage of £3 13s. 0d.,⁸ while a male laborer earning an average of 1.75d. per day would have earned at most only £2 2s. 7d.,⁹ and a female laborer only £1 4s. 4d.¹⁰ The value of the writer's pledges thus represented about three-quarters of a year's wages for a master craftsman, more than a year's wages for a male laborer, or more than two years' wages for a female laborer.

The fact that the writer of our letter borrowed the money from a Jewish pawnbroker suggests that he lived in or near one of the towns in England that had a Jewish community at this time. The Jews had come to England from Normandy following the conquest of England in 1066 by William, duke of Normandy. Their first community was established at London, and there is no evidence of any English Jewries outside London until the reign of King Stephen (1135–54). By 1159, however, there were Jewish communities in ten provincial towns, and by 1189 there were twenty-four provincial Jewries. Most were established in towns where the king or, in seigneurial boroughs, a baron, had a castle to offer protection to the Jews if they were physically attacked.[11]

For the most part the Jews lived in peace, if not in friendship, with their Christian neighbors, but probably never with a sense of real legal, economic, or physical security. Beginning in the late 1170s the English kings periodically targeted wealthy individual Jews, or the entire Jewish community, for heavy taxation. A series of attacks, lootings, and even massacres occurred at the beginning of the reign of Richard I in 1189–90, in which at least seven Jewish communities were attacked. Four were especially hard-hit: Lynn, which was wiped out permanently; York, which was destroyed for a period of years; Stamford, which survived in part through the efforts of Hugh of Avalon, bishop of Lincoln, only to disappear by 1194; and Bury, which suffered heavy casualties and from which, some months later, the survivors were expelled by Abbot Samson.[12] In 1210 King John, desperate for money to finance his foreign campaigns, ordered a "general captivity" of wealthy Jews. Some of those imprisoned were subjected to extortion, mutilation, or hanging, and the Jewish community as a whole was taxed £40,000. During the tumultuous years that followed many Jews fled: tax returns of 1221 show that the Jews of Coventry took refuge at Leicester, but those of Chichester, Hertford, Bedford, and Wallingford simply disappeared. The return for Gloucester listed only ten Jews, of whom four were women, three of them widows. Thus, during the reigns of Richard I (1189–99) and John (1199–1216), the number of Jewish communities in England was reduced from twenty-four to fifteen, although the Jewries of York and Stamford were revived a generation later, between 1217 and 1221.[13] In 1221 the seventeen Jewish communities were at Bristol, Cambridge, Canterbury, Colchester, Exeter, Gloucester, Hereford, Lincoln, London, Northampton, Norwich, Nottingham, Oxford, Stamford, Winchester, Worcester, and York. By 1241 Bedford, Dorchester, Marlborough, and Warwick had been added, for a total of twenty-one Jewries.[14]

Until *c.* 1180 the Jews of Norman England seem to have specialized in money-changing and dealing in plate and bullion as well as moneylending,[15] but they engaged in a variety of other characteristically urban enterprises as well, including pawnbroking, property-development, trading in bonds, dealing in rents,[16] and speculating in commodities such as grain. One Jew, Aaron of

Figure 6. Caricature of devils mocking a Jewish coin-clipper (in pointed hat) and male and female moneylenders. From the Rotulus Judeorum, 1233 (TNA: PRO, E 401/1565).

Lincoln (d. 1187), whose business activities embraced all of the above, amassed such an astounding fortune, worth the modern equivalent of £21.6 billion, that he has been named as the ninth-richest man in all of British history.[17]

A combination of political, economic, and legal developments in the reign of Henry II (1154–89) led English Christians to forsake large-scale money-lending and Jews to come to specialize in it. One major factor seems to have been the condemnation in 1163, by the church council held at Tours, of usury (lending money at interest) by Christians. This prohibition enabled Henry II to claim the estates of "manifest usurers."[18] It also seems to have led him to cease borrowing himself from Christian moneylenders and to turn instead to Jews.[19] The Jews in England began to concentrate primarily on moneylending, but until the 1190s they did this in cooperation with London-based Christian financiers. By about 1200, however, the latter had withdrawn from the business. In addition, beginning in the 1190s, the royal department that controlled Jewish affairs, the Exchequer of the Jews, enabled Jewish creditors to obtain or recover seisin (secure possession) of lands that had been pledged by defaulting debtors. Christian moneylenders did not achieve a comparable method of enforcing such debts until 1283. These conditions helped to give the Jews a near-monopoly on large-scale moneylending in England during the first half of the thirteenth century.[20]

As a result, after the disruptions of John's reign, the Jewish community in England was at its financial peak between about 1217 and 1240. In 1241–42 the English Jews collectively controlled about £133,333—close to 30 percent of the value of all the coin in England—and the richest Jew, Aaron of York, was worth the staggering sum of £40,000, or about eight percent of the value of all the coin in circulation in the country. However, between about 1240 and 1260 Henry III's financial exploitation of the nation (see DOCUMENT 35) bore heavily on the Jewish community, siphoning off as much as fifty percent of the capital of Jewish financiers and destroying their ability to lend on a large scale. In 1275 formal moneylending was forbidden to Jews by statute, and in 1290 the entire Jewish community, which by then numbered fewer than two thousand people, was expelled from England by Henry III's son, Edward I.[21]

NOTES

1 Add. 8167, fol. 99r.
2 The same phrase, "*suus per omnia*," occurs in the opening of a letter of 1286–90 from the prior of St Mary Huntingdon to John de Kirkby, bishop of Ely and treasurer of Edward I. TNA, PRO: SC 1/10/137.
3 Corrected in MS from *iudaissmo*.
4 *qui* in MS.
5 *pignoravit* in MS.
6 *set* expunged here in MS.
7 On English law regarding pledges and pawnbroking, see Brand, "Aspects of the Law of Debt," 19, 29–30. A similar letter was written *c.* 1269 × 86 by Richard de Gratia Dei to John de Kirkby (keeper of the rolls of Chancery, 1263–84; subsequently treasurer, 1284–90, and bishop of Ely, 1286–90). Richard wrote in very humble tones, and with elaborate references to Scripture and the Church Fathers, to request assistance in redeeming pledges from the Jewry and elsewhere. TNA: PRO, SC 1/8/72.
8 292 days at 3*d.* per day = 876*d.* or £3 13*s.* 0*d.*
9 292 days at 1.75*d.* per day = 511*d.* or £2 2*s.* 7*d.*
10 292 days at 1*d.* per day = 292*d.* or £1 4*s.* 4*d.* For the above wage-rates, see Colvin, ed., *Building Accounts of King Henry III*, 8–12 (wage-rates in southern England for the years 1220–27).
11 Joe Hillaby, "Jewish Colonisation in the Twelfth Century," in *The Jews in Medieval Britain: Historical, Literary and Archaeological Perspectives*, ed. Patricia Skinner (Woodbridge, Suffolk: Boydell, 2003), 15, 20–25, and Map 1.
12 Hillaby, "Jewish Colonization," 29–33; pers. comm., Robert Stacey.
13 Hillaby, "Jewish Colonisation," 32, 35.
14 Henry Gerald Richardson, *The English Jewry Under Angevin Kings* (London: Methuen, 1960), 14–16.
15 Robert C. Stacey, "Jewish Lending and the Medieval English Economy," in *A Commercialising Economy: England 1086 to c. 1300*, ed. Richard H. Britnell and Bruce M. S. Campbell (Manchester: Manchester University Press, 1995), 78–88.
16 Annuities in the form of fixed annual rents, due in perpetuity on certain properties.
17 Robin R. Mundill, "Christian and Jewish Lending Patterns and Financial Dealings During the Twelfth and Thirteenth Centuries," in *Credit and Debt in Medieval*

England c. 1180–c. 1350, ed. Phillipp S. Schofield and Nicholas J. Mayhew (Oxford: Oxbow Books, 2002), 42–43, 45–48.

18   Stacey, "Jewish Lending," 87–91.

19   According to H. G. Richardson, Henry II's borrowings from Christian moneylenders ceased abruptly in 1163–64 with the exception of Robert fitz Sawin, from whom he continued to borrow for some years. Richardson, *English Jewry*, 50–57.

20   Stacey, "Jewish Lending," 91–93.

21   Stacey, "Jewish Lending," 93–101; see also Barrie Dobson, "The Medieval York Jewry Reconsidered," in *Jews in Medieval Britain*, ed. Skinner, 149. On the amount of coin in circulation, see DOCUMENT 3.

13

A Letter of Response: Buying a Horse for One's Lord[1]

Litere responsales

Venerabili domino suo .A., B. salutem. Misistis michi nuper ut equum trium marcarum vobis emerem de denariis meis cuius precepto non ausus sum resistere. Incontinenti duarum mutuo accepi a Judeis ut negocium vestrum perficerem fideliter. Circuivi [*sic*] totam provinciam, ut quererem mannum ydoneum, et tandem inveni badium equum, sano dorso, oculis sanis perspicacibus, capite parvo,[2] pedibus sanis. Quid plura? Caret omni vicio. Set non possum eum extorqueri a domino suo, nisi prius dederim tres marcas et dimidiam. Quare vos exoro—si fas est dicere, consulo—ut mittatis .G. senescallum vestrum cum dimidia marca ad illum, videndum de predicto precio aliquid evellendum si posset.[3] Sciatis quod sine illius auxilio et consilio equum prefatum emere non audeo. Quare tantum faciatis ne ego culpam incurram et vos penitenciam agatis emcione. Valete.

A letter of response

To my venerable lord A., B. sends greetings. You sent to me lately to buy you a horse with three marks of my own money, which order I did not dare to refuse. Immediately I borrowed two marks from the Jews so that I might faithfully carry out your business. I rode around the entire county to find a decent cob, and I found a chestnut[4] horse with a sound back; healthy, sharp-sighted eyes; small head; [and] sound feet. What more can I say? It was free from every fault. However, I could not pry him away from his owner unless I first paid three and a half marks. Wherefore I pray—or, if I may, I recommend—that you send G. your seneschal to him with half a mark to see if he can get something knocked off the price. You should know that without his aid and counsel I dare not buy the horse. So I hope that you will act in such a way that I will incur no blame and that you do not regret the purchase. Farewell.

This letter may be connected with DOCUMENT 47, in which an earl writes to his agent ("*clienti*," perhaps a moneylender) to demand 100 shillings (£5) with which to purchase a palfrey, which was a top-quality riding horse. In this letter, the unnamed lord, again apparently short of cash, has ordered a man of means at his command, perhaps a business agent or a member of his affinity, to find a cob (a stocky, sturdy road horse used by both men and women) and buy it with three marks (£2) of his own money.[5] The recipient of this order has little ready cash himself and has had to borrow two marks in a hurry from Jewish moneylenders.[6] Presumably the lord has promised to reimburse him for these expenses. However, although the agent has tracked down a suitable horse, the seller is demanding more than the three marks stipulated by the lord, and the agent dares not carry out the purchase without the lord's express approval. He therefore begs the lord to send his seneschal to come with the extra cash to negotiate the price and complete the purchase.[7]

The amount demanded by the seller of the horse, 3½ marks (46s. 8d.), seems around mid-range for saddlehorses at this period. For example, when five horses belonging to a knight were impounded at Southampton in May 1219, at the time of the siege of Winchester Castle by Louis of France, they were valued, respectively, at 100 shillings, five marks (66s. 8d.), four marks (53s. 4d.), twenty shillings, and ten shillings.[8] Warhorses (known as destriers) and palfreys (discussed in DOCUMENT 47) were much more valuable.[9] Their typical price rose tenfold in the late twelfth and early thirteenth centuries, from £2 in the reign of Henry II (1154–89), to thirty marks (£20) in that of John (1199–1216).[10]

The description in the letter of the horse's features is an interesting literary touch that recalls Virgil's enumeration in the *Georgics* (29 B.C.) of the points of a perfect horse:

> . . . *His neck is high,*
> *His head clean-cut, his barrel short, his back*
> *Well-fleshed; his gallant chest ripples with muscle.*
> *(For colour, bay and roan are fine, the worst*
> *Are white and dun.) . . .*
> *His mane is thick, and falls on his right shoulder*
> *When tossed. A double ridge runs down his back.*
> *His hoof digs into the ground, its solid horn*
> *Making a heavy thud.*[11]

Figure 7. Count Thibaut VI of Blois (d. 1218) on his warhorse. From the window of the Labors of the Months and Signs of the Zodiac, Chartres Cathedral (*c.* 1220).

NOTES

1   Add. 8167, fol. 99v.
2   Corrected in MS from *partuo.*
3   Corrected in MS from *possit.*
4   Or bay (*badium*).
5   On the cob (*mannus*), see Anne-Marie Bautier, "Contribution à l'histoire du cheval au moyen âge," *Bulletin philologique et historique* (Paris, 1978, for 1976), 228–29. For this reference we are grateful to Andrew Ayton.
6   See DOCUMENT 12 for a discussion of Jewish moneylending in England at this time.
7   The seneschal or steward was the most senior officer in charge of the lord's estates; lords also often had a separate household steward.
8   Letter from the mayor and men of Southampton to Peter des Roches, bishop of Winchester, and Hubert de Burgh, justiciar of England, in Shirley, ed., *Letters*, vol. 1, 8–10 (now TNA: PRO, SC 1/1/52). For the suggested date of this letter, see ibid., p. xxxni n. Patricia Barnes, in *PRO Lists and Indexes*, No. XV, p. 5 (no. 52), dates this letter more vaguely to "[e]arly Henry III."
9   Matthew Bennett has, however, suggested that the medieval warhorse was very similar to the modern cob. "The Medieval Warhorse Reconsidered," in *Medieval Knighthood V: Papers from the Sixth Strawberry Hill Conference, 1994*, ed. Ruth E. Harvey and Stephen Church (Woodbridge, Suffolk: Boydell, 1995), 26.

10 Michael Prestwich, *Armies and Warfare in the Middle Ages: The English Experience* (New Haven: Yale University Press, 1996), 34 and n. 74.

11 Virgil, *The Georgics*, trans. Lancelot Patrick Wilkinson (Harmondsworth, Middlesex: Penguin, 1982), Book 3, lines 79–82, 86–88. Cf. the even more elaborate description of the points of a horse by Varro in *Rerum Rusticarum*, Book 2, 7:4–5, in *Marcus Porcius Cato, On Agriculture; Marcus Terentius Varro, On Agriculture*, trans. William Davis Hooper, revised by Harrison Boyd Ash (Cambridge, Mass.: Harvard University Press, and London: William Heinemann, 1935, rpt. 1960), 382–85.

----------- 14 -----------

A Letter of Refusal: Rejecting a Subordinate's Request for a Second Loan[1]

Litere negacionis

A. B. fideli suo salutem. Mandasti michi ut ego tibi tres marcas acomodarem, quibus possis a manibus iudeorum terram vestram redimere. Set vehementer admiror qua fronte hec [*sic*] fecisti cum tibi nuper .v. marcas acomodavi nec dum recepi.[2] Quare volo ut scias quod de cetero non amplius tibi acomodabo quam tibi dare [non][3] habeo in proposito, ideo enim mutuaris ut mutuo sumptum detineas. Et ideo te precor ne amplius me solicites. Vale.

A letter of refusal

A. to his faithful B., greetings. You sent word to me that I should lend you three marks with which you could redeem your land from the hands of the Jews. But I am astonished that you had the effrontery to do this, since I lately lent you five marks, and I have not yet received [them back]. Wherefore I wish you to know that henceforth I will no longer lend to you that which I have [no] intention of giving you, for you borrow in order to keep the money that was given to you as a loan. And thus I beg you not to ask me again. Farewell.

This curt letter of refusal is blunt and to the point, with few rhetorical flourishes. The sender, evidently a man of means, has received a request for a loan from a subordinate (only someone under the sender's authority would be addressed as "faithful"). The latter has asked to borrow three marks (£2) with which to redeem land that he has pledged to Jewish moneylenders. The sender is affronted at this request, because the subordinate has already borrowed five marks (£3 6s. 8d.)—a very substantial sum (see DOCUMENT 9)—from him and has not repaid this prior loan. He tells the subordinate roundly that he will no longer lend him anything because he keeps whatever he borrows instead of paying it back.

The man to whom this letter is addressed evidently has borrowed money from Jewish moneylenders on the security of land, rather than from pawnbrokers on the security of a pledge. The distinction here is important, because money borrowed on a short-term basis from a pawnbroker normally carried no interest penalty, since physical possession of the pledge insured the pawnbroker against the risk of non-payment. Instead, the pawnbroker's profit came from the value of forfeited pledges, which (as in DOCUMENT 12) were always worth much more than the value of the loan. Money lent on the security of land or other valuables not placed in the lender's possession, however, commonly included a percentage of concealed interest. This was because the lender did not take physical possession of the land or valuables at the time of the loan, and therefore risked the loss of the capital sum without the assurance of immediate compensation if the borrower defaulted. Also, such loans often were made for extended periods, during which the lender would have neither the use of the capital that he had lent to the borrower, nor the use of the borrower's collateral.[4] The interest rates on such loans could range from substantial to staggering: in 1225–27, for example, a ledger of Jewish loans in Norwich recorded annual interest rates in three different transactions of, respectively, ten percent, 25 percent, and 150 percent, with additional penalties for late payment.[5] The borrower in this letter, especially if he was known to be a poor credit risk, probably had received much less than three marks in cash when he pledged his land. The difference between what he had actually received and what he now owed represented the concealed interest that the lenders had charged for making the loan.[6]

NOTES

1   Add. 8167, fol. 100r.

2   Corrected in MS from *recipi*.

3   A negative seems to be missing here.

4   We are grateful to Robert Stacey for information on these points concerning Jewish pawnbroking and moneylending. On English law regarding pledges and pawnbroking, see Brand, "Aspects of the Law of Debt," 19, 29–31.

5   Mundill, "Christian and Jewish Lending Patterns," 45–46; see also 46–48. By comparison, an Italian bank ledger of 1211 records annualized interest rates for short-term loans (one to three months) of thirty percent, forty percent, 75 percent, and 95 percent (6*d.*, 8*d.*, 15*d.*, and 19*d.*, respectively, in the £ per month), while for longer periods the standard annualized rate was twenty percent (4*d.* in the £ per month). Geoffrey Alan Lee, "The Oldest European Account Book: A Florentine Bank Ledger of 1211," in *Accounting History: Some British Contributions*, ed. Robert Henry Parker and Basil S. Yamey (Oxford: Clarendon, 1994), 169–71, 173–76, 179–81.

6 In 1258, for example, the king himself paid a concealed interest rate of ten percent on a loan of £500 that he obtained on the security of gold and silver jewelry sealed with the seals of J. Mansel, treasurer of York, and Edward of Westminster. The king's acknowledgment of the receipt of this loan, which was made on May 7 and was to be repaid by January 1, reported that it amounted to £550, but a marginal note reveals that the king actually received only £500, and that the extra £50 was "for usury" (i.e., interest), which the Church forbade. *Calendar of Patent Rolls, 1247–58,* 629.

HOUSEHOLD PROVISIONING AND HOSPITALITY

———————— 15 ————————

Instructions for Writing Orders or Prohibitions: An Earl Orders His Steward to Send Him a Supply of Wine and Ale[1]

Precepciones et proibiciones sic debent fieri. Primo debet preponi salutacio, secundo[2] precepcio vel proibicio, tercio narracio, quarto conclusio, hoc modo.

A. Comes Glovernie .C. fideli suo salutem. Precipio tibi ut, visis literis istis, omni occasione et dilacione postpositis, michi mitti facias per latorem presencium, duos cados vini albi, et duas floscas vini castanei et unum doleum servisie defecate. Sciturus quod ego et commitissa mea fleubotomati sumus apud .N. Tantum ergo facias ne nos in iram commoveas propter tuam negligenciam. Vale.

Orders and prohibitions ought to be done thus. First should come the greeting; secondly, the order or prohibition; thirdly, the explanation; fourthly, the conclusion; in this manner.

A., earl of Gloucester, to his faithful C., greetings. I order you that, when you have seen these letters, having put aside every argument and delay, you have two barrels of white wine and two flasks of chestnut wine and one tun of filtered ale sent to me by the bearer of this letter. You shall know that I and my countess are having our blood let at N. Therefore see to it that you do not move us to anger by your negligence. Farewell.

This is the first of a group of ten letters (Documents 2–8, 15, 47, and 85) that illustrate how to write orders and also how to refuse them. Here an earl writes to one of his officers, probably his household steward; only someone in the earl's employ or under his authority would be addressed as "faithful." He orders his officer to send him supplies of wine and ale, and to do so at once. The earl's tone is peremptory—he is addressing someone inferior to him in rank and under his control, and he is giving a command, not making a request.

The ostensible writer of this letter, "A., earl of Gloucester," is possibly intended to be identified with Amaury de Montfort, fourth earl of Gloucester, who is also the putative or possible author of as many as eight other letters in this collection (see DOCUMENT 2). Nothing in DOCUMENT 15 would exclude the possibility that Earl Amaury was its author, and its association with him must therefore be regarded as possible, though not certain. Its unusually circumstantial details are intriguing, however; it may at least be based on a genuine letter by an earl or other lord, even if not by Amaury himself.

In the letter, the earl orders the wines and ale to be sent to "N." ("name"—nomen in Latin—a signal to the writer to fill in the blank here with the appropriate name). This may have been a monastic house, a castle or manor house, or a town. The earl and countess are having their blood let there, presumably as part of a health regimen. The two casks of white wine and the tun of fine-quality ale could have been intended for the consumption of the earl and countess and their traveling staff, and perhaps also for sharing with their hosts if they were staying at a religious house or as guests in another household.[3] The two flasks of chestnut wine are an unusual touch. They evidently represent a special treat or therapeutic drink, perhaps the equivalent of a fine liqueur or "medicinal" brandy today. They may have been designed as an appropriate gift for a thoughtful host, but more likely they were intended for the earl and countess to drink, to assist their recovery from bloodletting. According to the thirteenth-century encyclopedia *De proprietatibus rerum* (*On the Properties of Things*) by Bartholomæus Anglicus (Bartholomew the Englishman), roasted or boiled chestnuts were nourishing, bred "good humors," relieved dryness of the body and breast, and were an effective remedy for nausea and *ieiunium* (the depletion caused by fasting), which were common after-effects of bloodletting.[4] An English poem on courtly manners and behavior, *Urbanus Magnus* (c. 1180), recommended bloodletting to clarify, cleanse, and invigorate the body and the senses, and prescribed a special diet for those who had had their blood let.[5]

Bloodletting (phlebotomy) had been used by Greek physicians as a therapy for illness, as a diagnostic tool, and as part of a seasonal health regimen, and it formed part of the scientific legacy of classical antiquity in the medieval world.[6] Its concept was drawn from the doctrine of the humors, the theoretical basis of classical and medieval medicine. The human body's digestive processes were thought to produce four fluids or "humors": black bile, yellow bile (choler), blood, and phlegm (mucus). These corresponded to the four basic elements that made up the universe: earth, air, fire, and water. Each of these universal elements and their corresponding bodily humors shared essential characteristics of heat or coldness, and moistness or dryness. Earth (cold and dry) corresponded in the body to black bile; air (hot and wet) to blood; fire (hot and dry) to yellow bile; and water (cold and wet) to phlegm. Bodily health was believed to depend on the four bodily humors remaining in balance; if one's humors were out of balance, illness would result. To learned Christian, Muslim, and Jewish physicians of the medieval world, therefore, the appropriate treatment for illness was to discover the nature of the humoral imbalance and then attempt to correct it.[7]

A common method for correcting an imbalance in the humors was to change the patient's food and drink. The patient might also be prescribed medicines and physical treatments to purge the body of its evil humors through sweating, vomiting, evacuating the bladder and bowels, or bloodletting.[8] Medieval treatises on phlebotomy identified more than thirty places in the body from which a practitioner might let blood.[9] The appropriate vein was identified by sight and touch, and raised with warmth and rubbing, by a ligature, or (if the vein was in the arm) by having the patient grip hard on a stick. The raised vein was then pierced with a lancet to produce a gush of blood. Care was taken to avoid piercing any nearby artery, nerve, or ligament. The bleeding was stopped when enough blood had been let.[10] Therapeutic bloodletting was often performed by barbers.[11] In May 1265, for example, Eleanor, countess of Leicester, spent 2*s.* 8*d.* to bring a barber from Reading, on a hired horse, to her castle at Odiham in Hampshire, to let the blood of an unnamed "damsel" (*Domisella*), perhaps the countess's daughter Eleanor.[12] Patients might also travel to have their blood let by a specialist, or to receive special care. In a letter written perhaps in 1273, the unnamed writer (possibly Edmund de Caldecotes) described his activities at Dunwich on the king's behalf, and reported that he then left town "for the pressing need I had of being bled, for the illness which I had" (*pur grant mester ke jeo aveie de seiner, pur la maladie ke jeo aveie*).[13]

Then as now, physicians advised their patients to eat and drink sensibly and to keep in good physical condition as a means of preventing illness, and to this many people added a prophylactic regimen of bloodletting and of purging with emetics, diuretics, and laxatives.[14] Periodic bloodletting as part of a seasonal health regimen had been practiced institutionally in monastic houses since at least the ninth century,[15] and monastic custumals (collections of the regulations and customs of individual religious houses) of the later middle ages record that regular prophylactic bloodletting was common. The canons of the Augustinian priory of Barnwell in Cambridgeshire, for example, were bled an average of seven times a year, and the Benedictine monks of Ely every six weeks.[16] At the Benedictine abbey of Westminster, healthy monks were probably bled by a hired barber about seven or eight times a year in the mid-thirteenth century.[17] Regular bloodletting was recommended in health treatises called dietaries, which suggested appropriate seasonal diets and health regimens. For example, the earliest known dietary in Dutch, dating from 1253, recommended bleeding in February, April, and November, but warned against blood-letting in March, late July ("after St Margaret's day," July 20), and August.[18] However, it is always difficult to determine to what extent prescriptive literature of this kind was actually followed in practice by individuals. This model letter thus provides clear evidence for the practice of bloodletting as part of an aristocratic health regimen, used by both men and women.

NOTES

1 Add. 8167, fol. 97r.

2 *narracio* expunged here in MS.

3 The casks of wine probably contained about 30 U.S. gallons (114 liters) each, and the tun of ale probably held 252 U.S. gallons (about 954 liters). Although there were a number of attempts to standardize weights and measures in medieval England, including in Magna Carta (1215) itself, many local variations persisted. See, e.g., Zupko, *Dictionary of English Weights and Measures* (1968); *A Dictionary of Weights and Measures for the British Isles: The Middle Ages to the Twentieth Century* (Philadelphia: American Philosophical Society, 1985); and "Weights and Measures, Western European," in *Dictionary of the Middle Ages*, ed. Strayer, vol. 12, 585. For a discussion of the measures of wine and ale and levels of consumption, see Labarge, *Baronial Household*, 109–12.

4 *On the Properties of Things: John Trevisa's Translation of Bartholomæus Anglicus, De Proprietatibus Rerum. A Critical Text*, ed. Michael Charles Seymour et al., vol. 2 (Oxford: Clarendon, 1975–88), 978 (Book 17, Chap. 88, *De castanea*, especially lines 21–30). We are grateful to Linda Ehrsam Voigts for this reference, and for information on the after-effects of bloodletting. For his discussion of the medicinal uses of chestnuts, Bartholomew cites Isaac Judaeus or Israeli ("the Jew," died *c.* 932), *De dietis particularibus et universalibus*, in the Latin translation of Constantine the African (d. 1087).

5 Daniel of Beccles, *Urbanus Magnus Danielis Becclesiensis*, ed. Josiah Gilbert Smyly (Dublin: Hodges, Figgis & Co., 1939), lines 2676–96. This portion of the text was also printed and translated by Frederick J. Furnivall in *The Babees Book*, Early English Text Society, original ser., 32 (1868), "Modus Cenandi," 46–47, lines 154–74.

6 On medieval phlebotomy, see Linda E. Voigts and Michael R. McVaugh, "A Latin Technical Phlebotomy and Its Middle English Translation," *Transactions of the American Philosophical Society*, 74, pt. 2 (1984), 1–69 (especially 1–4); and Pedro Gil-Sotres, "Derivation and Revulsion: The Theory and Practice of Medieval Phlebotomy," in *Practical Medicine from Salerno to the Black Death*, ed. Luis García-Ballester,

Roger French, Jon Arrizabalaga, and Andrew Cunningham (Cambridge: Cambridge University Press, 1994), 110–55 (especially 110–19, 123–32).

7 Melitta Weiss Adamson, *Medieval Dietetics: Food and Drink in Regimen Sanitatis Literature from 800 to 1400*, German Studies in Canada, 5 (Frankfurt am Main: Peter Lang, 1995), 10–15; Carole Rawcliffe, *Medicine and Society in Late Medieval England* (Stroud, Gloucestershire: Sutton, 1995, rpt. London: Sandpiper, 1999), 29–40, 53–54.

8 Rawcliffe, *Medicine and Society*, 34, 51–53.

9 Voigts and McVaugh, "Latin Technical Phlebotomy," 4–5.

10 Gil-Sotres, "Derivation and Revulsion," 140–54.

11 Gil-Sotres, "Derivation and Revulsion," 120–22.

12 Turner, ed., *Manners and Household Expenses*, 31.

13 Shirley, ed., *Letters*, vol. 2, 321, 372 (Anglo-Norman text and English translation); this letter is now TNA: PRO, SC 1/8/42.

14 Rawcliffe, *Medicine and Society*, 61, 64–67.

15 Voigts and McVaugh, "Latin Technical Vocabulary," 1–2.

16 Rawcliffe, *Medicine and Society*, 66–68.

17 Barbara Harvey, *Living and Dying in England, 1100–1540: The Monastic Experience* (Oxford: Oxford University Press, 1993), 96–99; cf. 77n.

18 Oxford, Bodleian Library, MS Junius 83, printed in Alphonse van Loey, *Middelnederlands Leerboek* (Antwerp: De Sikkel, 1947), 330–32; available online with a rough English translation by Eli Steenput at http://www.geocities.com/ulfberth/Diet.htm [seen May 24, 2006]. See also Falconer Madan, Herbert Henry Edmund Craster, and Noël Denholm-Young, *A Summary Catalogue of Western Manuscripts in the Bodleian Library at Oxford*, vol. 2, part 2 (Oxford: Clarendon, 1937), pp. 981–82; Willy Braekman and Maurits Gysseling, "Het Utrechtse Kalendarium van 1253 met de Noordlimburgse gezondheidsregels," *Verslagen en Mededelingen der Koninklijke Vlaamsche Academie voor Taal- en Letterkunde*, (1967), 575–635; and Maurits Gysseling, *Corpus van Middelnederlandse Teksten (tot en met het jaar 1300)*, ser. 2, vol. 1 (The Hague: Nijhoff, 1977), 345–47. For a fifteenth-century monthly regimen for diet and bloodletting in Middle English, see Linne R. Mooney, "Diet and Bloodletting: A Monthly Regimen," in *Popular and Practical Science of Medieval England*, ed. Lister M. Matheson (East Lansing, Mich.: Colleagues Press, 1994), 245–61.

16

A Friend Warns Another to Buy Grain Against a Coming Dearth[1]

B. mandat C. ut muniatur de blado contra annos futuros

Karissimo amico suo A., B. salutem. Quoniam promocionem vestram desidero, ideo vos premunire volo, ut bladum queratis ad emendum ubicumque invenire poteritis. Scimus enim quod terra seminata male respondet agricolis, et nisi deus prospiceretur, caritudo nascetur per totam terram antequam nova messis inhorretur, gelu namque satis suffocat. Et ideo tantum faciatis ut providencia vestra vobis et vestris valeat p[ro]desse[2] et aliis indigentibus. Valete.

B. sends word to C. to stock up on grain against the coming seasons

To his dearest friend A., B. sends greetings. Since I am zealous for your welfare, I wish to warn you to seek out grain to buy wherever you can find it. For we know that the sown earth is repaying the farmers badly and, unless God should provide, there will be dearth throughout the entire land before the new harvest bristles forth, for the frost quite smothers [it]. Therefore, I hope that you will act in such a way that your foresight may benefit yourself and your own people, and other needy people. Farewell.

Poor harvests were a recurring fact of life in medieval Europe. Even in good years, harvest yields were frighteningly low by modern standards. For example, on the bishop of Winchester's estates between 1225 and 1249, a period of generally high grain yields compared with those of the following two centuries, the ratio of grain harvested to seed sown averaged only 4.14:1 for wheat, 4.75:1 for barley, and 2.71:1 for oats.[3] Thus, a farmer who sowed one bushel each of wheat, barley, and oats in a single year would have reaped, on average, about four bushels of wheat, 4¾ bushels of barley, and only 2¾ bushels of oats. From those totals, moreover, the farmer would have had to deduct one bushel each of seed for sowing the following year. In addition, a tenant-farmer had to pay a percentage of his crop in rent (either in cash or grain, or a combination of the two), and a further percentage would be due from any grain that he ground at the lord's mill (see DOCUMENT 1). Finally, all farmers would have lost a percentage of their stored grain to waste, spoilage, and vermin. As a result, even in the comparatively good years of the second quarter of the thirteenth century, the profit margins of arable farming in a lord's demesne (home-farm), which owed no rent, would have been modest at best, while those of tenant-farmers, both free and servile, would have been dangerously slim.

This letter sounds as if it was written during an unusually cold, late spring when the frostbound fields showed no sign of sprouting grain. Spring was usually the hungriest time of the year. The previous autumn's harvest bounty was a fading memory; gardens and fruit trees were bare; the poultry were not laying eggs; the cows, ewes, and nanny-goats were dry of milk; and many pigs and other livestock were unsuitable for slaughter because they were pregnant, too young, too thin, or needed for work, wool, or breeding. Because of this annual scarcity the early Church, making a virtue of necessity, decreed the forty-day Lenten fast to commemorate the fasting of Jesus in the wilderness for forty days and nights (Matthew 4:2). During Lent the consumption of all meat, poultry, and dairy products was forbidden.

The sender of this letter anticipates that, as a result of the bitter weather, there will be a dearth in which grain will be scanty and expensive, although he does not predict an outright famine. His advice to his friend—to stock up now, so as to provide for dependents and for the poor—recalls the biblical story of Joseph, who counseled Pharaoh to store up surplus grain in the good years at hand in order to have it to use in the lean years to come (Genesis 41).

NOTES

1 Add. 8167, fol. 101r. On the discrepancy in initials between heading and text, see DOCUMENT 33, n. 1.
2 *pdesse* in MS.
3 Bruce M. S. Campbell, *English Seigneurial Agriculture, 1250–1450* (Cambridge: Cambridge University Press, 2000), Table 7.12.

17

An Archdeacon Sends Word to a Dean About an Impending Visitation by the Bishop[1]

Archidiaconus mandat decano ut muniat presbiteros et personas de cibis multimodis contra eius adventum

Archidiaconus decano salutem. Preceptum domini episcopi heri suscepi ut munirem[2] omnes presbiteros et personas qui in hoc episcopatu sunt ut unusquisque illorum, sicut consuetudo est, competens[3] officium illi. Veniet enim ante sex dies in has partes et tunc primum vult[4] facere mansionem mecum secundo tecum commoraturus. Quare vos premunio ut premuniti sitis contra eius adventum cibis multimodis, ut petens apud vos inveniat hospicium et convenienter ibi reficiatur. Et tantum faciatis[5] ne inveniat occasionem vobis malignandi.

An archdeacon sends word to a dean that he should give notice to priests and incumbents[6] about the many sorts of provisions for his visit

An archdeacon to a dean, greetings. I received yesterday a writ of the lord bishop that I should warn all priests and incumbents in his diocese that each of them, according to custom, [is to] assemble [to pay] respects to him. For he will come to these parts within six days, and he wishes to stay at first with me, and later with you. Because of this I am cautioning you to be stocked up for his arrival with all sorts of food, so that when he arrives at your house he will find lodging and an appropriate table.

And I hope that you will act in such a way that he will not find an excuse to speak badly of you.

Hospitality was a vexed subject in the Middle Ages. A bishop on a visitation of his diocese, as here, depended on the hospitality of his subordinates, but this raised pressing issues of both cost and reputation. An episcopal visitation would have involved considerable expense to any host of lesser station. Prelates might travel with a substantial household of servants and chaplains, sufficient to cause difficulties to their hosts. In the 1190s Gerald of Wales criticized his fellow archdeacons who went around demanding hospitality and indulging their appetites for food and drink rather than correcting clerical abuses. He talked of the many courses of fine food and the spiced wines that bishops, archdeacons, and officials expected their hosts to provide.[7]

A damaged letter survives from the 1190s in a fragment of a lost formulary that preserves the complaints of the incumbent of the Yorkshire parish of Kirkby Lonsdale concerning the demands about to be made on him by a visitation from the vice-archdeacon of Richmond. The priest is writing to the abbot of Furness, a monastery with which his parish had some undefined connection. He is anxious about the very things discussed in DOCUMENT 17— that is, the cost of entertainment and the consequences of failure in that department: "John, incumbent of Kirkby to . . . by the grace of God abbot of Furness, greetings. Your excellency should know that the lord Theobald, vice-archdeacon of [Richmond], will be entertained on Friday and that . . . I have no idea what I shall serve him. So I beg your worship to instruct your fishermen to catch [suitable?] fish for his needs, and [that] whatever they take they keep till Friday . . . [so] that I do not lose my reputation for hospitality by lack of food."[8] The canons issued by the Council of London (1237) therefore urged archdeacons on visitations that "they should not drag hangers-on around with them, but take just a few servants and horses."[9] Episcopal visitations were likely to be even more burdensome, especially to rural deans, whose houses, as here, were often the bishop's headquarters during his progress through the diocese. Bishops could be ostentatious travelers. One of the principal complaints in 1191 against William Longchamp, bishop of Ely and justiciar, was that he would arrive at monasteries "in such a swarm of men, horses, dogs and hawks, that the monastery where he was to stay the night could scarcely be restored to its former state in three years."[10] His colleague at the court of Henry II, Stephen de Fougères, later bishop of Rennes, regarded this practice as objectionable and wrote around 1160 that "the luxury of this world is an odious thing, a man of self control rejects and distances himself from it; a man who rides out with too great a retinue embarrasses the host where he seeks lodging."[11]

The core of the dilemma for hosts such as this dean was the expectations of the guest.[12] Early thirteenth-century moralist Raoul de Houdenc reckoned that entertaining was comprehended within the virtue of largesse, and that "it is a very good thing to give a banquet." A man's ability to entertain was thus a measure of his prowess (*proece*), which meant that men of standing were expected to compete for distinction in entertaining.[13] It is for this reason that the archdeacon in the letter above not only tells the dean to stock up on provisions against the bishop's arrival, but warns that if he fails to do so, the bishop could "find an excuse to speak badly of you." The dean's reputation would then inevitably suffer in the poor report that the bishop's household would make of him, as the priest of Kirkby Lonsdale feared would happen if he failed to entertain the vice-archdeacon suitably.

The demands of elite hospitality were described by Daniel of Beccles in his verse handbook on courteous behaviour, *Urbanus Magnus* (*c.* 1180):

> Should a clergyman or knight arrive as a guest, you should come out to meet him and greet him warmly. If he is a good friend of yours offer him hugs and kisses. The best you have should be laid out on the table in a show of honor. All the household should be respectfully put at his disposal, with hay for his horses, and the occasion should call forth sufficient supplies. The guest should not encounter smoky and reeking fires; no hearth should be lighted in the hall if it is overheated. The abundance of the feast should make the diners cheerful; an ever-open hand should add distinction to the food and drink. The offering of food and drink should satisfy the guests; cheerful speech should be refreshed by a worthy audience; the harmony of all sorts of song should follow on from the serving of wine; as you dine you should toast your guests. . . . A free hand in throwing dinners bestows a reputation for generosity.[14]

Entertainment in the middle ages was about more than hospitality, or even obligation. It was part of the interplay of patronage and status that dominated society. Walter Map, archdeacon of Oxford, joked that he was urged by his household servants to offer generous hospitality as part of a strategy to promote his reputation and secure higher office.[15] Much the same social consciousness is on display in this letter.

NOTES

1 Add. 8167, fol. 102v.

2 Corrected in MS from *muniatrem*.

3 *Sic* in MS; perhaps something like *competendum [facere]* was originally intended.

4 *wlt* in MS.

5 *facientes* in MS.

6 An incumbent (*persona*) was a cleric who occupied a benefice.

7 Gerald of Wales, *Speculum Ecclesiae*, in *Giraldi Cambrensis Opera*, ed. John Sherren Brewer, vol. 4. Rolls Series, 21 (London: Longman, 1873), 329–30.

8 Nicholas Vincent, "William Marshal, King Henry II and the Honour of Château-roux," *Archives*, 25 (2000), 15.

9 *Councils and Synods*, vol. 2, no. 1, p. 254. Jean Scammell, "The Rural Chapter in England from the Eleventh to the Fourteenth Century," *EHR*, 86 (1971), 13, describes the complaints of the clergy of Holderness in the early 1280s about the level of enforced hospitality, saying that in the previous generation they had been obliged to entertain only the archdeacon's official, the rural dean, and a couple of clerks.

10 *Gesta Henrici Secundi*, ed. William Stubbs, vol. 2, Rolls Series 49 (London: Longman, 1867), 200.

11 R. Anthony Lodge, ed., *Le Livre des manières* (Geneva: Droz, 1979), lines 433–36.

12 See Julie Kerr, "The Open Door: Hospitality and Honour in Twelfth/Early Thirteenth-Century England," *History*, 87 (2002), 328–29.

13 Keith Busby, ed., *Le Roman des Eles* (Amsterdam: John Benjamins, 1983), lines 239–51.

14 Daniel of Beccles, *Urbanus Magnus*, lines 2344–56, 2359 (translation by David Crouch).

15 *De Nugis Curialium*, ed. and trans. Montague Rhodes James, Christopher N. L. Brooke, and Roger A. B. Mynors (Oxford: Oxford University Press, 1983), 20–22; discussed by Julie Kerr in "Food, Drink and Lodging: Hospitality in Twelfth-Century England," *Haskins Society Journal*, 18 (2006), 72–73.

18

A Rural Dean Warns a Priest of an Imminent Visit from the Bishop and Advises Him to Obtain an Appropriate Variety of Foods[1]

Decanus presbitero ut premuniat se de cibis

Decanus presbitero salutem. Scias quod dominus episcopus cras tecum commedet, quare tibi consulo ut amico meo ut premunitus sis contra adventum suum cibis multis,[2] multi enim secum venient clerici et laici et oportet omnibus satisfacere. Hii volunt vinum, hii digni sunt vino; hii carnes appetunt, qui digni sunt carnibus; hii pisces optant—unicuique datur secundum quod est [dignum].³ Tantum ergo faciatis ut a domino episcopo grates habeatis.

A rural dean to a priest that he should ready himself concerning food

A dean to a priest, greetings. You should know that the lord bishop will be dining with you tomorrow, and so I would advise you as my friend to be ready for his arrival with a variety of foods, for many clergy and laypeople are coming with him, and it is in your interest to satisfy them all. Some want wine, and others are entitled to wine; some are eager for meat, [and] some are entitled to meat; some prefer fish—let each be given what is [appropriate]. Therefore, you should act in such a way that you may have thanks from the lord bishop.

This letter reflects the ripple effect of the impending visit by a bishop to the clergy of his diocese, as discussed in DOCUMENT 17. In that letter an archdeacon alerted a subordinate, a rural dean, to prepare food for the bishop's arrival. Here we see how the effort and expense of providing hospitality to the bishop and his entourage are being partly shifted to one of the dean's subordinates, a parish priest. (For the organization of the church in medieval England, see DOCUMENT 44.) The dean advises the priest that the bishop's party will be demanding and the burden of hospitality great, but that it is very much in the priest's best interests to accommodate his guests as best he can so as to earn the bishop's gratitude.

The dean's letter also testifies to the fact that written communication was routine by this date among all ranks of clergy, including rural deans and parish priests. It represents the clerical parallel to the correspondence in this volume by all ranks of the laity, including shopkeepers and peasants. Among the clergy, it is clear that such correspondence was normally channeled up and down the chain of command between people of equal or adjacent rank: in DOCUMENTS 17 and 18, for example, each cleric corresponds directly with an immediate inferior or superior, rather than with someone two or more grades in rank above or below him. Among the laity, although (except in relationships of direct authority and dependence) the hierarchical chain could be less explicit, it also was most common for correspondence to take place between people who were of equivalent or adjacent rank, as in DOCUMENTS 62 and 65.

NOTES

1   Add. 8167, fol. 103r.
2   *multibus* in MS.
3   Word supplied to preserve the sense of the text.

----------- 19 -----------

The King Orders a Sheriff to Commandeer Wine for His Use and Transport for It, and to Deal Sharply with Any Resistance[1]

Rex mandat vicecomiti ut capi faciat vina contra eius adventum et equos ad tra[h]endum[2] vina usque ad aulam eius

> Rex vicecomiti salutem. Tibi mando atque firmiter precipio ut, omni occasione et dilacione remotis, vina que apud .B. invenire poteris ad opus meum capi facias. Precipio at[que][3] veredos et equos quoscumque et in villis proximis reperieris capi facias et vina prefata educi facias. Et siquem rebellum inveniris pone eum per vadium et plegium quod ad curiam regis veniat et de presumpcione regi respondeat. Vale.

The king sends word to a sheriff to commandeer wine in advance of his arrival and horses to transport the wine to his hall

> The king to a sheriff, greetings. I direct and firmly command you that, with no excuse or delay, you cause what wine you can find at B. to be commandeered for my use. I also order you to arrange whatever wagons and horses you can discover in the nearby villages to be taken, and cause the said wine to be transported. If you find anyone who resists, place him on pledge and surety to come to the king's court and answer to the king for his defiance. Farewell.

There is no royal writ that parallels this one. King William Rufus (1087–1100) was notorious for allowing his court to steal and pillage its supplies as it passed through a locality. By contrast, his successor Henry I (1100–1135) gave notice of his movements so that merchants and provisioners could meet his court and provide for the court's needs. Kings thereafter were careful in managing the requisition of goods. The king might very well draw supplies from royal manors, but this writ conjures up the idea of a king arbitrarily seizing luxury goods and commandeering the means to transport them. To that extent, the writ is a fanciful product conjuring up a picture of outright royal tyranny, but a similar situation is alluded to in DOCUMENT 33.

In fact, the writer here is depicting a pervasive practice called "prise," which was the king's right to "take" goods for his use. The prise of wine, an expensive import (see DOCUMENT 2), was particularly valuable to the king. Not only did the court consume a lot of it, but the king also frequently offered gifts of tuns of wine as patronage. In 1243, for instance, the king ordered forty tuns of the best of the new wines arriving at Southampton from Gascony to be taken for his use to Westminster. But the king had to pay for wine taken in this way, so his agent was commissioned to appoint a panel of independent valuers to assess the value of the wine taken, and pay the assessed price to the merchants from whom the wine had been taken.[4] That at least was the ideal.

It is possible to see this letter as having been inspired by the defects of the prise system. The king's men might be slow to pay the merchant, who in any case might well think he could get a better price elsewhere. The inconvenience and dissatisfaction that are obliquely expressed in this letter might well refer to the crisis in the wine trade of the 1230s, when the government attempted to fix wine prices with an assize. The result was a disruption in the wine trade in England. When the trade resumed, merchants resisted the prise because the king was insisting on a price of half the market value. Merchants' stocks were seized and detained until the king's agents could secure the amounts they required. The agents themselves could and did exploit their position by reselling the wine at a large profit. As a result, the administration of the king's "chamber of wines" collapsed.[5]

Further evidence that this letter reflects wider discontent may be found in the Petition of the Barons of 1258, the statement of grievances against Henry III's personal rule. Two clauses deplore the king's poor administration of prises, claiming that the king's agents took more than the king actually required for his use, sometimes two or three times more, and sold the excess for their own profit. The other major complaint was the king's poor record of payment, which impoverished native merchants and discouraged foreigners.[6]

NOTES

1   Add. 8167, fol. 108v.
2   *traend'* in MS.
3   *at* in MS.
4   *Close Rolls, 1242–47*, 131, 136.
5   Robert Stacey, *Politics, Policy and Finance Under Henry III, 1216–1245* (Oxford: Oxford University Press, 1987), 106–8.
6   Reginald F. Treharne and Ivor J. Sanders, eds., *Documents of the Baronial Movement of Reform and Rebellion, 1258–1267* (Oxford: Oxford University Press, 1973), 84–86.

ACCOUNTS

—— 20 ——

The Manner of Keeping Accounts[1]

Siquis voluerit scire compota ordinare et formam et artem inbreviandi, in hoc rotulo omnia que neccessaria fuerint[2] secundum quod capitula in margine rotuli ordinati destincta fuerint invenire poterit. Primo, de numeris et postea de subsequentibus. [S]iquis[3] et de marcis libras facere[4] voluerit et numerus earum, ternarie ductum[?];[5] subiaceat[6] tercia parte remota marcarum, remanet numerus librarum. Set si forte remaneat .i. marca. de ternaria duccione, interd[etur?];[7] vero[8] due que faceunt .i. libram[9] ii.[10] et dimidiam marcam. Si autem volueritis de libris facere marcas, numero librarum adde medietatem sui et h[ab]ebis[11] marcas si par numerus est. Si autem inpar, pro una que inparalitatem facit adde marcam et dimidiam. Hic incipies ordinare capitula margini hoc modo.

If anyone should wish to know how to keep accounts and the form and art of brevement,[12] he will be able to find in this roll everything that will be necessary by following the separate chapter-headings that are listed in the margin of the roll. The first chapter concerns numbers, and afterward other topics follow. And if anyone should wish to make pounds from marks, [for] the number of them, let him cast out a deduction by threes; with the third part of the marks removed, the number of pounds remains. But if it should happen that one mark remain from the deduction by threes, let it be distributed; and two [marks remaining] make one pound and half a mark.[13] If you should wish to convert pounds to marks, to the number of pounds add half again and you will have the [number of] marks, if it is an even number. If, however, it is an odd number, for the one [pound] that makes it an odd number, add a mark and a half. Here you begin to list the headings of the margin in this manner.

The keeping of private financial accounts had begun in England by c. 1139, and perhaps earlier still in the twelfth century, when Robert I, count of Meulan and earl of Leicester (d. 1118), granted revenues from his exchequer to his collegiate church of St. Mary de Castro in Leicester Castle. The description of the grant, in a charter of his son Earl Robert II (d. 1168), makes it clear that by c. 1139 the earl's estates (which were divided into units called "sokes") produced written accounts at an annual exchequer session in Leicester Castle. The most likely model for the accounting practices of the earl's exchequer would have been the new royal Exchequer (first established by Henry I c. 1106–10), which from its beginning may have kept annual account rolls.[14] Further evidence of the keeping of private financial accounts dates from the mid-twelfth century. In a celebrated legal case that spanned five years, from 1158 to 1163, Richard of Anstey took his cousin Mabel de Francheville to court to gain possession of her father's lands. Anstey's expenses in connection with this lawsuit came to almost £350, and he later described them in detail in a lengthy memorandum, which must have been based on records that he had kept at the time.[15] The earliest English household account to survive is an undated fragment of the late twelfth century.[16]

DOCUMENTS 20–23 represent the earliest known *instructions* from medieval England for keeping private financial accounts, and also the earliest known examples from England of specimen (model) accounts.[17] From the introductory sentence in the document above, and a similar reference in DOCUMENT 22, it is clear that the original versions of these texts were written on parchment rolls, which was the usual form for keeping accounts in England until the years around 1400, when accounts began to be kept instead in paper books.[18]

The systems described here for converting marks to pounds and pounds to marks, which look so cumbersome to modern eyes, reflect the difficulties of doing sums using Roman numerals, in which multiplication and long division were impossible. A pound contained 20 shillings or 240 pence; a mark was two-thirds of a pound, and contained thirteen shillings fourpence (13*s.* 4*d.*, or 160*d.*). To convert marks to pounds using Arabic numerals is simple: one multiplies the number of marks by two-thirds. To convert pounds to marks one multiplies the pounds by one and a half. For example, nine marks contained six pounds ($9 \times 2/3 = 6$), while six pounds contained nine marks ($6 \times 3/2 = 9$). Medieval accountants working in Roman numerals, however, had to use addition or subtraction in place of multiplication or division. Converting marks to pounds required "casting out threes." That is, from the total number of marks one would subtract three; from the remainder one would subtract another three; and so on, until no marks were left. Then one mark would be deducted from each group of three (or, alternatively, one-third of the groups of three would be deducted), and the remaining marks would represent the number of pounds. Thus, nine marks contained six pounds.[19] Converting pounds to marks using Roman numerals was simpler: to the number of pounds one added half again, and the total represented the number of marks. Thus, six pounds contained nine marks.[20]

Converting marks to pounds always resulted in a whole number if the number of marks was divisible by three. Thus, three marks contained two pounds.[21] If the number of marks was *not* divisible by three, there was always a remainder of either one or two marks. For example, four marks contained two pounds with one mark (13*s.* 4*d.*) left over, and five marks contained two pounds with two marks (26*s.* 8*d.*) left over. The instructions in the text above for converting marks to pounds provided a simple rule for calculating these fractions. If a single mark remained after casting out one-third, it was simply added to the sum as 13*s.* 4*d.* Thus, four marks made £2 13*s.* 4*d.* (£2 plus 13*s.*

4*d*.). If two marks remained, one pound plus half a mark were added. Thus, five marks made £3 6*s*. 8*d*. (£2 plus £1 6*s*. 8*d*.). Similarly, according to the instructions above, one converted odd numbers of pounds to marks by subtracting one pound, adding half again to the even number of remaining pounds, and then adding a mark and a half for the missing pound. Thus, five pounds contained seven and a half marks.[22]

Only two other accounting treatises dating from before the reign of Edward I (1272–1307) are known from medieval England. One, written by a clerk called John "de Morbiria" (Marbury-cum-Quoisley, Cheshire), includes some brief instructions for keeping accounts, together with a set of specimen accounts dated 1258–59.[23] The other formed part of the formulary compiled between 1261 and 1268 by the bailiff Robert Carpenter II of "Hareslade" (Haslett, near Shorwell, Isle of Wight).[24] Carpenter's formulary, which contains a considerable number of texts in common with those in Article 5 of Add. 8167, also includes instructions for keeping accounts and specimen accounts. Neither Marbury's nor Carpenter's instructions or specimen accounts replicate those in Add. 8167.

NOTES

1 Add. 8167, fols. 131v–132r.
2 *fuerit* in MS.
3 There is a blank space in the MS at the beginning of this word, evidently for a capital "S."
4 Fol. 132r. commences here.
5 *dc'm* in MS. The Latin text here from *numerus* to *dimidiam* is murky, but the meaning is clear; see below.
6 *subiacereat* in MS.
7 *interd'* in MS.
8 *ii°* in MS.
9 Or possibly *vel* (*l'* in MS).
10 It is unclear whether "*ii.*" here is a mistaken duplication of the "*due*" above, or if instead the sense of this passage is: "and two [remaining marks] make one pound [into] two, plus half a mark." Whichever is correct, the overall meaning of the passage is the same. See below.
11 *hebis* in MS.
12 Entering accounts.
13 In other words, if one mark remains, add 13*s*. 4*d*. to the sum; if two remain, add £1 6*s*. 8*d*. See below.
14 On the Leicester and royal exchequers, see David Crouch, *The Beaumont Twins: The Roots and Branches of Power in the Twelfth Century* (Cambridge: Cambridge University Press, 1986), 163–67. On the earliest known royal Exchequer roll or "pipe roll" (1124), see Mark Hagger, "A Pipe Roll for 25 Henry I," *EHR*, 122, no. 495 (2007), 133–40. The earliest known medieval accounts of domestic expenditure to have survived from continental Europe are those of the Count-King Berenguer

IV of Catalonia for 1156–57. Christopher M. Woolgar, ed., *Household Accounts from Medieval England*, 2 vols., British Academy, Records of Social and Economic History, new ser., 17–18 (Oxford: Oxford University Press, for the British Academy, 1992–93), vol. 1, 16.

15 See Paul A. Brand, *The Origins of the English Legal Profession* (Oxford: Blackwell, 1992), 1–2. For the text of Anstey's memorandum, see Raoul C. van Caenegem, ed., *English Lawsuits from William I to Richard I*, vol. 2, *Henry II and Richard I*, Selden Society, 107 (London, 1991), 397–404. An English translation of part of Anstey's memorandum can also be found in David C. Douglas and George W. Greenaway, eds., *English Historical Documents*, vol. 2, *1042–1189* (London: Eyre and Spottiswoode, 1953), 456–57.

16 This fragment records the daily expenses of an unidentified household at London, Westminster, and Windsor for twenty-two days between October 4 and November 1. The days of the week and holy days mentioned in the account would fit the years 1168, 1174, 1185, 1191, 1196, and 1202. Woolgar, ed., *Household Accounts*, vol. 1, 10–11, 107–10. Woolgar implies (p. 10) that this account dates from the 1180s, which would mean that its correct date is 1185. On manorial accounts, including a transcript of an account from 1258, see Bailey, trans. and ed., *English Manor*, 98–120.

17 Margaret Wade Labarge erroneously reported that there was a French as well as a Latin version of these instructions on folios 132 and 137 of Add. 8167; there is no such French text anywhere in the manuscript. Labarge, *Baronial Household*, 189 and n. 1. Dorothea Oschinsky noted that only three other accounting treatises from England are known before 1270. Oschinsky, "Medieval Treatises on Estate Accounting," *Economic History Review*, 17, no. 1 (1947), 54, 58; cf. eadem, *Walter of Henley and Other Treatises on Estate Management and Accounting* (Oxford: Clarendon, 1971), 235–37.

18 E.g., accounts for Edward Courtenay, earl of Devon, for 1384–85, and for Margaret Beauchamp, countess of Warwick, for 1405–6, were kept on rolls, while those of of Margaret Plantagenet, countess of Norfolk (1394–95) and of Richard Mitford, bishop of Salisbury, for October 1406 to June 1407 were kept in books. See Woolgar, ed., *Household Accounts*, vol. 1, 30–31, 38, 262; vol. 2, 698; TNA: PRO, E 101/513/12 (Beauchamp roll).

19 $9 - 3 = 6$; $6 - 3 = 3$; $3 - 3 = 0$; $2 \times 3 = 6$.

20 $6 + 3 = 9$.

21 Three less one-third leaves two $(3 - 1 = 2)$.

22 $5 - 1 = 4$; $4 + 2 = 6$; $6 + 1\frac{1}{2} = 7\frac{1}{2}$.

23 Bodleian Library, Oxford, Rawlinson MS C. 775, pp. 117–26.

24 Gonville & Caius 205/111, pp. 341–66. Both of these treatises were discussed by Noël Denholm-Young in *Seignorial Adminstration in England*, 121–22, and by Dorothea Oschinsky in "Medieval Treatises on Estate Accounting," 54, 56, 58, and *Walter of Henley*, 39, 43, 228–29, 236, 237–39. A later version of Gonville & Caius 205/111 was written by Robert Carpenter II's son and namesake, Robert Carpenter III, between 1283 and 1300. It is now CUL, MS Mm. I. 27. See Denholm-Young, "Robert Carpenter and the Provisions of Westminster," *EHR*, 50 (1935), 22–35; rpt. in idem, *Collected Papers on Mediaeval Subjects* (Oxford: Basil Blackwell, 1946), 96–110; and again in idem, *Collected Papers* (Cardiff: University of Wales Press, 1969), 173–86. See also Oschinsky, *Walter of Henley*, 36–37, 239; and Martha Carlin, "Cheating the Boss: Robert Carpenter's Embezzlement Instructions (1261 × 1268), and Employee Fraud

in Medieval England," in *Markets and Entrepreneurs in the Middle Ages: Essays in Honour of Richard Britnell*, ed. Ben Dodds and Christian Liddy (Woodbridge, Suffolk: Boydell, 2011), 183–97.

21

Model Manorial Account for a Six-Year Period
[September 29, 1222–September 29, 1228][1]

A. serviens de B. et C. prepositus reddunt compota eiusdem manerii a festo sancti michaelis anno regni regis H. tercii .vi°. usque ad festum sancti michaelis anni eiusdem .xii°. Recepta prima de redditu. Item reddit [*sic*] compotum. de .iiii^xx. libris et xix. solidis. [v][2] denariis. et obolo de redditu assiso et de .x. solidis de incremento unius termini. Summa. iiii^xx. librarum. et .xxix. s'. et .v. d' et ob'. Quietancia redditus. In servicio unius prepositi .v. s'., et unius forestarii .v. s'., et unius vaccarii et beccar[ii][3] et porcarii .xv. s'., unius bedelli .iiii. s'. et .vi.d'., et trium carucariorum .xv. s'. Summa. xliiii. s'. et sex den'. et remanet de gabulo reddibili lxxix. librae. et. iiii. solidi. et .xi. denarii et obolus.

A. the bailiff[4] of B., and C. the reeve, render the accounts of the same manor, from the feast of Michaelmas in the sixth year of the reign of King Henry III to the feast of Michaelmas in the twelfth year of the same [September 29, 1222–September 29, 1228]. First, receipts from rent: Item, he [*sic*] renders account of £80 19s. [5]½d. of rent of assize, and of 10s. of the increase of one term.[5] Total, £80 29s. 5½d. Discharge of rent:[6] For the service of one reeve, 5s.; and of one forester, 5s.; and of one cowman, shepherd, and pigman, 15s.; of one beadle, 4s. 6d.; and of three plowmen, 15s. Total, 44s. 6d. And there remains to be rendered from the land-gavel £79 4s. 11½d.[7]

For most of the twelfth century, great landholders typically leased the bulk of their estates to tenants. As a result, they had no need to keep detailed financial records for each manor. Between *c.* 1180 and *c.* 1220, however, rapid inflation and rising debt among landholders led to a major change in English estate management: great landlords began to exploit the economic value of their estates more fully by managing them directly (through professional stewards), rather than leasing them out *en bloc* at rents that would be eaten up by inflation. This prompted the landlords to require their estate officers to keep annual financial accounts (*compota*). The first such accounts to survive are those of the bishopric of Winchester, which begin in 1208–9. Early *compota* could vary widely in form, but their financial year often began on the feast of St. Michael the Archangel, known as Michaelmas (September 29), by which time the autumn harvest would have been in.[8]

Only about a dozen manorial accounts are extant for the period before 1250, and the model account here is the earliest specimen (model) manorial account known from medieval England.[9] It reads as if it were based on a genuine account, one perhaps rendered by a single accountant (the "he" of the second sentence),[10] for an unnamed manor (the "same" manor mentioned in the opening sentence, which evidently was the subject of a preceding account). It is a summary of six years' worth of rental income and six years' payment of wages that were charged against those rents. The fixed annual rental income for this manor totaled £80 19*s*. 5½*d*., or one halfpenny short of £13 9*s*. 11*d*. per annum. An extra ten shillings in rental income are reported for a single term, perhaps representing the lease of additional property from the manor.

From the rental income was deducted the cost of annual wages: 40*s*. (10*d*. each per annum) for the service of eight manorial officers and workers, and 4*s*. 6*d*. (9*d*. per annum) for the service of the manor's beadle.[11] That left a net rental income due to the current landlord of £79 4*s*. 11½*d*. for the six years, or one halfpenny shy of £13 4*s*. 2*d*. per annum, plus the additional 10*s*. for one term only.

The list of officers and workers makes it clear that the lord of this manor kept some of it in demesne (i.e., he did not lease it out), so as to provide produce for his own use or to sell. The list also reveals that the lord's demesne practiced a mixed husbandry, with arable acreage that was plowed and planted for crops, and land that was used for the pasturage of cows and sheep and the keeping of pigs.

NOTES

1   Add. 8167, fol. 132r.
2   The amount of pence is left blank here in the MS, but can be supplied from the totals below.
3   *beccar* in MS.
4   For the translation of *serviens* as "bailiff," see DOCUMENT 50, below.
5   A rent of assize was a fixed (not variable) annual rent, payable to the current landlord.
6   A "discharge of rent" was an expense charged against the rental income. A similar usage occurs in the formulary of 1261 × 68 compiled and written by Robert Carpenter II of "Hareslade" (now Haslett Farm) on the Isle of Wight, who was an estate bailiff of William de Insula. Gonville & Caius College 205/111, pp. 366, 370. We are

grateful to Paul Hyams for his assistance with the interpretation of this term. On Robert Carpenter and his formulary, see DOCUMENT 4.

7   Here land-gavel rents are used synonymously with rents of assize (see above).

8   See Bailey, trans. and ed., *English Manor*, 19–20, 105, 107–8; and Paul D. A. Harvey, "The English Inflation of 1180–1220," *Past and Present*, 61 (November 1973), 3–30; rpt. in Rodney Hilton, ed., *Peasants, Knights and Heretics: Studies in Medieval Social History*, Past and Present Publications (Cambridge: Cambridge University Press, 1976), 57–84. Sidney Painter found that average manorial revenues increased by 51 percent to 64 percent between 1220 and 1250. Painter, *Studies in the History of the English Feudal Barony* (Baltimore: The Johns Hopkins Press, 1943), 160; cited in Harvey, "English Inflation," 69, n. 53.

9   On early manorial accounts, see Paul D. A. Harvey, "Manorial Accounts," in *Accounting History*, ed. Parker and Yamey, Chap. 3.

10 However, it was more usual for early manorial accounts such as this to be rendered jointly by the bailiff and the reeve, rather than by a single officer. See Paul D. A. Harvey, "Agricultural Treatises and Manorial Accounting in Medieval England," *Agricultural History Review*, 20 (1972), 173.

11 On manorial officers and their responsibilities, see Bailey, trans. and ed., *English Manor*, 99.

22

Instructions for Keeping a Travel Account, Followed by a Daily Household Account[1]

Siquis voluerit compotum ordinare ad modum itinerancium, primo debet ponere in margine rotuli nomen loci[2] et inde in pagina infra margina nomen diei, et postea, secundum[3] officina curie, expensas ordinare hoc modo.

Die martis proxima post ramos palmarum. Dispensa in pane. v. s'. In gausape, iii. s'. In salsario, iij. d'. In cultell', vi. d'. In servisia, iiii. s'. In vino, vi. s'. In cyphis emptis, vi. d'. In costrellis emendendis, v. d'. In novis costrellis emptis, xviii. d'. Expensa coquine. In allece, ii. s'. In macherell',[4] iii. s'. In muluell', xi. s'. In lupis aquaticis, x. s'. In salmone, xx. d'. In ostris, xv. d'. In congr', xxxi. d'. In pectini[bu]s,[5] xi. d'. In barbell', viii. d'. In albo pisse, x. d'. In pipere, v. d'. In alveis, ii. d'. In mustardo,[6] v. d'. In craticulis emendendis, ii.d'. In ollis et cacabis perarandis, xii. d'. In scutellis, xii. d'. Expensa equorum. In feno, x. d'. In avena, xii. d'. In littera, vi. d'. In busca. xiii. d'. In alba candela, iii. den'. In pelvi[bu]s[7] emptis ad avenam mensurandam, v. d'. Expense [*sic*] camere. In cera, ii. s'. In aliis luminaribus, ij.d'. Summa[8] l. et viii. s'. et ob'.[9]

If anyone should wish to keep an account in the manner of travelers, first he should put in the margin of the roll the name of the place, and then on the page within the margin the name of the day, and afterward, according to the offices of the household, he should list the expenses, in this manner.

Tuesday after Palm Sunday. Spence:[10] For bread, 5s. For a tablecloth (*gausape*), 3s. For sauce, 3d. For a knife (or knives), 6d. For ale, 4s. For wine, 6s. For cups purchased, 6d. For repairing costrels, 5d. For buying new costrels, 18d. Kitchen expenses: For herring, 2s. For mackerel, 3s. For cod (*mulvell'*), 11s. For pike, 10s. For salmon, 20d. For oysters, 15d. For conger eels, 31d. For *pectinibus*,[11] 11d. For barbel,[12] 8d. For *albo pisse* (whitefish or whiting), 10d. For pepper, 5d. For troughs, 2d. For mustard, 5d. For repairing gridirons, 2d. For engraving pots and cauldrons, 12d. For bowls, 12d. Expenses of the horses: For hay, 10d. For oats, 12d. For litter, 6d. For firewood, 13d. For tallow candles, 3d. For basins bought for measuring out oats, 5d. Expenses of the chamber: For wax, 2s. For other lights, 2d. Total: 58s. 1/2d. [*recte* 54s. 0d.]

Although the instructions that preface DOCUMENT 22 are intended for an account of travel expenses, the specimen account that follows represents a household account, since (contrary to the instructions) the location is not identified, and since it includes some expenses, such as the purchase and repair of kitchen utensils and tableware, and the purchase of wax, which would have been much more typical of a household account than a travel account. This suggests that the instructions were rather carelessly grafted onto an extract from an existing household account, possibly a genuine one, rather than that the account above was written as a model to illustrate the instructions. Similarly, the incorrect total at the end of the account may indicate that the compiler or copyist has omitted one or more items (totaling 4s. 1/2d.) from an existing genuine or model account.

Only about a dozen household accounts from before 1250 have survived from England. Most of them, like the examples in DOCUMENTS 22 and 23, are daily or "diet" accounts, which list their entries in a sequence that represents the standard departments into which large medieval households were organized. However, only two of the surviving accounts contain a heading that actually names a household department.[13] DOCUMENTS 22 and 23, which may date from the 1220s (see DOCUMENT 23), and certainly date from before 1250, thus are the earliest English accounts to use headings that name a full array of household departments, which the instructions to both documents call the "offices" (*officina*). The first of these household departments or offices was the "spence" or storeroom (*dispensa*). The spence represented an amalgam of the offices that in later years were generally divided into pantry, saucery, and buttery. The pantry stored and issued bread and table linens; the saucery stored and issued sauces; and the buttery stored and issued drink and drinking-vessels. The second department listed in DOCUMENTS 22 and 23 was the kitchen, which was responsible for producing cooked meals. The third department was the stable, also called the "marshalsea" because it was headed by an officer called the marshal, who was responsible for the household's horses. The final department was the chamber, which encompassed both the treasury and the private quarters of the lord or lady who was the head of the household. DOCUMENTS 22 and 23 are the earliest English accounts to name both the spence and the chamber as household departments. The chamber expenses listed in DOCUMENTS 22 and 23 include purchases of luxury items such as wax and spices. Such purchases, especially when made in bulk, later came to be handled by a separate department, known as the wardrobe.[14]

The account in DOCUMENT 22 is identified as dating from the Monday after Palm Sunday—that is, the Monday in Holy Week, the last week of Lent before Easter Sunday. During the forty days of Lent all meat, game, poultry, and dairy products were forbidden (see DOCUMENT 16). Even for wealthy households that could afford fresh fish, shellfish, and crustaceans, the unrelentingly fishy Lenten diet was a trial to be endured rather than a discipline to be embraced. For modest households that could afford only dried, salted, or smoked fish, and for poor households that could afford little or no fish at all, the Lenten fast was a meager time indeed.

The knife or knives purchased for 6*d.* for the use of the spence may have been intended for the preparation of bread for the table. Special knives were used for paring burnt crusts from loaves of bread, for cutting the pared loaves into slices, and for smoothing and squaring slices of trencher bread, the coarse, four-day-old bread that was used in great households as disposable plates.[15] Medieval ovens were brick chambers that baked food through retained heat alone. First, a fire was built inside the open oven and left until it had burnt down and the bricks were glowing hot. The embers were then swept out and the sooty floor of the oven was quickly swabbed with a wet cloth on a pole. Then the rounds of bread dough or other foods such as meat pies were put into the oven with a wooden peel (a flat shovel), the oven door was closed, and the foods were left to bake.[16] In baking, the crusts of the loaves or pies were often burnt or blackened by soot, especially the bottom crusts. No respectable household was served with burnt or blackened bread, so each loaf or roll was pared or "chipped" before it was served at table. Walter de Bibbesworth's *Tretiz* (*c.* 1250–1300), an Anglo-Norman language manual in verse that describes many daily household activities, says that the bread should be pared and sliced, and the parings given as alms (*Taillez ceo pain que est paré;/ Les bisseaus seient pur Deu doné*).[17] A model household inventory of *c.* 1300 included among the contents of the pantry "two great knives for paring bread" (*duo magni cultelli ad parand' pan'*).[18]

Another intriguing entry in the account above is the 12*d.* paid "for engraving pots and cauldrons" (*In ollis et cacabis perarandis*). Since these were kitchen utensils, the engraving cannot have been purely for decoration, but must instead have been done for some practical purpose, most likely to mark the pots (like plates) with a sign of the owner's identity, such as an initial or heraldic symbol.[19] Metal cookware was expensive, and engraving it would have been a useful deterrent to theft, since an engraved pot could not safely be kept by a thief, or disposed of to anyone else other than a metalsmith who could rework it. The engraving may have been done on the rim of the pots, since the sooty outsides of cooking pots were seldom washed.[20]

NOTES

1   Add. 8167, fol. 132r–v.
2   Fol. 132v commences here.
3   *scdm* in MS.
4   Corrected in MS from *machelrell.*
5   *pectinis* in MS.
6   Corrected in MS from *murstardo.*
7   *pelvis* in MS.
8   Corrected in MS from *S^aumma.*
9   This total is incorrect; the correct total is 54*s.* 0*d.*
10   For the office of the Spence (*dispensa*, storeroom), see below.
11   Small flatfish or a type of shellfish, possibly a scallop, Woolgar, ed., *Household Accounts*, vol. 1, 92.
12   A freshwater fish of the carp family.
13   Woolgar, ed., *Household Accounts*, vol. 1, 10, 12–13. One account, from 1225–26, names the marshalsea, and the other account, from c. 1240–70, names the kitchen.
14   The development of separate wardrobe accounts may have begun in the largest households, and those closest to the Crown, by the beginning of the 1220s. Woolgar, ed., *Household Accounts*, vol. 1, 14.
15   Cf. John Russell's *Book of Nurture* (c. 1460), which advised, "In the pantry, you must always keep three sharp knives, one to chop the loaves, another to pare them, and a third, sharp and keen, to smooth and square the trenchers with," and "Always cut your lord's bread, and see that it be new; and all other bread at the table one day old ere you cut it, all household bread three days old, and trencher-bread four days old." Edith Rickert, *The Babees' Book: Medieval Manners for the Young: Done into Modern English from Dr. Furnivall's Texts* (London: Chatto and Windus, New York: Duffield and Co., 1908), 50; translating Russell's Middle English text, edited by Furnivall in *The Babees Book*, 120, lines 50–56.

16 See, e.g., John M. Steane, *The Archaeology of Medieval England and Wales* (Athens: University of Georgia Press, 1985), 268.

17 Walter de Bibbesworth, *Le Tretiz*, ed. William Rothwell, Anglo-Norman Text Society, Plain Texts Series, 6 (London, 1990), lines 1055–56.

18 BL, Add. MS 41201, fol. 4r.

19 Since worn or damaged metalware could be reworked, little domestic plate or metal kitchenware survives from this period. For a pewter saucer of c. 1290 punched on the rim with the initial "P" (Southampton City Museums), and for two silver spoons of *c.* 1410 (Mercers' Company), engraved with the arms of Sir Richard Whittington, mayor of London (d. 1423), see Jonathan Alexander and Paul Binski, eds., *Age of Chivalry: Art in Plantagenet England, 1200–1400* (London: Royal Academy of Arts, 1987), 280, 283.

20 Dishes and pots were scoured with warm water, straw, and ashes. Although tableware was thoroughly washed, normally only the insides of cooking pots were cleaned, since the outsides would get black and sooty again as soon as they were put on the fire. Bridget Ann Henisch, *Fast and Feast: Food in Medieval Society* (University Park: Pennsylvania State University Press, 1976), 90, 152–53. For examples of sooty kitchenware found in archaeological excavations, see Steane, *Archaeology of Medieval England and Wales*, 269–70.

23

Further Instructions for Keeping Travel Accounts, Followed by Another Daily Household Account[1]

Set si advenerit quod aliqua expensa facta fuerint per diem carnis et in proprio manerio, servaris tantum nomen loci et nomen diei et officina, sicut superius demonstravimus.[2] In hac forma procedendum est.

Die lune in crastino pasche. Dispensa panis [super][3] instauramenta manerii, et de empto, v. s'. In servisia super instauramenta, v. s'. In vino, x. s'. In coquina boum, bac', multonum, sals' super instauramenta, x. s'. In bove frisco, iiii. s'. In porco recente,[4] ii. s'. In gallinis super instauramenta [*no amount given*]. In agnis, xx. s'. In pipere, ii. d'. et ob'. In cimino [*sic*], ii. d'. Dispensa marscall' [*sic*]. In feno et avena, super instauramenta, et in alba candela, xx. d'. In littera super instauramenta, x. d'. Dispensa camere. In cera, ii. s'. In speciebus, iii. s'. In oblacionibus, x. d'. Summa, xxix. s'. et .viii. d'. et ob'. [*recte 64s. 8¹/₂d.*]

If it should happen that some expenses be made on a flesh-day in [the lord's] own manor, keep only the name of the place and the name of the day and the offices, as we showed above. You should proceed in this manner.

Monday the morrow of Easter. Spence: Bread from the stock of the manor, and by purchase, 5s. For ale from stock, 5s. For wine, 10s. In the kitchen: Salt beef, bacon, [and] mutton, from stock, 10s. For fresh beef, 4s. For fresh pork, 2s. For hens from stock, [*no cost given*]. For lambs, 20s. For pepper, 2½d. For cumin, 2d. Expenses of the marshalsea [*i.e., stable*]: For hay and oats from stock and for tallow candles, 20d. For litter from stock, 10d. Expenses of the chamber: For wax, 2s. For spices, 3s. For oblations [*i.e., church offerings*], 10d. Total: 29s. 8½d. [*recte 64s. 8½d.*]

This account for the day after Easter Sunday is notable for the quantity and variety of meats, both preserved and fresh, that appear in the kitchen account. The household is clearly celebrating the end of Lent with a carnivorous rapture that includes spring lamb and fresh beef, pork, and chicken, as well as salt beef, pork, and mutton, well seasoned with imported pepper, cumin, and other spices, and washed down with copious amounts of ale and wine.

The church offerings are another distinctive item in this account. A penny a day probably was a common offering for a wealthy lord or lady; even Eleanor de Montfort gave an average of only about 3½d. per day in oblations.[5] Most people probably made an annual offering at Easter; those who could afford it may have made additional offerings during the year to commemorate other religious holidays and important personal events, such as a marriage, a baptism, a funeral, or the anniversary of a loved one's death. The 10*d*. reported here is thus quite generous. It may represent the lord's or lady's Easter oblations or an offering made to commemorate some special event.

The grand total for this account is incorrect, as is the grand total in DOCUMENT 22. Although the incorrect totals in these documents may well represent poor copying by the compiler or copyist of this text, incorrect totals were a common feature in medieval accounts, and reflect the difficulties of using Roman numerals to add up long sums. For early accounts such as this, which were written in blocks of text rather than in a columnar list, the accountant also had to tease out the separate sums from the surrounding text before adding them up. This complicated the process still further and made incorrect totals even more likely.

This account bears a strong resemblance in general character and contents, and in the daily expenditure of around three pounds, to the daily account in DOCUMENT 22. The circumstantial details in these two accounts suggest that both may derive from a genuine account-roll of a lay household, perhaps one dating, like DOCUMENT 21, from the 1220s. If so, it must have been the household of a very great magnate indeed, since a daily expenditure at the rate even of 54*s*. (as in DOCUMENT 22) would come to £985 10*s*. 0*d*. per annum, exclusive of the payment of wages and fees; the purchase of horses, jewels, plate, or cloth; the bulk purchases of foodstuffs, wine, or spices; the giving of·gifts; and other similar expenses. In thirteenth-century England, there were at any one time some eighty to ninety lay magnates, fifteen bishops, and twenty-five to thirty abbots and priors who had annual net incomes of £400 or more from which to maintain their state, but very few even of these were in a position to spend £1000 and more per annum.[6]

NOTES

1 Add. 8167, fols. 132v–133r.

2 Fol. 133r commences here.

3 *sive* or *sine* (*siii'*) in MS, but the sense here appears to require *super*.

4 *recente* repeated here in MS.

5 In 1265, between Easter Sunday (April 5) and the Octave of Trinity (June 7), "*prima die computata*" ("including the first day," i.e., during sixty-four days), Eleanor gave a total of 19s. 1d. in oblations, or an average of 3.58d. per day. Turner, ed., *Manners and Household Expenses*, 33. The king was much more generous; see Henry III's alms roll for 1238–39, TNA: PRO, C 47/3/44. (For this information we are grateful to Robert Stacey.) At the end of the century, in 1299–1300, Edward I ordinarily gave 7d. per day in "common oblations," though more on special occasions. Arnold Taylor, "Royal Alms and Oblations in the Later Thirteenth Century: An Analysis of the Alms Roll of Edward I (1283–84)," in *Tribute to an Antiquary: Essays Presented to Marc Fitch by Some of His Friends*, ed. Frederick G. Emmison and Roy Stevens (London: Leopard's Head Press, 1976), 113–16.

6 Christopher M. Woolgar, *The Great Household in Late Medieval England* (New Haven: Yale University Press, 1999), 4. See also Painter, *Studies in the History of the English Feudal Barony*, Chap. 7.

CHAPTER 2

War and Politics

WAR

24

An Earl Summons His Knights to Military Service Overseas[1]

Comes militibus ut muniantur equis et armis

R. Comes Cestrie omnibus militibus suis salutem. De dileccione vestra quamplurimum confisi, vobis mandantes (*precipimus; attentissime petimus*)[2] quatinus pro amore nostro parati sitis cum equis et armis in die tali coram nobis ubicumque fuerimus. Scituri[3] quod dominus rex nos sicut alios fecit summoniri et cum eo transfretaremus cum totis viribus nostris sicut amorem suum desideramus. Quare tantum faciatis ut domino regi placere poterimus et fideliter servire in necessitatibus[4] [suis].[5] Valete.

An earl orders his knights to equip with horses and arms

R., Earl of Chester, to all his knights, greetings. We, putting the highest trust in your love, order you (*we have ordered; we have most earnestly besought*) that, for the sake of our love, you be prepared with horses and arms on such a day before us wherever we may be. You shall know that the lord king has caused us, like others, to be summoned, and we are to take ship with him with all our men, as we desire his love. Therefore, I trust that you will act in such a way that we may be able to please the king and faithfully serve him in his needs. Farewell.

This text gives us an unparalleled glimpse into the military organization of medieval England. Very few texts survive that record the procedures for summoning an army in the twelfth or thirteenth century, which has led many scholars to assume that written summonses were rarely issued. This text, however, clearly shows the king's summons to a lord being transmitted down the chain of command in the form of a private writ (formal order), in Latin, to the lord's military tenants (that is, those who held land of him by knight service).

Like DOCUMENT 2, which may be based on a genuine letter of Amaury, earl of Gloucester, this private writ of summons may well be based on an original text. There are several reasons for believing that this document may have a genuine letter behind it. The first is that the "Earl R." who issued it seems likely to be Ranulf III, earl of Chester (1181–1232), sometimes known as Ranulf de Blundeville. It is even possible to suggest likely dates for Earl Ranulf's original document. Summonses were issued by the king to his barons for service overseas on several occasions during Ranulf's tenure of the earldom. The writ on which the text above probably was based may have been a response to the summons of King Richard I (1189–99) for service in Normandy in 1196. Ranulf is also known to have answered summonses by John (1199–1216) in 1213 for service in Poitou in 1214, and by Henry III (1216–72) in 1229 for the Breton campaign of 1230. Of these three possibilities, we can eliminate both 1196 and 1229–30. In 1196, the king asked that his magnates bring no more than seven knights with them, at most.[6] DOCUMENT 24, however, says that the earl has been ordered by the king to mobilize all his men. A text of Henry III's actual writ of summons to Earl Ranulf in 1229 also survives.[7] It did not specify the level of service required of the earl, and in 1230, as the campaign's muster roll tells us, Ranulf was asked only to bring twenty knights with him.[8]

The likelihood, therefore, is that if there was an original writ upon which the text above was based, it was issued in 1213. There is some possible support for this in the title that the earl uses. In 1217, Ranulf was awarded the earldom of Lincoln as well as Chester, and he took that double title until his death. Earlier in his career, between 1188 and 1199, he also enjoyed another multiple title: duke of Brittany and earl of Chester and Richmond. Here, however, he calls himself simply "earl of Chester," which was indeed Ranulf's only title in 1213. However, Ranulf did not use his multiple titles at all consistently, and in any case he might very well have called himself simply "earl of Chester" when addressing the tenants of his earldom, so, although suggestive, the evidence of his title is not conclusive.[9]

It can be argued from other evidence that in France and England knights had been summoned for feudal service by the writs or letters of their lords for well over a century before this sample writ was entered into the formulary. Previously, the earliest text of a military summons was thought to be a writ of

1072 supposedly sent by King William the Conqueror (1066–87) to Abbot Aethelwig of Evesham, summoning him for the five knights he owed the king, but there are strong reasons to suspect that this writ is in fact a forgery of the later twelfth century.[10] However, there is a reliable early reference (1081 × 87) to such a summons in a Norman act of William the Conqueror, which mentions that an abbey's tenants may be liable for a summons to military service, by writ.[11] Another is in a private charter (1088 × 1106) of Robert fitz Hamo, lord of Gloucester, to a man to whom he had granted a tenancy, that "when I instruct [him] by my letter (*litteras meas*) he should appear for my service."[12] Mention of a military summons is a feature in other early grants of this type, including one original surviving Warwickshire example of the late 1120s or early 1130s.[13] In the northern French romance *Le Couronnement de Louis* (c. 1130), Count William of Orange sends out his writs (*ses briés*) to his knights summoning them to join him for military service.[14] In another such literary incident in the *Chanson d'Aspremont* (*c.* 1190), Duke Girart of Burgundy summons his army in haste and causes his writs (*briés*) to that effect to be sealed and sent.[15] The fact that counts and dukes communicated with their tenants by sealed instruments is such a literary commonplace in the twelfth century that it must reflect actual practice.

But although it seems that, by the decades around 1100, writs of summons were routinely issued by kings to their magnates, and by magnates to their knights, very few texts actually survive, even of royal summonses. That is what gives this document its extraordinary value. Most summonses were ephemeral documents, written for a particular occasion and purpose and soon discarded. On a single night in 1188, for example, the clerks of Count Richard of Poitou (the future Richard I) allegedly drew up more than two hundred letters (*letres*) summoning Richard's knights and barons as he traveled in haste to escape his father, King Henry II (1154–89).[16]

A surviving summons of Henry II of England can be dated to that same fateful campaign of 1188 in which the king fell out with his son, Count Richard. Its text was also copied into a formulary, compiled in the north of England around 1200 and later sliced up by a clerk to make seal tags, which is how it was preserved. It is probably the earliest known text of an individual writ of military summons and runs as follows: "Henry, by the grace of God, king of England, greets William Marshal. I request that you come to me fully-equipped as soon as may be, with as many knights as you can get, to support me in my war, and [that you let me know] how many and what sort of troops will be in your company. You have ever so often moaned to me that I have bestowed on you a small fee.[17] Know for sure that if you serve me faithfully I will give you in addition Châteauroux with all its lordship and whatever belongs to it [as soon as] we may be able."[18] Note here that the summons applies only to the Marshal himself. But the king expects Marshal to appear with the rest of his military household and offers the handsome inducement of the great French honor of Châteauroux in Berry, whose heiress was at the time in Henry's wardship.

The form of summons probably took a while to stabilize.[19] A little more formal is the general summons contained in a letter of Richard I to Archbishop Hubert Walter in 1196:

> We instruct you to cause all those who have baronies-in-chief[20] in Normandy to cross the sea without delay. You should also summon everyone who owes us the service of a knight in England, except for William de Briouze, William d'Aubigné and the barons of the Welsh March, that they may all join us overseas in Normandy the Sunday before Pentecost [June 2] with horse and arms, ready for service, and that they should come ready for a long time in our service, so that they need not encumber themselves by too many knights nor bring more than seven with them at most. Also, you should summon the bishops and abbots who owe us knight service so that they should oblige us with knights in a way that will do them credit and earn our thanks.[21]

Here again the king is not levying the full service owed to him by his barons, but only a fraction. His reason is that such a small number will be less of a logistical and financial burden for his barons. But this mandate at least gives a date and place for the levy to assemble. The model writ in DOCUMENT 24 is just the sort of follow-up that the earl would have made to such a summons, although it has been edited so that specific dates and locations have been changed to generic phrases such as "on such a day" and "wherever I may be." A genuine writ would have specified the date and place of assembly, as in King Henry III's summons to Earl Ranulf himself in 1229:

> The king to his beloved and faithful Ranulf, earl of Chester and Lincoln, greetings. Know that, at the request of certain of our friends overseas and on the advice of our earls and barons of England, we are determined, God willing, to cross the sea, so that we will be at Portsmouth a fortnight after Michaelmas [October 13] ready and able to board our ships. So we instruct you, firmly enjoining you by the faith in which you are bound to us, to be with us on the said day and in the said place with twenty knights,

ready to cross with horse and arms with us, and so by this you may earn our gratitude. Witnessed by myself. St. Neots. July 27 [1229].[22]

This is the basic form of the summons as it became formalized in the course of the thirteenth century, although, of course, each royal summons was tailored to the nature of the campaign and the particular needs of the king.[23]

The final significance of DOCUMENT 24 is what it tells us about the internal organization of a great English honor.[24] The text makes it clear that the earl has lists of his knights and the services that they owe him, since without such lists he could not have gauged the knights' response to his summons. Contemporary literature suggests that many magnates kept rolls of the names and obligations of their followers. In Thomas of Kent's *Le Roman de toute chevalerie* (late 1170s or early 1180s), for example, great lords register their followers so that they will know who should be in their hosts and who has defaulted.[25] In the mid-thirteenth century the earldom of Chester owed the king eighty knights for Cheshire itself and the lands across the frontier with Wales, as well as at least 112 more knights for lands in England outside Cheshire—quite a large number to keep track of.[26] There is a reference to a register preserved at Chester by the earl's clerks in the time of Ranulf III. Such a register might well have included a list of knights and the service they owed.[27]

NOTES

1   Add. 8167, fol. 98v.

2   The italicized words shown in parentheses here are part of the text and represent variant phrasings supplied by the author or compiler of the formulary. Similar variant phrasings can be found in DOCUMENTS 5 and 32.

3   *Sciturus* in MS.

4   Corrected in MS from *necessitabtibus*.

5   Word inserted to preserve the sense of the document.

6   The text of this writ is given below.

7   The text of this summons is given below.

8   *Close Rolls, 1227–1231*, 248; Ivor J. Sanders, *Feudal Military Service in England: A Study of the Constitutional and Military Powers of the* Barones *in Medieval England* (London: Oxford University Press, 1956), 121.

9   For Ranulf's various titles, see Geoffrey Barraclough, ed., *The Charters of the Anglo-Norman Earls of Chester*, Record Society of Lancashire and Cheshire, 126 (1988), nos. 202–437. The act analyzed here is not in Barraclough's collection.

10   David Bates, ed., *Regesta Regum Anglo-Normannorum: The Acta of William I (1066–1087)* (Oxford: Clarendon, 1998), 449–52. Professor Bates notes the reasons for doubting the Evesham writ's authenticity, but equivocates on the grounds that its uniqueness is what largely condemns it. But it would seem to be compromised by its ostentatious support for the abbey's assessment as owed in the 1159 aid and the 1166

royal inquisition on service owed the crown. The only text is to be found in a late thirteenth-century cartulary of the abbey. J. H. Round noted grounds for suspecting it, but dismissed them by saying that there was not "anything to be gained by forging a document which admits, by placing on record, the abbey's full liability." John Horace Round, "The Introduction of Knight Service into England," in idem, *Feudal England: Historical Studies on the XIth and XIIth Centuries* (London: Allen & Unwin, 1964), 238. But there were many reasons why the abbey should do so, especially if a later king were attempting to increase the assessment. Nonetheless, the Evesham writ has value, at the very least in indicating the possible shape of a late twelfth-century writ of summons. On the subject of military mobilization, see David Crouch, *The English Aristocracy, 1070–1272: A Social Transformation* (New Haven: Yale University Press, 2011), 20–30.

11   Bates, ed., *Regesta Regum Anglo-Normannorum*, 261.

12   Peter R. Coss, ed., *The Langley Cartulary*, Dugdale Society, 32 (Stratford-upon-Avon, 1980), 10.

13   This was a serjeantry granted by Osbert of Arden to Thurkil Fundu. BL, Cotton Charter xxii. 3, translated with commentary in David Crouch, *Tournament* (London: Hambledon, 2005), 163.

14   Ernest Langlois, ed., *Le Couronnement de Louis*, Classiques français du moyen âge, 22 (Paris: Champion, 1984), line 1997.

15   Louis Brandin, ed., *La Chanson d'Aspremont, chanson de geste du XIIe siècle. Texte du manuscrit de Wollaton Hall*, 2 vols., Classiques français du moyen âge, 19, 25 (Paris: Champion, 1919–21), 1: line 1512.

16   Anthony J. Holden and David Crouch, eds.; Stewart Gregory, trans., *History of William Marshal*, 3 vols., Anglo-Norman Text Society, Occasional Publications Series, 4–6 (London, 2002–7), 1: lines 8248–49.

17   A "fee" translates the Latin word *feodum*, which means a piece of land subject to particular sorts of service, mostly military.

18   The text and the extraordinary story of its discovery are in Nicholas Vincent, "William Marshal, King Henry II and the Honour of Châteauroux," *Archives*, 25 (2000), 15. The translation is that offered in David Crouch, *William Marshal: Knighthood, War and Chivalry, 1147–1219,* 2nd ed. (London: Longman, 2002), 61.

19   Helena M. Chew, *The English Ecclesiastical Tenants-in-Chief and Knight Service* (London: Oxford University Press, 1932), 75, makes this point, even though she did not know of the evidence mentioned here.

20   A "barony" was an estate inherited by a baron, which would consist of at least several knights' fees, and might be hundreds. A "barony-in-chief" is one held directly of the king.

21   Translated from Ralph de Diceto, *Radulfi de Diceto decani Lundoniensis opera historica*, ed. Wlliam Stubbs, vol. 2, Rolls Series, 68 (London: Longman, 1876), lxxix–lxxx.

22   *Close Rolls, 1227–1231*, 248. The assignment of a ship to Earl Ranulf in September 1229 is noted in ibid., 252.

23   For numerous examples of the military summonses of Edward I, see Francis Palgrave, ed., *The Parliamentary Writs and Writs of Military Summons*, 2 vols. in 4 (London: Records Commission, 1827–34), 1:193ff. For comments on the situation in the earlier thirteenth century, see Michael R. Powicke, *Military Obligation in Medieval England* (Oxford: Clarendon Press, 1962), 65–67; and J. S. Critchley, "Summonses to Military Service Early in the Reign of Henry III," *EHR*, 86 (1971), 79–95, although this article deals rather with the schedules attached to the actual initiating summons.

24 An "honor" was the complex of estates and rights that belonged to a great English magnate.

25 Thomas of Kent, *Le Roman de toute chevalerie*, ed. Brian Foster, 2 vols., Anglo-Norman Text Society, 29 and 31 (London, 1971–73) 1: lines 1063–64, 3339–40.

26 Figures extrapolated from Ivor J. Sanders, *English Baronies: A Study of Their Origin and Descent, 1086–1327* (Oxford: Clarendon, 1960), 32n.

27 David Crouch, "The Administration of the Norman Earldom," in *The Earldom of Chester and Its Charters*, ed. Alan T. Thacker, *Journal of the Chester Archaeological Society*, 71 (Chester, 1991), 94–95.

25

A Knight Responds to a Summons for Military Service by Asking for a Cash Loan to Meet His Expenses[1]

Huiusmodi litere sunt responsales et postea petentes

Dilecto amico suo A., B. salutem. Mandastis michi ex parte domini regis ut munitus essem cum equis et armis, quod mandatum non ausus sum transgredi. Michi providi inquantum melius potui set moneta michi deficit ad tam magnum iter arripiendum, quare dileccioni vestre pias preces effundens, attencius rogans .xx. marcas michi acomodetis. Sciturus quod .C., famulus meus, vobis redditurus est quam cito poterit vendere bladum vel lanam. Quare tantum faciatis ne pro defectu nummismatis iter meum inpediatur. Valete.

Replies and requests (given hereafter) use this form of letter

To his dear friend A., B. [sends] greetings. You sent me word on the king's behalf that I should be equipped with horses and arms, which is an order I did not dare disobey. I have provided for myself as best I could, but I do not have the money for setting out on so long a journey, and so, pouring out my dutiful prayers to your kindness, I request most earnestly that you lend me twenty marks. You will know that C., a member of my household, will repay you as soon as he can sell grain or wool. So I hope that you will act in such a way that my journey will not be hindered for lack of cash. Farewell.

This letter provides an unprecedented look into military relations between a magnate and his knights. It is written in response to the summons to appear for knight service for a royal campaign in DOCUMENT 24. The magnate (who in DOCUMENT 24 is R[anulf], earl of Chester) has communicated the king's

summons to the knights of his honor, or barony, or at least to those whom he
wishes to take with him. Here a knight replies, acknowledging his duty to
appear but citing financial difficulties.

The customary duty (*servitium debitum*) that he has been asked to fulfill
was known as campaign (*expeditio*) or army (*exercitus*) service. The Angevin
kings of England not infrequently issued writs to assemble armies in such a
way. In the long reign of Henry III (1216–72), a feudal army was summoned
to serve in Wales in 1223, 1231, 1245, 1257, 1258 and 1264. Other such armies
were summoned against Scotland and for overseas service in France.[2] Once
the knight had been summoned, there was the issue of his costs. According to
Norman sources from the reign of William the Conqueror (1066–87), a knight
called up as a result of such a summons had to finance his own travel and
service for a term of days (given variously as sixty or forty). Beyond that, the
lord had to pay the knight's costs if he wished to retain him for the rest of the
campaign.[3] Slightly fuller evidence about the conditions of service in England
comes from a charter of around 1156 in which the king's marshal, John fitz
Gilbert, sells a knight's fee (an estate to support a knight) in Somerset: "Know
that I have granted Hugh de Raleigh my land of Nettlecombe, for him and his
heirs to hold in fee and inheritance for the service of a knight, by this condition that, if there is war, Hugh should provide me with a knight available for
two months, and if peace, then for forty days, doing such service as knights
can reasonably be expected to do for any English magnate."[4]

It may have been this time restriction that made lords, and the kings who
summoned them, unwilling to take large contingents overseas, since they
would quickly have to meet substantial expenses. The costs of full quotas of
knights from large honors (if they all appeared and served more than forty
days) would have been prohibitive, even with the resources of the king behind
the summons. At the end of the twelfth century the honor of Chester, for
example, was supposed to muster eighty knights from Cheshire and 118 from
the rest of England. In fact, however, when a summons to serve abroad was
issued to the earl in 1229, he was asked to bring only twenty knights (see
DOCUMENT 24, above). It was not unusual for a limit of this sort to be
imposed, nor for such contingents to be reckoned in multiples of five and ten.
In 1165, Richard fitz Gilbert, earl of Striguil, served in the king's army in Wales
with twenty knights and forty mounted serjeants (cavalry troopers armed less
heavily than knights).[5] His lands, however, were actually supposed to answer
for a hundred knights.

Henry II had begun limiting the numbers of knights summoned to war by
1157, when he called up an army for service in Wales "in such a way that,
throughout England, every two knights fit out (*pararent*) a third."[6] That is,

two-thirds of the knights whose service he could have demanded were excused from the campaign, and they in return provided money and arms to support the other third. In this way, the king picked knights who served at a reduced cost. His sons Richard I and John used similar arrangements when they called up the feudal host.[7] As early as 1100, another option was for the king to take "scutage" payments from knights (called after the *scutum*, or shield) instead of having them serve in person. He would then use the money to hire companies of professional soldiers or pay royal household troops. In this way, he would have a small but elite and willing army, which would serve until the end of the campaign. So it was that in 1159, in assembling his great army to attack Toulouse, we are told that Henry II, "considering the distance and difficulty of the route, rather than trouble the knights of the countryside, the townsfolk and peasantry," took scutage of sixty shillings per fee across his realm. With these funds, he then "took with him his chief barons and a few men, but innumerable *paid* knights."[8]

By the reign of King John (1199–1216), a knight's daily wage was around two shillings. A force of twenty knights in the field would have cost their lord two pounds sterling a day in their wages alone.[9] The knight in the letter above knows very well that he himself will have to pay the heavy cost of the first part of his service, and he is not happy about it. By the customary rates, before he could expect wages, he would have to find at the very least the large sum of four pounds sterling for his own maintenance and that of his servants, as well as fund his travel to the point of embarkation and equip himself with horses, arms, and armor. No wonder he is driven to ask his lord for a loan, to be secured on the grain or wool that his estate will produce that year. Knights who haggled and negotiated over their customary obligations, however, like the knight in the letter above, were not the type of knight who would have been most welcome to their lords on campaign.

NOTES

1   Add. 8167, fol. 99v.
2   Powicke, *Military Obligation*, 65–66.
3   Charles Homer Haskins, *Norman Institutions*, Harvard Historical Studies, 24 (Cambridge, Mass.: Harvard University Press, 1918), 20–21, gives this evidence. See a review of the question in C. Warren Hollister, "The Annual Term of Military Service in Medieval England," *Medievalia et Humanistica*, 13 (1960), 40–47. Hollister perceives a negotiated reduction in the term from sixty to forty days during Stephen's reign, seeing the sixty-day term as a relic of service in the *fyrd* (the Anglo-Saxon militia), but his deduction depends on a mistaken early date range for the fitz Gilbert charter (p. 45).
4   *Collectanea Topographica et Genealogica*, 2 (London, 1835), 163. Discussed, but misdated, in Frank M. Stenton, *The First Century of English Feudalism, 1066–1166*, 2nd ed. (Oxford: Clarendon, 1961), 177–78.

5   *Pipe Roll of 11 Henry II*, 13. Striguil was the lordship based on Chepstow in South Wales. For the figures given here, see Thomas K. Keefe, *Feudal Assessments and the Political Community Under Henry II and His Sons* (Berkeley: University of California Press, 1983), passim.

6   Robert de Torigny, *Chronica*, in *Chronicles of the Reigns of Stephen, Henry II and Richard I*, ed. Richard Howlett, Rolls Series, 4 vols. (London: Longman, 1886–89), 4:193.

7   See comments in Robert Bartlett, *England Under the Norman and Angevin Kings, 1075–1225* (Oxford: Clarendon, 2000), 263–64.

8   Torigny, *Chronica*, 202 (emphasis added).

9   For the intricacies of knight service at a national level, see Sanders, *Feudal Military Service*.

26

A Man Asks a Friend to Make His Excuses to the King for Being Unable to Respond to a Summons[1]

Litere excusationis

Karissimo amico suo A., B. salutem. Mandatum domini nullo modo relinquerem imperfectum nisi necessitate magna inpeditus essem. Pater enim meus ultimum diem vite sue clausit hora qua literas vestras accepi, unde celebratis exequiis illius, oportet me ire London', et debita[2] illius persolvere ibi et domino meo reddere relevium;[3] quod nisi fecero cum festinacione patrimonium amittere possum. Quare supliciter vos exoro ut habeatis me excusatum coram domino rege. Sciturus quod si scire potero quod me excusaveris dabo tibi unum palefridum trium marcarum. Tantum ergo faciatis ne per meam absenciam regi incurram offensam. Valete.

A letter of excuse

To his dearest friend A., B. [sends] greetings. I would never leave a lord's request unanswered unless I was hindered by pressing business. For my father passed away on the very day on which I got your letter, and so after his funeral I was obliged to go to London, to settle his debts there and to pay a relief to my lord; had I not done it promptly, I could have lost my inheritance. Therefore I humbly request that you make my excuses to the lord king. Bear in mind that, should I learn that you will get me excused, I will give you a palfrey worth three marks. So take care of this in such a way that I may not cause offense to the king by my absence. Farewell.

This letter addresses a very vexed area in the life of a medieval landowner: the hereditary succession to a fee or property. Other letters (e.g., DOCUMENTS 29 and 36–38) show how elite landholders were affected by the customary obligations attached to property, rights over the marriage and custody of heirs, and obligations for military service. The letter above touches on another sensitive area, the right of a lord to demand a "relief" (*relevium*) from his tenant—a sort of entry-payment or inheritance tax—on succession to an estate. This gave the overlord of an estate a significant occasional boost to his income, so its non-payment or denial was a frequent source of litigation. It was also a source of concern to the tenant, for unless the money was paid and the act of homage performed, he did not technically possess his father's land. The legal position is laid out in the 1180s in the legal tract known as *Glanvill*: "When anyone's father or ancestor dies, the lord of the fee is immediately bound to receive the homage of the right heir, whether the heir is a minor or of full age, provided that he is male. For women may not by law do homage, though they generally swear fealty to their lords . . . it is a general principle that no-one may demand service, whether it be a relief (*relevium*), or something else, from an heir, whether of full age or a minor, until he has received his homage for the tenement in respect of which he claims to have the service."[4]

The importance of this payment is underlined in the letter above by the fact that the writer, who received a summons to the royal court on the very day on which news reached him of his father's death, ignored the king's summons in order to attend the funeral and then went to London to settle his father's debts, presumably those owed to moneylenders. It was customary to settle outstanding claims on a person's estate on the day of the funeral, as a sort of extension of the deathbed obligation to wind up one's moral and spiritual affairs on one's deathbed. Medieval funerals normally followed within a day or two of death, though in some cases the funeral was delayed, especially if the corpse had to be transported to a distant burial site, such as a family's monastic foundation.[5]

The writer of the letter above chose family obligations and the protection of his own inheritance over his duty to the king, but some put their duty to the king above that to their family. In 1194, William Marshal received a summons to attend King Richard, who was newly returned from Crusade and captivity, at the same time as he heard of his brother's death at Marlborough, and he determined that his self-interest lay in serving the king:

> At the time when the king arrived, the Marshal was at Striguil [Chepstow]. Hear now what happened to him there. The bitter news reached him that his brother, Sir John, had died. He was so

distressed at this news of his brother, when he heard it, that he almost died of grief. And it would have been a very cruel blow to him had there not been another piece of news, thanks be to God, which he found most pleasing, for there appeared before him an eloquent, courtly and wise messenger who informed him that the king of England had arrived in his own land. . . . The body [of Sir John] was carried into the church for a magnificent funeral service. The king's messengers went there to hurry the Marshal along, and prevented him from going to the place where his brother was to be buried. All his men went to Bradenstoke, carrying the body in high estate and giving it a magnificent burial; he was buried with great ceremony in the place where his ancestors lie. The Marshal went to join the king, but he took with him only three knights, since his men had gone with his dead brother.[6]

In William Marshal's case there was every reason for him to get to King Richard quickly. His brother had been in revolt when he died—or possibly was killed—and the latter's lands were at the king's disposal. Marshal had to get to the king to make sure of his elder brother's inheritance, and that took precedence over attending his brother's burial.

William Marshal had some reason for insecurity about succession in his day. His father, John Marshal the elder, had held land from the archbishop of Canterbury, and in 1163 Archbishop Thomas Becket had refused to take homage for it. Since John Marshal had not been able to do homage, the archbishop had argued that he was within his rights to dispossess him of the estate and he did so. This case triggered a debate in England about hereditary right to succeed to an estate that resulted in a legal process to establish possession independently of the mechanism of homage and service, a process called *nouvel disseisin*.[7] The sender of DOCUMENT 26 clearly feared that some legal chicanery would challenge his right to his father's estate. He chose to pay someone to make his excuses, and risk the king's displeasure, rather than to risk losing his inheritance.

NOTES

1   Add. 8167, fols. 99v–100r.
2   Fol. 100r commences here.
3   *relevum* in MS.
4   George Derek Gordon Hall, ed., *The Treatise on the Laws and Customs of the Realm of England Commonly Called Glanvill* (London: Thomas Nelson & Son, 1965), 103–4.
5   For deathbed and funeral practices in the middle ages, see Ronald C. Finucane, "Sacred Corpse, Profane Carrion: Social Ideals and Death Rituals in the Later Middle

Ages," in *Mirrors of Mortality: Studies in the Social History of Death*, ed. Joachim Whaley (London: Europa, 1981), 40–60; David Crouch, "The Culture of Death in the Anglo-Norman World," in *Anglo-Norman Political Culture and the Twelfth-Century Renaissance*, ed. C. Warren Hollister (Woodbridge, Suffolk: Boydell & Brewer, 1997), 157–80; Christopher Daniell, *Death and Burial in Medieval England, 1066–1550* (London: Routledge, 1997), 44–64. For the settling of claims on estates after funerals, see David Crouch, "Death in Medieval Scarborough," *Yorkshire Archaeological Journal*, 72 (2000), 68.

6   Holden and Crouch, eds., *History of William Marshal*, vol. 2, lines 10018–32, 10065–80.

7   Mary Cheney, "The Litigation Between John Marshal and Archbishop Thomas Becket in 1164," in *Law and Social Change in British History*, ed. John A. Guy and H. G. Beale, Royal Historical Society Studies in History, 40 (London, 1984), 9–26.

27

A Man Cautions a Friend That He Should Provide for the Knights Committed to His Custody or His Fortune Might Suffer at Court[1]

Amicus mandat amico ut muniatur militibus sibi traditis incarceratis bene et honorifice custodiendis

Karissimo amico suo A., B. salutem. Comoditatem vestram non minus desiderans quam propriam, illud nos amovere propono quod non minus vobis quam vestris credere profuturum, ut milites quos de precepto domini regis tenetis incarceratos benigne custodiatis et diligentem curam eis inpendatis. Scituri quod si de [hoc][2] querelam fecerint in presencia regis, dominus rex bona vestra confiscabit ut ei placeat [et][3] in propriam convertet peccuniam. Quare tantum faciatis pro prefatis militibus ne aliqua mergat occasio unde vester tardetur[4] effectus.

A friend sends word to a friend that he should provide handsomely and honorably for the knights given him to keep imprisoned

To his dearest friend A., B. [sends] greetings. Desiring your advantage as much as my own, I suggest that we set about something that we trust will benefit you no less than your own people: that you take good care of the imprisoned knights whom you have in custody by the king's command, and don't stint on their maintenance. Bear in mind that if they were to create a fuss about [this] in the king's presence, the lord king will seize your goods as it suits him [and] convert them into cash for himself. So treat those knights in such a way that no excuse might emerge by which your fortunes might suffer a setback.

Prisoners were a lucrative source of income in medieval northern Europe, but also potential sources of great trouble for their captors and jailers. DOCU-MENTS 27 and 28 demonstrate this very starkly. The prisoners mentioned here are knights taken in warfare or rebellion against the king. The king could grant such men to his courtiers as a form of reward, for the prisoners would then be held until they paid the ransom of money or land that would secure their release. Unfortunately it did not always work out that way. In 1184, for example, the Limousin poet Bertran de Born recorded the complaints of Gaston, lord of Béarn and Pau, who had received prisoners from Henry II of England with the intention of collecting their ransoms, but got nothing because they would not pay up.[5]

Worse dangers were represented by the possibility of escape. An early example of just how serious this might be was the escape in 1101 of a state prisoner, Bishop Ranulf Flambard, from the Tower of London. The constable of the Tower, Geoffrey de Mandeville, was so crippled by the punitive fines imposed on him by the king that it took his family two generations to repair the losses.[6] Penalties such as these were by no means unusual. In 1130, the sheriff and courtier Aubrey de Vere owed £550 and four palfreys for, among other things, the escape of prisoners in his custody.[7] In a similar way, Henry II of England fined the northern baron Robert de Vaux a hundred marks in 1186 for a variety of offenses, including that he had allowed his prisoners to escape.[8] These sorts of fines were exploited ruthlessly by the Angevin kings of England, especially King John (1199–1216), and DOCUMENT 28 is a direct consequence of their harshness in such matters.[9]

The costs of guarding and maintaining prisoners were the responsibility of the jailer, as was the liability should they escape.[10] In the twelfth century it was only rare state prisoners, such as Duke Robert of Normandy (held at Devizes from 1106 until 1126, and subsequently at Bristol and Cardiff until his death in 1134)[11] or Bishop Peter of Beauvais (held at Rouen from 1197 to 1199), whose costs were paid for by the royal exchequer in England or Normandy.[12] High-ranking prisoners could be very demanding, and this may have been the source of the difficulty highlighted in this letter. It seems that the prisoners in the custody of the recipient were sufficiently well connected to be able to have their complaints heard at court. Under such circumstances, it was clearly important for their jailer to try to make them comfortable.

NOTES

1   Add. 8167, fol. 100v.
2   Word inserted to preserve the sense of the passage.

3 Word inserted to preserve the sense of the passage.
4 Corrected in MS from *dardetur.*
5 *Poésies complètes de Bertran de Born*, ed. André Antoine Thomas, Bibliothèque meridionale, première ser., 1 (Toulouse, 1888), 50.
6 C. Warren Hollister, "The Misfortunes of the Mandevilles," *History*, 58 (1973), 315–33.
7 *Pipe Roll of 31 Henry I*, 53, 113. See generally Ralph B. Pugh, *Imprisonment in Medieval England* (London: Cambridge University Press, 1968), 232ff.
8 *Pipe Roll of 32 Henry II*, 98.
9 Nicholas Vincent, "Hugh de Neville and His Prisoners," *Archives*, 20 (1992), 190–91.
10 Jean Dunbabin, *Captivity and Imprisonment in Medieval Europe, 1000–1300* (Basingstoke, Hampshire: Palgrave, 2002), 53–55.
11 For the duke's imprisonment, see William Aird, *Robert Curthose, Duke of Normandy* (Woodbridge, Suffolk: Boydell, 2008), 248–52.
12 *Pipe Roll of 31 Henry I*, 144, 148; Dunbabin, *Captivity and Imprisonment*, 55.

28

A Man Advises His Friend to Guard Well the Imprisoned Knights in His Charge[1]

Amicus mandat amico ut custodiat firmiter milites incarceratos

Karissimo amico A., B. salutem. Habetis in domo vestra milites incarceratos, quos nisi melius solito custodieritis, ipsi vobis iacturam machinabuntur, ipsi enim cotidiano more famulos vestros inebriant ut possint invenire locum exeundi. Quod si invenerint rex omnia bona vestra confiscabit. Set absit ut hoc eveniat, et ne sic fiat, adibeatis illis novos custodes vobis fideles et obsides duros, qui nec prece nec precio possint molliri. Et tantum faciatis ne dominus rex inveniat occasionem vobis malignandi. Valete.

A friend sends word to a friend that he should keep a close guard on some imprisoned knights

To his dearest friend A., B. [sends] greetings. You are keeping knights imprisoned in your house who will be the cause of your downfall if you do not keep a closer guard on them than you have been doing, for every day they get your servants drunk so that they can find a means of escape. If they do find a way out, the king will seize all your possessions. I hope that this never happens, but to make sure it doesn't,[2] you should impose new jailers on them—men who are faithful to you, so that they cannot be softened either by pleading or by bribe—and tough pledges. Handle this in such a way that the king may find no excuse to do you harm. Farewell.

This letter is comparable to DOCUMENT 27 but is prompted by different concerns about the keeping of prisoners. It reflects a danger that had actually threatened a number of magnates in the reign of King John (1199–1216). A concern of the barons who negotiated Magna Carta in 1215 was the king's practice of levying "amercements" (fines) to regain his good will after an offense.[3] The king's need for money could lead to the imposition of crippling fines on offending magnates, such as the 1200 marks (£800) levied on the northern baron Robert de Ros when a captured French knight whom Robert was guarding escaped with the help of one of his own guards. Robert was himself imprisoned until he paid up, and he found himself fined a further 300 marks (£200) in 1207 by King John after another prisoner escaped from his custody (though he was later pardoned for this).[4]

An even more extreme example of this kind of exploitative fine is that imposed on Hugh de Neville (d. 1234), the chief forester of Richard I and John. Following John's Irish campaign of 1210, Hugh was given custody of two knights who subsequently escaped. The king used their escape as part of his justification for fining Hugh the astonishing sum of 6000 marks (£4000), along with outstanding arrears of other debts to the Exchequer. Nicholas Vincent has drawn attention to the consequences of this for Hugh's later prisoners. In 1216 he was holding several rebel knights. Nervous about the possibility of their escape, Hugh got his clerks to draw up bonds for five prisoners by which they undertook not to escape from his prison, and promised to indemnify Hugh for his losses if they did escape. Hugh even had seals made for the captive knights so that they could properly transact the deeds. The bonds ran as follows:

> Know that in consideration of the honor which Sir H[ugh] de Neville has done me while I was in prison in his custody and because he has firmly promised not to remove me from his custody to be imprisoned elsewhere, I have given my word and sworn on holy relics, I shall not attempt any trick or strategy to deceitfully escape from his prison. I have also sworn and given my word and confirmed by this charter that if by the siege of the castle or any other means I may be taken or liberated from prison, and if King John of England may wish Hugh to be prosecuted or fined for this, I will return in person to his prison, or if not I will reimburse and indemnify Hugh for the money the king demands from him and look to his interests in all things. If I cannot do this, I will hand over my estates to Hugh to hold or to mortgage to whomever he

wishes, from year to year for a reasonable length of time until the money is paid.[5]

Jailbreaks during sieges actually happened. Around 1194, for example, when John himself was besieging Salisbury castle, several prisoners escaped from the castle when his troops broke in.[6] DOCUMENT 28 clearly reflects the world and concerns of men such as Robert de Ros and Hugh de Neville. The writer warns his friend that his prisoners are likely to escape, which will leave him liable to the sort of punishment that Robert and Hugh experienced from Kings Richard I and John. He advises better guards and the taking of serious pledges, which are reminiscent of the bonds that Hugh required from his prisoners in 1216.

NOTES

1   Add. 8167, fol. 100v.

2   Literally, "so that this happens, and not that."

3   The charter states (clause 21) that "Earls and barons shall not be amerced except by their peers and only in accordance with the nature of the offence." James C. Holt, *Magna Carta,* 2nd ed. (Cambridge: Cambridge University Press, 1992), 457.

4   *Pipe Roll of 9 Richard I*, 61; Thomas Duffus Hardy, ed., *Rotuli de oblatis et finibus in Turri Londinensi asservati* (London: Record Commission, 1835), 413. See James C. Holt, *The Northerners* (Oxford: Clarendon, 1961), 25.

5   Translated by David Crouch from Vincent, "Hugh de Neville and His Prisoners," 196–97.

6   See Pugh, *Imprisonment in Medieval England*, 218–19, for this and other examples.

29

The Sheriff of Cambridge Orders the Serjeants of a Hundred to Summon Those Who Owe the King Military Service to Assemble at Portsmouth to Go Overseas[1]

Vicecomes Cantebrig' servientibus hundredi salutem. Mandatum domini regis suscepi quatinus comuniter summonicionem per totum comitatum Cantebrig' facerem[2] omnibus qui debunt servicia domino regi. Et ideo vobis mando quatinus illam summonicionem faciatis ita quod omnes qui debunt domino regi servicia parati sint apud Portesmutiam in crastino sancti .N. ad transfretandum sicut se et tenementa sua diligunt, ne pro defectu terre eorum in manus domini resaysientur. Valete.

The sheriff of Cambridge to the serjeants of a hundred, greetings. I have received the lord king's writ that I should make a common summons

throughout Cambridgeshire of all who owe the lord king service. Therefore I order you to make that summons so that everyone who owes
service to the lord king may be ready to make the crossing at Portsmouth, on the morrow of the feast of St N., as they care for themselves
and their properties, lest their lands be taken back into the king's hand
for their default. Farewell.

This writ, sent by a sheriff to his subordinate officers, is a rare glimpse of a
level of administration for which records barely survive. In this case, the sheriff
is transmitting onward the king's general summons to the knights of the shires
for military service abroad. His subordinates, the hundred serjeants, are to
have the summons read out at their hundred courts.[3] English local government was already well developed before the Normans conquered the country
in 1066. The south and west of England (Wessex) had been divided into shires
as early as the tenth century. Each shire was administered on the king's behalf
by his sheriff ("shire-reeve"). Shires were subdivided into smaller districts
called hundreds, which had their own reeves, subordinate to the sheriff. This
system was extended to the center of England (Mercia) after its re-conquest
from the Vikings in the tenth century, and then further extended into Yorkshire and the north in the eleventh century, though here and in parts of the
north Midlands another unit called a wapentake either took the place of the
hundred or was an intervening level between it and the shire. The last English
shires (Cumberland and Westmorland) were formed at the end of the twelfth
century.[4]

   This model writ follows quite closely the genuine form of a royal summons
to service, and it may be drawn from an authentic document. However, it has
been rendered into a generic form by deleting all details except the name of
the port of embarkation, and by giving the date of assembly as the day after
the feast of St "N." This stood for the Latin word *nomen* ("name"), and was
the equivalent of saying, "fill in the blank." The sheriff's writ has close parallels
in the summons by the earl of Chester to his knights in DOCUMENT 24, and
also in a summons for service in Brittany issued by Henry III in 1234: "Henry
king of England, etc., greets his beloved and faithful Henry de Turberville. We
send you this instruction, asking that, as you love and honor us, you be at
Portsmouth with four other knights promptly at the feast of the Ascension in
the eighteenth year of our reign (June 1, 1234). Depart fully equipped with
horses and arms to cross the sea to the aid of the count of Brittany and ready
to remain in our service as the said count may more fully instruct you on our
behalf, so that we may owe you our gratitude."[5] The main difference between
DOCUMENT 29 and the summons of 1234 is that the latter is directed to a man

important enough to have an individual summons. The writ in DOCUMENT 29 was for lesser men, royal tenants of no more than local importance, who are being summoned collectively rather than individually.

NOTES

1 Add. 8167, fol. 126r.
2 *facere* in MS.
3 On the hundred courts, see DOCUMENT 42.
4 For these developments, see James Campbell, ed., *The Anglo-Saxons* (London: Penguin, 1982), 172–73; and Helen M. Cam, *The Hundred and the Hundred Rolls* (London: Methuen, 1930), 1–19.
5 Thomas Rymer, *Fœdera conventiones litteræ et acta publica*, ed. Adam Clarke and Frederick Holbrooke (London: Record Commission, 1816–69), vol. 1, pt. 1, 211.

30

The King Writes to the Earl of Chester Requesting Aid Against the Welsh Under Prince Llywelyn[1]

H. dei gratia, rex Anglie et cetera, dilecto et fideli suo comiti Cestrie salutem. Iniquum est merita sua suo premio defraudare. Nichilominus est equitati consonum transgressiones et iniurias ulcissi. Satis datum est nobis intelligi quod per experienciam congnovimus: quam fideliter [et][2] integre predecessoribus nostris et nobis vos devotes et fideles in servicio bono prebueritis, et quanta pro nobis pericula in transmarinis partibus iamdudum sustenueritis. Restat, igitur, ut in hiis partibus solitam probitatem vestram et probissime familie[3] vestre fortitudinem nostri infestantes senciant inimici, Walenses precipue, qui sub principe suo Leulino regni nostri partes australes invaserunt. Quosdam enim de militibus nostris in insidiis sedicione captos detinet in carcere, quosdam autem interfecerunt. Ad quorum ulcionem vos et alios fideles nostros invitamus, ut perfida gens Walensis, viribus Anglorum repulsa, nemorum suorum latibulam querere compellatur et ad habitaciones defugere ferinas.

H[enry] by the grace of God king of England, etc., greets his beloved and faithful earl of Chester. It is unfair to deprive someone of reward for his merits; likewise, it is only reasonable to avenge offenses and injuries. We have been told what we have ourselves observed: how faithfully and completely you have offered your devoted and loyal self in sterling service to our predecessors and us, and how many dangerous missions

you have undertaken for us overseas in days gone by. It remains, therefore, that our turbulent enemies in these parts should experience your
usual prowess and the might of your veteran military household, especially the Welsh, who under their prince, Llywelyn, have invaded the
southern part of our kingdom. For he is holding in prison some of our
knights, captured by treachery in ambushes; others the Welsh have
killed. To avenge them, we are summoning you and our other vassals,
so that the traitorous Welsh people, routed by the power of the English,
will be forced to seek a refuge in their forests and flee back to their
bestial lairs.

Though there is no known original of this letter, there are some that are comparable. In 1220 William Marshal II, earl of Pembroke (d. 1231), wrote to
King Henry III to complain about the problems he was having with the same
Prince Llywelyn mentioned above. He described the many attacks that the
prince had made on his lands in the southern March of Wales, and referred to
the several letters that he had written to the king about them. He also stigma-
tized the prince as a liar.[4] Henry III's own letters about Llywelyn tended to
be more circumspect in their language than the one above.[5] This was hardly
surprising, since in 1205 Llywelyn had married the king's elder half-sister Joan
(d. 1237), and Henry was thus Llywelyn's brother-in-law and the uncle of
Llywelyn's heir, Dafydd.

Llywelyn ab Iorwerth came to sole power in the northwestern Welsh principality of Gwynedd in 1201, after several decades of rivalry among the sons and
grandsons of Owain Gwynedd (d. 1170). Llywelyn had to compete with the
rival principality of Powys and the military power of his father-in-law, King
John (d. 1216). By the conclusion of the Barons' Wars in 1217, however, Llywelyn had broken the power of Powys and secured the submission of most of
the important Welsh magnates. Thereafter, Llywelyn dominated Wales until
his death in 1240, commencing a castle-building program and ruling his grow-
ing realm in princely style. His wife Joan styled herself as "lady of Wales" and
Llywelyn called himself "prince of Aberffraw and lord of Snowdon," evidently
in allusion to the way the king of England bolstered his status by employing
multiple titles (such as "King of England, Lord of Ireland, and Duke of
Normandy").[6]

The racial rhetoric deployed here in relation to the Welsh is by no means
unprecedented. The characterization of Celtic peoples in Britain as barbaric
and bestial is evident in the early twelfth century in the historical writings of
Anglo-Norman chroniclers, not least in those of William of Malmesbury.[7]
Such rhetoric justified any sort of atrocity, and had been a feature of Norman

writings about the Bretons in the previous century. The Welsh, like the Bretons, were characterized by the English as a pastoral, primitive people, without settled habitations or towns, whose lack of self-discipline led them to treachery and vicious violence. An Anglo-Norman baron, William de Briouze, told the royal clerk, Walter Map, about a Welsh lord who was a neighbor of his. According to the baron, this Welshman was devout and austere in the practice of his religion, fasting and keeping vigil in prayer naked on a cold floor, but in warfare there was no deed too abominable for him to contemplate.[8] As a result of such characterizations, the English regarded themselves as justified in any harsh action they took against the Welsh, including forced dispossession and massacre. This is clearly the sentiment behind DOCUMENT 30, and can also be seen in DOCUMENT 31, which follows.

NOTES

1 Fairfax 27, fol. 4r.
2 Word supplied to fit the sense of the passage.
3 *tue* expunged here in MS.
4 Shirley, ed., *Royal Letters*, vol. 1, 143–44.
5 See, for example, a letter dated 1233 to the constables of the border castles of Clun and Whitchurch, in Shirley, ed., *Royal Letters*, vol. 1, 423–24.
6 See Huw Pryce, "Negotiating Anglo-Welsh Relations: Llywelyn the Great and Henry III," in *England and Europe in the Reign of Henry III, 1216–1272*, ed. Björn K. U. Weiler and Ifor W. Rowlands (Aldershot, Hampshire: Ashgate, 2002), 13–29; Huw Pryce, ed., *The Acts of the Welsh Rulers, 1120–1283* (Cardiff: University of Wales Press, 2005), 26–29.
7 John Gillingham, "The Context and Purposes of Geoffrey of Monmouth's *History of the Kings of Britain*," *Anglo-Norman Studies*, 13 (1990), 106–9; idem, "Conquering the Barbarians: War and Chivalry in Twelfth-Century Britain," *Haskins Society Journal*, 4 (1992), 67–84. For similar hostile descriptions of the Welsh in the thirteenth century, see Sir Maurice Powicke, *The Thirteenth Century, 1216–1307*, 2nd ed. (Oxford: Clarendon, 1962), 383–84.
8 Walter Map, *De Nugis Curialium*, trans. Montague Rhodes James, ed. Christopher N. L. Brooke and Roger A. B. Mynors (Oxford: Clarendon, 1983), 146.

31

The King Summons an Army to the Defense of His Interests in Wales[1]

H. dei gratia rex Anglie, et cetera, dilectis et fidelibus suis baronibus et militibus et libere tenentibus salutem. Satis vobis[2] omnibus innotuit qualiter dominia nostra Walenses iam devastaverunt, damna nobis multa faciendo. Nos enim illam gentem omnino delere proponimus, et totius Wallie[3] nobis universa adversancia destruere municipia. Set quia in suffragio nostro hec non possumus facere, vobis mandando precipimus, quatinus cum equis et armis et omni aparatu bellico nobiscum contra Walenses veniatis, ut per vos illius gentis[4] et alios fideles nostros falcitatem adnichiliare valeamus.

H[enry] by the grace of God king of England, etc., greets his beloved and faithful barons and knights and freeholders.[5] It is well known to all of you how the Welsh are currently laying waste our lordships, doing us many injuries. Now we plan to annihilate that race completely, and to destroy every settlement hostile to us in the whole of Wales. But because, in our judgment, we cannot do this [unaided], we issue this instruction to you, ordering that, with horses, arms, and all military supplies, you march with us against the Welsh, so that through you and our other faithful vassals we shall be able to eliminate the treachery of that race.

This writ of summons to an army for war against the Welsh is rather more literary in style than one would expect. The writ issued by Henry III in June 1245 to all his feudal tenants to muster against the Welsh under Prince Dafydd ap Llywelyn is much more laconic, simply stating the cause of service and the time of the muster.[6] The author of DOCUMENT 31 knows the correct form of address of a king to his tenants, but the rest of this undoubtedly fictional text is a rhetorical exercise, portraying Henry III as a justly enraged monarch, determined, as in DOCUMENT 30, to destroy a treacherous, barbarous race with the aid of his loyal subjects. In fact, in 1245 King Henry had been reluctant to move against his nephew, Prince Dafydd, who had been at war with the Marcher barons since the previous summer.[7] The writ above does, however, echo the fact that the military demands on the cash-starved king were causing him to press for full feudal knight service from his tenants. This actually happened in 1245, and would happen again with increasing frequency during the later thirteenth century.[8]

NOTES

1 Fairfax 27, fol. 4r.
2 *nobis* in MS.
3 *Walense* in MS.
4 *gentes* in MS.
5 Freeholders were holders of land not bound by peasant service. These could be quite considerable landowners who were not knights.
6 *Close Rolls, 1242–47*, 357.

7   On Anglo-Welsh relations at this period, see Robert Rees Davies, *The Age of Conquest: Wales, 1063–1415* (Oxford: Oxford University Press, 1987).

8   Sanders, *Feudal Military Service*, 130–35.

--- 32 ---

The King's Liege Men Warn Him About Secret Confederacies Between Some of His Own Men and the Welsh, Which Threaten the Success of His Campaign[1]

Excellentissimo domino suo salutem. (*H. dei gratia, et cetera, sui fideles et ligii semper ad servicia.*)[2] Gentis Walensis[3] versuciam et machinamenta delere defacili possetis, nisi quidam de vestris privatim Walensibus consentirent. De quorum privata confederacione[4] diligenter inquiratis[5] et, illis ab expedicione remotis,[6] inter vos et inimicos[7] vestros conflictis inhibeantur,[8] ne tantarum transgressionum[9] eorum impunitas amplioris fiat eius occacio presumcionis. Penitus enim frivola fiet et inutilis est expedicio, si iunctim super inimicos nostros procedant vestri fideles, et Walentibus confederatis.

To their most excellent lord, greetings. (*To H[enry], by the grace of God, etc., his faithful and liege men, always at his service.*)[10] You could easily destroy the craftiness and trickery of the Welsh people, were not some of your own men secretly conspiring with them. You should make a careful inquiry into their confederacy and, having removed those men from the campaign, you should not let them be employed in the fighting between you and your enemies, lest their exemption from punishment for such treasonable activities should give them an opportunity for even greater plotting. For the campaign [*against the Welsh*] will be completely worthless and pointless if your faithful vassals should jointly advance upon your enemies, and those men [*i.e., the English traitors*] are already confederated with the Welsh.

The March of Wales, the region on the Welsh-English frontier that was controlled by English barons rather than Welsh princes, was built up by the piecemeal conquests and strategic marriages of Anglo-Norman aristocrats between the 1080s and 1170s. By the 1150s, the name "March" (a Germanic word meaning "border region") was in general use. Though ruled by English lords and colonized by English peasants and townspeople, the March was not England. The king had influence there, because he was the overlord of the

Marcher barons for their English lands, and sometimes he himself ruled over Marcher lordships for long periods of time. But English law and the king's administration had no authority there. Marcher lords had their own courts and governments within their lordships. They conducted war and relations with the Welsh, and with one another, as it suited them, not the king. There was a good deal of intermarriage in the twelfth and thirteenth centuries between the families of Marcher lords and the Welsh princely dynasties of Deheubarth, Gwynedd and Powys,[11] and on occasion Welsh princes and Marcher lords cooperated militarily, sometimes even in warfare against the king. It was, for instance, the backing of troops from Welsh kings that made the rebellion of Earl Robert of Gloucester against King Stephen possible in 1139. The support of Prince Llywelyn ab Iorwerth of Gwynedd against King John allowed the Briouze family to recover its lands in the March in the warfare of 1215–16.[12]

It is therefore not surprising that this document alleges that a party among the king's own English subjects was conspiring against him with the Welsh. As early as 1145, informers insinuated to King Stephen of England (1135–54) that Earl Ranulf II of Chester wanted to lure the king into the March, where the Welsh would do away with him. The king believed them and had the earl arrested on the strength of the allegations.[13] There is, however, little in the historical record to justify the allegations made in DOCUMENT 32. In 1228 the young King Henry III (1216–72) summoned a large army to Ceri in support of the earl of Pembroke against Prince Llywelyn, but a vigorous Welsh counter-response led to an inconclusive campaign. The contemporary historian Roger of Wendover picked up rumors—probably from disgruntled courtiers—that "there were many among the magnates in the king's army who were allied with Llywelyn and merely pretended to follow the king."[14] But it is unlikely that the Ceri campaign could have provided the material for this letter. It is more likely that its paranoia is rooted in the suspiciousness of medieval courts toward any group—like the Marcher barons—that aspired to independence from royal control.

NOTES

1   Fairfax 27, fol. 4r–v.
2   The italicized passage here, as in DOCUMENTS 5 and 24, represents a variant phrasing included in this model text.
3   *Walense* in MS.
4   *consideracione* in MS.
5   Corrected in MS from *inquirastis*.
6   In MS, the words *et ne* follow *remotis*; they do not make sense in this context.
7   Fol. 4v commences here.

8   *inhiantur* in MS.

9   *tante transgressiones* in MS.

10   The italicized passage represents a variant salutation included in this model text.

11   For a comprehensive study of its origins and development, see Max Liebermann, *The March of Wales, 1067–1300: A Borderland of Medieval Britain* (Cardiff: University of Wales Press, 2008).

12   David Crouch, "The March and the Welsh Kings," in *The Anarchy of King Stephen's Reign*, ed. Edmund King (Oxford: Clarendon, 1994), 276–78; Ifor W. Rowlands, "King John and Wales," in *King John: New Interpretations*, ed. Stephen D. Church (Woodbridge, Suffolk: Boydell, 1999), 284–87.

13   Kenneth R. Potter and Ralph Henry Carless Davis, ed. and trans., *Gesta Stephani* (Oxford: Oxford University Press, 1976), 192–96.

14   *Flores Historiarum*, ed. Henry G. Hewlett, vol. 2, Rolls Series, 84 (London: Eyre and Spottiswood, 1886–89), 350; for comment, see Ron F. Walker, "Hubert de Burgh and Wales, 1218–32," *EHR*, 87 (1972), 481–82.

33

A Warning to a Friend to Get His Grain off the Road, Because the King Is About to Go to Wales and Will Seize All Provisions That He Finds Along the Way

D. mandat E.[1] ut movet bladum suum a via regis

Karissimo amico suo A., B. salutem. Rex profecturus in Walliam capiet omnia cibaria que invenire potest per viam et transitum. Quare bladum vestrum a via eius submoveatis. Scituri quod quicquid ceperit nunquam revocetis nec eius precium, et ita provideatis vobis ne dampnum incurratis contra eius adventum. Valete.

D. sends word to E. to get his grain off the royal highway

To his dearest friend A., B. sends greetings. The king, who is about to go to Wales, will seize all the food that he can find on the road and the route. Therefore, get your grain off his road. You will know that you will never recover whatever he seizes, or its price, and thus you should watch out lest you incur any loss because of his coming. Farewell.

This letter gives a vivid picture of the depredations caused by royal purveyors (provisioning agents). King John's abuse of purveyance was so notorious that a remedy for it was sought in Magna Carta (1215). The king was required to stipulate, for example, that "No constable or any other of our bailiffs shall take any man's corn [i.e., grain] or other chattels unless he pays cash for them at once or can delay payment with the agreement of the seller" (clause 28). King John also had to guarantee that "No sheriff or bailiff of ours or anyone else is to take horses or carts of any free man for carting without his agreement" (clause 30).[2] The problem was not usually that provisions were seized without any compensation (as the writer of the letter above fears), but that payment was delayed and did not match the value of what was taken. For a discussion of royal purveyance of goods and transport, see DOCUMENT 19.

Although Henry III made four military expeditions to Wales before 1250 (see DOCUMENTS 25 and 30), it is unlikely that this letter was inspired by any particular campaign, but the royal right of "prise" or seizure was a contentious issue. The language of this letter, while it makes no mention of war, nevertheless implies that the king is heading for Wales with a very large party under conditions of such urgency that the royal purveyors are not purchasing grain in the local markets in an orderly fashion, but simply seizing it wherever they find it. The warning to the addressee to get his grain off the road suggests that this letter may reflect conditions around the time of the autumn harvest, when cereal crops—wheat, rye, oats, and barley—were being carted to manorial granges and to markets. If so, it may indeed have been inspired by one or more of Henry III's Welsh campaigns, all of which took place in the autumn months.

NOTES

1   The discrepancy in the initials of the sender and recipient between the heading ("D. to E.") and the body of this letter ("B. to A.") reflects the rather careless manner in which it was copied from another letter collection. Similar examples can be found in DOCUMENTS 10, 16, 50, 70, and 90.

2   Holt, *Magna Carta*, 459. For these two clauses of Magna Carta, see also the Articles of the Barons, clauses 19 and 20, and the re-issue of Magna Carta in 1225, clauses 20 and 21, in ibid., Appendices 5 and 12.

POLITICS

34

King Henry III of England Requests an Aid for the Marriage of His Sister[1]

Rex mandat comitibus[2] et baronibus[3] ut adiuvant ei ad sororem maritandam

Henricus dei gratia Rex Anglie, dominus hybernie, dux Normannie et Aquitannie, comes Andegavie, comitibus et baronibus et omnibus fidelibus suis salutem. Ad honorem et commoditatem nostram vos et omnia vestra de iure vestre fidelitatis exponere tenemini. Quoddam enim speciale dominium regi solummodo debitum est corpora vestra pro me ponere. Vobis igitur mandamus ut inter vos provideatis in quantum ad sororis mee maritagium nobis auxiliari velitis, et tantum super hoc facientes ut de vestra bona voluntate et voluntatis exsecucione personas[4] vestras debeamus commendare. Valete.

The king sends word to his earls and barons to aid him in arranging for the marriage of his sister

Henry, by the grace of God, king of England, lord of Ireland, duke of Normandy and Aquitaine and count of Anjou, to his earls, barons and all his faithful men, greetings. We are justified in disposing of you and all your goods for our own honor and convenience, as follows from your oath of fealty. For it is a special prerogative due to a king alone to dispose of you for my own advantage. Therefore, we command you that you take thought among yourselves as to how much you might wish to aid us for the marriage portion of my sister, acting in such a way in this matter that we may owe you our thanks for your good will and for your performance of our wish. Farewell.

This model document, although fictional, nonetheless reflects the actual political situation in England in the mid-1230s. It is based on a contemporary debate over the extent of the king's power to tax his subjects, based on his rights as their feudal lord.

By the end of the twelfth century it was established that a lord might exact money payments, known as "aids" (*auxilia*), from his tenants on a number of occasions when he might need cash for particularly heavy expenses. A Northamptonshire landowner of the early 1180s defined these occasions as follows: "if need shall arise [my tenants] shall help to ransom my body and to make my eldest son a knight and to give in marriage my eldest daughter."[5] But it is never suggested by any contemporary source that a lord might levy an aid for the marriage of a sister. When the barons imposed their view of aids on King John in Magna Carta (1215), the king and barons stated the custom in similar terms, though with an added restriction on the marriage of the eldest daughter: "No scutage or aid is to be levied in our realm except by the common counsel of our realm, unless it is for the ransom of our person, the knighting of our eldest son or the first marriage of our eldest daughter; and for these only a reasonable aid is to be levied." The charter laid out the same terms for the levying of aids by any lord.[6]

The issue resurfaced in 1235, when Henry III (1216–72) married his sister Isabel to the German emperor Frederick II (1215–50), and the king asked his subjects for an aid. Isabel's marriage portion of 30,000 marks (£20,000) was a huge sum, and its payment caused a financial crisis in England. The government of Henry III was driven to a variety of desperate measures in order to meet the installments, the last of which was not paid until 1237.[7]

A council of barons and prelates granted the necessary sum as an aid early in the summer of 1235.[8] They imposed a levy of two marks on each tenant-in-chief for every knight's fee, and on the English clergy of one-thirtieth of their income.[9] The slow rate of payment drove the king to extend the tax to his Irish barons and clergy in 1236. The exceptional nature of this tax is noted by the king in the writ that he sent to his sheriffs in July 1235 concerning its collection. He said that his barons "conceded us a worthwhile aid to further our important business, *of their own free will and without creating any precedent.*"[10]

The letter above reflects the baronial distrust of the monarchy that was fanned anew by the events of 1235. It presents a stark statement of the royal position on aids in the king's declaration that "We are justified in disposing of you and all your goods for our own honor and convenience, as follows from your oath of fealty." We may doubt very much whether this is a genuine letter of Henry III to his barons, but it may nonetheless preserve one of the positions in the debate between the king's counselors and his magnates. As such, it has a wider significance yet. The crisis of 1235 added to escalating problems between Henry III and the political community that grew, in 1258 in the Provisions of Oxford, into a demand for the permanent reform of royal government by the magnates and bishops, united as the "whole community of England." The underlying cause of the events in 1258 was the same as that in 1235: the king's political weakness, which stemmed from his continual need for cash to fund his foreign ventures.

NOTES

1   Add. 8167, fol. 105r.
2   Corrected in MS from *commilitibus* to *commitibus*.
3   *boronibus* in MS.
4   *persona* in MS.
5   Stenton, *First Century*, 277.
6   Holt, *Magna Carta*, clauses 12 and 15, p. 455.
7   Stacey, *Politics, Policy and Finance*, 98–99.
8   It was specifically an aid for the marriage of Henry's sister, although it was also referred to as a "scutage," "tallage," and "carrucage."
9   Sydney Knox Mitchell, *Studies in Taxation Under John and Henry III* (New Haven: Yale University Press, 1914), 208–14. A tenant-in-chief was a landowner holding his

estates directly from the king; a knight's "fee" was the amount of land thought necessary to support him. Opinions vary as to how much land that needed to be.

10   William Stubbs, *Select Charters and Other Illustrations of English Constitutional History*, ed. Henry William Carless Davis, 9th ed. (Oxford: Oxford University Press, 1913), 357 (emphasis added).

35

A Magnate Replies to the King Acknowledging the King's Right but Reminding Him Not to Overburden His Subjects When He Has Income of His Own[1]

Responsio ad predictas

Excellentissimo regi, et cetera. Sciatis[2] [quod][3] connovimus quod quicquid[4] possumus et quantum ex debito ligancie nostre vobis tanquam domino nostro debemus, set dominium super nos habeatis tantum in debitis exaccionibus; nos non gravare debetis. Si vestre sororis maritagium[5] tesauros[6] vestros in magna parte consumsit, ut quid ad nos recuritis cum redditus et firmas habetis quibus tesauros vestros tesaurare valeatis? Absit a regia dignitate liberos subditos in debitis molestare consuetudinibus, et ab eis exigere que nunquam facere solebant.

A reply to the aforesaid letter

To the most excellent king, etc. Know that we acknowledge that we owe to you as our lord whatever and as much as we can [give], as due from our allegiance, but you ought to have lordship over us only for payments that are actually owed to you; *you* have a duty not to harm *us*. If the marriage portion of your sister has taken most of your wealth, why then do you resort to us, when you have rents and farms[7] with which you might enrich your treasury? Let it be far from the royal dignity to harass your free subjects concerning the customary payments due [to you], and to demand from them what they used never to do.

This letter is a response to the royal position on taxation presented in Document 34. Although a purely fictional exercise in composition, the attitude that it records may well reflect a genuine debate between the king and his subjects at the time of the marriage of the king's sister Isabel in 1235. This letter evidently is intended to be a remonstrance from the magnates and barons of England to Henry III for attempting to impose an unaccustomed and unacceptable demand for money to pay for his sister's marriage portion. Written representations of this sort were actually made at times, the earliest known being a letter directed to King John from the barons of Leinster and Meath in 1207, which does not survive but is known from the outraged monarch's irate response.[8]

An interesting point in this letter is the argument that the king has enough rents and farms by which he may finance his projects without having to trouble his subjects. This may well be the earliest manifestation of the opinion that a monarch should live off his own resources, a view that became a perennial feature of debates between the sovereign and the nation into the seventeenth century. The other argument that this letter contains is a protest against innovations. This echoes the king's disclaimer (discussed under DOCUMENT 34) that he did not intend his request for an aid to create a precedent. The refusal to countenance demands beyond those allowed by custom is much older than the view that the king should live off his own resources, and recurs in every generation after the Conquest.

NOTES

1 Add. 8167, fol. 105r–v.
2 *scintatis* in MS.
3 *quod* missing in MS.
4 *quicquit* in MS.
5 Fol. 105v commences here.
6 *teusaros* in MS.
7 A farm (*firma*) or fee-farm was an annual fixed charge paid to the Crown by a "farmer" in return for a body of rights, such as the right to collect tolls or taxes. The farmer made his profit on what he could extort on top.
8 *Rotuli litterarum patentium*, 72.

36

The Bishops and Church Dignitaries Recommend to the Magnates and Knights of England that They Take Counsel over the King's Position on Taxation[1]

Pontifices et prelati mandant comitibus et baronibus tocius Anglie, habendi consilium de rege precepcione

Pontifices et prelati tocius Anglie, comitibus et baronibus et militibus, salutem in domino. Communi negocio et ad omnium commodum est insistendum, et siquis [dis]senterit[2] in quantum unanimiter est ei resistendum. Maior enim est universitas subditorum quam sit alicuius domini super subditos constituti dignitas[3] aud[4] dominium. Set dominus rex, iuri iusticieque [. . .]⁵ constituere in titulo quibusdam adulatoribus hec ad eum adientibus.⁶ Cuius propositum cum equitate sit contrarium modis omnibus quassare studeamus, cum ex tali proposito nos et successores nostri gravari possumus in posterium. Quod⁷ enim monemus [?melius] est quam ad⁸ omnem regis exigenciam iustam vel iniustam favorabiles existere. Si sic procedere posset sicut iam incepit in scutagiis et aliis auxiliis exig[e]ndis,⁹ quis tam dives quis tam habundans in tali casu subsisteret? Certe plus a nobis posset exigere quam nos omnes ei possimus facere. Conveniamus igitur et provideamus quid et qualiter respondeamus, et ab omnibus nobis tanquam ab uno nostrum responsum accipiat. Nullo quia modo sustineamus ut unius tam avaricia nos et heredes nostros confundat inperpetuum.

The bishops and prelates send word to the earls and barons of England, for taking counsel concerning the king's order

The bishops and prelates of all England to the earls, barons and knights, greetings in the Lord. It is necessary to pursue a common problem to the benefit of everyone, and if anyone [should dissent], he is to be unanimously opposed as much as possible. For the community of all subjects is more important than might be the dignity or estate of any one lord set over subjects. But the lord king, after certain flatterers had appealed these matters to him, [?blind] to law and justice, [?has refused] to constitute [this principle] as an established right.¹⁰ Since it is contrary to equity, we should endeavor to suppress their proposal by all means, since, as a result of such a proposal, we and our successors can be harmed in future. For indeed we declare [?this better] than to appear favorable to every royal demand, whether just or unjust. If the king is allowed to carry on as he has now begun to do in demanding scutages and other aids, who could survive in such circumstances, however rich, however abounding in wealth? It is a fact that he can demand more from us than we all combined could produce for him. So let us come together and consider what we should say in response and how, and let him receive our answer from all of us as if from one of us [*i.e., let him receive the same answer from one and all of us*]. Because in no way ought we to allow that so much greed of one man might ruin us and our heirs¹¹ forever.

This is the third of three letters, the others being DOCUMENTS 34 and 35, that appear to derive from the debate about the aid for the marriage portion of the king's sister Isabel in 1235. On that occasion, the clergy of England granted the king a tax of one-thirtieth of the value of their income, while the lay magnates allowed a levying of scutage on their knights' fees. It is not surprising, therefore, to find this letter linked with the others. What is interesting is to find the prelates of England (the bishops, abbots, priors, and cathedral dignitaries) depicted as consulting with the magnates to organize a common front against the king. Again, it is unlikely that a genuine letter lies behind this one, but it may well represent its author's understanding of the interplay between clergy, laity, and king in the financial crisis of 1235. No such early letter of the prelates of England survives, though it is by no means unlikely that they could have written as a body. Matthew Paris, for example, preserved an extensive list of the complaints of the Church in 1257 against the government of Henry III in the name of the bishops of England.[12]

Together, these three letters are important in elucidating an otherwise little-known crisis in Henry III's government in the mid-1230s. DOCUMENT 36 illustrates how his constant need for money, which caused him to resort to new and extortionate demands, became a grave and persistent irritant in the relations between the king and his country.

NOTES

1   Add. 8167, fol. 105v.
2   *senterit* in MS.
3   *dingnitas* in MS.
4   *Sic* for *aut.*
5   A phrase evidently is missing here; something like *"cecus negavit"* would fit the sense.
6   Corrected in MS from *adiacentibus.*
7   *quidam* in MS.
8   Corrected in MS from *ead.*
9   *exigndis* in MS.
10   The gaps in the text mean that this can only be an approximate sense of the passage.
11   The term "heirs" here is used in the sense of successors in ecclesiastical office, to which real property such as knights' fees was attached. In addition, numerous bishops acquired knights' fees by purchase, which they bequeathed to blood-relations.
12   *Councils and Synods*, 2:1, 539–48.

37

A Knight Seeks Advice Concerning the King's Supposed Willingness to Marry Noble Young Women to Men Below Their Social Station[1]

Miles mandat militi ad habendum consilium de rege qui vult[2] maritare filiam inliberiori quam deberet

Miles militi salutem. Communi periculo communiter est occurendum.
Rome vicinitas, vicino vicinus in necessitatis articulo consilium et auxilium prebere tenetur. Quasdam novas et³ inconsuetas dominus rex con-
suetudines vult⁴ introducere, satellitibus suis generosas filias nostras et
neptas volens coniungere coniugali copula. Ignot' nobis est cuius sint
condicionis quibus matrimoniali foedere⁵ filie nostre debeant copulari.
Quidam enim in sua provincia sutores erant, quidam porcarii, et quidam
inveniendus est quam generosam innobili copulare. Hinc indiscreto
domini regis proposito modis omnibus satagamus obviare, et humilimis
precibus et si necesse fuerit muneribus regiam voluntatem flectere
studeamus.

*A knight sends word to a knight to get his advice about the king's intention to
marry a daughter to a man of lower station than he ought*

A knight to a knight, greetings. It is necessary to combine when under a
common threat. As a province to Rome, so a neighbor is bound to give
aid and counsel to his neighbor in the face of an emergency. The lord
king wants to introduce certain new and unprecedented customs, pro-
posing to unite our noble daughters and granddaughters to his hangers-
on in a bond of marriage. It is unknown to us of what condition are
those men to whom our daughters might have to be joined in marital
union. For some were shoemakers in their own shires, some swineherds,
and the man has yet to be found who would couple a girl of such noble
birth to a man of ignoble origins. So let us busy ourselves to thwart in
every way this unwise proposal of the lord king, and endeavor to divert
the king's will with the humblest of prayers—or, if necessary, with
bribes.

The issue of "disparagement" (*dispargacio*; see DOCUMENT 38) is prominent
in complaints of English and French barons against their king for much of the
twelfth century. Put simply, disparagement was the marriage of a noble person
to someone of inferior rank or standing.⁶ The king was entitled to use the
wardship of noble girls and boys, and the disposal of their marriages and those
of noble widows, to reward his allies and servants. When, however, the ally or
servant was of comparatively low birth and connections, the marriage was
considered degrading ("disparaging") to the noble spouse, whether male or
female, but the outcry was loudest when the injured party was female.⁷ The
issue would seem to have been a heated one when King Henry I came to the
throne of England in 1100. In his coronation charter he felt obliged to assure

his subjects that, "if when one of my barons or other men die leaving a daughter as heir, I will not give her in marriage except according to the advice of my barons."[8] The intention here seems to have been to reassure his magnates that noble heirs would be treated responsibly by making their marriage conditional on baronial advice. It was this level of monitoring that the barons wanted over King John in 1215 when they were negotiating Magna Carta, although the eventual settlement drew back from that position. In the end, Clause 6 read simply: "Heirs shall be given in marriage without disparagement (*disparagacione*), yet so that before a marriage is contracted it shall be made known to the heir's next of kin."[9]

It would appear that the king's exploitative treatment of female heirs (whether daughters or widows) had antagonized the Anglo-Norman aristocracy as early as the reign of William Rufus (1087–1100), since his brother Henry I was so keen to distance himself from the practice in the aftermath of his seizure of the throne. But, as commentators have noted, Henry (like his successors) continued to make the most of his rights of wardship throughout his reign, making widows pay if they wished to be free of his control of their marriage, and selling and granting wardships to his favored officers.[10] The potential for revenue and patronage implicit in the control of marriage was too much for the Norman and Angevin kings to leave alone.

We have some indications in contemporary literature that the same resentment was current in the parts of France where the king could control wardships. In the earliest portion of the epic *Raoul de Cambrai*, which dates from around 1150 and was composed in the northeast of France, the malevolent King Louis proposes to marry the widow of the count of Cambrai to a low-born courtier, no more than a hired soldier, to the disgust of the nobles who considered it to be "coupling a mongrel with a greyhound."[11] There is an earlier English literary parallel to this in Geoffrey Gaimar's *Estoire des Engleis* (c. 1138 × 40), in which Argentille, the heiress to the kingdom of Lindsey, is outrageously obliged by her wicked uncle and guardian to marry a cook.[12] A parallel example to Gaimar's comes from two or three decades later, in the northern French romance-epic *Garin le Loherenc*, in which Count Dreux of Amiens urges Baldwin of Flanders to marry off quickly his widowed sister Helisent, since he has heard that the king of France intends to marry her off "to one of his kitchen scullions who roasts his chickens."[13] In the French historical epic the *Roman de Thèbes* (1150s), a royal princess, Antigone, reluctantly spurns the advances of a knight, Parthenopus, for not being "of such *linage* that you might be *de mon parage*," a phrase that anticipates the verb *desparager* by some decades.[14]

It seems fair to conclude from this evidence that behind DOCUMENTS 37 and 38 lay over a century of aristocratic insecurity in both France and England about the fate of noble children and widows, and a long-running item on the agenda of business between kings and their magnates. In fact, barons may not have been quite so exercised on the subject as this letter implies. To begin with, the disparagement itself was not necessarily committed by the king, but by the person who obtained the wardship from him. It seems also that Richard I and John married off noble heiresses to relatively humble royal servants without incurring any known condemnation.[15] Nonetheless, the barons brought the issue forward in 1215. Indeed, in 1218 the Flemish writer known as the Anonymous of Bethune singled out the clause on disparagement as a major issue between the king and barons when he described the negotiation of Magna Carta, and disparagement was an issue with which Earl Ranulf III of Chester had to deal in 1215 when his own tenants demanded a charter of liberties.[16]

The letter above is a literary exercise, and a rather overblown one. The king certainly could not be accused of wanting to marry off girls of noble family to any artisans and peasants who had the money to buy superior marriages. Such accusations recall the absurd literary mismatches in the romance-epics of the previous century. Furthermore, as the canon law of marriage developed in the late twelfth and thirteenth centuries, it was impossible for any ward to be forced to marry someone to whom he or she objected.[17] However, the charges do reveal a willingness in their author to question the king's intentions toward aristocratic heiresses. They also portray Magna Carta as a bastion against the king's inclination to disparage girls in marriage. Why was this? One possible explanation is that social rank was becoming more self-conscious and structured in the first decades of the thirteenth century. As this happened, the possibility of disparagement became increasingly threatening and offensive to an emerging social order. As a result, the king was demonized, especially by the social group that had only recently secured recognition as nobles, the knights. These letters seem, therefore, to reflect a strengthening feeling of hierarchical class within English society.[18]

DOCUMENT 37 is addressed by a knight to another knight. The sender is evidently the senior or more important of the two, since he puts himself first, but both of these county knights are depicted as defensive about their social standing—fearful that they will be linked with men of lesser rank, not only artisans and peasants but, by implication, also tradesmen and nonnoble landowners, men of no birth or social standing. To these knights, Magna Carta is their guarantor of noble status, their bulwark against being lumped forcibly into the lower orders, and they take it very seriously. What is clear is that county knights were well acquainted with the text of Magna Carta. For instance, among the surviving papers of a Northamptonshire knight, Richard Hotot, compiled in the 1240s, was a copy of the 1225 reissue of Magna Carta.[19]

NOTES

1 Add. 8167, fols. 105v–106r.

2 *wlt* in MS.

3 Fol. 106r commences here.

4 *wlt* (i.e., *vult*) added in caret here in MS.

5 *federe* in MS.

6 A *par* (in English, "peer") is a person's equal. "Disparagement" literally means a slight to one's "parage," a term that comprehends status through noble connections. See David Crouch, *The Birth of Nobility: Constructing Aristocracy in England and France, 900–1300* (London: Longman, 2005), 135–48. It has been suggested that the word *disparagacio* was coined in England in the reign of John, as a result of the intensive exploitation of wardships by Richard and John. See Scott L. Waugh, *The Lordship of England: Royal Wardships and Marriages in English Society and Politics, 1217–1327* (Princeton, N.J.: Princeton University Press, 1988), 80n. However, the word itself first appeared in Latin in 1194 (*Pipe Roll of 6 Richard I*, 238), and occurred earlier still in the French past participle form *desparagee*, in the Anglo-Norman romance *Protheselaus*, which was composed in England between 1180 and 1190. See Hue de Roteland, *Protheselaus*, ed. A. J. Holden, vol. 2, Anglo-Norman Text Society, 47–49 (London, 1989–93), 118, line 10734. The sudden appearance of the word in French and Latin forms at the end of the twelfth century may well be a consequence of English royal exploitation of underage heirs, but its earliest occurrences clearly pre-date John's reign.

7 It should be noted that the first occurrence of the word in English royal records relates to money paid in 1194 for the marriage of a Gloucestershire boy heir "where he may not be disparaged"; it does not concern a girl. *Pipe Roll of 6 Richard I*, 238.

8 Latin text in Holt, *Magna Carta*, 425 (translation by David Crouch).

9 Holt, *Magna Carta*, 452, 453.

10 See observations in Frank Barlow, *William Rufus* (London: Eyre Methuen, 1983), 255–56, noting Orderic Vitalis's comments about the excessive fines demanded by Rufus from his barons. See also Judith A. Green, *The Government of England Under Henry I* (Cambridge: Cambridge University Press, 1986), 84–86, and particularly James C. Holt, "Feudal Society and the Family in Early Medieval England: IV. The Heiress and the Alien," *Transactions of the Royal Historical Society*, 5th ser., 35 (1985), 24–25, who lists the social disparities between Henry I's servants and the noble brides they were awarded but does not see significant resistance to the practice at the time.

11 *Raoul de Cambrai*, ed. and trans. Sarah Kay (Oxford: Clarendon, 1996), lines 214–16.

12 Geoffrey Gaimar, *L'Estoire des Engleis*, ed. Alexander Bell, 3 vols., Anglo-Norman Text Society, 14–16 (1960), lines 97–167. As noted in Holt, "Feudal Society and the Family in Early Medieval England: IV. The Heiress and the Alien," 25.

13 *Garin le Loherenc*, ed. Anne Iker-Gittleman, 3 vols., Classiques français du moyen âge, 117–19 (Paris: Champion, 1996–97), 1: lines 2617–21.

14 *Le Roman de Thèbes*, ed. Francine Mora-Lebrun (Paris: Lettres Gothiques, 1995), lines 4256–29.

15 Holt, "Feudal Society and the Family in Early Medieval England," 26–28.

16 Francisque Michel, ed., *Histoire des ducs de Normandie et des rois d'Angleterre* (Paris: Société de l'histoire de France, 1840), 149. The "Magna Carta of Cheshire" granted by Earl Ranulf III to his tenants in mid-1215 deals with disparagement (clause 8): "Neither a widow nor an heir should be married where disparagement occurs (*disparigetur*), but by permission and gift of their family." Barraclough, ed., *Charters of the Anglo-Norman Earls of Chester*, 389.

17 See the review of the issue in Sue Sheridan Walker, "Free Consent and Marriage of Feudal Wards in Medieval England," *Journal of Medieval History*, 8 (1982), 123–34. Those disappointed men who bought the marriages of wards who then refused to marry as directed were offered financial compensation from the ward's estate.

18 Other later thirteenth-century attacks on the king's alleged misuse of grants of marriages focused on the grants to "aliens," unworthy foreign favorites. Matthew Paris was a writer particularly exercised by this issue. Scott L. Waugh, "Marriage, Class and Royal Lordship in England Under Henry III," *Viator*, 16 (1985), 181–82, 202–3.

19 On the Hotot papers, see Edmund King, "Estate Records of the Hotot family," in idem, ed., *A Northamptonshire Miscellany*, Northamptonshire Record Society, 32 (Northampton, 1983), 1–58.

38

His Colleague Reassures the Knight that Disparagement Is Against the Articles of Magna Carta, and Assures Him of His Assistance[1]

Responsio ad predictas

Militi miles salutem. Similis rerum omnium disposicio[2] communi debet ordinari consilio, set tamen res ille tangant et exigant periculum vestrum. Michi vestris literis significastis quod non minus quam me alios tangit et solicitat. Cum meam filiam[3] coniungamus sic ut de ipsa idem casum eveniat quo et vos gravari pertimescitis. Non regis set regni deo dante constitucio servabitur, [quam][4] rex[5] et predecessores [eius][6] nobis concesserunt.[7] Materia [in][8] eorum cartis continetur quod filias nostras sine dispargacione maritare possimus. Deum testor—et per experienciam probare poteritis—quod in hoc negocio me fidelem habeatis auxiliarium et auxiliatorem. Ad quod dicam, vestra providencia, negocium istud commune profectum perducatur ad effectum, omnibus vestris commilitonibus consilium et auxilium vobis inperpendentibus. Valete.

A reply to the previous letter

To a knight, a knight [sends] greetings. The appropriate outcome of all matters should be decided by common deliberation, but nevertheless those matters might concern and involve your own peril. You told me in your letter that it touches and concerns others no less than me. Since we are marrying off my daughter, the same circumstance may occur as regards her that you fear may affect you. The constitution—not, God willing, of the king, but of the realm—will be preserved, [which] the king and his predecessors granted to us. The matter is included in their charters: that we can marry off our daughters without disparagement. God is my witness—and you can prove this by past experience—that you may count on me in this business as a faithful aid and assistant. To which, may I say, this common business may be brought to an effective conclusion by your prudence, bearing in mind the aid and counsel given you by all your fellow knights. Farewell.

The central issue of this letter—disparagement (the marriage of a person of noble family to one of lesser rank)—is also the focus of DOCUMENT 37, where it is discussed in full. Both letters also dwell on the insecurity and even paranoia of the landowning classes as to the king's intentions concerning Magna Carta. Here the knights have heard rumors that the king may not honor the provisions of Magna Carta, although it was reissued by Henry III's advisers and ministers during his minority in 1217 and again in 1225. In fact, no such thing was contemplated by the king, but that it was feared is evident enough from this letter. The clauses of Magna Carta had already, by 1220, become catch-phrases for the politically active among the aristocracy and urban classes in their local courts. In 1226, for example, the knights of Lincolnshire were in hot dispute with their sheriff about just how Magna Carta affected the regularity of the sessions of the county court.[9] DOCUMENTS 37 and 38, therefore, though probably written as classroom composition exercises, offer glimpses into the psychological world of the early thirteenth-century knights and their families.

NOTES

1 Add. 8167, fol. 106r.
2 *dispocicio* in MS.
3 *mea filia* in MS.
4 Word inserted to preserve the sense of the passage.
5 *reg'* in MS.
6 Word inserted to preserve the sense of the passage.
7 *concessores ruunt* in MS.
8 Word inserted to preserve the sense of the passage.
9 Holt, *Magna Carta*, 390–93.

CHAPTER 3

Lordship and Administration

LAW AND ORDER

39

A Constable Orders His Bailiffs to Discover Who Are the Robbers Plaguing Their Jurisdictions and to Stop Them[1]

Constabularius ballivis ut[2] faciant inquiri[3] qui sunt vispiliones qui spoliant homines

[Constabularius][4] A., B., C., ballivis salutem. Vobis mando ex parte domini regis et firmiter precipio ut, istis audituris, sine omni contradiccione et omni [dilacione][5] remota, faciatis inquiri per ballivas vestras qui sunt vispiliones qui transeuntes spoliant homines et occidunt. Ad audienciam vero regis perventum est quod nemo solus transire potest per ballivas vestras quin occidatur et in aqua proiciatur. Quare tantum faciatis ne malefactores tales in ballivis inveniantur. Valete.

A constable orders his bailiffs to discover the criminals who are robbing men by night

[A constable] to his bailiffs, A., B., and C., greetings. I am sending you word on the king's behalf and firmly ordering you that, when you have heard this letter, you will, with no argument or delay, have an inquiry made throughout your jurisdictions as to who are the criminals who are robbing and killing travelers by night. For it has come to the king's attention that no man can travel alone through your jurisdictions without being killed and dumped in the river. Therefore, make sure that no such evildoers be found in your jurisdictions. Farewell.

This letter, like DOCUMENT 29, provides a rare glimpse of the personnel who had responsibility for local administration and law and order in medieval

England. The office of constable was an ancient one, going back in origins to the households of the Merovingian kings of the Franks, where the constable (*comes stabuli*, "count of the stable") was a high official in charge of the horses and mounted attendants of the king. As the idea of a princely household evolved in France in the eleventh century, the *conestabularius* and his colleague, the marshal, became the officers who commanded the household guards.[6] The constable usually carried the gonfanon, or banner, at the head of his lord's troops. So Gerald of Wales refers to his ancestor and namesake in 1092, Gerald of Windsor, as the "constable and leader" (*constabularius suus primipilusque*) of the troops of Count Arnulf de Montgomery, and commander of his castle of Pembroke. In the twelfth century, "constable" became the usual title for the commander of a castle garrison.[7] It was the attachment to the command of castles and their tributary districts that appears to have led to the transfer in England of the word "constable" to the officer responsible for law enforcement in administrative districts, such as shires, hundreds, and boroughs.[8] This happened in 1205, when England was threatened with invasion after the fall of Normandy to King Philip Augustus. King John issued a proclamation ordering the appointment of a national network of constables, distinct from the castle constables. Each shire was to have a chief, or high, constable (an office soon annexed to that of sheriff), and within each shire the chief constable was to appoint constables for each hundred, city or lesser borough. Their duties were given as follows: "All the local constables are to obey the chief constables of the shires, and at the chief constables' order (or communally if the chief constables are absent) all the local constables are to appear with their armed levies, and everything they need for the defence of the realm and the keeping of the peace against foreigners or whoever else disturbs the peace."[9]

It seems most likely that the constable of DOCUMENT 39 is a local (hundred) constable, not the high constable of the county (an office that, as has been said, soon disappeared into that of the sheriff), and that his "bailiffs" are village or town officials. They may have been the village constables who are known to have existed in Henry III's reign, and whose duties included police functions,[10] or else possibly the "serjeants of the peace" who began to be appointed in many shires in 1241.[11] It is interesting to note that the constable expects the bailiffs to "hear" his letter rather than to read it for themselves. Presumably it is to be read out to them by the constable's envoy or messenger, who may also translate it for them from Latin into English, or possibly into Anglo-Norman, the dialect of French that was used in many elite households and legal and business circles in England at this time. (For a similar reference to a charter being read aloud, see DOCUMENT 42.)

How often did the hundred constables and their officers have to deal with homicide? Evidence presented by juries to the royal justices touring the counties of England (itinerant justices or "justices in eyre") not infrequently referred to dead bodies found in fields or by the roadside, and suspicious deaths were investigated. For instance, in 1226 or 1227 a mutilated and unidentifiable corpse was found within the bounds of Leighton Buzzard, Bedfordshire. A sixty-year-old charter of Walter Giffard, earl of Buckingham, was found on the body, so the justices in Bedford sent a copy of the charter on to the sessions in neighboring Buckinghamshire to see if anyone there could shed light on the matter.[12] In the plea rolls for Devon for the year 1238, the jurors of the hundred of Axminster reported that, during the previous decade, seven people had been found dead within their bounds, five of whom were unidentifiable vagabonds and strangers. In Devon the hundred juries reported that 144 people had been found dead within the county in the same decade (an average of just over fourteen per year). Twenty-two of the dead were unidentified travelers, the likeliest prey of criminals. Most were vagabonds, but they also included two merchants and a pilgrim, and many were probably victims of violence.[13]

Although the roads of England in the mid-thirteenth century were clearly dangerous for unaccompanied travelers, the case described in DOCUMENT 39 is nonetheless exceptional. The king's direct intervention in the keeping of the peace was not a common event, and its occcurence here implies that matters had gotten seriously out of control. The *vispiliones* (criminals who preyed by night) sound like gang members who were attacking travelers along a main road, perhaps near a bridge crossing, from the reference to bodies being tossed in a river. James Given has estimated that in thirteenth-century England, more than 60 percent of those charged with robbery and murder belonged to gangs of four or more. It was rare that such groups had sufficient organization or leadership to allow them to prey on an area for any length of time, but a situation similar to that described in DOCUMENT 39 occurred in the vicinity of Winchester early in Henry III's reign. Conditions were so bad that they prompted a letter (1218 × 21) by Pandulf, the papal legate, to Peter des Roches, bishop of Winchester: "My lord bishop, the complaints of the poor and of women ought especially to move you, that nobody can travel near Winchester without being held up, robbed, and worst of all—should there not be enough goods on them—people are being killed. Truly, because this sort of thing is a disgrace to the lord king, and to you, and it is going on to the scandal and disorder of the whole kingdom, we ask, advise and firmly instruct your wisdom, as you value the forgiveness of your sins, that you cause this business to be sorted out, so that we hear no further complaints."[14] The reference in Panduf's letter, as in DOCUMENT 39, is plainly to brigandage, although the crime wave at Winchester may have been sparked by aristocratic violence, since he was writing in the turbulent aftermath of the Barons' Wars (1214–17).

NOTES

1 Add. 8617, fol. 98v.

2 *vero* in MS.

3 "*v*" expunged here in MS.

4 In the manuscript, DOCUMENT 39 actually begins *Dilecto amico suo* ("To his beloved friend"). This must be a slip, since, as the heading makes clear, the letter is an order from a constable to his bailiffs.

5 *dilacione* missing in MS but required by the sense of the passage. Similar phrasing can be found in DOCUMENTS 2, 15, and 19.

6 For an overview of the evolution of the princely and noble household, see David Crouch, *The Image of Aristocracy in Britain, 1000–1300* (London: Routledge, 1992), 281–93.

7 [Gerald of Wales,] *Itinerarium Kambriae*, in *Giraldi Cambrensis Opera*, ed. John Sherren Brewer, James Francis Dimock, and George F. Warner, vol. 6, Rolls Series, 21, 8 vols. (London: Longman, 1861–91), 89. For the castle constables of late twelfth-century England, see Richard R. Heiser, "Castles, Constables and Politics in Late Twelfth-Century Governance," *Albion*, 32 (2000), 19–36.

8 Shires or counties were divided into local administrative districts called hundreds; in some counties these were called wapentakes or wards.

9 Gervase of Canterbury, *The Historical Works of Gervase of Canterbury*, ed. William Stubbs, 2 vols., Rolls Series, 73 (London: Longman, 1879–80), 2:97.

10 Helen M. Cam, *The Hundred and the Hundred Rolls* (London: Methuen, 1930), 188–94.

11 Helen M. Jewell, *English Local Administration in the Middle Ages* (Newton Abbot, Devon: David & Charles, and New York: Barnes and Noble, 1972), 166–67.

12 TNA: PRO, JUST 1/2, m. 13.

13 Henry T. Summerson, ed., *Crown Pleas of the Devon Eyre of 1238*, Devon and Cornwall Record Society, new ser., 28 (1985), for Axminster hundred, pp. 9–13. As some loose comparison with modern times, the Devon and Cornwall constabulary recorded thirteen homicides for both counties in the year May 2005 to April 2006, http://www.crimestatistics.org.uk. The statistics on homicide in James Given's *Society and Homicide in Thirteenth-Century England* (Stanford, Calif. Stanford University Press, 1977), unfortunately, are marred by problematic assumptions, methodologies, and data. See, e.g., the reviews of Given's book by Edwin B. DeWindt in *Canadian Journal of History*, 13:2 (1978), 248–52; by John S. Beckerman in *American Journal of Legal History*, 22:3 (July 1978), 254–56; and by Thomas A. Green in *Speculum*, 54, no.1 (January 1979), 137–40.

14 Shirley, ed., *Letters*, 1:167.

40

The King Orders a Sheriff to Find and Hang the Thieves Who Have Been Burgling Village Homes by Night[1]

Rex vicecomiti ut faciat inquiri qui sunt vispiliones nocturno tempore villis vicinis malo[2] invadentes

> Rex vicecomiti salutem. Conquesti sunt nobis homines de B. predones in partibus illis nocturno tempore habitantes villis vicinis invadunt. Habitantes ville ligant et vero[3] occidunt illos, omnia asportantes que inveniunt. Quare tibi precipimus ut nemora vicinia cum manu armata abcidas et secretos[4] recessus inquiri facias, donec vispiliones prefatos invenieris, quos inventos suspendi committas. Scias pro vero si hoc pigre facias te pro eis affligemus. Vale.

The king [writes] to a sheriff that he should have an inquiry made as to who are the criminals attacking neighboring villages at night

> The king to a sheriff, greetings. The inhabitants of B. have complained to us that robbers in their district are attacking by night people living in surrounding villages. They tie up the villagers and even kill them, carrying off everything they find. Therefore, we order you to comb the surrounding woodlands with an armed band and cause a search to be made for hiding places until you discover the said evildoers, whom, when they are found, you should sentence to be hanged. You should know for a fact that if you take your time about this, we will punish you severely in their place. Farewell.

This royal writ provides an abundance of information about crime and law enforcement in thirteenth-century England. The robbers in Document 40 are preying on the villages around B. from their hideout in nearby woodlands. The forest was a place of resort for all sorts of marginal characters in medieval society. Hermits were drawn to woodlands, and sometimes their cells became the core of later monastic communities, such as Luffield in Northamptonshire.[5] But more famous marginal characters in forests were outlaws and dissidents, including Fulk fitz Warin, a notorious Marcher baron in the reigns of Richard the Lionheart and John. Fulk's family had a claim to the lordship of Whittington in Shropshire, and his father had made a serious bid to recover it. In 1200, Fulk's own attempt to secure it was passed over by King John in favor of Fulk's rival, Meurig son of Roger of Powys, a member of an important Welsh-Norman dynasty. Fulk murdered Meurig in early 1200 and was outlawed. He was not pardoned until 1203, and in the interval, according to the verse romance later written about him, Fulk and his gang survived by their wits in forests and the wild.[6] It is possible to see the antecedents of the Robin Hood stories in such incidents, though the legendary outlaw was not a dispossessed aristocrat, but came from the rural freeholder class.[7]

The woodland dwellers in DOCUMENT 40 were marginal characters of a different sort. They were members of a criminal gang who lived on the edges of the cultivated land and preyed on local peasants. There is nothing fictional about such groups. The justice rolls of the thirteenth century reveal that much crime was gang-related and focused on housebreaking, during which assaults and even murders frequently occurred. Most gangs numbered four or more. Some operated out of towns, where they might sell their stolen goods. In 1267, in a case very similar to that described in this writ, bandits arrived at dusk in the hamlet of Honeydon, Bedfordshire, and broke into the houses, wounding and killing the householders and carrying off their goods. Then they moved on to the neighboring village of Goodwick, eventually escaping when the hue (the alarm by shouts and horns) was raised against them.[8]

As noted in DOCUMENT 39, it was not common for the king to intervene personally in local peacekeeping matters. The fact that the residents of B. have complained directly to him suggests that they have previously complained to their county sheriff but have been ignored. This would explain the king's very harsh threat of retribution against the sheriff himself if he does not act promptly.

For the sufferings of a victim of the outrages described in DOCUMENT 40 and the response of his neighbor, see DOCUMENTS 91 and 92.

NOTES

1 Add. 8167, fol. 108r.

2 Corrected in MS from *maleo*.

3 In the MS, this word is rendered as an "n" with a bar over it, which is usually an abbreviation for "*non*." This is probably a mistake for "*vero*," for which the abbreviation looks similar. The same error occurs in DOCUMENT 69.

4 Corrected in MS from *secretas*.

5 For example, between 1118 and 1120, Robert II, the earl of Leicester, then in his teens, "granted in alms to Mauger the monk, the servant of God, a small clearing . . . for building huts and a chapel there." Gerald Ranking Elvey, ed., *Luffield Priory Charters*, vol. 1, Northamptonshire Record Society, 22, 26 (Northampton, 1968–75), 15.

6 Ernest Jackson Hathaway et al., eds., *Fouke le Fitz Waryn*, Anglo-Norman Text Society, 26–28 (London, 1968–70), xiii–xv, xxvii–xxxiv.

7 James C. Holt, *Robin Hood* (London: Thames & Hudson, 1989), 62–65.

8 Given, *Society and Homicide*, 113–20.

41

The Sheriff Informs the King of the Result
of His Pursuit of the Robbers[1]

Responsum ad preceptum quid fecerit

Regi vicecomes salutem. Iniunxit michi vestra excellencia ut ego cum armata manu nemora proxima illius loci in[vest]igarem[2] et latrones[3] ibidem habitantes extrahere.[4] Preceptum illud pro posse meo exsecutus sum; silvas predictas investigavi interius. Custodi vero reliqui aliquem angulum intactum[5] donec latrones inveni et inventos ligavi et incarceravi et in tanto artu tenui illos ut ego coegi duos socios [?revelare][6] qui ab illis [electi][7] sunt ducere. Cognitis autem nominibus et locis unde essent [?homines meos][8] ad eos misi oculte et eos capi feci et cum aliis sociis incarceravi. Vos autem significetis inde michi voluntatem vestram.

The reply the sheriff made to the writ

To the king, the sheriff [sends] greetings. Your Excellency commanded me to comb the woods near such-and-such a place with an armed band and to flush out the robbers living there. I have carried out your order to the best of my ability; I have combed the woodlands closely. I left any untouched corner under guard until I found the villains, and those who were found I bound and imprisoned, and I kept them in such close confinement that I forced two of their fellows [?to reveal] who were the ones chosen by the others to lead. As soon as I learned their names and the places where they are from, I sent [?my men] secretly to them and I had them taken and imprisoned with their other associates. So inform me of your wishes concerning them.

This document provides a fascinating insight into the operations of law officers in thirteenth-century England. Here a sheriff, in what reads like a response to the writ in DOCUMENT 40, writes to the king to announce his success in rounding up a gang of criminals near "such-and-such a place" (presumably the village or town of "B." mentioned in DOCUMENT 40). The sheriff, perhaps goaded by the king's threat in DOCUMENT 40 to punish him if he fails to act promptly, reports that he searched the robbers' woodland hideout and staked out remote corners until he captured and locked up the gang. He then compelled two of the prisoners to divulge the identities of the gang's chosen leaders, who evidently were living elsewhere and were not captured in the forest with the rest. As soon as the sheriff learned the leaders' names and where they could be found, he sent his men secretly (presumably so as not to alert the leaders) to arrest them. Now that he has the whole lot in custody, he asks the king for instructions as to what to do with them.

NOTES

1   Add. 8167, fol. 108v.
2   *indigarem* in MS.
3   *latrone* in MS.
4   *extraere* in MS.
5   *intacitum* in MS.
6   Some such word as *revelare* ("to reveal") appears to be missing here.
7   *elegati* in MS.
8   The sense of this passage seems to require *homines meos* ("my men") or something similar here.

42

A Landowner in the King's Service Complains to a Sheriff that His Men Are Being Harassed by the Sheriff's Officers for Suit of County and Hundred Despite His Exemption[1]

Karissimo amico suo. G. de B., R. salutem et amicicias. Bene scitis quod sum[2] in servicio domini regis et[3] quod omnes mei res possessiones et terre mee sunt in eius proteccione. Et ideo multum admiror quod homines meos iniuste[4] vexatis, et a servientibus et ballivis vestris vexari permittaris, pro secta comitatus et hundredi quam, sicut [bene][5] scitis,[6] non debeo, quia cartam libertatum mearum sepius audistis. H[oc][7] est quod vos requiro: quatinus a vexacione hominum meorum desistatis et servientes vestros desisse faciatis, ne opporteat me querelam facere domino regi de iniuria michi illata [dum in eius sum servicio. Valete.][8]

To his dearest friend G. de B., R. [sends] greetings and friendly salutations. You know well that I am in the lord king's service, and that all my goods and lands are in his protection. And so I am very much surprised that you are unlawfully troubling my men, and are allowing them to be harassed by your serjeants and bailiffs for suit of county and hundred, which, as you well know, I do not owe, because you have often heard the charters of my exemptions. This is what I request of you: that you cease troubling my men and cause your servants to do the same, so that

I do not have to complain to the lord king of any injury done me while I am in his service. Farewell.

"R.," the man of property who is the sender of the letter above, is away from home in the king's service. He may be attached to the royal household, as in DOCUMENTS 77 and 100, or he may be serving on a legal commission or a military or diplomatic mission, as perhaps was the case in DOCUMENT 75. In any case, R. is exempt during his period of service from his ordinary obligation to attend the meetings of the county and hundred courts.

Every county had a court that met regularly, commonly once a month. County courts were mainly courts of law that dealt with civil matters, including pleas of land, debt, and trespass, but they shared with the folkmoot court of London a unique jurisdiction over outlawry. From the reign of Henry I (1100–1135) onward, they also became increasingly important in criminal jurisdiction, since they played host to touring commissions of royal justices (justices in eyre). Each county was divided into smaller administrative districts called hundreds,[9] many of them in private hands, and each hundred also had its own court, which generally met once every four weeks. The hundred courts handled only civil (non-criminal) cases, and did not hold pleas of land; they dealt mostly with actions of debt and trespass. The county court was presided over by the sheriff; the court of a hundred in private jurisdiction was presided over by the lord's steward; and the court of a hundred in the king's jurisdiction was presided over by the bailiff to whom the sheriff had let the hundred to farm.[10] Attendance at ("suit to") these courts was among the burdens attached to the tenure of freehold land, and fixed obligations to attend were assigned to individual holdings ("tenements"). The suitors (that is, the more substantial local landholders), not the presiding officers, made the judgments at these courts.[11]

In the letter above, "G. de B.," the recipient, is evidently the sheriff.[12] His officers have been harassing the men of the writer, "R.," for suit at the county court and hundred court. The sheriff's officers are harassing R.'s men because suitors who were away from home could be represented at both courts by their steward or, if the steward was also unavailable, by the reeve, priest, and four men of each village held by the suitor.[13] R., however, has written proof of his exemption from attending these courts in the form of a charter of his exemptions or "liberties" (cartam libertatum mearum). In fact, R. rather sarcastically points out, the sheriff himself has often heard this charter read out (sepius audistis), quite possibly at the very county court at which R.'s presence is being demanded.[14] Now R. wants the harassment of his men to stop. If it doesn't, he warns, he will complain to the king.

There had long been a consensus that the possessions of men who were away from home in the king's service should be safe from molestation. In 1086, for example, the jurors for Buckinghamshire made a point of complaining to the Domesday commissioners that Bertram de Verdun's neighbors had committed some form of trespass upon his manor of Farnham Royal while he was overseas on the king's business.[15] The first written protections for the lands of men overseas on the king's service date from much later, however. One of the earliest is this example from 1199:

> G[eoffrey] fitz Peter earl of Essex [the king's justiciar] greets the lord king's justices at Westminster. We have received a writ from the king as follows: "The king etc. greets his beloved and faithful G[eoffrey] fitz Peter earl of Essex. We instruct you that you safeguard and protect the lands [and] goods of our beloved John de Lascelles while he is abroad on our service with horse and arms. You should not allow him in the meantime to be subject to any lawsuit or be troubled in any way." Therefore we instruct you that the king's writ be followed to the letter. Witness: Master R. of Stoke. Lincoln, 6 September [1199].[16]

Pleas before the king's justices on the grounds that their protections while on the king's business have been ignored are very common in the judicial sources after 1200. Sometimes such protections could be exploited unreasonably by those who had them. John de Lascelles, for example, managed to delay a pressing lawsuit for eight years after the date of the above writ in his favor.

In DOCUMENT 42, R.'s threat to complain to the king if the sheriff does not call off his men was a serious matter, since the sheriff held his office at the king's pleasure.[17] R.'s resentment of the sheriff's unreasonable insistence on his attendance at the local courts was widely shared, and was among the baronial grievances that eventually found their vent in the Provisions of Oxford in 1258.[18]

NOTES

1   Add. 8167, fol. 126r–v.
2   *cum* in MS.
3   *et* inserted above line.
4   Fol. 126v commences here.
5   *un[de]* in MS.
6   *sitis* in MS.
7   *hinc* in MS.
8   The words in square brackets were added at the end of the text in a different hand.

9   Or, in some counties, wapentakes or wards.
10   That is, the sheriff had entrusted the administration of the hundred to the bailiff in return for a fixed annual rent.
11   Sir Frederick Pollock, Bart., and Frederic William Maitland, *The History of English Law Before the Time of Edward I*, 2 vols., 2nd ed. (Cambridge: Cambridge University Press, 1898), 1:538–43, 547–58; and Paul Brand, *The Origins of the English Legal Profession* (Oxford: Blackwell, 1992), 6 and 163, n. 35.
12   The initials "G. de B." seem unusually specific for a generic model letter. In the late twelfth to mid-thirteenth centuries, members of the Beauchamp family, who were hereditary sheriffs of Worcestershire throughout this period, included men named William ("Guillaume" or "Guillelmus") and Walter ("Gautier" or "Gualterus"). A. Hughes, *List of Sheriffs for England and Wales from the Earliest Times to A.D. 1831*, Public Record Office, London, Lists and Indexes, 9 (1898; rpt. with additions, New York: Kraus Reprint, 1963), 157.
13   Brand, *Origins of the English Legal Profession*, 6–7.
14   William Alfred Morris, *The Medieval English Sheriff to 1300* (Manchester: Manchester University Press, 1927), 218. For another reference to the reading aloud of documents, see DOCUMENT 39.
15   *Domesday Book* i, fol. 151v.
16   Doris Mary Stenton, ed., *Pleas Before the King or His Justices, 1198–1202*, vol. 1, Selden Society, 67, 68, 83, 84 (London, 1948–67), 411–12.
17   Morris, *Medieval English Sheriff*, 143–44. The potentially grave consequences of such a complaint can be seen in other documents in this volume, such as DOCUMENTS 27 and 40.
18   Morris, *Medieval English Sheriff*, 169–70.

--- 43 ---

A Man Asks a Sheriff to Release Goods Seized for an Unpaid Fine Owed to the King[1]

Karissimo[2] et cetera, et quicquid potest honoris et servicii. Scias quod C. serviens hundredi cepit nameam ea q[ue][3] fine, quam debeo domino regi, nec vult[4] ea dimittere per vadium et plegium. Et vos requiro, quatinus si placet nameam meam michi dimittatis, et ego manu capio adquietare vos ad scakarium, in crastino sancti Michaelis, ita quod non eritis in aliquo perdens pro defalta mea. Valete.

To his dearest [friend], etc., and whatever can be of honor and service. You ought to know that C., the serjeant of the hundred, took naam for the fine that I owe to the lord king, and does not wish to release it in exchange for a pledge and surety. I request of you, if it please you, that you release my naam to me, and I undertake to acquit you at the Exchequer on the day after Michaelmas [September 30], so you will not be losing in any way for my default. Farewell.

"Naam" was property—valuables, livestock, or other goods—that was confiscated in order to put pressure on a defaulter to carry out an unperformed duty or service. In the case above, the naam was taken by a sheriff's officer to force the payment to the king of an unpaid fine.

Naam was taken in a forcible act called "distraint" (*districtio*). The naam could be redeemed for a pledge offered by its owner or by a third party, until the whole business was settled in court. The word comes from a family of Germanic words, such as Old English *niman* or the German *nehmen*, meaning "to take." Originally perhaps the taking of naam was a violent and intimidatory act, an eye for an eye. But by the 1110s, when it was mentioned in an English legal tract called "The Laws of Henry I," it was a more formalized process. The right to take naam was monitored. It had to be done by the license of a court. However, the naam was not the property of the lord or officer who seized it, or of the court. Rather, it was held only until a pledge was offered that the offender would perform the required duty or answer the case in court.[5]

The writer of this letter is caught up in just such a process. He has had naam taken from him by "C.," the serjeant of the hundred (the local unit of county administration), who has refused to release it in return for a pledge. Now the owner is writing, evidently to the sheriff (whom, like the writer of DOCUMENT 42, he addresses as his "dearest friend"), to request the release of the naam. He promises to indemnify the sheriff, who is the king's administrative officer in charge of the county, at the royal Exchequer at Westminster on September 30, when the sheriff would be required to present his accounts for their annual audit.

The taking of naam was much resented because of the potential for violence and intimidation in the process; it was almost licensed brigandry, and sometimes it was resisted by force. In 1255, for example, some royal foresters attempted to take naam in the form of livestock from the residents of two Northamptonshire villages, who had refused to appear before a royal inquest into alleged depredations on the forests of Rockingham and Saucey. The villagers swore an oath of confederation, posted lookouts on top of church towers and windmills, and attacked the king's officers and seized their arms when they tried to enter the manors.[6]

There were attempts by some landowners to get exemptions from the taking of naam in case they got into trouble over payments. Bruern Abbey, a Cistercian house in western Oxfordshire, is a case in point. It held an estate in the Cotswold Hills at Sezincote in Gloucestershire, from the Beauchamp family, hereditary sheriffs of Worcestershire, in return for knight service. This burdened it with dues for which the monks could be fined for non-payment:

compulsory attendance ("suit") at the Beauchamp seigneurial court in distant Worcestershire; castle guard at the Beauchamp castle of Elmley in Worcestershire; and a whole range of minor forms of taxation, called "feudal incidents" by legal historians. Luckily for the abbey, at some time, perhaps in the 1240s, William de Beauchamp was persuaded to relinquish all such claims on the estate except for scutage (a money payment in lieu of military service), and also to allow "that neither I nor my heirs will take any naam from the monks for any failure to pay up on what they owe . . . except for any rent due."[7] The letter above exemplifies the difficulties into which landholders could fall if they were not shielded by such an exemption.

NOTES

1 Add. 8617, fol. 126v.
2 *H'mo* in MS.
3 *quod* in MS.
4 *wlt* in MS.
5 Pollock and Maitland, *History of English Law*, vol. 2, 574–77.
6 *Calendar of Inquisitions Miscellaneous Preserved in the Public Record Office*, 8 vols. (London: H. M. Stationery Office, 1916–2003), 1:71–72.
7 Emma Mason, ed., *The Beauchamp Cartulary*, Pipe Roll Society, new ser., 44 (London, 1980), 49.

44

A Man Asks a Friend to Come to London with Him to Act for Him in a Canon Law Suit[1]

Amicus amico mandat ut veniat London' placiturus pro se

Karissimo amico suo A., B. si placet salutem et se totum.[2] Vobis mando et diligenter exoro, quatinus pro amore et servicio mei, ven[i]atis[3] mecum London' acturus pro me (*vel placiturus*)[4] contra adversarium meum. Sciatis pro vero quod ipse novas literas impetravit a domino papa. Quare tantum faciatis ut facundia vestra cornu eius obrumpat et [aspir]acionem[5] eius confundat. Valete.

A man asks his friend to come to London to plead [a case] for him

To his dearest friend A., B. (if it please) [sends] greetings and his entire self. I charge you and earnestly implore that, for the sake of my love and service, you come to London with me to act for me (*or plead for me*) against my adversary. You should know for a fact that he has obtained a new letter from the lord pope. So take good care that your eloquence may overwhelm his courage and confound his hopes. Farewell.

The reference to the pope in this otherwise generic letter suggests that it concerns a forthcoming case in an ecclesiastical rather than a secular court. The church in medieval England had its own judicial system, and this reflected the church's general administrative organization.

For ecclesiastical purposes, the country was divided administratively into two large provinces (archbishoprics), headed respectively by the archbishop of Canterbury and the archbishop of York. Both provinces were divided into dioceses (bishoprics), each of which was headed by a bishop. Dioceses in turn were divided into archdeaconries, each headed by an archdeacon; archdeaconries were divided into deaneries, each headed by a dean; and deaneries were divided into parishes, each headed by a vicar or rector. Although there were local exceptions and variations to this arrangement, there were thus five main administrative levels in diocesan administration. The parish clergy reported to their local dean, the deans to their archdeacon, the archdeacons to their local bishop, and the bishops of each province to their archbishop. The geographical divisions of ecclesiastical administration were based in part on the secular administrative divisions of the country: generally, a bishopric corresponded to one or more counties, an archdeaconry to a single county, and a deanery to a hundred.[6]

The medieval church claimed jurisdiction over its own clergy and property, and also over certain church-related matters that affected the laity, such as matrimony (since marriage was one of the seven sacraments), the probate of testaments (which often concerned not only matrimonial issues and legitimacy, but also deathbed decisions and pious legacies), heresy, and defamation.[7] Cases could be initiated either by clerics or laypeople,[8] and courts were held regularly by archdeacons, bishops,[9] and archbishops, or by their deputies (known as "officials"). Generally speaking, low-level judicial matters that concerned a single archdeaconry were handled in the local archdeacon's court; cases that concerned more than one archdeaconry within a single diocese were handled by the bishop's consistory court; and cases affecting more than one diocese were handled in the archbishop's provincial court. As with the royal courts, cases that began in local ecclesiastical courts might be transferred to higher courts, and in some cases, where there was no satisfactory resolution, an appeal might be made to Rome. Important plaintiffs might also take their cases directly to the papal court.[10] Oxford itself, where the formulary containing this letter evidently was written, had been a center of ecclesiastical courts since the 1170s.[11]

In the letter, the case in question was to be heard in London. Its venue might thus have been the archdeaconry, episcopal, or archiepiscopal court, but the allusion to a papal letter makes it much more likely that the case was to be heard before a panel of three judges delegate, that is, local judges who were appointed by the pope to hear suits that had been appealed to papal jurisdiction.[12] Such cases were heard in various venues in England; in London, they were heard on at least seven occasions between 1206 and 1254, most commonly in St Paul's Cathedral.[13]

A plaintiff wishing to open a suit before papal judges delegate first had to obtain a mandate from the pope, and this is probably the "new letter from the lord pope" that in this document the writer's unnamed adversary has obtained (*impetravit*). A mandate was based on the plaintiff's written "impetration" (application), which was submitted to the papal Curia. The impetration was then read at a public sitting of the papal Chancery, at which time the defendant could lodge an objection to it through a proctor, if he had one. However, not all defendants retained a proctor in Rome, and many impetrations must have been read unchallenged. The plaintiff's impetration specified the local judges to whom the plaintiff wished the case to be delegated, and since the venue for the case was largely based on the judges' convenience, this gave the plaintiff the double advantage of being able to name the judges and, indirectly, the venue.[14]

In this letter, the writer asks his "dearest friend" to come with him to London to "act" or "plead" for him against his adversary. It sounds as though the writer has received a peremptory (final) summons, and he must now appear before the judges delegate or risk excommunication, imprisonment, and the loss of his case through default.[15] The "friend" whose assistance he is requesting may indeed be a personal friend, but it is more likely that the writer wishes to employ him as either his advocate (lawyer) or his proctor to represent him in court.

Canon lawyers had been serving as paid advocates and experts in ecclesiastical courts in England since at least the mid-twelfth century, well before the appearance of professional lawyers in the common law courts,[16] and canon law was taught at English as well as Continental schools and, by the early years of the thirteenth century, universities. Advocates were trained in canon (ecclesiastical) law and could offer expert advice and written opinions to clients, but their main function was to plead cases in court—that is (in the words of an early procedural manual), to "set out one's claim or that of one's friend in court . . . or to oppose the claim of another."[17]

Proctors, who served as litigants' representatives and agents rather than as their professional counsel, did not necessarily have any formal legal training.

Unlike advocates, proctors could act only in civil suits, and could take oaths on behalf of their principals. Proctors advised clients on the choice of advocates, and might also hire the advocate, negotiate his fee, and instruct him in the client's wishes. They also navigated cases through the court system, saw to the collection and copying of required documents, organized the appearance of witnesses, and paid all necessary fees on the client's behalf. Until it was forbidden in 1237, proctors were often, it seems, employed on a day-by-day basis. By mid-century, however, they were becoming increasingly professionalized, and their skills at case-management made them essential to litigants.[18]

In this letter, the writer's wish to have the recipient "plead" for him and the reference to the latter's "eloquence" suggest that the writer wishes the recipient to act as his advocate rather than as his proctor. For other requests for legal assistance, see DOCUMENTS 45 and 46.

NOTES

1   Add. 8167, fol. 98v.
2   *setotum* in MS. For other examples of this expression, see INTRODUCTION, p. 16.
3   *veneratis* in MS.
4   The italicized phrase in parentheses represents a variant included in the text. Similar variant phrasings can be seen in DOCUMENTS 5, 24, 32, 46, 47, and 62.
5   In the manuscript this word is given as *desperacionem* ("hopelessness" or "despair"), which does not fit the context.
6   On diocesan organization and administration, see Robert E. Rodes, Jr., *Ecclesiastical Administration in Medieval England, the Anglo-Saxons to the Reformation* (London: Notre Dame University Press, 1977), 100–107. On the administrative divisions of English counties, see DOCUMENT 42.
7   See, e.g., Jane E. Sayers, *Papal Judges Delegate in the Province of Canterbury, 1198–1254: A Study in Ecclesiastical Jurisdiction and Administration* (London: Oxford University Press, 1971), 166–68, 204–12.
8   Sayers, *Papal Judges Delegate*, xxii–xxv.
9   Including suffragan bishops, who deputized for the diocesan bishop.
10 Sayers, *Papal Judges Delegate*, xxii–xxv, 2–8, 219. For additional discussion of ecclesiastical courts, see DOCUMENT 54.
11 Leonard E. Boyle, O.P., "Canon Law Before 1380," in *The History of the University of Oxford*, vol. 1, *The Early Oxford Schools*, ed. Jeremy I. Catto (Oxford: Clarendon, 1984), 533.
12 Those appointed as judges delegate were often bishops and their officials, archdeacons, rural deans, senior cathedral clergy, abbots and priors, senior Augustinian canons, and masters of law. There were provisions for providing alternate judges if the original appointees were unwilling or unable to serve. Sayers, *Papal Judges Delegate*, 109–33, 135–43.
13 Sayers, *Papal Judges Delegate*, 59–60, 290–91.
14 Sayers, *Papal Judges Delegate*, 54–63, 109–17, 161–62. Many of the litigants were religious houses and, according to Sayers (p. 215), "Most of the larger religious communities employed standing proctors at Rome."

15 On summonses and procedures of the court, see Sayers, *Papal Judges Delegate*, 70–99, 150–61.

16 For example, when Richard of Anstey went to law in 1158 against his cousin, Mabel de Francheville, to obtain her inheritance on the grounds that she was illegitimate, a case that took five years to conclude, his expenses included payments to two Italian canon lawyers who had assisted him in the English ecclesiastical courts. See Paul Brand, *The Origins of the English Legal Profession* (Oxford: Blackwell, 1992), 1–2.

17 On the study of canon law at Oxford, see INTRODUCTION, pp. 12–13; see also Leonard E. Boyle, O.P., "Canon Law Before 1380," 531–64. On the study and practice of canon law on the Continent as well as in England in the later twelfth and early thirteenth centuries, see James A. Brundage, *The Profession and Practice of Medieval Canon Law* (Aldershot, Hampshire: Ashgate, 2004); and idem, *The Medieval Origins of the Legal Profession: Canonists, Civilians, and Courts* (Chicago: University of Chicago Press, 2008), 222–48, 344–53 (definition of "to plead," 351). For English masters at Bologna in the late twelfth and early thirteenth centuries, see Sayers, *Papal Judges Delegate*, 38.

18 Sayers, *Papal Judges Delegate*, 221–38; Brundage, *Medieval Origins of the Legal Profession*, 353–64.

45

A Letter to a Friend Requesting Legal Assistance on Another's Behalf[1]

Litere petentes pro aliquo ut sibi adiuvet in causa sua

Karissimo amico suo A., B. salutem. Pro G. latore presencium vobis preces effundo[2] huberimas [*sic*], petens attencius[3] quatinus, pro amore meo[4] et servicio mei, illum adiuvetis in causam contra S. Sciturus quod si ille laborem vestrum non sufficit remunerare, ego pro ea supplebo vices remunerandi, et quod ipse minus egerit ego pro posse mea in omnibus vobis satisfaciam. Et ideo tantum faciatis pro eo ut in redditu meo grates vobis debeam persolvere. Valete.

Letter seeking legal assistance on behalf of another

To his dearest friend A., B. sends greetings. I pour out the richest prayers for G., the bearer of this letter, asking earnestly that, for the sake of my love and service, you aid him in his case against S. You will know that, if he does not sufficiently repay you for your labor, I shall make up the difference, and what he shall be less able to do I shall make good to you in all respects, to the best of my ability. And therefore, act in this in such a way toward him that I may owe you my thanks along with my reimbursement. Farewell.

Here, as in Documents 44 and 46, a man writes to ask for legal assistance, this time on a friend's behalf rather than his own. The nature of the case and its venue are not identified, but the lack of any ecclesiastical references suggests that it was a matter of common law rather than canon law. Although the writer salutes the recipient as his "dearest friend" and addresses him in the respectful plural (*vos*), his desire that the latter provide the requested assistance "for the sake of my love and service" (a phrase that also appears in Documents 10, 44 and 46), and his wish that the addressee will act in such a way that he will deserve the writer's gratitude (similar expressions also appear in Documents 5 and 18), make it clear that the addressee was subordinate in rank to the writer. The addressee's apparent legal expertise, and the fact that he was to be paid for his labor, suggest that he was a professional lawyer.

The study and practice of common law were stimulated in England by the establishment of the national courts of the General Eyre, Exchequer, and Common Bench under Henry II (1154–89), and of King's Bench under his grandson Henry III, in or a little before 1234.[5] By the 1240s, when the formulary that includes this document was compiled, there were two types of common lawyer in England: attorneys and serjeants. Attorneys, who appeared in court in place of one of the parties to a case, first occur in the second half of the twelfth century (see Document 46). In the reign of John (1199–1216) at least some attorneys were acting in a "proto-professional" fashion, using their special expertise (in some cases, perhaps gained from holding office in the courts or the Exchequer) to attract clients and receiving fees for their work, though not necessarily enough to support them in full. By the 1240s, a litigant could choose as his attorney someone who represented clients for a fee, but he could also, as in earlier days, simply choose a relative, friend, or servant to represent him. An attorney was formally empowered to act in place of his principal, and his representation could not subsequently be disavowed.[6]

Serjeants, in contrast, were skilled "pleaders" or litigators who were expert in the ever-changing intricacies of the common law. They spoke on behalf of their clients but, unlike the attorneys, were not formally empowered to do so, and thus their representation could be disavowed by their principals. Although there is one case of a "pleader" appearing in the king's court in the late 1150s, the first clear example of a serjeant speaking in court on a defendant's behalf dates from 1207.[7] By the later 1220s to early 1230s, when much of the legal treatise known as *Bracton* was composed,[8] the use of professional serjeants to represent litigants in the Common Bench appears to have become usual, though not universal. By 1239 a small number of identifiable serjeants regularly practiced in the Common Bench and were, to all appearances, a genuinely professional group. In the other royal courts, non-professional serjeants were common until after the middle of the century. However, in 1247 the king began to employ a lawyer, Lawrence del Brok, to represent him both as an attorney and, evidently, as a serjeant in the court of King's Bench as well as in the Common Bench, and in the same year at least three Common Bench serjeants also appeared at the Buckinghamshire eyre, presumably to represent clients. The earliest known deed of retainer of a Common Bench serjeant, however, probably dates from the time of the Essex eyre in 1262.[9]

In DOCUMENT 45 above it is unclear whether the writer is hoping to engage the services of an attorney or of a serjeant. This vagueness may be deliberate, intended to make a single model letter serve for either purpose. However, the letter's very presence in this formulary, together with that of DOCUMENTS 44 and 46, supports the evidence discussed above that the retention of paid legal representation was routine in at least some of the royal and ecclesiastical courts by the late 1240s.

NOTES

1   Add. 8167, fol. 99r–v.
2   Corrected in MS from *effeundo.*
3   Corrected in MS from *atthencius.*
4   Fol. 99v commences here.
5   In the General Eyre, the country was divided into judicial circuits and panels of royal justices traveled the circuits to hold courts. The courts of Exchequer and Common Bench normally sat at Westminster, and the court of King's Bench followed the king wherever he was in England. Brand, *Origins of the English Legal Profession*, 2–3, 14–25, 32.
6   Brand, *Origins of the English Legal Profession*, 43–46, 50–54.
7   The term *serviens* ("serjeant") did not come into use for this kind of practitioner until the second half of the thirteenth century. In the first half of the century the term used was *narrator* or *advocatus*, or possibly, in some cases, *placitator* or *causidicus*. Brand, *Origins of the English Legal Profession*, 46–49.
8   On the date of *Bracton*, see Paul Brand, "The Age of Bracton," in *The History of English Law: Centenary Essays on "Pollock and Maitland,"* ed. John Hudson, Proceedings of the British Academy, 89 (Oxford: Oxford University Press, for the British Academy, 1996), 65–89 (especially 75).
9   Brand, *Origins of the English Legal Profession*, 54–65.

46

A Man Asks a Friend for the Services of His Attorney to Appear in His Place at the Royal Court[1]

[B.] mandat [A.][2] ut commodat sibi legatum suum ad legandum in loco suo

Dilecto amico suo A., B. salutem. De dileccione vestra quamplurimum confisus, humilime peticionem effundo, petens attencius quatinus pro amore meo et servicio mei michi acomodetis G., legatum vestrum, quem possum mittere in loco meo ad me excusatum (*vel essoniandum*)[3] in curia domini regis, siquis me vocaverit ante iusticiarium. Scituri quod summonicionem semel habui ut coram rege vel eius iusticiario comparerem, responsurus[4] A. [*sic*] de una hyda terre quam teneo iure hered-[it]areo,[5] set predictus A. dedit domino regi intelligendum quod pater meus predictam hydam ei iniuste detenuit (*sive deforciavit*).[6] Quapropter tantum faciatis ad presens ut G., qui prudens est in sermone, prof[ic]-iscatur[7] ad curiam et ibi me assoniare coram iusticiarium si aliquis versum me loqui voluerit. Valete.

[B.] sends word to [A.] to lend him his attorney to represent him

B. to his beloved friend A., greetings. Having complete trust in your love, I humbly pour forth a request, asking earnestly that for the sake of my love and service you lend me G., your attorney, whom I can send in my place to get me excused (*or essoined*) in the lord king's court, if anyone should call me before the justiciar. You will know that I have had my first summons to appear before the king or his justiciar to reply to A. [*sic*] concerning a hide of land that I hold by hereditary right, but the said A. gave the lord king to understand that my father unjustly withheld the said hide from him (*or deprived him of it*). Therefore, I hope that you will ensure that G., who is an excellent speaker, may go to the court and there make my excuses before the justiciar if anyone should wish to make a case against me. Farewell.

In DOCUMENT 45 the writer is apparently hoping to engage the services of a lawyer—either an attorney or a serjeant—to represent a third party in a forthcoming case. In DOCUMENT 46, however, it is evidently an attorney (*legatus*) whose services are sought.

The important legal treatise *Glanvill* (*c.* 1180) mentions people called "repliers" (*responsales*) who were appointed by one of the parties in a case to act in their place in court. A generation later the word "attorney" (*attornatus*), which derived from the French word for "deputize," became the standard term for such a representative.[8] The word *legatus*, used for "attorney" in the letter above, is not used at all in legal sources. It is a literary Latin word that recalls the legates or envoys of emperors and popes who were sent to transact high-level negotiations in their master's name.

The writer of DOCUMENT 46 is seeking the services of a skilled attorney to "essoin" him (make his excuses) for his non-attendance in court. Essoining is first mentioned in 1170 in a proclamation of King Henry II that stressed that essoiners were liable for arrest if they failed to provide pledges for their principals' eventual appearance, or if their principals failed to appear when required.[9] *Glanvill* considered at length the issue of delays and excuses in law cases, so it was plainly already a major problem by 1180. According to *Glanvill*, there were legitimate excuses for failing to respond to the king's summons, and illness was one of them. If such an excuse reached the court, it had to be accompanied by a "pledge"—that is, the name of a man willing to present the excuse and swear to its truth. If the argument was accepted, then three successive postponements might be allowed, if the excuses were appropriately presented. By the fourth summons the defendant had to appear either himself or by means of an attorney, who had "power to win and lose." Other forms of essoin mentioned by *Glanvill* include service overseas or service on the king's behalf.[10]

There is a lot at stake in this letter. The property over which B. is being sued was a hide in extent. Before the Conquest, estates in England were assessed for taxation purposes in hides. The origins of the "hide" are ancient and wrapped up in mystery, but it probably represented a piece of land sufficient to maintain a freeman's household. Originally the assessment may have represented a particular amount of land, but by the time of *Domesday Book* the hide could not be defined by any standard measurement; it is best seen as a unit of tax value.[11] However, the word continued to be used throughout the twelfth century as a description of the value of an estate, and the hide remained a unit of the assessment of the old Anglo-Saxon tax known as geld until its abandonment by King Henry II in 1162.[12] The point of its use here is that it evoked the idea of an estate of moderate but not insignificant value.

The nature of the legal process alluded to in this letter is as follows. B.'s hereditary right to the land has been challenged by his adversary on the grounds that B.'s father had denied the litigant's right to it. A writ of *novel disseisin* ("recent dispossession") has been obtained from the king, which directed that the arguments of both sides should be heard and the nature of the right to the land should be investigated through a jury of local knights, or "grand assize." The reference in this letter to the "king or his justiciar" hearing the case indicates that the case is to be heard in one of two royal courts: Common Bench, which sat principally at Westminster, or King's Bench, which followed the king wherever he was in England. (For these courts, see Document 45.)

The process of essoin was one way in which a canny defendant could delay a court case by not appearing. A convincing advocate was therefore very necessary, as this letter indicates. The strategy behind delaying a case like this was to postpone judgement and wear down the determination and also the finances of the rival litigant. Frequently a compromise settlement (recorded in a document called a "foot of fine") was reached before the case actually came to judgement, and the plaintiff and defendant thus cut their potential losses. Often the plaintiff had only started it speculatively in any case, hoping that the defendant would settle out of court.

NOTES

1   Add. 8167, fols. 100v–101r.
2   *A. mandat B.* in MS, but in the text, B. is the sender and A. the recipient of this letter.
3   The italicized parenthetical phrase is included in the text as a variant of the preceding phrase. Similar variant phrasings can be found below in this text and in DOCUMENTS 5, 24, 32, 44, 46, 47, and 62.
4   Fol. 101r commences here.
5   *heredareo* in MS.
6   The italicized words in parentheses here represent another variant phrasing.
7   Corrected in MS from *prosfiscatur* to *profiscatur*, a slip for *proficiscatur*.
8   Brand, *Origins of the English Legal Profession*, 43–49.
9   "Assize of Essoiners," in Stenton, ed., *Pleas Before the King or His Justices,* 1:152–53. Paul Brand, "Henry II and the Creation of the English Common Law," in *Henry II: New Interpretations*, ed. Christopher Harper-Bill and Nicholas Vincent (Woodbridge, Suffolk: Boydell & Brewer, 2007), 225–26, considers and affirms the claims of this passage to be considered a royal assize, though he has reservations about the date assigned to it.
10 George Derek Gordon Hall, ed. and trans., *The Treatise on the Laws and Customs of the Realm of England, Commonly Called Glanvill* (Oxford: Clarendon, 1993), 6–8.
11 Thomas M. Charles-Edwards, "Kinship, Status and the Origins of the Hide," *Past & Present*, 56 (1972), 3–33; John F. McGovern, "The Hide and Related Land-Tenure Concepts in Anglo-Saxon England, A.D. 700–1100," *Traditio*, 28 (1972), 101–18. The idea that hides were nominal tax units by 1086 is found in John Horace Round, "Domesday Book," in idem, *Feudal England* (London: Allen & Unwin, 1964), 82–88.
12 Judith A. Green, "The Last Century of Danegeld," *EHR*, 96 (1981), 241–58.

LORDSHIP AND MANORIAL ADMINISTRATION

——————————————— 47 ———————————————

An Earl Asks an Agent to Get Him Money for a Replacement Mount[1]

Comes clienti suo precipit sic

D. comes Cestrie dilecto et fideli suo A. salutem. De fidelitate tua[2] quamplurimum confisi, tibi mandantes (*precipimus, preces preceptis adiungentes*),[3] ut pro amore nostro et fide quam nobis debes, C. solidos facias nos habere ad unum equum emendum. Sciturus quod palefridus noster mortuus est et non habemus equum cui possimus confidere. Quare tantum facias ne negocium nostrum admittatur pro defectu equitature. Vale.

An earl orders his agent as follows

D., earl of Chester, to his beloved and faithful A. greetings. We have put our highest trust in your loyalty, ordering you (*we have ordered, adding entreaties to our commands*), that, for the love and faith you owe us, you provide us with 100 shillings to buy a horse. You will know that our palfrey has died and we do not have a horse in which we can trust. Therefore, make sure that our business is not hindered for want of a mount. Farewell.

There was no "D." who was earl of Chester in the twelfth or thirteenth century, although for the possibility that this letter may reflect contemporary correspondence, see DOCUMENT 2. Whether or not it was based on a genuine document, however, this letter refers to a genuine problem of the day: the high attrition rate in road horses. It brings to mind the experience of Richard of Anstey, the celebrated litigant of the early years of Henry II. When he reckoned the expenses of his epic lawsuit between 1158 and 1163, they included the replacement of two pack horses and two riding horses.[4]

The sort of horse that the earl required here was a palfrey (*palefridus*), the Rolls Royce of riding horses. Palfreys were pacers, trained to move their left and then right legs forward together in an even pace, giving a comfortable ride. Unlike other saddle horses, palfreys could moderate their pace to a comfortable amble, between a walk and a trot.[5] William fitz Stephen's "Description of London" (*c.* 1173) speaks appreciatively of such mounts: "It is a joy to see the pacing horses with glossy coats ambling, that is to say, raising and putting down their feet on each side together."[6] The word "palfrey" dates from the Late Roman period, when a *paraverdus* was a post horse. In the tenth century the meaning of palfrey shifted to "road horse," and around 1200 English scholar Alexander Neckam traced the etymology of *palefridus* to the Latin phrase *passu lenu frænum ducens*, which refers to its gentle gait.[7]

The sum of money requested by the earl in the letter above indicates that he was expecting to buy a very expensive mount. Palfreys could be had for as little as one mark (13*s.* 4*d.*) in Richard of Anstey's day, though some were priced at more than five pounds sterling, a price that was standard for a palfrey by the fourteenth century.[8] Under King John (1199–1216), palfreys were often used in settlement or part settlement of Exchequer debts. In DOCUMENT 26, a palfrey worth two pounds (three marks) is offered as an inducement for the granting of a loan. In the 1230s, it became increasingly common for Henry III to present palfreys to prelates as gifts, and to receive palfreys from them. (Prelates had a special interest in breeding palfreys, since they had no use for the more expensive warhorse, or destrier.)[9]

In the heading to the letter above, the earl's addressee is called his *cliens*. This was a relatively unusual word in medieval Latin, and it generally signified a dependent or attendant of some sort. In the early twelfth century, for example, Norman baron Richard de Redvers made a grant of his chapel of Néhou to fund the prebend (living) of a canon who was to share with his seneschal the oversight of Richard's affairs and of the conduct of his dependents (*clientes*) in the town.[10] In the late twelfth-century story of Hereward the Wake, William the Conqueror's kitchen is depicted as bustling with attendants (*clientes*) and servants (*garciferi*).[11] In DOCUMENT 47, the sense of *cliens* seems to be something like "agent," a man with whom the earl has regular dealings and in whose loyalty he trusts. In this instance, the *cliens* may be an urban agent who arranges loans on the market for aristocrats who need ready cash, or he may be a moneylender himself.

NOTES

1   Add. 8167, fol. 98r–v.

2   Fol. 98v commences here.

3   The italicized words in parentheses represent a variant phrasing included in the text, as in DOCUMENTS 5, 24, 32, 44, and 46.

4   For the Anstey case, see DOCUMENT 44, note 16. For the list of Anstey's expenses, see Raoul C. van Caenegem, ed. and trans., *English Lawsuits from William I to Richard I*, vol. 2, *Henry II and Richard I*, Selden Society, 107 (London: 1991), 397–404.

5   Anthony Austen Dent, "Chaucer and the Horse," *Proceedings of the Leeds Philosophical and Literary Society*, 9 (1959), 6. We owe this and other references to the kindness of Andrew Ayton.

6   For the various types of riding horse, and for the passage from fitz Stephen's "Description of London," see Ralph Henry Carless Davis, *The Medieval Warhorse* (London: Thames & Hudson, 1989), 66–67.

7   *Palefridus, sic dictus quasi passu lenu frænum ducens* ("The palfrey is called that as its gentle pace pulls only lightly on the bit"). Alexander Neckam, *De naturis rerum*, ed. Thomas Wright, Rolls Series, 34 (London: Longman, 1863), 260. For this and other reflections, see Anne-Marie Bautier, "Contribution à l'histoire du cheval au moyen âge," *Bullétin philologique et historique* (1976), 218–20.

8   For the value of palfreys in the fourteenth century, see Andrew C. Ayton, *Knights and Warhorses: Military Service and the English Aristocracy Under Edward III* (Woodbridge, Suffolk: Boydell & Brewer, 1994), 40, 206–7. For attrition rates among mounts on campaign, see ibid., 257, 263–65. The pipe rolls of Richard I (1189–99)

and John (1199–1216) note palfreys valued variously at £6 13*s.* 4*d.* (ten marks), £3 6*s.* 8*d.* (five marks) and 40*s.* (two pounds). Charles Gladitz, *Horse Breeding in the Medieval World* (Dublin: Four Courts, 1997), 299, n. 268.

9 Gladitz, *Horse Breeding in the Medieval World*, 171–73. In fact, as early as *c.* 1170 Wace of Bayeux could talk of a Norman duke exercising patronage through gifts of fabrics, arms, armor, and *pallefroiz*. *Le Roman de Rou*, ed. Anthony J. Holden, vol. 1 (Paris: Société des anciens textes français, 1970–73), 2, line 4128.

10 Lucien Musset, "Récherches sur les communautés de clercs seculiers," *Bullétin de la société des Antiquaires de Normandie*, 55 (1961, for 1959–60), 37–38; Robert Bearman, ed., *Charters of the Redvers Family and the Earldom of Devon, 1090–1217*, Devon and Cornwall Record Society, new ser., 37 (Exeter, 1994), 56. Neither editor comments on the nature of this curious grant.

11 Ernest O. Blake, ed., *Liber Eliensis*, Camden Society, 3rd ser., 92 (London, 1962), 184.

48

A Lord Responds with Threats to an Attack on His Dependents[1]

A. mandat B. quare hominibus suis iniuriam fecerit

A. B. salutem, id quod. meruit. Miror et vehementer admiror que temeritas te compulerit hominibus meis in[i]uriari,[2] cum scires me virum sanum et incolumem. Set volo ut scias quod me habebis inimicum quam diu vixero nisi michi cicius satisfacias de iniuria illata. Quare tantum facias, si sapias, cito venies ad satisfaccionem, ne pena debita peccatum sequatur. Vale.

A. asks of B. why he has done harm to his men

A. greets B., as much as he deserves. I marvel and am completely astonished at the impudence that might have motivated you to do harm to my men, since you know that I am a man in full possession of my powers and perfectly secure in my position. But I want you to know that you will have me for a mortal enemy unless you promptly make satisfaction to me for the injury you caused. Therefore, if you are wise, you should see to it that you come to a settlement quickly, so that your offense is not followed by the punishment that it deserves. Farewell.

Brief though it is, this letter gets right to the dark heart of medieval lordship. For magnates to act effectively at court or in the countryside they had to be feared, not so much for what they had done as for what they might do if they were so moved. Menace was the way in which many magnates exerted pressure. In 1174, for example, Jordan Fantosme wrote that Earl Robert III of Leicester (d. 1190) boasted that in his part of England that there was hardly a knight whom he could not overthrow if the knight refused him aid.[3]

Lords, like the lord in this letter, could not tolerate challenges to their prestige or reputation. To flatter a lord, one used the sort of language employed by Geoffrey of Monmouth when he dedicated editions of his *History of the Kings of Britain* in 1136 to both Robert, earl of Gloucester (d. 1147), and Waleran, count of Meulan (d. 1166): "You have learned through your father's precedent, to be a terror to your enemies and a protection to your own people. Faithful defender as you are of those dependent on you, accept under your patronage this book which is published for your pleasure."[4]

In this letter, a lord finds that his ability to protect his dependents is being directly challenged. He retaliates forcefully, addressing his rival in blunt and insulting terms, using the familiar "*tu*" instead of the respectful "*vos*," and threatening "mortal enmity" if the offender does not make prompt reparations. This phrase does not necessarily mean that he would seek to harry his enemy to death, but that he would be his enemy "for as long as I shall live" (*quam diu vixero*).

Mortal enmity was used as a social sanction throughout medieval Europe, even in England, which had a high reputation for public peace.[5] The phrase "mortal enemy," which owes something to Roman law, occurs in England as early as 1091.[6] The French equivalent phrase occurs in the Anglo-Norman history of the conquest of Ireland (*c.* 1190), in which King Domnall Mac Donnchadh of Osraige, who had attacked Earl Richard of Striguil's father-in-law, is described as the earl's *enemi mortel*.[7] It was the custom to inaugurate such a state of enmity by a formal defiance of the adversary, and the letter above may be interpreted as just such a defiance.

Mortal enmity could embrace families and friends as well as individuals. In 1205, the viscount of Aulnay was contesting a divorce, and he objected to all three of the clerical judges appointed to try the case, including the bishop of Quimper, because he was a relative of the viscount's mortal enemy (*capitalis inimicus*). Furthermore, the viscount objected to the venue, since it was "the land of his enemies where he cannot go without danger of death, and he has no letters of safe conduct and even if he did he could not trust in his mortal enemies."[8] In 1215, according to the writer called the Anonymous of Bethune, a Flemish knight, Walter Bertaut, was on a boat that was driven ashore in the county of Holland. This terrified him because he was the first cousin of the count of Loos, who had challenged Count William of Holland for his lands, and so Count William "hated Walter to the death."[9]

The use of menace and threat in relations between a magnate and a lesser man, as in the letter above, is characteristic of the sort of society described by the historian K. Bruce McFarlane as "bastard feudal." By this he meant that magnates attracted men to their "affinities" (followings) by a variety of means, such as by offering fees, offices, or general goodwill. By recruiting such affinities, magnates could both dominate particular localities and enhance their power at the royal court. McFarlane saw a "bastard feudal" order succeeding an older "feudal" order (one based on knight service and feudal tenure) at the end of the thirteenth century.[10] More recent debate has pushed back the history of the affinity as a form of magnate power-play back into the twelfth century.[11] The inclusion in a formulary of a model letter such as this, in which a magnate responds to an injury to his dependents by threatening mortal enmity, clearly presumes a society in which magnates were already recruiting retinues and offering them protection. It was also a society in which the same magnates used menace and threats as readily as patronage and courtesies to support and protect their followers and their own standing.

NOTES

1 Add. 8167, fol. 101r.

2 *inuriari* in MS.

3 *Jordan Fantosme's Chronicle*, ed. and trans. Ronald C. Johnston (Oxford: Clarendon, 1981), 70.

4 *The Historia Regum Britanniae of Geoffrey of Monmouth*, vol. 1, *Bern, Burgerbibliotehek, MS 568*, ed. Neil Wright (Cambridge: D. S. Brewer, 1984), xiii–xiv.

5 For the European background, see Robert Bartlett, "Mortal Enmities," in *Feud, Violence and Practice: Essays in Medieval Studies in Honor of Stephen D. White*, ed. Belle S. Tuten and Tracey L. Billado (Farnham: Ashgate, 2010), 197–212. For England, see David Crouch, *The English Aristocracy, 1070–1272: A Social Transformation* (New Haven: Yale University Press, 2011), 124–29.

6 Goscelin of Canterbury, *Historia translationis sancti Augustini episcopi*, in Jacques-Paul Migne, ed., *Patrologiae cursus completus: series Latina*, 221 vols. (Paris: Garnier, 1844–64), vol. 155: col. 19.

7 *La Geste des Engleis en Yrlande*, ed. and trans. Evelyn Mullally (Dublin: Four Courts, 2002), lines 2143–44.

8 Bartlett, "Mortal Enmities," 10, citing a letter of Innocent III that became the basis of a later decretal.

9 Francisque Michel, ed., *Histoire des ducs de Normandie et des rois d'Angleterre* (Paris: Société de l'histoire de France, 1840), 156.

10 For the classic statement of this, see K. Bruce McFarlane, "Bastard Feudalism," reprinted in *England in the Fifteenth Century*, ed. Gerald L. Harriss (Oxford: Oxford University Press, 1981), 23–44, and generally, Michael Hicks, *Bastard Feudalism* (London: Longman, 1995). For the historiographical background, David Crouch, *The Birth of Nobility: Constructing Aristocracy in England and France, 900–1300* (Harlow: Longman, 2005), 265–73.

11 David Crouch, "From Stenton to McFarlane: Models of Societies of the Twelfth and Thirteenth Centuries," *Transactions of the Royal Historical Society*, 6th ser., 5 (1995), 194–97.

49

A Villein Refuses a Request for the Loan of a Plow and Oxen Because He Needs Them Himself[1]

Litere responsales de acomodatu boum

Dilecto amico suo A. et cetera. Significati michi per nuncium vestrum ut vobis boves meos acomodarem,[2] cum aratro, quod nullo modo possum facere, quia non habeo nisi duo iuga boum et ex illis me oportet[3] servicium domini mei perficere, quod nisi fecero graviter puniam. Quare vobis consulo ut alios boves vobis perquiratis. Valete.

Letter of response concerning the loan of oxen

To his beloved friend A., etc. You sent me word by your messenger that I should lend you my oxen, with the plow, which I can in no way do, because I have only two yoke of oxen and with these I have to perform my lord's service, and unless I do so I shall be severely punished. So I suggest that you seek other oxen. Farewell.

Is it plausible that a villein (or one who held at least some land by servile tenure) would have sent a formal letter, in Latin, in response to a request for the loan of his oxen and plow? It seems unlikely, but perhaps not wholly impossible. Under ordinary circumstances, one would expect such a request to have been made and answered verbally, and in person. Here, however, we are told that the request was made through a messenger. This suggests that the "beloved friend" who made the request lived at some distance. He was not the villein's own lord, but he evidently considered himself entitled to request—or even to demand—such a substantial favor. Perhaps the villein was in some way indebted, or in debt, to him, or he was a person of standing or authority whom the villein did not dare to offend. If so, a simple verbal refusal might have seemed inadequate or the messenger untrustworthy to convey the message accurately, and a formal reply in writing, explaining the reason for the refusal, might have been deemed more desirable. (In just this way the skinner in DOCUMENT 8 wrote a polite letter of refusal to the earl who had asked him to supply furs on credit; the skinner, too, addressed the earl as his "beloved friend" and used the formal *"vos"* rather than the familiar *"tu."*) In such a situation, the villein presumably would have obtained aid in composing and writing the letter from a local priest or from someone else schooled in Latin.

While such a scenario is possible, it seems much more likely that this particular letter, like the letter allegedly written by one villein to another in DOCUMENT 93, is wholly fictitious, and perhaps even the product of a school exercise in formal letter-writing (*dictamen*) in which the task was to compose a polite but firm letter of refusal in an everyday fashion, with no rhetorical flourishes, suitable for the subject and the writer. Even so, it provides us with a rare, sympathetic glimpse into the world of the medieval villein, whose life was circumscribed by obligations to his lord that he dared not contravene, but who might be subject to requests and demands from others whom it was also dangerous to offend.

For a discussion of the manorial dues owed by villeins to their lords, see DOCUMENT 1.

NOTES

1   Add. 8167, fols. 101v–102r.
2   Corrected in MS from *acomodarens.*
3   Fol. 102r commences here.

50

A Tenant Informs on a Landowner's Corrupt Bailiff[1]

G. mandat H.[2] de moribus infidelis servi[entis][3] eius

Venerabili domino suo. A., B. salutem. Nolo vos latere, R. famulus vester res vestras minus fideliter quam deberet. Vendit enim staurum vestrum oculte et precium sumit et in propriis expendit. Et quod hoc sit verum traho in testimmonium D., C., fideles vestros, qui hoc viderunt ubi presens interfuit. Quapropter, si utile fore credetis, sine mora castigetur vel ab officio eius deponatur, ne magis dampnum vobis eveniet. Valete.

G. sends word to H. about the practices of his unfaithful bailiff

To his venerable lord A., B. [sends] greetings. I will not keep you in the dark: R. your bailiff [is attending to] your business less faithfully than he ought. For he is selling your stock behind your back, and keeping the proceeds and spending them on his own account. And that this is true I call to witness D. [and] C. your loyal men, who actually saw him doing it. Therefore, if you think it beneficial, let him be punished without delay or let him be discharged from his office, so that he may cause you no further loss. Farewell.

This is the first of three letters concerning an allegation of fraud against a manorial officer. The heading of the letter above refers to the officer in question as a "serf" (*servus*; here given in the genitive case as *servi*), probably a slip for "serjeant" or "bailiff" (*serviens*; *servientis* in the genitive case). In the body of the letter he is called a *famulus*, which literally means "member of household" or, more generally, "servant." In DOCUMENT 51 neither his office nor his name is given, but in DOCUMENT 69 he is called "*W. serviens*," and DOCUMENTS 21, 53, 98 and 99 also concern the activities and responsibilities of the *serviens* of a manor.[4]

In the thirteenth century, *serviens* was an all-purpose term for an officer. It is commonly translated as "serjeant," but in a manorial context, as here and in the other documents listed above, a *serviens* was a bailiff.[5] Bailiffs (*ballivi*) were mid-level officers, responsible for the administration of one or more manors. Their duties (which are also discussed in DOCUMENTS 53, 98, and 99) included superintending the farm work, ordering repairs, buying supplies, selling livestock and produce, and keeping the accounts. The Anglo-Norman treatise on estate administration (*Rules*), compiled by Bishop Robert Grosseteste of Lincoln (1235–53) for the use of the widowed countess of Lincoln (see DOCUMENT 51), recommended that each bailiff have his own copy of the enrolled details of all the rents, customs, usages, bond services, franchises, and demesne lands that belonged to his office.[6] The anonymous Anglo-Norman treatise on estate management known as *Seneschaucy* ("stewardship"), written in England before 1276, includes a detailed description of the bailiff's duties.[7] Bailiffs were answerable to the estates steward or seneschal (*senescallus*), who was the lord's or lady's most senior officer, often of knightly rank, and responsible for the overall administration of all the estates (see DOCUMENT 51). Bailiffs themselves supervised the manorial reeves (*prepositi*), generally peasants (either freemen or villeins), who were the overseers or foremen in charge of the day-to-day work of the manors.[8]

By the twelfth century there was a considerable literature about the prevalence of corruption among manorial officers. For example, in the *Romance of Thebes* (c. 1150 × 63), King Etiocles grants a handsome estate to found a nunnery for his sister Ismene, and observes that "if the bailiff of the lordship which surrounds it does not cheat her, she will have a very comfortable life on those estates."[9]

With the sharp inflation that occurred around 1180–1220, and the consequent shift by great landowners from leasing out their demesne lands on fixed rents to farming them directly, the owners began to demand regular financial accounts from their manorial officers (see DOCUMENT 21). An officer who refused to present his accounts could be sued by his lord. In 1249, for example, a plea was lodged before the justices in eyre by Walter of Neweport against one Richard of Barewell, "that he should deliver a reasonable account (*rationabile compotum*) of the time when he was bailiff" in 1248.[10] Bishop Grosseteste's *Rules*, evidently written for the countess of Lincoln, speak of bailiffs offering annual accounts as a matter of course, and of how strict audits can reveal both the diligence and the shortcomings of bailiffs and other manorial officers.[11] Grosseteste's warning about the importance of careful auditing was well founded since, without it, bailiffs and reeves had ample opportunities for fraud. One manorial bailiff, Robert Carpenter II of "Hareslade" (Haslett) on the Isle of Wight, actually wrote a detailed description of various methods by which an unscrupulous bailiff could defraud his master, frauds that are very similar in character to those alleged in DOCUMENT 50.[12]

In this letter, "B.," the sender, is not identified, but in DOCUMENT 51, the accused bailiff calls him his "neighbor." B.'s opening salutation to his "venerable lord" suggests that he may be one of the lord's tenants or dependents, which would have made an unfounded allegation against the bailiff a dangerous venture for him. B., however, prudently cites two witnesses who will support his allegation—a reminder to users of this model letter (as similarly in DOCUMENT 70) always to bolster a serious accusation with strong evidence.

NOTES

1   Add. 8167, fol. 102r.
2   In the body of the letter the sender is called "B." and the recipient is "A." Evidently, in the exemplar from which this model letter was taken, the sender was "G." and the recipient "H." Similar cases of careless copying can be found in DOCUMENTS 10, 16, 33, 70, and 90.
3   *servi* ("serf") in MS.
4   Bruce R. O'Brien, *God's Peace and King's Peace: The Laws of Edward the Confessor* (Philadelphia: University of Pennsylvania Press, 1999), clause 32, p. 190. For *gerefa*, see Raymond Ian Page, "*Gerefa*: Some Problems of Meaning," in *Problems of Old English Lexicography: Studies in Memory of Angus Cameron,* ed. Alfred Bammesberger (Regensburg: Pustet, 1985), 211–28; Paul D. A. Harvey, "*Rectitudines singularum personarum* and *Gerefa*," *EHR*, 108 (1993), 1–22.
5   Dorothea Oschinsky, *Walter of Henley and Other Treatises on Estate Management and Accounting* (Oxford: Clarendon, 1971), 65.
6   Oschinsky, *Walter of Henley*, 388–89.
7   Oschinsky, *Walter of Henley*, 268–75.

8 Oschinsky, *Walter of Henley*, 65–67.

9 Francine Mora-Lebrun, ed., *Le Roman de Thèbes* (Paris: Lettres Gothiques, 1995), lines 7081–82.

10 The missing account was for the manor of Elmedon in Northamptonshire. TNA: PRO, JUST 1/777, m. 13.

11 Oschinsky, *Walter of Henley*, 191–97, 394–95; Denholm-Young, *Seignorial Administration in England* (London: Oxford University Press, 1937), 121–22. The traditional date for the *Rules* of 1240 × 42 has been challenged by Michael Burger, who argues for the broader date of 1235 × 53. Michael Burger, "The Date and Authorship of Robert Grosseteste's *Rules for Household and Estate Management*," *Historical Research*, 74 (2001), 206–16.

12 Oschinsky, *Walter of Henley*, 461–62; see also the comments in *Seneschaucy* (ibid., 273). On Carpenter, see Martha Carlin, "Cheating the Boss: Robert Carpenter's Embezzlement Instructions (1261 × 1268), and Employee Fraud in Medieval England," in *Markets and Entrepreneurs in the Middle Ages: Essays in Honour of Richard Britnell*, ed. Ben Dodds and Christian Liddy (Woodbridge, Suffolk: Boydell, 2011), 183–97.

51

The Same Bailiff Sends His Rebuttal to His Lord[1]

Ipse de quo in predictis[2] literis agitur querela mandat domino suo

Venerabili domino A., B. salutem. Mallivolus ubique querit occasionem malignandi. Illum e[3] facto ledere non potest, illi crimen inponit ut ore confundat quem opere non potest. R. vicinus meus, immo pocius adversarius, erga vos michi crimen inposuit, dicens quod ego staurum vestrum vendidi et in propriis usibus expendidi. Re vera, quatuor caseos vendidi, et bladum ad opus famulorum vestrorum emi. Et ut verum sit, traho in testimonium[4] senescallum vestrum, qui enumeravit et qui dicam habuit contra me de caseis et aliis rebus vestris. In[de][5] quapropter vobis supplico, ne fidem de cetero habeatis suis sermonibus. Valeat dileccio vestra.

The man of whom a complaint was made in the previous letter sends word to his lord

To his venerable lord A., B. [sends] greetings. An ill-disposed fellow is always looking for occasion to do harm. A man whom he cannot attack for anything specific, he accuses of fraud, so that he may cause trouble for someone by speech whom he cannot trouble by deed. R., my neighbor, or rather my enemy, has accused me of fraud against you, saying that I sold your stock and spent the proceeds on myself. In fact, I sold four cheeses and bought grain for the use of your household servants, and that this is true, I call to witness your steward, who counted them out, and who, I might add, held me to account for the cheeses and other things of yours. In light of this, I beg you to put no trust whatsoever in that man's allegations in the future. May your love flourish.[6]

In this letter, the bailiff replies to the allegations made against him in Document 50. Like his accuser, the bailiff is careful to cite a credible witness to his version of events. However, while the accuser cited as witnesses two of the lord's tenants or dependents, men presumably of similar rank to himself, the bailiff cites his own superior, the lord's estates steward or seneschal (*senescallus*), who was a person of much higher standing than any of them.

By the 1240s the estates steward was the senior officer in charge of of a lord's entire complex of estates. The title was an ancient one, originally signifying a domestic officer of the Merovingian kings of the Franks in the seventh century. The word *senescallus*, which was Frankish in origin, lost currency to more classical equivalents such as *dapifer* and *discifer* in the eleventh and early twelfth centuries, but it was revived in Latin texts of the second half of the twelfth century. By then, the duties of the "seneschal" (as the officer was called in French and Anglo-Norman) were often divided into two offices: the household steward or steward of the hall, who was responsible for the management of a lord's domestic household, while the estates steward was responsible for the overall administration of all or part of the lord's estates.[7]

It is difficult to date with precision the emergence of seneschals as recognized estate officials. The domestic seneschals of the earlier twelfth century, like any officials of a lord's court, dealt with a variety of administrative duties, including acting as their lord's deputy in his seigneurial court. This lack of specialization clouds the chronology, but seneschals were supervising blocks of the earl of Chester's estates in Warwickshire and Lincolnshire by the 1190s,[8] and in the 1190s and early 1200s several great churches undertook expensive litigation to extinguish hereditary seneschalcies attached to their estates, probably to enable them to appoint their own chosen officers to a post of increasing importance and responsibility.[9] This chronology fits well with the steep inflation of *c.* 1180–1220 that caused great landowners to shift from leasing out their demesne lands on fixed rents to farming them directly, since lords could not have managed their own demesnes without the assistance of estate officers such as stewards and bailiffs (see Documents 21 and 50).

The job of an estates steward in the first half of the thirteenth century was thus central to the whole process of seigneurial administration. It is for that reason that the steward featured largely in some of the earliest handbooks on the subject. In Bishop Grosseteste's *Rules* for the countess of Lincoln (1235 × 53), for example, he is called the "chief steward" (*graunt seneschal*), and it is to him that a lord or lady entrusts everything in his or her "ward and government." The chief steward is also a person of rank, whom lords and ladies address respectfully as "good sir" (*beau sire*).[10] One such steward was Simon of Senlis, the nephew or great-nephew of Simon III of Senlis, earl of Northampton (d. 1184). He served Ralph de Neville, bishop of Chichester and chancellor of England, from 1222 × 24 (when Neville was still bishop-elect) until about 1232. In 1227, while in Neville's service, Simon obtained the wardship and marriage of an heiress to estates in Rutland, and by 1235 he had married her and settled on the estates. He died in 1259, survived by at least three sons.[11]

The estates steward's qualifications and duties were described in detail before 1276 in the Anglo-Norman handbook on estate mangagement called *Seneschaucy* ("stewardship"). Among other things, the unknown author wrote:

> The estates steward [*seneschal*] ought to be knowledgeable and loyal and capable of administering the lands profitably; he ought to know the law of the country so that he can defend actions outside the lord's estate, can give confidence to the bailiffs who are under him, and can instruct them.
>
> The steward ought to make his circuit twice or three times yearly and visit the manors in his charge. On these occasions he ought to inquire into rents, services, and customary payments which have been concealed and are being withheld; and he ought to inquire also into franchises of courts, lands, woods, meadows and pastures, waters and mills, and of any other estates which belong to the manor and have been disposed of without warrant; by whom and why.[12]

The author of *Seneschaucy* also made clear the steward's supervisory function over the lesser estate officers: "On his visits to the manors the steward ought to inquire how the bailiff conducts himself within and without, how he looks after the manor, what improvements he makes and what growth and profit on the manor and in his office he has achieved and which are to his credit. In the same way he ought to inquire into the offices of the reeve, hayward, stockkeeper, and all the other servants and how each of them conducts himself. In this manner he will best be able to see who achieves profit and who causes loss."[13] Preventing loss and fraud was an important part of the steward's job. In DOCUMENT 51, the bailiff calls the steward to witness that he committed no fraud in selling the lord's cheeses, saying that the steward had counted them out and had held the bailiff to account for them. Apparently, the bailiff had to demonstrate at his audit that he could account for the sale of the cheeses and for his use of the proceeds to purchase grain for the lord's household. Now he is citing the steward's accounting procedures to establish his innocence in the fraud alleged against him.

NOTES

1   Add. 8167, fol. 102r.
2   *in* expunged after *predictis* in MS.
3   *illi qui pro* struck through and erased in MS, and replaced above the line with *illum e.*
4   *testeimonium* in MS.
5   *in* in MS.
6   At first glance, the phrase "*dileccio vestra*" might appear to be an honorific form of address, such as "Your Excellency" or "Your Worship." However, the same valediction (*valeat dilecio tua*) in used in DOCUMENT 53, a letter written by a man of property to his bailiff, whom he would not have addressed with an honorific. This suggests that in these letters *valeat dileccio vestra* (or *tua*) was simply a genteel way of closing, the equivalent to such modern valedictions as "Sincerely yours" or "Very truly yours."
7   See Frank M. Stenton, *The First Century of English Feudalism, 1066–1166,* 2nd ed. (Oxford: Clarendon, 1961), 73–79; Denholm-Young, *Seignorial Administration,* 66–69.
8   David Crouch, "Administration of the Norman Earldom," in *The Earldom of Chester and Its Charters,* ed. Alan T. Thacker, *Journal of the Chester Archaeological Society,* 71 (Chester, 1991), 93–94.
9   Paul Brand, "The Rise and Fall of the Hereditary Steward in English Ecclesiastical Institutions, 1066–1300," in *Warriors and Churchmen in the High Middle Ages: Essays Presented to Karl Leyser,* ed. Timothy Reuter (London: Hambledon, 1992), 159–60: Peterborough (1194, or soon after); St. Augustine, Canterbury (1197); Westminster (1198); See of Lincoln (1209). Brand also draws attention (157–58) to a clause in the late twelfth-century description of the seneschalcy of the abbey of Bury St Edmunds, which says that the hereditary steward had no business meddling in the administration of the abbey's estates. This implies that estate administration was by then a normal part of a seneschal's job.
10   Oschinsky, *Walter of Henley,* 390–91. On the date of Grosseteste's *Rules,* see Burger, "Date and Authorship," 206–16.
11   Jeanne and Lionel Stones, "Bishop Ralph Neville, Chancellor to King Henry III, and His Correspondence: A Reappraisal," *Archives,* 16, no. 71 (April 1984), 241–43.
12   Oschinsky, *Walter of Henley,* 88–89, 264–65.
13   Oschinsky, *Walter of Henley,* 266–69.

52

A Knight Orders a Bailiff Accused of Fraud to
Present His Accounts for Inspection[1]

Miles servienti salutem. Quia de fidelitate tua fidelique servicio confidens, te aliter quod deberes, quia datum est michi intelligi quod de
rebus meis ac si proprie essent tuam facis voluntatem, et quod minorem
capis curam de comodo meo faciendo[2] scilicet de domibus meis, et de
horreis[3] meis cooperiendis, et de sepibus meis circa curiam faciendis.
Quare tibi mando ut, in crastino sancti Andree, ad me venias promptus
et paratus reddere compotum tuum, et adducas[4] tecum prepositos[5] duos
et de legalibus hominibus meis, qui michi dicere velint veritatem ex
omnibus que audivi. Quia si f[a]l[su]m[6] est quod de te audivi, illos qui
talia michi dixerunt de [te][7] non credam, et tibi pro ut meruisti dabo
mercedem. Vale.

A knight to a bailiff, greetings. Because I trusted in your good faith and
loyal service, you [evidently have been behaving] otherwise than you
ought, because I have been given to understand that that you have been
making free with my possessions as if they were your own, and that you
have been negligent in doing your work for me, namely, in roofing my
houses and barns, and making fences around my manor house (*curiam*).
Therefore, I order you that on the day after the feast of St Andrew
[December 1] you are to come to me ready and prepared to render your
account, and bring with you two reeves from among my sworn servants
who will tell me the truth about all the things that I have heard. Because
if what I have heard of you is false I shall give no credit to those who
have said such things about [you], and I shall pay you the wages that
you have earned. Farewell.

The presentation of written accounts by manorial officials at the end of their
term of office was a universal practice by the middle of the thirteenth century,
though very few of these written accounts survive (see DOCUMENTS 20–23 and
50). Here, in what may have been intended as a conclusion to the exchange of
letters in DOCUMENTS 50 and 51, a knight orders his bailiff to render his
accounts because the bailiff has been accused of fraud, and to bring with him
two reeves (manorial foremen) who will tell the knight the facts of the matter.
For the present, the knight is keeping an open mind; he assures the bailiff that
if the allegations prove false, he will put no credence in them, and he will pay

the bailiff the salary that is due to him. However, the knight is clearly suspicious that the bailiff has not merely performed his job badly, but has abused his trust. Such an offense would undoubtedly be punished harshly, since it would have injured not only the knight's purse and feelings, but also his reputation as a wise and strong lord whom no lesser man would dare to harm (see DOCUMENT 48).

NOTES

1   Add. 8167, fols. 129v–130r.
2   Corrected in MS from *faceendo*.
3   *horibus* in MS.
4   Fol. 130r commences here.
5   *propositos* in MS.
6   *fl*[m] in MS.
7   Word supplied to preserve the sense of this passage.

53

A Landowner Sends a List of Instructions to His Bailiff[1]

A. de C. N. servienti suo salutem. Mitto tibi literas meas directas domino G. de .C., precipiens, quod statim visis literis istis, eas ad dominum R. et deferas[2] ei literas meas quas tibi mitto. Et sicut me diligis, quam cito poteritis consilium adibeas quod mer[em]ium[3] meum sit apud M., quia dei gratia preparabo domum meam, faciendam cum tempus et saysona adveneri[n]t.[4] Ad[hi]beas[5] quod wanagium meum procedat, et de omnibus agendis sicut alias tibi mandavi te intromittas, quod provedenciam tuam merito debeam commendare. Et deferas alias literas priori de M. quas tibi transmitto. Valeat dilecio tua.

A. de C. to N. his bailiff, greetings. I am sending you a letter from me addressed to Sir G. de C., ordering that, as soon as he has seen it, you go to Sir R. and hand on to him the letter that I am sending you. And, as you love me, find out as quickly as you can what timber I might have at M., because, God willing, I will be building my house when the time and season are right. Make sure that the cultivation of my land continues, and that you get busy on all the things that need to be done that I previously sent word to you about, so that I may have reason to commend your good stewardship. And take the other letter that I am sending to you to the prior of M. May your love flourish.[6]

This list of urgent tasks is so breathless—indeed, almost incoherent—that it could be considered a burlesque, were it not for the fact that there are very similar letters among the surviving correspondence of the period. In one such letter, Simon of Senlis, steward to Ralph de Neville, bishop of Chichester and chancellor of England, reports to his master that he has seen to the supplying of the bishop's London house with firewood and has purchased lambskins for the household's winter clothing. He asks Neville to think about buying sheep from the Cistercian abbey of Vaudey in Lincolnshire and sending them to the bishop's estates in Sussex, and inquires if he has spoken with Sir Robert of Lexington about some oxen for the larder in London. He also wishes to know when the bishop expects to come to London, and suggests that part of the bishop's old wheat at Westmill in Hertfordshire be threshed and sent to London against his arrival.[7] In another letter, Simon reports his progress on completing an even more dizzying list of tasks in Chichester and in several of the bishop's manors in Sussex:

> Know, lord, that William de St John is not in these Sussex parts, so that I cannot at present complete the business which you enjoined me; but as soon as he shall be come into these Sussex parts, I will strive with all my might to expedite and complete it, as I shall see it result to your honour. I send you fourscore and five ells of cloth, bought for the use of the poor, and to be distributed. I am not able to sell for your advantage the wine which is in your cellar in Chichester, on account of the too great abundance of new wine which there is in the town of Chichester. Know also, lord, that a certain burgess of Chichester holds one croft, which belongs to the garden granted to you by the Lord King, for which he pays every year 11 shillings, which (*quos*) the sheriff of Sussex exacts (*exigit*) from him. Wherefore since the said land belongs to the said garden, and has been of old time subtracted from it, about the aforesaid rent be pleased to signify your advice to me. In your manor of Selesey I am marling effectually, so that, on the departure of this, five acres have been marled. Please to intimate to me your will upon the premises and other matters, as I will show myself vigilant and watchful, to the utmost of my strength, about taking care of and completing your business. May your excellency prosper in the Lord.[8]

NOTES

1   Add. 8167, fol. 130r.
2   *differas* in MS.

3   *merium* in MS.
4   *advenerit* in MS.
5   *adybeas* in MS.
6   For a discussion of this valedictory expression, see DOCUMENT 51.
7   TNA: PRO, SC 1/6/149 (*c.* 1226 × 32). On Simon of Senlis, see DOCUMENT 51.
8   TNA: PRO, SC 1/6/134 (1226–27); translated by W. H. Blaauw in "Letters to Ralph Neville," *Sussex Archaeological Collections*, 3 (1850), 72.

ECCLESIASTICAL ADMINISTRATION

54

Bishop H[ugh] of Lincoln Orders His Official to Prohibit Two Men from Leaving a Town Until a Major Lawsuit Between Them Has Been Settled by a Forthcoming Diocesan Assembly[1]

Episcopus mandat officiali suo ne permittat illum, nec illum, transgred[i][2] a villa antequam lis [magna][3] inter eos mota coram discretos fuerit terminata

H. dei gratia Lincolniensis episcopus officiali suo salutem. Pro[h]ibemus[4] tibi ne permittas D. et C. transgred[i][5] extra villam. Scituri quod lis magna inter eos movetur non potest terminari nisi coram magna discrecione. Unde volumus ut, partibus convocatis, accedentibus abbatibus et prioribus et aliis personis idoneis, res ab origine inquirend[e][6] sunt, et consilio bonorum virorum tene[an]tur.[7] Tantum ergo faciatis ne inter viros predictos fiat transaccio. [Valete].[8]

A bishop orders his official not to permit this or that man to leave the town before a major lawsuit commenced between them has been settled in the presence of learned men

H[ugh] by the grace of God, bishop of Lincoln, to his official,[9] greetings. We forbid you to allow D. and C. to leave the town. You will know that a major lawsuit between them is in progress. It cannot be settled except in the presence of much gathered wisdom. So, when the parties have been summoned, together with the abbots, priors, and other suitable clergy, we want the matters to be investigated right from their beginning, and to be settled by the advice of good men. Therefore, see to it that there is no private dealing between the said men. [Farewell.]

This letter reads as if it were based on an original act of Bishop "H." of Lincoln, but which one? There were two bishops of Lincoln with that initial in the late twelfth and early thirteenth centuries: Hugh of Avalon (1186–1200; canonized 1220) and Hugh of Wells (1209–35). Numerous written records are extant for the episcopacy of the later bishop, Hugh of Wells. He is the first English bishop whose episcopal register survives, and the texts of some 450 of his acts and letters have come down to us.[10] For Hugh of Avalon, some 215 acts (*acta* or official documents) have been published.[11] The compiler of this formulary included within it at least one other act of Hugh of Avalon, and another document (DOCUMENT 1) that may have had some association with his episcopate.[12]

The letter above does not appear in any published collection. Its opening formula, "H. by the grace of God, bishop of Lincoln," was in use in the diocese from the 1120s to the 1250s, and so could refer to either bishop. Since Hugh of Wells's surviving acts usually concluded with the date and place of issue, both of which are lacking in this letter, their absence might indicate that the letter relates to the earlier bishop. However, such specific details are lacking in most of the other documents in this formulary and thus could well have been deleted by the compiler.

The contents of the letter, however, are more suggestive of the episcopate of the earlier Hugh, since the case here between the characters D. and C. is to be settled at a forthcoming assembly of abbots, priors, and other clergy of the diocese. Such assemblies, sometimes called "synods" and at other times "chapters," had been meeting in the English church since the Conquest, for a variety of purposes. By the end of the eleventh century synods had developed a judicial function, and were dealing, at least on occasion, with such matters as church rights or the misdemeanors of laypeople.[13] Between about 1150 and 1200, however, the judicial functions of diocesan synods, which normally met only twice a year, were largely taken over by a new episcopal court, the consistory. These new courts developed along with the contemporary new field of canon law and the emerging professionalization of its practice. After 1200, English synods rarely engaged in judicial activity.[14]

This suggests that DOCUMENT 54 is more likely to have been based on a genuine act of the earlier bishop, Hugh of Avalon, than of his successor, Hugh of Wells. In either case, however, it provides an interesting glimpse into the ecclesiastical courts and diocesan administration in England at a time of rapid development and change.[15]

NOTES

1   Add. 8167, fol. 102v.
2   *transgredere* in MS.
3   Word in square brackets added in margin of MS, in same hand as main text.

4   *proibemus* in MS.
5   *transgredere* in MS.
6   *inquirendi* in MS.
7   *tenetur* in MS.
8   *vob'* (for *vobis*) in MS, seemingly in error for *Val[ete]* here.
9   On the office of the bishop's official, see DOCUMENT 56.
10 The texts of Hugh's acts are collected in William P. W. Phillimore, ed., *Rotuli Hugonis de Welles episcopi Lincolniensis*, 2 vols., Lincoln Record Society, 3 and 6 (Lincoln, 1912–13); and David M. Smith, ed., *The Acta of Hugh of Wells, Bishop of Lincoln, 1209–1235*, Lincoln Record Society, 88 (Lincoln, 2000).
11 For Hugh of Avalon's acts, see David M. Smith, ed., *English Episcopal Acta IV: Lincoln 1186–1206* (London: Oxford University Press, for the British Academy, 1986).
12 On fol. 118r–v of Add. 8167 (not printed in the present volume) is partial copy of a mandate by Bishop Hugh of Avalon concerning scholars of Northampton, of which the complete text survives in Walters MS W. 15, fol. 80v. The Latin text was printed by H. G. Richardson in "The Schools of Northampton in the Twelfth Century," *EHR*, 56 (1941), 596; see also *Formularies Which Bear on the History of Oxford*, ed. Salter, Pantin, and Richardson, 2:276, no. 8. It is summarized and discussed in Smith, ed., *English Episcopal Acta IV: Lincoln, 1186–1206*, no. 135. (For this reference we are grateful to Philippa Hoskin.) DOCUMENT 1 is a revised version of an earlier document (of which a copy survives in Walters MS W. 15, fol. 81r), which is dated to the year in which Bishop Hugh [of Avalon] died. See INTRODUCTION, pp. 7–8, and DOCUMENT 1.
13 Martin Brett, *The English Church Under Henry I* (London: Oxford University Press, 1975), 158–61.
14 Colin Morris, "From Synod to Consistory: The Bishops' Courts in England, 1150–1250," *Journal of Ecclesiastical History*, 22 (1971), 115–21.
15 On the administrative organization of the English church, see DOCUMENT 44.

55

An Archdeacon Writes to a Rural Dean to Charge Him with the Collection of a Clerical Tax, and to Order Him to Correct the Misbehavior of Chaplains in His Deanery[1]

Archidiaconus decano salutem. Mandatum domini pape distincte suscepimus. Omnem censum qui domino pape contingit in decanatu vestro colle[g]imus,[2] et ideo vobis idem preceptum iniungimus faciendum. Ceterim datum est nobis intelligi quod cap[e]llani[3] de decanatu vestro minus honeste vivunt, irregulariter se gerentes sub pretextu quod non sunt presbiteri parochiales. Tabernas enim ut audivimus frequentant inconvenientem et illicitam habentes cum laycis[4] societatem, ut de illis videatur impletum quod dicitur et erit populus sicut et sacerdos. Quod

ne vestre possit imputari pigricie predicti capellani⁵ siqui tales in decanatu vestro fuerint, sic corrigere studeatis, ut ceteris delinquentibus delin-
quendi m[iseri]am⁶ adnuatis, [saluti]⁷ commissarum vobis animarum
vigilanter insistentes.

An archdeacon to a rural dean, greetings. We have received a mandate
in no uncertain terms from the lord pope. We have assembled all the
taxation assessment material that relates to the lord pope in your deanery, and so we order you to see that his precept is carried out. In the
meantime, we have been given to understand that chaplains in your
deanery live in less than upright fashion, and behave in this way on the
pretext that they are not parish priests. For they go to taverns, as we
have heard, where they have inappropriate and illicit association with
laypeople, with the result that those who say that priests are no different
from laypeople are justified. In order that in the future it cannot be said
that, as a result of your laziness, such chaplains have been found in your
deanery, bestir yourself to correct these matters. Point out to the other
delinquents the wretchedness of their misbehavior, vigilantly pursuing
the salvation of those souls committed to you.

The archdeacon's censure here of the impropriety of clergy mingling in taverns
with layfolk was not the personal idiosyncracy of a teetotal bureaucrat, but
rather official church policy emanating from Rome itself. In 1215 the Fourth
Lateran Council (Lateran IV), the most important medieval council of the
Latin church, issued seventy-one canons (church laws) on a wide variety of
topics. These canons, which defined the basic beliefs and religious duties
required of all Christians, and which set forth procedures for ecclesiastical
administration at all levels, were drawn up at the instance of Pope Innocent
III (1198–1216), who convened the council and oversaw the speedy passing of
its agenda.

Canons 14–20 of Lateran IV dealt with clerical behavior and performance
of duties. These canons represented one of the responses by Pope Innocent to
anticlerical movements such as Waldensianism, which had been provoked by
the widespread perception that many clerics led lives of self-indulgence and
immorality and failed to live up to the ideals of "apostolic poverty" that
reformers associated with Jesus and the apostles. Two of these canons in particular lay behind the injunctions in the archdeacon's letter above: Canon
15, which ordered all clergy to abstain from drunkenness and from drinking
competitions, and Canon 16, which forbade clergy to enter taverns, except
when necessary on a journey. Since Canon 6 required the holding of annual

provincial councils and diocesan synods to examine and, where necessary, correct the morals of the clergy, and also required that "discreet" and "honest" persons be placed in each diocese to observe and report on any misbehavior to the archbishops and bishops, the archdeacon may also have been protecting himself from charges of maladministration by officially putting the rural dean on notice to clean up the misbehavior of the chaplains in his deanery.[8]

For accusations of misconduct by parish clergy, see also DOCUMENTS 57, 72, and 73.

NOTES

1   Add. 8167, fol. 130r–v.
2   MS damaged here.
3   *capllani* in MS.
4   Fol. 130v commences here.
5   *capellanos* in MS.
6   Word uncertain; *m$^{a^\cdot}$* in MS.
7   Or possibly *salvacioni*; this word is given as *solucioni* in MS.
8   For an English translation of the canons of Lateran IV, see Harry Rothwell, ed., *English Historical Documents, III, 1189–1327* (London: Eyre and Spottiswoode, 1975), 643–76. On the diocesan administration of the church, see DOCUMENT 44; on diocesan synods, see DOCUMENT 54.

56

A Bishop's Official Writes to an Archdeacon's Official to Certify the Credentials of a Chaplain Who Wishes to Move to the Latter's District[1]

Officialis officiali salutem. Quia sanam [non][2] sufficit habere conscienciam nisi similiter habeamus testimonium ab hiis foris sunt, vestre discrecioni [?commendare][3] volumus presencium latorem R. capellanum, de cuius ordine [non][4] dubitamus. Literarum sui ordinatoris [?testamur illum][5] ostendisse[6] sufficienciam [et][7] viva voce coram nobis ordines[8] probasse; diu eciam in partibus nostris divinam celebrasse; sicut eciam testantur illi cum quibus conversatus est eius vita [ir]reprehensibilis[9] est et honesta conversacio. Talem igitur tantum que virum cum in partibus vestris moram facere proposuerit si placet ad ex[secu]cionem[10] sui officii potestis admittere, quia talem periculo carere testamur admiscionem. Valete.

An official to an official, greetings. Because to have a thorough understanding is [not] possible unless we similarly have evidence from those

from elsewhere, we wish to [recommend] to your discretion R. the chaplain, the bearer of this present letter, of whose qualifications we have
[no] doubts. [We certify that] he has demonstrated the sufficiency of the
letters of the man who ordained him, and that his orders were pronounced valid in his interview before us, and also that for a long time
now he has celebrated mass in our district. Also, those with whom he
has spent his life testify that he is blame[less] and of honest conversation.
Such a man—and only such a man—when he proposes to live in your
district, you may, if you wish, admit to the performance of his office,
because we bear witness that such an admission would be free from risk.
Farewell.

This is a singularly corrupt text, which has the appearance of having been
intended to offer two variant appraisals (positive and negative) of a job candidate and of the validity of his qualifications. As a result, it has been necessary
here to edit it in such a way as to reflect one of these senses. In this version, a
chaplain wishes to move from one ecclesiastical district to another. In preparation for this, he has submitted his credentials to his bishop's official for verifi-
cation. The official has interviewed the chaplain personally, and has checked
his references with those who could testify to his character and to his performance of ecclesiastical duties. Now the bishop's official has written a letter of
recommendation for the chaplain to take to the official of the archdeacon of
the district into which he wishes to move. The letter certifies the chaplain's
qualifications and character, and authorizes the archdeacon's official to permit
him to officiate in his clerical capacity.

"Officials" were specialists in canon law delegated by bishops and archdeacons to preside over their courts in their absence and, as in this case, to conduct necessary investigations.[11] The "orders" that the official is investigating
here are three of the four senior grades of ordained ministry: sub-deacon,
deacon, and priest. The orders of deacon and priest had to be obtained from
the hands of a bishop (the fourth and highest grade).

Inquiries of various kinds were regularly made before men were appointed
to ecclesiastical benefices. Proof of legitimacy might be demanded, since the
illegitimate were barred from ordination;[12] peasants were examined to see if
they were of servile status; and candidates for the orders of priest and bishop
might be questioned as to whether they had reached the minimum age
required for consecration. As in this letter, there might also be background
checks of credentials and character, and these could be of critical importance.[13]
Around 1250, the Franciscan master, Adam Marsh, recalled some enquiries
that he had made about a candidate presented to the bishop of Lincoln for the

rich Oxfordshire vicarage of Bloxham. The people whom he had consulted assured him that the candidate was a man of good reputation, but later the news reached him that the man was carrying on a clandestine affair with a woman and that she had borne him a child.[14]

As in the letter above, a cleric's credentials and character were checked if he moved into a different jurisdiction. A thirteenth-century English ecclesiastical formulary includes a similar letter concerning a cleric who wishes to transfer from one diocese to another. It is addressed by "H." (presumably Hugh), bishop of Lincoln, to "T.," archdeacon of Wiltshire, and testifies to the good personal and priestly standing of the bearer.[15] This sort of checking was important, since cases of imposture were known. In 1211, for example, a certain Roger "le Chaplain" of Bishop's Stortford in Essex was arrested for pretending sometimes to be a clerk and sometimes a knight.[16] References would also be checked if a priest wished to be restored to duty after having suffered ecclesiastical punishment. In one such case in 1266, the dean of York wrote a letter on behalf of a priest called Mauger of Ripon, who had been suspended for having received his orders from foreign bishops without the permission of his own bishop. The dean certified that, following an examination of Mauger's life and accomplishments, he had restored his standing as a priest.[17] A priest who could not produce satisfactory credentials or testimonials when required was in danger of losing his livelihood altogether (see DOCUMENT 57).

Another letter in Add. 8167, from a bishop to an abbot, provides an interesting counterpart to this letter. The bishop writes that the abbot has sent his beloved clerk R. to him with a letter of recommendation, asking that R. be provided to a particular church. The bishop notes that the abbot's commendation was not necessary because R.'s honest life has long been well known and has been attested by such-and-such men. He has therefore admitted R. to the cure of souls and has ordered the local archdeacon to put him in physical possession of the living.[18]

Letters such as the latter reflect not only the ordinary business of church administrators but also (as in DOCUMENTS 17, , 73, 78, 86–87 and 95–96) the culture of favor-exchange that played such an important role in medieval life, ecclesiastical as well as secular.

NOTES

1   Add. 8167, fol. 131r–v.
2   The sense of the text appears to require a negative here.
3   In MS, *constare*, which does not fit well with the sense of the passage.
4   Here again the sense of the text appears to require a negative.
5   Several words of this sort evidently have been dropped from this sentence.
6   Word unclear; in MS, *osten*[iie].

7 q[uia] or q[ue] in MS.
8 Fol. 131v commences here.
9 Once again a negative seems to be required here.
10 excusacionem in MS.
11 See Morris, "From Synod to Consistory," 118–21. On the hierarchy of diocesan administration, see DOCUMENT 44.
12 Cf. a letter in Fairfax 27, fol. 3r (not printed in the present volume), reporting on the apparent illegitimacy of a candidate for a benefice.
13 Clause 16 of the Constitutions of Clarendon (1164) required that any peasant who was to be ordained had to get the permission of his lord. William Stubbs, *Select Charters, and Other Illustrations of English Constitutional History*, ed. Henry William Carless Davis, 9th ed. (Oxford: Oxford University Press, 1913). On age and educational requirements for ordination in this period, see Julia Barrow, "Grades of Ordination and Clerical Careers, c. 900–c. 1200," in *Anglo-Norman Studies*, 30, ed. Christopher P. Lewis (Woodbridge, Suffolk: Boydell, 2008), 41–61.
14 *Adae de Marisco Epistolae*, in *Monumenta Franciscana*, ed. John Sherren Brewer, vol. 1, Rolls Series, 4 (London: Longman, 1858–82), 108–9.
15 Lambeth Palace Library, MS 105, fol. 271v, middle column, letter headed: *Siquis clericus ab una diocesi ad aliam transmigrare voluerit a prelato suo huiusmodi litteras debet inpetrare*. This archdeacon "T" was fictitious, *Fasti Ecclesiae Anglicanae, 1066–1300, 4, Salisbury*, ed. Diana E. Greenway (London: University of London, 1991), 35.
16 *Curia Regis Rolls*, 6:146.
17 Christopher R. Cheney, "Letters of William Wickwane, Chancellor of York, 1266–1268," *EHR*, 47 (1932), 638.
18 Add. 8167, fol. 129r–v. This letter is not included in the present volume.

57

A Chaplain Who Is Worried About Losing His Job Writes to a Fellow-Chaplain for Advice and Help[1]

Capellanus capellano salutem. Generalis[2] ad nos iam pervenit citacio, ut unusquisque nostrorum illo die vel a quo fuerit ordinatus paratus sit edocere, de vita et similiter de moribus et de conversacione respondere. Super hiis a vobis consilium et ausilium appeto, quia—nescio quo casu—perdidi [?scriptum][3] quod de mea ordinacione habui, et nec [sic] ordinacionis mee sufficiens habeo testimonium. Insuper decanus michi multum adversatur, dicens me taberne frequentatorem esse et aliatorem, et liberalitatem meam convertens in scandalum, nec aliud est in causa nisi quod bursam meam nititur emungere. Tamen illud unicum habeo solacium, quod me solum gravare non poterit talium obieccio, pauci enim sane sunt in hoc episcopatu presbiteri qui de premissis immunes se scenciunt. Levius enim tolleratur quod a pluribus autem sustinetur;

comunis pena mitior esse solet. Quid michi sit agendum litteratorie significetis, et si neccese fuerit mecum stare velitis. Eandem cum locus et tempus exigerit recompensacionem rescipituri.

A chaplain to a chaplain, greetings. A general citation has now reached us that each of us must be prepared to show on what day or by whom he was ordained, and to answer concerning his life and, similarly, his moral character and associations. I need your advice and assistance concerning these matters because I have lost—I know not how—the [documentation] that I had concerning my ordination, and [now] I don't have sufficient evidence about my ordination. In addition, my rural dean really has it in for me, saying that I am a frequenter of the tavern and a gamester, and turning my generosity into scandal, for no other cause than that he is trying to clean out my purse. Nevertheless, I have one solace: that I can't be the only one accused of these things, since there are precious few priests in this diocese who can claim to be immune from such charges. For something is more easily borne if it is shared by many; a communal punishment is generally milder [*i.e., than an individual one*]. Please let me know by letter what I ought to do, and if you would be willing to support me, if necessary. When place and time shall require it, you will receive the same help [from me] in return.

In the manuscript, the letter that precedes this one is a general citation from a rural dean to all the priests of his deanery, ordering them to bring in their certificates of ordination to the archdeacon for inspection.[4] Now a panicky chaplain writes to a friend for advice and help, because he has lost the written record of his ordination and doesn't know what to do. He is especially fearful because, he says, his rural dean is out to get him, and is making him out to be a tavern-haunter and habitual gambler, whereas in fact the chaplain has simply been generous. The chaplain's only comfort is that all the other priests in the diocese have been doing the same things, and a communal punishment falls more lightly than an individual one. He begs his friend for advice on what to do, and for assurances that the friend will stand by him, if that should become necessary, and promises to do the same for his friend someday if needed.

This letter opens a window onto the world of ecclesiastical politics at the lowest level, that of the parochial clergy. The chaplain here is not a parish priest nor the holder of some other benefice with a lifetime tenure. In the early thirteenth century, a chaplain (*capellanus*) was a cleric who exercised his function as priest or deacon within a wealthy lay or ecclesiastical household. In this fashion, by 1200 most vicars and rectors of any substance in England maintained several chaplains on salary to assist them in their pastoral duties. Bishops approved highly of this, since the chaplains performed valuable assistance in the parishes but were not supported at diocesan expense.[5]

In this letter, the writer holds a stipendiary position that he is in serious jeopardy of losing if he cannot produce his ordination credentials, especially if his rural dean tells the archdeacon that his behavior is notorious. A chaplain who lost his job under such conditions would have had a very difficult time finding another. If the chaplain's friend cannot help him, ruin stares him in the face, and he knows it.

NOTES

1   Fairfax 27, fol. 3v.
2   Corrected in MS from *Generacolis*.
3   There is a gap in the text here about one-half inch (1.25 cm) long. It must represent a neuter word meaning something like "record" or "documentation"; *scriptum* would be one possibility.
4   Fairfax 27, fol. 3v. This letter, which is not included in the present volume, begins as follows: *Decanus de illo loco capellanis omnibus de decanatu suo salutem. Ab archideacono generalis emanit citacio, ut omnes presbiteri tam parochiales quam alii coram illo tali die et tali loco compareant, super ordinacione sua certitudinem ei facientes.* On the hierarchy of diocesan administration, see DOCUMENT 44.
5   Simon Townley, "Unbeneficed Clergy in the Thirteenth Century: Two English Dioceses," in *Studies in Clergy and Ministry in Medieval England*, Borthwick Studies in History, 1 (1991), 38–64.

FORESTS AND HUNTING

--------------------------------- 58 ---------------------------------

The King Orders a Sheriff to Inquire into the Poaching of Game in a Royal Forest[1]

Rex vicecomiti mandat de feris suis qui destruuntur

Rex vicecomiti. salutem. Ad audientiam nostram perventum est quod foresta nostra destruitur et fere nostre furtim occiduntur. Quare tibi mandamus atque precipimus ut, visis literis istis, inquiri facias per comitatum tuam[2] qui solent esse infames de foresta nostra, et eos facias atachiari per vadia firmentalia, et si plegios ad libitum tuum invenire non poterint, pone corpora eorum in carcere donec coram nobis vel iusticiariis nostris comparuerint. Vale.

The king asks a sheriff about his animals that are being killed

The king to a sheriff, greetings. It has come to our attention that our forest is being damaged and our animals secretly slaughtered. Therefore, we order and command you that, as soon as you have seen this writ, you have an inquiry made throughout your county as to who are the persons of ill repute in our forest, and have them attached by secure pledges, and if they are unable to find suitable pledges, imprison them until they can appear before us or our justices.[3] Farewell.

A large part of England was designated as royal forest. This was area reserved by the king for his hunting and forestry, within which a special form of customary law called "forest law" applied. The area designated might be wooded (*alta foresta*, or "deep forest"), or it might be heathland, or it even might be agricultural land.[4] The area of royal forest reached its greatest extent in the reign of Henry II (1154–89), when the entire county of Essex, and much of the counties of Berkshire, Hampshire, Huntingdonshire, and Northamptonshire, were under forest law.[5] A network of forest justices, chief foresters, and foresters enforced the law assiduously across England, and Henry II established a periodic "forest eyre," a national circuit of forest courts that examined pleas of "vert" (offenses against woodland) and "venison" (offenses against the king's game animals). However, as the writ above demonstrates, the king could also order a sheriff to investigate and punish poachers and other forest offenders.

People of all social classes resented forest law and jurisdiction, for the king's officers could fine inhabitants of the forest areas for a range of offenses and levy payments on them for farming in an area devoted to game. Foresters, themselves often heavy-handed and corrupt (see DOCUMENT 59), were among the most hated of the king's officers. Disputes over forest jurisdiction were among the earliest grievances that counties and local communities sought to negotiate with the king. These complaints reached their high point in 1217 with the "Charter of the Forest." Like Magna Carta, it was a product of the "Barons' War," a confrontation in fact between the king and the entire nation, not just the aristocracy. The Forest Charter addressed five principal abuses: the extension of the royal forest since Henry II's accession in 1154; the overzealousness of royal foresters in imposing fines for farming and for keeping dogs within forest boundaries; the frequent summons to forest courts not only of those who lived within the forest, but also of people who lived outside the bounds; the trespass of royal officers into exempt private woodland within the forest; and the imposition of corporal and capital penalties on those convicted of forest offenses.[6]

The Forest Charter put an end to the harsh Forest Law practice of mutilating or executing those who poached game in royal forests, and introduced fines and imprisonment instead. It also permitted prelates and magnates traveling through a royal forest to take one or two deer for their own use, providing they did so under supervision of the king's foresters, or at least sounded their horns as they hunted the beasts, "so that they do not appear to be doing it illegally" (clause 11). As this letter shows, poaching was a frequent problem. The rolls of the forest justices in the later thirteenth century give a picture of quite how widespread and pervasive poaching was in royal forests. It took in the full social spectrum, from archbishops to the poorest of peasants, although barons and knights were the most prominent offenders. Hunting deer with bows and dogs was a definitive aristocratic recreation, and many aristocrats enjoyed illegal sport in the king's forest, or took more game than was permitted to them while passing through.[7]

The king's game was also poached by forest residents and other ordinary people, including the household servants, huntsmen, and woodsmen employed by wealthy landowners, who went into the king's forests on their own account without their masters' knowledge. The judicial records reveal that poaching, like other criminal activities (see DOCUMENTS 39–41), could also be highly organized, and that gangs sometimes systematically plundered royal woodland. They took venison to order for criminal receivers for illegal sale, or for wealthy clients for their own consumption. In the 1250s, for example, Walter of Okle and William Baterich were persistent offenders in the Forest of Dean in Gloucestershire. They and others like them obtained venison from a ring of poachers (who worked in groups of up to a dozen men), on commission from local aristocrats, and even from the monks of Tintern abbey and the canons of St Augustine, Bristol. William apparently supplied venison to contacts and receivers in the town of Bristol, across the Severn estuary from the forest. One of his associates was a local butcher.[8] Poaching the king's game in the thirteenth century, an activity that embraced the entire social spectrum, was often widely tolerated in society.

The king's view was otherwise, of course. The fact that the writ above is directed to his principal county officer, the sheriff, rather than to the castellan or forester in charge of an individual forest, indicates that in this case the offense was widespread or particularly severe. Poaching gangs were not afraid to resist, assault, or shoot at royal foresters and verderers (forest officials in charge of timber and animal pasture). One of the miracles attributed to St Thomas Becket, for example, was the healing of a forester who had been shot in the throat by poachers (Fig. 8).[9] On two occasions in 1272 poachers cut off a deer's head and placed it on a stake in Rockingham Forest in Northamptonshire. On the first occasion they placed a spindle in the deer's mouth and the second time a billet of firewood, turning its head to the sun, "in great contempt of the king and his forester."[10] It was outrages such as these that probably inspired the model writ above.

Figure 8. Adam the Forester is shot in the throat by men poaching deer, from the Becket Miracle Windows, Canterbury Cathedral (*c.* 1213–20).

NOTES

1   Add. 8167, fol. 107v.
2   Corrected in MS from *tuuam.*
3   I.e., the prisoners could be released if they were able to produce pledges of sufficient value to serve as their bail, otherwise they were to be imprisoned.
4   It is often assumed that far more of England was wooded in the middle ages than today, but surveys have shown that in fact the wooded area was not much more extensive in the thirteenth century than in the mid-twentieth century, though there have been major changes since then. Oliver Rackham, *Trees and Woodland in the British Landscape* (London: J. M. Dent, 1976), 173.
5   Margaret Bazeley, "The Extent of the English Forest in the Thirteenth Century," *Transactions of the Royal Historical Society*, 4th ser., iv (1921), 140–72, map at p. 60.
6   Stubbs, *Select Charters*, 344–48; translated in Rothwell, ed., *English Historical Documents, III, 1189–1327*, 337–40.
7   Jean Birrell, "Who Poached the King's Deer? A Study in Thirteenth-Century Crime," *Midland History*, 7 (1981), 11–13.
8   Birrell, "Who Poached the King's Deer?" 14, 20.

9   For the early thirteenth-century window in Canterbury Cathedral that illustrates this miracle, see M. A. Michael, *Stained Glass of Canterbury Cathedral* (London: Scala, 2004), 16–17, 120–21.

10 Birrell, "Who Poached the King's Deer?" 16.

59

The King Orders a Sheriff to Arrest the Corrupt Foresters Under His Command Who Have Been Selling Oak Trees from the Royal Forest[1]

Rex mandat vicecomiti de quercis in foresta sua destructis

Rex vicecomiti salutem. Significavit nobis vicinus tuus quod ministri tui qui sub te forestam nostram custodiunt[2] quercus foreste nostre vendunt ad suum placi[t]um,[3] et de hoc precipue certificavit me v. [vel][4] vi. magnas quercus comparavit et a silva reduxit. Quare tibi mandamus atque precipimus ut, omni occasione et dilacione remotis, predictos ministros tuos quot[5] sint incarcerari facias, nec dimittas illos per vadium nec per plegios donec breve nostrum habueris. Preterea precipimus ut capias caucionem de illis qui forestam nostram [?destruere][6] et robora nostra comparare consueverunt, ut veniant coram nobis responsuri et iuri parituri qua fronte ausi sunt hoc facere. Tantum facias nobis molliri. Vale.

The king sends word to a sheriff about oak trees being felled in his forest

The king to a sheriff, greetings. A neighbor of yours has informed us that your officers who keep our forest under you are selling oak trees from our forest at will, and in particular he has certified to me that he has purchased five or six great oaks and has taken them from the woodland. Therefore, we command and order you that, having put aside every argument and delay, you have those officers imprisoned, however many of them there may be, and you are not to release them by pledge or sureties until you have our writ. Furthermore, we order you to take bail from those who have been accustomed to damage our forest and sell our oaks, so that they may come before us to answer and produce their defense for having had the effrontery to do this. Deal with this in such as way as to make us less angry [*i.e., with you*]. Farewell.

This letter illustrates another of the common abuses of the forest, offenses against the "vert" or "greenwood." Most of these were minor and usually resulted in fines. Such offenses included unlicensed farming in woodland clearings (*purpesture*), and illegal pasturing of pigs (*pannage*) or collecting of firewood (*estover*) where there was no customary right to do so.[7] There are instances of foresters illegally disposing of firewood and timber for their own profit, including one Norman Sampson, who was accused in 1255 of selling three oaks from the king's forest of Huntingdonshire, and of giving stolen wood from the king's woods at Weybridge to his landlord's daughters, which they sold at Huntingdon for money to buy him food.[8] The offense described in the writ above was much more serious, since it involved widespread and organized corruption among the foresters under the sheriff's command, and extended to other men to whom they were fencing the stolen trees. Chief foresters might, however, as perquisites of their office, have the right to take the loppings of trees, and even to make an occasional gift of a royal tree; this is discussed in DOCUMENTS 95 and 96.

NOTES

1   Add. 8167, fol. 108r.
2   Corrected in MS from *costoditunt*.
3   *placidum* in MS.
4   *q[ui]* in MS.
5   *quot quot* in MS.
6   Some such verb as this appears to be missing here.
7   Charles Young, *The Royal Forests of Medieval England* (Philadelphia: University of Pennsylvania Press, 1979), 108–11.
8   George James Turner, ed., *Select Pleas of the Forest*, Selden Society, 13 (London, 1899), 21, 25.

------------------------------ 60 ------------------------------

A Sheriff Tells the King that He Cannot Comply with a Command to Provide Venison, Because the Adjoining Forests Belong to the King of Scots, Whose Foresters Refuse to Allow Him to Take Game There[1]

Excellentissimo domino suo regi Anglie, vicecomes de C. salutem et fidele servicium.[2] Omnia que literis vestris michi mandastis pro posse meo fideliter adimplevi. Restat tamen de venacione ad opus vestrum capiendam, quod facere non potui, quia foreste que terris vestris in balliva mea vicine pertinent ad dominum regem Scoticorum, et forestarii eius nolunt sustinere quod aliquam ibi capiam venacionem. Quare, si placet vobis, alibi super hoc provideatis.

To his most excellent lord the king of England, the sheriff of C[am-bridge] sends greeting and faithful service. I have faithfully carried out everything that you ordered in your letter to me, so far as I was able. The only exception is the taking of venison for your use, which I could not do because the forests that abut your estates in my shire belong to the lord king of Scots, and his foresters refuse to allow me to take any venison there. Therefore, if it please you, you need to make arrangements for this elsewhere.

The identification of the shire here as Cambridge is based on the fact that the king of Scots periodically held the honor of Huntingdon, which had large estates in that county.[3] Between 1165 and 1237 the honor of Huntingdon was in the hands of Earl David II and Earl John of Huntingdon (cadets of the Scottish royal house), so if this letter is based on a sheriff's actual response to a royal writ, it belongs after 1237, when Huntingdon reverted to King Alexander II (1214–49).[4]

An especially interesting feature of this document is what it reveals about the increasing degree of territorial autonomy that a lord's estate officers could claim, even against the officers of the king of England. The barons' desire to defend and extend their "liberties" was a pronounced feature of the thirteenth century. In the 1260s and 1270s, for example, Earl John de Warenne of Surrey (1250–1304) jealously guarded his forests in Sussex, even at the king's expense, as the king of Scots was supposedly doing in Cambridgeshire in this letter. In the 1260s, through his court at Lewes, the earl's bailiffs harried those who sought to encroach on his timber and game, while in the 1270s one of his tenants alleged that his bailiffs had for some time been forcibly excluding the king's officers from his woodland. The earl's passion for hunting his parks and forests was conducted at his neighbors' expense. He put their lands under his own forest law as it suited him, and chased deer over their fields with his dogs and an armed retinue. His parks were stocked with so many deer that they were driven to forage for food in his unlucky neighbors' fields, damaging their crops.[5]

NOTES

1 Add. 8167, fol. 129v.
2 For other examples of this salutation, see DOCUMENTS 69 and 99.
3 In the counties of Cumberland and Kent (*Cantia* in Latin), which also had the initial "C," the kings of England and Scotland did not possess adjoining estates.
4 On the lands of the Scottish royal family in England in the twelfth and thirteenth centuries, see Keith J. Stringer, *Earl David of Huntingdon: A Study in Anglo-Scottish History* (Edinburgh: Edinburgh University Press, 1985).

5   For the rise of the baronial liberty in the thirteenth century, see Crouch, *English Aristocracy*, Chap. 10. For the Warenne forests, see *Rotuli Hundredorum*, ed. William Illingworth, vol. 1 (London: Record Commission, 1812–18), 208–10; *Records of the Barony and Honour of the Rape of Lewes*, ed. Arnold J. Taylor, Sussex Record Society, 44 (1939), passim.

61

A Baron Asks Another Baron to Send Him Game and Fish to Stock His New Park and Fishpond, and in Return He Sends Hunting Dogs, Hawks, and Falcons[1]

Baro baroni salutem. Bona communicata pluribus proficiunt. In loco competenti parcum, in parco vivarium feci. Loci considerans amenitatem, communicare mecum velitis ferarum vestrarum et piscium abbundanciam quam habetis? Scilicet, damulas et capriolas de parcis vestris, lucios et perticos et rochias de vivariis vestris, michi transmittatis? Licencius et dilectabilius, cum ad partes illas veneritis, venari poteritis et piscari. Mitto vobis duos leporarios et unum canem lupinarium, tres brachios, et unum hispinelium[2] et unum lutericium[3] et alium investigatorem, nisum sorum, hostorium mutatum, tercellum ramagium, falconem altanum,[4] et duos lanarios, que munuscula, si placet, gratanter accipiatis, sicut si preciosiora vobis destinassem.

A baron to another baron, greetings. When good things are shared, they benefit more people. I have made a park in a suitable place, and in the park I have made a fishpond. Considering the pleasantness of the place, would you be willing to share with me the abundance of game and fish that you have? Namely, would you send me does of fallow deer (*damulas*) and of roe deer (*capriolas*) from your parks, and pike (*lucios*), perch, and roach from your fishponds? [That way,] you will be able to hunt and fish all the more freely and pleasurably when you come here. [In return,] I am sending you two grayhounds (*leporarios*) and a wolfhound (*canem lupinarium*), three brachets (*brachios*)[5] and one spaniel (*hispinelium*), and an otter-hound (*lutericium*), and another tracker-dog (*alium investigatorem*), a sorehawk (*nisum sorum*),[6] a mewed goshawk (*hostorium mutatum*),[7] a ramage tiercel (*tercellum ramagium*),[8] a peregrine falcon (*falconem altanum*), and two lanner falcons (*lanarios*), which little gifts, if it please you, accept freely, since, were they even more precious, I would have chosen [them] for you.

Hunting and hawking were iconic recreations of the medieval aristocracy. They were done both on foot and on horseback, with the assistance of special breeds of dogs and hunting birds. In this letter, a baron writes that he has created a hunting park with a fishpond in it. He asks his fellow-baron, who has multiple parks and ponds of his own, to send two kinds of deer and three kinds of fish for stocking the writer's park and pond. As inducements (in the kind of gift-exchange that was so important in elite culture), the writer notes that his stocked park and pond will then provide sport for the other baron to enjoy when he visits, and he sends his friend nine hunting dogs and six hunting birds of his own, a valuable present that he disarmingly dismisses as "little gifts" ("*munuscula*").

The keeping of game parks served to demarcate elite status as clearly as did the possession of a castle.[9] Such parks were large areas of woodland or heathland that were enclosed by ditches, banks, and palisades to keep the game within their bounds. When Geoffrey de Clinton, a rising royal officer, acquired the royal manor of Kenilworth around 1125, he laid out his park there first, before he began serious work on the large castle that was to be his other great social statement.[10] The kings of England maintained very extensive hunting territories (see DOCUMENTS 58 and 60) and, as the model letter above makes plain, wealthy landholders were willing to invest heavily in the creation and maintenance of parks and fishponds, in stocking them with suitable game and fish, and in obtaining and training hunting dogs, hawks, and falcons. The possession of a park was both an assertion of aristocratic standing and a source of patronage, even for those who did not hunt. In the 1180s, for example, the wealthy abbot of Bury St. Edmunds had parks on his estates, and although he could not himself hunt them, he offered them to favored neighbors and sat in a hilltop pleasance or viewing platform to watch them enjoy themselves.[11]

Three kinds of deer were used for stocking game parks in medieval England: red deer (in Latin, *cervus*, a large breed), fallow deer (*dama* or *damus*, a medium-sized breed), and roe deer (*capreolus*, a small breed). Harts (male red deer over six years in age, with large, tined antlers) were by far the favorite deer for the chase, but bucks (adult male fallow deer), hinds (female red deer), and does (female fallow deer) were also hunted, as were the smaller roebuck (adult male roe deer) and roe does.[12] In this letter, the writer's request for does of fallow and roe deer suggests that he already has some bucks and now wishes to establish breeding herds.

The favorite manner of hunting deer was for groups of hunters to chase a single hart or buck on horseback with dogs. The quarry was pursued until, exhausted, it turned at bay; one of the hunters then dismounted and killed it by hand with a sword or knife, a dangerous act requiring much skill and training. Deer were also hunted in groups, on foot: servants drove them in herds past the hunters, who were stationed at designated places called "trysts" from which they shot at the running animals with bows.[13] This, too, could be hazardous for the men as well as the deer. In 1100, for example, King William Rufus was killed while hunting in the New Forest when a badly placed companion shot an arrow that passed over a deer and struck the king instead.[14] Milo, earl of Hereford, died in a similar hunting accident in 1143.[15] Hares, like harts and bucks, were chased ("coursed") on horseback with grayhounds. They provided such good sport that they shared with harts the status of favorite quarry.[16]

Although there was no statutory close season ("fence month") for game in this period, there were recognized seasons that were considered best for hunting various types of deer and other game because that was when they were in their best condition. In late medieval England, bucks and harts were hunted from June to September, hinds and does from September to February, and roebuck from Easter to Michaelmas (September 29). Foxes and boar were hunted in the cold-weather months, and otters from the end of February until midsummer; but hares, martins, badgers, rabbits, and (probably) wolves were generally hunted all year round.[17]

Fishponds (*vivaria*), while expensive to build and maintain, were much more common than game parks, and they were a feature of ecclesiastical as well as lay estates. They were especially useful because in medieval England the consumption of meat was forbidden on Fridays and Saturdays (and, in many households, on Wednesdays), as well as during Lent and on the eves ("vigils") of important festivals such as Christmas.[18] Like game parks, fishponds provided some of the most elite foods to grace the medieval table. Pike, perch, and roach (the three types of fish discussed in the letter above) were all highly regarded, especially pike,[19] but the inclusion of pike in a fishpond with other fish was risky. According to *Fleta*, a treatise on manorial and household administration written about 1290, fishponds, lakes, and other fisheries should be stocked with bream and perch, but not with pike, tench, or eels because they would devour too many fish.[20] Fishing as a sport is poorly documented before the late medieval period, and it has been argued that "it was not a recognized sport of the upper classes" at all.[21] The letter above, however, makes it clear that recreational fishing was indeed enjoyed by at least some noble sportsmen by the 1240s.

Of the six breeds of dog mentioned in this letter, at least four—the wolfhound, otter-hound, brachet, and the other tracker-dog—would have been used for hunting game: wolves and otters in the case of the first two breeds, and deer in the case of the latter two. The earliest medieval European treatise on deer-hunting (*De arte bersandi*), which dates from the time of Emperor Frederick II (d. 1250), devotes several chapters to the training of brachets to follow deer, and recommends that the hunter reward the successful brachet by patting it on the head and showing it "good will," because that is what brachets like.[22] The two grayhounds and the spaniel mentioned in the letter above may have been intended for use either in hunting or in hawking.[23] In another letter in the same formulary, a man asks a friend for the loan of a hawk (*nisum*), and also of a grayhound (*leporarium*) "with which my young grayhounds might learn to course."[24] Emperor Frederick II, who himself in the 1240s wrote a magisterial book on the art of hunting with birds (*De arte venandi cum avibus*), observed that the swiftness of grayhounds made them useful in assisting falcons against large, aggressive birds such as cranes and herons.[25] However, he noted, to be suitable, the grayhounds must be brave, willing to wade or swim through water, and able to run over difficult ground. Frederick recommended using only male dogs so that they would always be fit to hunt, unlike females, which might be in heat or pregnant when needed. He gave detailed instructions for training grayhounds to assist falcons in the hunt, recommending, among other things, that a dog be given treats of cheese, bread, "or other food that he likes" to reinforce its training.[26] Gaston Phoebus, count of Foix, who in the 1380s wrote a celebrated treatise on hunting called the *Livre de chasse*, reported that spaniels (*espaignolz*, or *chiens doysel*, "bird dogs") were especially useful in flushing partridge, quail, and other small game, and that, when taught to swim, they could also be sent against diving birds and used to retrieve waterfowl. However, he cautioned, spaniels could be quarrelsome and undisciplined, and they barked too much.[27]

Hawking was as aristocratic a sport as hunting, and while hunting seems to have been a predominantly male sport, hawking was enjoyed by women as well as men (see DOCUMENT 62). The goshawk, peregrine falcon, and lanner falcons named in the letter above were among the three species of falcons (peregrines, gyrfalcons, and lanners) and two of hawks (goshawks and sparrowhawks) that represented the five main kinds of hunting birds used in thirteenth-century England.[28] Hunters used falcons and hawks to hunt other birds, especially cranes, herons, and duck.[29] They preferred to use female birds, which were larger and stronger than the males ("tiercels"), although the latter were used, too; one young tiercel is mentioned in the letter above, and another is the subject of DOCUMENT 62.

For hunting purposes, the principal differences between hawks and falcons lie in the shape of their wings and the manner in which they hunt and kill their prey. Falcons have narrow, pointed wings and tails and fly with a rapid, steady wing-beat; they attack other birds by plummeting ("stooping") from a great height at great speed, striking their prey with tremendous force with their talons, and splitting or decapitating it with one blow. Because of this, falcons hunt best over open country. Gyrfalcons and peregrines were considered the finest falcons; they were flown principally against cranes, herons, and duck, though also, at least occasionally, against other birds such as rooks. Lanner falcons, which were considered less strong, swift, and bold than gyrfalcons or peregrines, and were of lesser value, were flown at partridges, crows, and magpies. Cranes, herons, duck, and partridge were all prized for eating, but not rooks, crows, or magpies; the latter were evidently hunted purely for sport (and, perhaps, for feeding to the falcons and hawks).[30]

Hawks have shorter, rounder wings and a longer tail than falcons; their gliding flight is broken with a stutter for three or four wing-beats, and they fly at low levels. They kill their prey by gripping and puncturing it with their long talons, and sometimes by slashing it with their beak. In England, both goshawks (the more highly valued hawk) and sparrowhawks were flown most often against duck, although there are non-English accounts of the use of goshawks against cranes and herons as well. Because of their maneuverability and low-altitude flying, hawks, unlike falcons, could be used in brush or woodland, where they were flown against pheasants, partridges, and rooks.[31]

The use of specialized terminology for hawking and hunting, so prominently displayed in DOCUMENT 61, was typical of the period. John of Salisbury noted sarcastically in *Policraticus* (1156–59), "In our day this knowledge [of hunting jargon] constitutes the liberal studies of the higher class."[32] In a model letter such as the one above, the inclusion of such terminology would also have served to teach Latin vocabulary to its audience of students and other readers. However, in the letter's proud display of technical vocabulary, as well as in its representation of some of the expensive demands of the sport, it encapsulates the flavor of the aristocratic obsession with hunting.

NOTES

1 Fairfax 27, fol. 4v.
2 Corrected in MS from *hispinalium*.
3 *lucercium* in MS.
4 *altatum* in MS.
5 Hounds that hunt by scent.
6 A hawk in her first year, before she molts, when her plumage is still reddish (sorrel-colored). Robin S. Oggins, *The Kings and Their Hawks: Falconry in Medieval England* (New Haven: Yale University Press, 2004), 12.
7 A goshawk that has molted and is thus more than a year old. See Frederick II, Emperor of Germany, *The Art of Falconry, Being the* De arte venandi cum avibus *of Frederick II of Hohenstaufen*, trans. and ed. Casey A. Wood and F. Marjorie Fyfe

(Stanford, Calif.: Stanford University Press, and London: Oxford University Press, 1943), "Glossary of Falconry Terms," s.v. "mew," 622.

8   A young male bird that has left the nest for nearby branches. Oggins, *Kings and Their Hawks*, 12.

9   For parks, see Rackham, *Trees and Woodland*, 142–51. On hunting, see Crouch, *Image of Aristocracy*, 305–10.

10   David Crouch, "Geoffrey de Clinton and Roger Earl of Warwick," *Bulletin of the Institute of Historical Research*, 55 (1982), 116–18.

11   *The Chronicle of Joscelin of Brakelond*, ed. H. E. Butler (London: Nelson, 1949), 28. Hunting and fowling, and the keeping of hunting dogs and falcons, were formally forbidden to clerics in 1215 by Canon 15 of the Fourth Lateran Council. Rothwell, ed., *English Historical Documents, III, 1189–1327*, 653; cf. DOCUMENT 55.

12   Richard Almond, *Medieval Hunting* (Stroud, Gloucestershire: Sutton, 2003), 18, 61–65, 73, 87.

13   Almond, *Medieval Hunting*, 73–75, 82–84.

14   Frank Barlow, *William Rufus* (London: Methuen, 1983), 123.

15   Thomas Jones, ed., *Brut y Tywysogyon; or, The Chronicle of the Princes. Red Book of Hergest Version* (Cardiff: University of Wales Press, 1955), 118.

16   Almond, *Medieval Hunting*, 67–68. The Latin word for grayhound was *leporarius*, or "harrier."

17   In the later medieval period, however, the highly prized harts (but not the hinds), were given the privilege of a close season from early February until May or June in England. Almond, *Medieval Hunting*, 84–87.

18   See Christopher Dyer, "The Consumption of Fresh-Water Fish in Medieval England," in *Medieval Fish, Fisheries and Fishponds in England*, ed. Michael Aston, vol. 1, B[ritish] A[rchaeological] R[eports] British Series, 182 (1988), 27–28. For a brief overview of the design and construction of fishponds, see also John M. Steane, *The Archaeology of Medieval England and Wales* (Athens: University of Georgia Press, 1985), 171–72.

19   According to Christopher Dyer, eels were the principal freshwater fish consumed in aristocratic households, followed by bream, perch, pike, roach, and tench. While all were caught in rivers, "they were also the most common species to be kept in ponds." Dyer, "Consumption of Fresh-Water Fish," 31.

20   *Fleta* (c. 1290), ed. and trans. Henry Gerald Richardson and George Osborne Sayles, vols. 2–4 (vol. 1 never published), Selden Society, 72, 89, 99 (1955–84, for the years 1953, 1972, 1983), vol. 2: 247. On the design, maintenance, and stocking of fishponds, including the transport of live fish to stock them, see also C. J. Bond, "Monastic Fisheries," in *Medieval Fish, Fisheries and Fishponds*, ed. Aston, vol. 1, 94–96; and C. F. Hickling, "Prior More's Fishponds," *Medieval Archaeology*, 15 (1971), 118–23.

21   Charles Homer Haskins, *Studies in Mediaeval Culture* (New York: Oxford University Press, 1929), 118. On the fifteenth-century literature on fishing, see Richard C. Hoffmann, *Fishers' Craft and Lettered Art: Tracts on Fishing from the End of the Middle Ages*, Toronto Medieval Texts and Translation, 12 (Toronto: University of Toronto Press, 1997).

22   Haskins, *Studies in Mediaeval Culture*, 117–18, 130–31.

23   A description of the royal household made shortly after the death of Henry I (1135) lists the king's hunting dogs as greyhounds (*veltrarii*) and running hounds (*liemarii*), both used for hunting wolves; bloodhounds; greater and lesser staghounds; and small

hounds (*braconarii*, evidently brachets). However, there is no mention in this treatise of royal hawks, falcons, or falconers. *Constitutio Domus Regis*, in *English Historical Documents*, vol. 2, *1042–1189*, ed. David C. Douglas and George W. Greenaway (London: Eyre and Spottiswoode, 1953), 422–27 (dogs, 426–27). See also the recent edition of this document in *Constitutio Domus Regis: Disposition of the King's Household*, ed. and trans. Stephen D. Church (Oxford: Clarendon, 2007).

24 *cum quo iuvenes leporarii mei curere discant.* Fairfax 27, fol. 6r. Unfortunately, portions of this letter are cut away and its full contents cannot be known.
25 Frederick II, *Art of Falconry*, 267–70, 288–90, 328–31.
26 Frederick II, *Art of Falconry*, 267–70.
27 Almond, *Medieval Hunting*, 59–60; also Oggins, *Kings and Their Hawks*, 32. On the literature of hunting before 1300, see also Charles Homer Haskins, "The Latin Literature of Sport," *Speculum*, 2 (1927), 235–52.
28 Oggins, *Kings and Their Hawks*, 10.
29 Oggins, *Kings and Their Hawks*, 13–14, 16, 32.
30 Oggins, *Kings and Their Hawks*, 10–17, 152 (nn. 16, 19, 21).
31 Oggins, *Kings and Their Hawks*, 10–12, 16.
32 Quoted in Oggins, *Kings and Their Hawks*, 129. On the date of *Policraticus,* see *Oxford DNB*, s.n. "Salisbury, John of (late 1110s–1180)."

62

A Baron Asks a Baron to Have the Latter's Son Train His Goshawk, Which He Sends[1]

Baro baroni salutem. A quodam milite socio vestro[2] didicimus, quod filius vester perydoneus est ad hosterios[3] reclamandum. Unum autem habemus, quem a muta[4] noviter extraximus, set ad illum reclamandum intendere non possumus et ad vos illum transmittimus, rogantes attencius quatinus illum filio vestro tradatis ad reclamandum. Et cum reclamatus fuerit per eundem filium vestrum nobis remittatur, ut illum volare videre[5] valeamus.[6] Et filio vestro laboris sui per optime premium suum (*vel mercedem*)[7] persolvemus.

A baron to a baron, greetings. From a certain knight, a friend of yours,[8] we have learned that your son is excellent at training[9] goshawks. We have one, which we have newly taken from the mews, but we cannot plan on training him, and [so] we send him to you, asking earnestly that you hand him over to your son for training, and when he is trained by him, let him be brought back to us by your son, so that we can see him fly. And we shall pay your son an especially good recompense (*or fee*) for his labor.

As noted in DOCUMENT 61, hawking and hunting were consuming aristocratic passions, and falcons and hawks were emblems of aristocratic life. Harold II, the last Anglo-Saxon king of England (d. 1066), was reputed to have written a book in English on the care of hawks,[10] and most great noble households included falconers and hawkers, such as those of the twelfth-century earls of Chester, who employed both.[11] In this letter, a baron sends a young male goshawk[12] to another baron, whose son is reputed to be good at training these birds, and requests that the latter's son undertake its training, for which the writer will remunerate him.

The training of falcons and hawks was complex, time-consuming, and expensive, and required considerable skill and patience. Young birds were captured in the wild rather than bred in captivity. Many were taken as nestlings, or in May, when they were just ready to leave the nest, but others were taken later. They were kept in small buildings called mews, which contained perches at various heights for the accommodation of birds at different stages of training. Mews were often built in walled compounds that also contained a bath for the birds, stables, kennels, accommodation for the falconers, a dovecote, and sometimes also a house for cranes, which were used in the training of falcons.[13]

When it was time to begin training a young bird, it was "seeled" (blinded) by having its eyelids sewn shut. This was done to eliminate, for the time being, the visual stimuli that governed the hawk's actions and reactions.[14] It also had its talons blunted; its feet fitted with leather thongs, called jesses, to which a leash could be attached; and a small bell tied to one foot. The bird was then put on its trainer's gloved fist and gently carried around in a darkened room for a long period (ideally, a day and a night), during which it was kept awake and not fed. This was to accustom it to human contact. Then the bird was fed a chicken leg or something similar, while the trainer sang it a musical phrase or bar of a song. This call was subsequently repeated whenever the bird was fed, so that it would associate the call with food. Gradually, the bird was introduced to brighter rooms and its sight was partially restored by loosening its stitches; it was then carried outside on foot and, finally, on horseback. When it was fully accustomed to all this, it was "unseeled."[15]

Up to this point, the training of falcons and hawks was identical, but thereafter it diverged, because falcons were trained to return to the ground by means of a lure (a long strap with bird wings and meat at one end), while hawks were trained to return to the trainer's gloved fist without the use of a lure. Both hawks and falcons were trained to hunt ducks by being taught to circle above the trainer's head until the ducks were flushed into the air. Falcons were also trained to hunt large, aggressive birds such as cranes and herons.

Figure 9. Seal of Aubreye de Harcourt, widow of William Trussebut, from British Library, Additional Charter 47736 (1175 × 1205).

They were first flown at live or dummy hares, and then at small birds, such as snipe or partridge. Then they were flown at live cranes or herons, but initially these were weakened birds, whose beaks and eyes were bound and whose talons were blunted, and who had meat tied to their backs to attract the falcon. Only gradually were these handicaps removed, until finally the falcon was flown at free-flying, unhandicapped quarries.[16]

Although hunting was predominantly a masculine sport, hawking was enjoyed by many elite women and girls as well as by men and boys. Queen Eleanor of Provence's wardrobe accounts for 1252–53, for example, record that she owned a mewed hawk and that she bought gloves for falconry for her daughter Beatrice as well as for her son Edmund.[17] In the late twelfth to early thirteenth centuries, many women of elite status chose to have themselves represented on their personal seals holding falcons or hawks on their wrists while standing or riding (Fig. 9),[18] whereas most aristocratic men used equestrian seals that showed them brandishing a sword or lance, though a few showed them engaged in falconry or sounding horns while riding at a full gallop.[19]

Many noble hunters trained their own birds, but others left the training to professionals. The letter above reveals that at least some of those who earned money by training hunting birds were themselves from elite families. The particular facility of some young aristocrats in training falcons and hawks is commented on by Arnaut-Guilhem de Marsan, an Aquitainian aristocrat of the 1170s, in his handbook of noble conduct. He thought it a skill desirable in his household squires.[20] This would have been one of the few paid occupations, other than those offered by the church or the sword, that were open to young men of gentle birth.

NOTES

1 Fairfax 27, fols. 4v–5r.
2 Or possibly *nostro* ("ours" instead of "yours").
3 I.e., *asturcos*, goshawks.
4 *mitta* in MS.
5 Fol. 5r commences here.
6 *valiamus* in MS.
7 The italicized words here appear to represent the kind of variant phrasing that occurs in other model letters in these formularies. See DOCUMENTS 5, 24, 32, 44, 46, and 47.
8 Or "ours" (if the word here is *nostro* instead of *vestro*).
9 See Frederick II, *Art of Falconry*, "Glossary of Falconry Terms," s.v. "Reclaim" (p. 625): "To tame, gentle, and train a wild hawk." The Latin word used for "reclaim" by Frederick II was *mansuefacere*. Cf. *OED*, s.v. "reclaim," 3.a: "To reduce to obedience, tame, subdue (an animal, *esp.* a hawk, also rarely a person)."
10 The text does not survive, but it was cited by Adelard of Bath (died *c.* 1152) in his treatise "On Birds" (*De avibus*). Adelard of Bath, *Conversations with His Nephew*, ed. and trans. Charles Burnett (Cambridge: Cambridge University Press, 1998), 238–40. Harold is shown with a hunting bird in the Bayeux Tapestry.
11 We can even trace a hereditary succession of hawkers of Chester, with an estate assessed as a full knight's fee. Crouch, "Administration of the Norman Earldom," 79. For knight's fees, see DOCUMENT 34, note 9.
12 Female falcons and hawks were generally preferred over males for hunting, because of their superior size and strength. See the discussion under DOCUMENT 61.
13 Oggins, *Kings and Their Hawks*, 12, 20, 22.
14 Hoods for falcons and hawks were unknown in Europe until they were introduced by Emperor Frederick II (d. 1250), who learned about them from Arab usage. Oggins, *Kings and Their Hawks*, 24, 26. Seeling was eventually superseded by the use of hoods. Frederick II, *Art of Falconry*, "Glossary of Falconry Terms," s.v. "Seel," p. 626.
15 Oggins, *Kings and Their Hawks*, 24–25.
16 Oggins, *Kings and Their Hawks*, 26–30.
17 Margaret Howell, *Eleanor of Provence: Queenship in Thirteenth-Century England* (Oxford: Blackwell, 1998), 81, citing TNA: PRO, E 101/349/18.

18 This seal was printed in *Early Yorkshire Charters*, vol. 10, *The Trussebut Fee*, ed. Charles Travis Clay, Yorkshire Archaeological Society Record Series, Extra Series 8 (1955), Plate II, and p. 35, no. 7. We are grateful to Nigel Ramsay for referring us to this volume. This seal is no. 61 in Johns, *Noblewomen, Aristocracy and Power*, App. 1.

19 Paul D. A. Harvey and Andrew McGuinness, *A Guide to British Medieval Seals* (Toronto: University of Toronto Press, 1996), 43–50. On women's seals from England and Normandy, see Susan M. Johns, *Noblewomen, Aristocracy and Power in the Twelfth-Century Anglo-Norman Realm* (Manchester: Manchester University Press, 2003), Chap. 7 ("Seals"), and Appendix 1 (catalogue of 142 women's seals from the twelfth and early thirteenth centuries). Among the early-thirteenth-century seals in Appendix 1 that include images of hawks or falcons are those of Matilda de Auberville of Sandwich (no. 8), Joanna de Cor[n]hill' (no. 35), Alice countess of Eu (no. 42), Ela countess of Alençon (no. 77), and Isabel countess of Pembroke (no. 100).

20 Arnaut-Guilhem de Marsan, *L'Ensenhamen d'Arnaut-Guilhem de Marsan, ou, Code du parfait chevalier*, ed. Jacques de Cauna, trans. Gérard Gouiran (Mounenh-en-Biarn [Monein]: Pyrémonde, 2007), lines 9–22.

TOURNAMENTS

63

An Earl Invites a Baron to Join His Tournament Retinue[1]

Comes mandat baroni ut veniat secum ad tornamentum

Comes baroni salutem. Generosi sanguinis exigit affluencia et ex innata vestra bonitate provenit quod milicie vere semper[2] sitis amatores, quia[3] degenerare multum esset inconveniens. Vos ortor, precor, et moneo quod predecessorum nostrorum vestigiis—in erratis omni dissimilite pretermissa!—tornamentum quoddam cum milite nostro iam affidavimus, ad quosdam nostros amicos in armis instructos invitare[4] nos oportet,[5] ne cum nominato ad locum tornementi venirimus commilitonibus nudi videamur. Sane delectabilis est ludus torneamenti, [et][6] ab re constitut[us][7] inter milites, cum in[8] tempore pacis torneamento dic[i][9] valeant qualiter hostibus in bello resistere debeant. Ad honorem igitur nostrum conservandum et vobis laudem perquirendum, illuc, si placet, veniatis et ad nostrum vexillum intendentes esse velitis. Cum hoc, deo dante, et[10] minimum sequi valeatis emolumentum, et de cetero vobis teneri debemus obnoxiores.

An earl sends word to a baron to come to a tournament with him

An earl to a baron, greetings. An abundance of noble blood demands (as does your own natural integrity) that you must always be a lover of true knighthood, since you cannot act contrary to nature. I urge, beg, and advise you that, [following] in the footsteps of our ancestors—although we haven't exactly done so![11]—we have lately sworn a tournament with a knight of ours, to which it is fitting for us to invite those of our friends who have training in arms, so that when we come with the said knight to the appointed place for the tournament we may not appear wholly devoid of companions. The recreation of a tournament is healthy and delightful, [and] it is held among knights for good reason, since those who are fit to be called to a tournament in time of peace will be all the more able to withstand enemies in war. So, to uphold our honor, and to win praise for yourself, you should—if you wish—come to that place and be prepared to rally to our banner. Should this [happen], God willing, you should be able both to attain a modest reward and also we shall be all the more obliged to you.

The tournament, or to be precise, the mêlée tournament, was a major preoccupation of the western aristocracy from at least the end of the eleventh century until the fourteenth century. It was a horseback recreation staged at a variety of recognized sites across Europe. By the end of the twelfth century it had spread from its place of origin in northeastern France to every corner of Latin Christendom, from Spain to Poland and the Crusader States.

From the beginning, the central event of the tournament was a mounted charge between two teams, made up of a variety of military households of magnates and unattached knights who just turned up on the day. However, the charge (called in French the *estor*) was only one part of the tournament. It was framed by a variety of events, social and sporting. The tournament was kicked off on the first evening by preliminary jousts (encounters between two knights), followed by lavish receptions. On the following day, parades followed by further jousts preceded the main *estor*. The tournament concluded with a dinner given by the host, at which a prize was awarded to the most successful knight on either side.[12]

Tournaments were very costly events and required careful planning by their sponsors. When a tournament was planned the usual term for this was "fixed" (*captum*), though a tournament could also be "sworn," as here and in DOCUMENT 65. In 1194, for example, King Richard I's regulations for the holding of tournaments in England required the organizers to take oaths that the participants would not breach the king's peace in traveling to the site.[13] Other oaths may have been taken to guarantee the organizers' expenses; this is hinted at in Chrétien de Troyes's *Erec et Enide*, when two knights stand surety for a planned tournament.[14] We know that invitations to tournaments, such as the one above, were sent by their sponsors, though very few such invitations survive. The most unusual one was written in verse, and was commissioned in the early 1180s by the count of Toulouse from the poet Bertran de Born. It was intended to rouse the knights of Languedoc to join the count in a three-day event to be staged outside the city of Toulouse against the knights of the king of Aragon, and was probably circulated by means of traveling jongleurs, who are known to have gone around southern France at this time singing "*novas*" ("news bulletins"):[15]

> The count has sent in haste by means of Ramon-Luc d'Esparron for me to compose for him the sort of song by which a thousand shields might be dented, by which helms, hauberks, mail and padded coats may be frustrated and broken.
>
> So I must do as he wishes, since he has communicated to me what his reasons are. I can in no way refuse him this. But though it is advisable for me to obey, how the Gascons will take it out on me! But despite them, I must do my duty.
>
> The count will set up his gonfanon at Toulouse, towards Montaigut, on his meadows besides the quarter of Peyrou. When he has raised his tent we will settle ourselves around it and we will sleep there for three nights under the stars.
>
> The princes and the barons will be with us there, and the most celebrated fellow-knights the world can offer. The men who are regarded as the most wealthy, the most brave and the most accomplished will join with us there.
>
> As soon as they will have arrived to engage in the tournament across the fields, the Catalans and the Aragonese will fall often and with little effort, for they won't be able to keep in their saddles, such frequent blows will we belabor them with there.
>
> It cannot fail to happen that lances will be raised toward the skies, and that samite, satin and sendal will be unfurled, and that the cords, the tents, the fastenings, the posts, the marquees and the pavilions will be erected.
>
> The king who lost Provence [Alfonso II of Aragon], the lord of Montpellier, Roger, the son of Bernard Aton, and the lord count

Peter will fight together with the count of Foix, with Bernard and Sancho, the brother of the defeated king.

Let each man look to his arms, for he is awaited at Toulouse. I wish that the magnates would always be so eager against each other.[16]

Other sources mention that tournaments were publicized by criers and poets, perhaps by means of such songs, since the larger the attendance, the greater the honor for the sponsors .[17]

The invitation in DOCUMENT 63 is perhaps more typical of the way in which a patron would attempt to maximize attendance at a tournament by sending out letters to friends and acquaintances in order to round up as many as possible. The earl here has taken the responsibility for organizing one team, and one of his knights the other. To help make sure that his side looks impressive, the earl is soliciting a baron (a magnate of lower rank than an earl) to join his team, with the unspoken expectation that the baron will bring his household knights with him.[18] This could be a sizable group. In DOCUMENT 64, for example, the young Edmund de Lacy, constable of Chester and heir to the earldom of Lincoln, brings twenty knights to a tournament.

A number of social imperatives made the tournament popular, and in the letter above the earl elegantly evokes these to persuade the baron to attend: social exclusivity, honor to family and lineage, the obligations of friendship, the polishing and display of knightly skills, the importance of training for war, the lure of financial reward, and the culture of favor-exchange. In its allusions to training for war, this letter also represents tournaments, by implication, as playing an important role in the justification for a military aristocracy, a subject also addressed by contemporary poet Henry de Laon:

Tournaments were not originally held
as a way of capturing horses,
but so as to learn who was manly
in his conduct, and to do great deeds of arms,
because of which one would venture to trust such a man
to lead great companies of knights;
so that it would be known in truth and without doubt
that at need he would persist in the assault
and help and support his men
and perform great deeds;
and so that it would be known that he could wear a helmet—
despite the heat and lack of air within—
as lightly as he would wear his cloth cap.

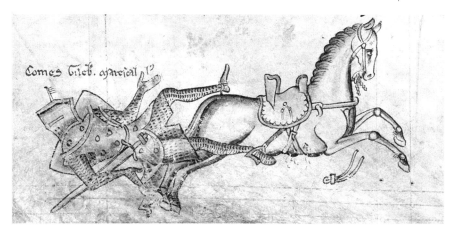

Figure 10. Death in a tournament of Gilbert Marshal, earl of Pembroke, 1241, by Matthew Paris, *Chronica Majora*, II, Corpus Christi College, Cambridge, MS 16, fol. 147v (148v).

> For the man who in such a situation is soaked
> in his own blood and sweat,
> this I call the high bath of honor.[19]

This poem speaks with reverence of the great days of the tournament as being in the past, just as the earl in the letter above represents himself as following in the footsteps of his own ancestors (although, he charmingly confesses, he has sometimes wandered off the path). In the late 1220s, the biographer of Earl William Marshal mourned that the great days of tourneying lay in the twelfth century, and urged the young King Henry III to revive them:

> But nowadays, high-ranking men
> have put Chivalry back in fetters too;
> errantry and tourneying
> have given way to formal contests.
> But, if God please, the young King Henry
> will restore fun, laughter
> and joy to the world.[20]

He was probably writing in response to the sporadic bans of tournaments imposed in England by John and continued under Henry III's minority government. The eagerness of the English nobility to hold tournaments once John was dead was remarked upon by a contemporary Flemish writer.[21]

The letter above clearly echoes a variety of aristocratic preoccupations of the early years of the reign of Henry III, and it is quite possible that it was based on a genuine letter from a great magnate recruiting a banneret to his side for a tournament that he had arranged. Specific details of place and time have been edited out, but the substance of the letter has all the characteristics of authenticity, and despite its lighthearted tone, it also gives a glimpse of the serious planning required of a tournament patron if he wished to make sure that the event was a success.

NOTES

1 Add. 8167, fol. 106r–v.
2 "*e*" expunged in MS after *semper*.
3 A second *quia* is expunged here in MS.
4 Fol. 106v commences here.
5 Corrected in MS from *oportest*.
6 *n[ec]* in MS, which does not fit the sense of this passage.
7 *constituta* in MS.
8 *torneamento* expunged in MS following *in*.
9 *dicere* in MS.
10 *ne* in MS, which does not fit the sense of this passage.
11 *in erratis omni dissimilite pretermissa*; literally, "every dissimilarity in our wanderings having been set aside." The exact meaning here is murky; an alternative translation to that above might be something like, "avoiding straying from their path!"
12 For this paragraph, the principal sources are Josef Fleckenstein, ed., *Das Ritterliche Turnier im Mittelalter: Beiträge zu einer vergleichenden Formen-und Verhaltensgeschichte des Rittertums* (Göttingen: Vandenhoeck & Ruprecht, 1985); Juliet R. V. Barker, *The Tournament in England, 1100–1400* (Woodbridge, Suffolk: Boydell & Brewer, 1986); and David Crouch, *Tournament* (London: Hambledon, 2005).
13 *Fœdera*, vol. 1, pt. 1, 65.
14 *Erec et Enide*, ed. Mario Roques, Classiques français du moyen âge, 80 (Paris: H. Champion, 1952), lines 2076–78.
15 On the circulation of *novas*, see the poem *Abril issi'e*, by Raimon Vidal de Besalú, in *Nouvelles occitanes du moyen âge*, ed. and trans. Jean-Charles Huchet (Paris: Flammarion, 1992), lines 38–47.
16 Bertran de Born, *Poésies complètes de Bertran de Born*, ed. André Antoine Thomas, Bibliothèque meridionale, première ser., 1 (Toulouse, 1888), 4–6 (English translation by David Crouch).
17 Crouch, *Tournament*, 29–30.
18 For the two sides in a tournament and their recruitment, see Crouch, *Tournament*, 72–74.
19 A. Långfors, "Le dit des hérauts par Henri de Laon," *Romania*, 44 (1914), 222–23 (English translation by David Crouch).
20 Anthony J. Holden and David Crouch, eds.; Stewart Gregory, trans., *History of William Marshal*, Anglo-Norman Text Society, Occasional Publications Series, 4–6 (London, 2002–7), 1: lines 2686–95.
21 Michel, ed., *Histoire des ducs de Normandie et des rois d'Angleterre*, 207.

—————————————— 64 ——————————————

A Knight Orders His Bailiff to Provide for His Arrival with Edmund de Lacy, Constable of Chester, and Twenty Knights, Who Are on Their Way to a Tournament at Blyth[1]

Miles servienti suo salutem. Noveritis quod in crastino Purificacionis cum tota familia nostra veniemus ad illam villam quam tue fidelitati commisimus custodiendam. Occuremus tibi cum domino E. de Lacy, constabulario Cestrie, qui partes illas cum xx. mil[it]ibus[2] transire faciet versus torneamentum de Blize. Quare tibi mando, procuracionem dicti constabularii et nostra in omnibus negociis provideas, ita quod de bono servicio tuo laudare valeam.

A knight to his bailiff, greetings. You will have heard that on the morrow of the Purification [February 3] we are to arrive with all our household at the estate that we have committed to your faithful keeping. We shall be coming to you with Lord E[dmund] de Lacy, constable of Chester, who will be traveling through those parts with twenty knights to the tournament at Blyth. Therefore I order you to provide for the needs of the said constable and myself in all matters, so that I may have cause to speak well of your service.

Blize, or Blyth, in Nottinghamshire, was a popular site for tournaments. It is first mentioned in Richard I's tournament regulations of 1194 as one of five sites in England where tournaments could be licensed. All five sites are expressed as pairs of towns; Blyth is paired with nearby Tickhill.[3] Tickhill is on the north side of the Yorkshire-Nottinghamshire boundary, and Blyth is three miles south of it on the Nottinghamshire side. The towns were closely linked in another way, as the joint centers of the great aristocratic estate ("honor") of Tickhill. Tickhill possessed the central castle of the honor, and the Benedictine priory of Blyth was its spiritual heart; in the twelfth century the honor is called Blyth or Tickhill interchangeably.[4]

The pairing of towns to define tournament sites was standard practice. All the great northern French tournament fields lay between two towns, such as the famous site between Gournay-sur-Aronde and Ressons-sur-Matz, which was in use between at least 1168 and 1240. The boundary between the counties of Clermont and Montdidier lay between Gournay and Ressons. The holding of tournaments on boundaries between principalities and lordships seems to go back to the earliest days of tourneying in France, and may have something to do with the knights' attempts to evade the peace legislation of the early eleventh century. The pairing of towns also allowed each side in the tournament to reside in a separate base, and thereby to avoid tensions and spread the burden of hospitality. By contrast, in England early tournament sites were described as being outside particular large towns. It is not until Richard I's regulations of 1194 that these paired sites appear in England, which suggests a conscious copying of the French practice by King Richard, himself an acclaimed veteran of the French tournament circuit. Like Tickhill and Blyth, two other pairs of sites in 1194 spanned county borders: Brackley (Northamptonshire) and Mixborough (Oxfordshire), and Stamford (Lincolnshire) and Wansborough (Northamptonshire), again echoing French practice.[5]

Blyth became a popular tournament venue. A metrical list of English towns, written in Anglo-Norman in the mid-thirteenth century, refers to Blyth as famous for both its blanket-making and its tourneyers.[6] The site of the action is thought to have been on fields to the north of Blyth, right on the county boundary. In the thirteenth century numerous tournaments were held there, and many others that were proposed were refused a license by the king.[7] It is no surprise, therefore, to find that the magnate and his knights in the letter above are on their way to a tournament at Blyth. The magnate himself is evidently a real person, Edmund de Lacy, son of John de Lacy, earl of Lincoln and constable of Chester (d. 1240). The Lacys were Yorkshire magnates, with their principal seat in the county at Pontefract castle, some fifteen miles to the northwest of Blyth.[8] Edmund claimed the honor of Tickhill as one of his estates, though the nature of his claim is not clear, since until 1244 it belonged to the countess of Eu, and in 1258 it was referred to as an estate of the Lord Edward, son of King Henry III.[9]

As one of England's greatest noblemen, Edmund de Lacy would certainly have been able to support a tourneying retinue of twenty knights. His appearance here allows a relatively narrow dating of this letter, and of the formulary into which it was copied, to the period between the summer of 1248 and 1250 (see INTRODUCTION, pp. 6–7). Edmund was born *c.* 1230. He was proclaimed of age at eighteen in May 1248 and succeeded to his lands and, eventually, to the earldom of Lincoln, though he was not formally invested as earl, perhaps because his mother Margaret (d. 1266), who was countess in her own right, was still living.[10] His own charters always call him "constable of Chester," though he is referred to as "earl" by others. He died, still a young man, on June 2, 1258.[11]

The nature of this letter opens up the strong possibility that a genuine document lies behind it, and even that the tournament referred to here can be dated. If E. de Lacy is Edmund, and it seems very likely that he is, he could not have attended a tournament with a military household until he was declared of age in May 1248. It is very likely that he was knighted on the occasion, although the first reference to him as knight is in 1255. So it is possible that the tournament referred to here might have been held in the first week of February 1249, as part of a tour to celebrate Edmund's status as a new ("tyro") knight. If so, it matches other evidence. King Henry III was notoriously hostile to tournaments, but he relaxed the prohibition on them briefly during 1248 and 1249 as a favor to his half-brother, William de Valence, also recently knighted. The chronicler Matthew Paris reports that William tourneyed at Newbury in March 1248, at Northampton on Ash Wednesday (February 17) 1249 (against the king's will), and at Brackley in October 1249. The tournament circuit was therefore very active between the autumn of 1248 and September 1249, when prohibitions once more began to be imposed.[12]

This letter gives us a glimpse of the amusements of the English aristocracy during the reign of Henry III. It was a very mobile world, and we see here a knight of the West Riding of Yorkshire providing hospitality (an essential aristocratic virtue) to one of the greatest nobles in the land to enable him to pursue a reputation for martial expertise, which was the defining characteristic of the thirteenth-century nobility. The unnamed knight's hospitality also linked him with the Lacy "affinity," the knights and landowners who aspired to Edmund's friendship, protection, and patronage. The knights in Edmund's retinue (who may have included the writer of this letter) may have pledged themselves to support him "in peace or war." This was the formula used in at least one early twelfth-century charter, and also in the formal tourneying contracts that first appear in 1297.[13] Their purpose was to guarantee that a magnate would always have an honorable escort, another requirement of noble standing.

NOTES

1 Add. 8167, fol. 128r.
2 *milibus* in MS.
3 *Fœdera*, vol. 1, pt. 1, 65.
4 For the honor of Blyth-Tickhill and its succession, see Reginald Thomas Timson, ed., *Blyth Priory Cartulary*, vol. 1, Thoroton Society, 27, 28 (Nottingham, 1973), cxv–cxxxv. For the Nottinghamshire-Yorkshire boundary at this point, see David Hey, "Yorkshire's Southern Boundary," *Northern History*, 37 (2000), 31–48.
5 Crouch, *Tournament*, 49–55.
6 Charles Bonnier, "List of English Towns in the Twelfth Century," *EHR*, 16 (1901), 501–3 (*blaunket de Blye*, 501; *turneur de Blye*, 502). Tickill was cited in the list (p. 502) as famous for its hose (stockings). For the revised date of this list, and for an English translation, see Rothwell, ed., *English Historical Documents, III, 1189–1327*, 881–84.

7   Timson, ed., *Blyth Priory Cartulary*, vol. 1, cxi–cxiii.

8   For the Lacy estates and succession, see William E. Wightman, *The Lacy Family in England and Normandy, 1066–1194* (Oxford: Clarendon, 1966).

9   Sir William Dugdale, *Monasticon Anglicanum*, ed. John Caley, Henry Ellis, and Bulkeley Bandinel, 6 vols. in 8 (London: Record Commission, 1817–30), 5:503; Ivor J. Sanders, *English Baronies: A Study of Their Origin and Descent, 1086–1327* (Oxford: Clarendon, 1960), 147.

10 It was for the widowed Countess Margaret that Bishop Grosseteste compiled the French version of his household *Rules* between 1240 and 1242 (see DOCUMENT 50).

11 *Complete Peerage*, vol. 7, 680–81; *Oxford DNB*, s.nn. "Lacy, John de, third earl of Lincoln (*c.* 1192–1240)"; and "Lacy, Margaret de, countess of Lincoln (*d.* 1266)."

12 For Valence and his tourneying circuit in 1248 and 1249, see Matthew Paris, *Matthæi Parisiensis, monachi Sancti Albani, Chronica Majora*, ed. Henry Richards Luard, 7 vols., Rolls Series, 57 (London: Longman, 1872–83), 5:17–18, 54–55, 83. A tournament to be held on September 22, 1249, at Worcester was prohibited, which heralded the resumption of the ban. Another to be held at Blyth in January 1250 was prohibited by an undated writ at the end of 1249. *Calendar of Patent Rolls, 1247–53*, 47, 77.

13 Michael Jones and Simon Walker, eds., "Private Indentures for Life Service in Peace and War, 1278–1476," in *Camden Miscellany*, 32 (1994), 2–3. For the twelfth-century charter (1130s), see Crouch, *Tournament*, 163.

65

The Earl of Warenne Beseeches the Count of Aumale to Come to a Tournament that He Has Sponsored, Because He and His Knights Are Rusty from Lack of Practice and Need His Help[1]

Comes Varenne comiti de Alba mara salutem. Desuetudinem[2] paravit id quod ab usu cessat. Milites inhibeamur[3] quam[4] colentes rudes; reddit longa perhendinacio desidie[5] que guttam renibus amovet milicie frequenciam. Tornamentum quoddam inter nos et O., comitem de illo loco, noveritis affidatum, ad quod ut veniatis quanta possimus affeccione obsecramus. Cum insanes,[6] in[7] probitate vestra tanquam municipio confidamus; ad vestrum enim triumphale vexillarium, tanquam ad castellum muris et vallo circumvallatum, lassorum et ab adversa parte gravatorum solet esse refugium. In nostro quoque peroptime solent presidio qui se vestre tuendos presidie [?per][8] potestatem[9] commiserunt. In[10] tanto eciam plus ibidem desideramus presenciam [vestram],[11] quanto credimus illam nobis fore necessariam.

The earl of Warenne to the count of Aumale, greetings. That which ceases from use has prepared the way for its own retirement. We knights are being kept from action like unskilled clodhoppers; this long interval of sitting around, which prevents the practice of knightly exercise, gives one kidney stones.[12] You will have heard that a certain tournament has been sworn between us and O., the earl of such-and-such a place. We beg you with our utmost affection to come to it. Since we are unfit, we trust in your integrity as to a city; to your triumphal banner as to a castle with its walls and surrounding moat, which is accustomed to be the refuge of the weary and of those oppressed by an adverse fate. And those who are accustomed to our protection in the best possible manner have committed themselves to being defended [by] the might of your protection. We also desire your presence there all the more because we believe it will be essential to us.

Before the Conquest of England in 1066 the Warenne family was important in Normandy, with an honor based on the castle of Bellencombre in the Pays de Caux. William I de Warenne, who after the Conquest had become a major landowner in Sussex, the West Riding of Yorkshire, and Norfolk, was created earl of Surrey at the end of 1088 by King William Rufus (1087–1100).[13] After the death in 1148 of his grandson, William III de Warenne, the earldom came successively to his daughter Isabel's husbands, William (d. 1159), son of King Stephen, and Hamelin (d. 1202), half-brother of King Henry II. Hamelin and his son, William IV de Warenne (d. 1240), took and perpetuated the Warenne name of Isabel's family. Their descendants continued to enjoy the earldom of Surrey until 1347, and the earls were known as both "of Surrey" and "of Warenne."[14]

The Norman counts of Aumale had enjoyed the English lordship of Holderness, which made up much of the East Riding of Yorkshire, from about 1096. After the death in 1179 of William le Gros, count of Aumale and sometime earl of York, the county of Aumale passed to his daughter Hawise, one of the great heiresses of England (d. 1213/14), and after her death to William II de Forz (d. 1241), Hawise's son by her second husband.[15]

The appearance of these two Anglo-Norman counts as the correspondents in this letter is perfectly plausible. Both families had connections with the sport of tourneying. In 1194, William de Warenne (later Earl William IV de Warenne) was among those who interceded with King Richard for a license to reopen the English tournament circuit.[16] William, who was probably born in the late 1160s or early 1170s, must have been quite a young man at that time. Raised in Normandy, he succeeded his father as earl in 1202, was deeply engaged in politics and warfare, and died in 1240. Since his son and heir John de Warenne was born in 1231, William IV de Warenne must be the purported writer of this letter. William II de Forz, count of Aumale, was a generation younger. He was born between 1191 and 1196 to Hawise, countess of Aumale and Essex, and her second husband, William de Forz (d. 1195), who had been one of Richard I's captains. The young count[17] came to England (perhaps from Poitou) in 1214 after his mother's death to obtain his inheritance. In 1219 he sponsored a tournament at Brackley in Northamptonshire that had been forbidden in the young king's name, and until the mid-1220s his career was marked by considerable political and military turbulence. In his later years, however, he collaborated with Henry III's government, and he was sent abroad on various diplomatic and military missions. He died on March 29, 1241, while on a pilgrimage to Jerusalem, and he was succeeded by his son and namesake, William III de Forz.[18] Earl "O.," the fellow-sponsor of the tournament with the earl of Warenne, may be entirely imaginary; equally, he may be a real person for whose name a fictional initial has been substituted.

Warenne's grumpy reference to "this long period of sitting around" (*longa perhendinacio desidie*), which has turned his knights into "unskilled clodhoppers" (*colentes rudes*) and rusted their martial skills, suggests that it has been a very long time since his last tournament. This fits well with the apparent date of this letter of 1214 $\times$ 40, between William II de Forz's succession to the county of Aumale in 1214 and William IV de Warenne's death in 1240.

Another point of interest in this letter is its language, which is extremely colorful. The gruffness and bluntness of the complaints about knights sitting around getting kidney stones sounds like the authentic voice of an aging aristocrat who longs for action. Equally striking, and quite poignant, is the remarkable image by which Warenne commits himself and his knights to the younger Aumale's command and banner, like refugees entrusting themselves to the might of a strong city or a walled and moated castle. Such a poetic image makes for a most unusual and lively invitation to a tournament. For another letter possibly by William IV de Warenne, see DOCUMENT 66.

NOTES

1   Fairfax 27, fol. 4v.
2   *Dissuitudinem* in MS.
3   *inibeamur* in MS.
4   *que* in MS.
5   *diffidie* in MS.
6   *infames* in MS.
7   *a* in MS.
8   A preposition that takes the accusative case, such as *per* ("by"), seems to be wanting here.
9   *potentem* in MS.
10   *On* in MS.
11   Word supplied to fit the sense of the passage.

12 Literally, "gout in the kidneys," an expression used for kidney stones.

13 Christopher P. Lewis, "The Earldom of Surrey and the Date of Domesday Book," *Historical Research*, 63 (1990), 329–36.

14 See *Oxford DNB*, s.nn. "Warenne, Isabel de, *suo jure* countess of Surrey (*d.* 1203)"; "Warenne, Hamelin de, earl of Surrey (*d.* 1202)"; and "Warenne, William (IV) de, fifth earl of Surrey (*d.* 1240)." For the Warenne family, see William Farrer and Charles T. Clay, eds., *Early Yorkshire Charters*, vol. 8, Yorkshire Archaeological Society (Leeds, 1914–65), 1–40.

15 *Oxford DNB*, s.nn. "Hawisa, *suo jure* countess of Aumale, and countess of Essex (*d.* 1213/14)"; and "Forz, William de, count of Aumale (1191 × 6–1241)." For the counts of Aumale, see Barbara English, *The Lords of Holderness, 1086–1260* (Oxford: Hull University Press, 1979), 6–54.

16 *Fœdera*, vol. 1, pt. 1, 65.

17 Although the Norman comté from which this title derived had been lost to the French in 1204, the title "count of Aumale" was still used by its English claimants.

18 *Oxford DNB*, s.n. "Forz, William de, count of Aumale (1191×6–1241)"; *Fœdera*, vol. 1, pt. 1, 65; *Patent Rolls, 1216–25*, 257.

66

An Earl Writes to Another Earl to Request a Brief Pause Between Tournaments, to Enable Everyone to Take a Little Break Before Resuming Combat[1]

Comes comiti salutem. Milicie frequencia modica quandoque perhendinacionem recreatur. Nec non pretermittitur, licet brevitate temporis interrumpatur. Quis enim in armis continue posset durare? Quod caret alterna requie durabile non est; arcus,[2] ni cesses tendere, lentus erit.[3] Post perhendinacionem et requiei beneficium acrius resurgimus ad miliciam;[4] post requiem resumptis[5] viribus ludum tornamenti delectabilem amplius affectamus. Predecessorum[6] nostrorum gesta recolentes—gesta ducis Macedonie et duodecim parium probitates—qui milicie nos ad frequenciam provocant. In pacis tempore torneando didicerunt, qualiter hostibus in bello resistere[7] debuerunt. Ad tornamendum non [?apprimendum][8] est, quem[9] timiditas[10] retrahit[11] aud expense trahunt;[12] domui remaneat, qui sonipedem [?audire][13] pertimessit. Ad honorem nostrum conservandum illuc veniemus, ut ibidem experiri valeamus. Cui gutta noceat, in armis [?si][14] quis fervencior existat![15]

An earl to an earl, greetings. An assembly for the practice of knightly skills is refreshed by a modest suspension. One should not cancel it, but let it be interrupted for a brief time. For who can fight without a pause? That which lacks daily rest cannot endure; a bow, unless you cease to draw it, will grow slack. After a break, and the benefit of rest, we rise up all the keener for our knightly exercise; after a rest, with our strength renewed, we strive all the more at the delightful sport of the tournament. We recall the deeds of our ancestors—the deeds of the duke of Macedon and the doughty deeds of the Twelve Peers—who rouse us to a gathering of knightly practice. They learned by tourneying in time of peace how they should withstand their enemies in war. One whom fear holds back, or costs constrain, should not [?be forced] to a tournament; one who is terrified to [?hear] the sound of the charge should stay at home. *We* shall come thither to preserve our honor, [and] so that we may put ourselves to the test there. And [if] anyone is more fervent at arms, may the gout take him!

This jocular letter makes a plea for a pause between tournaments by discoursing on the extreme physical demands that tourneying places on the participants. It also alludes to some of the other trials of the tournament circuit, especially the great expense and the risk of injury. The writer, in support of his argument, trots out a classical tag about how a bow that is drawn unceasingly will lose its spring. This line derives from Ovid's *Heroides*, a collection of fictitious letters written by heroines of classical mythology to the lovers who abandoned or rejected them. In Poem IV (lines 89–92), Phaedra attempts to seduce her stepson Hippolytus by advising him to relax from his rigidly moral principles, saying: "that which lacks its alternations of repose will not endure; . . . The bow . . . if you never cease to bend it, will grow slack" (*quod caret alterna requie, durabile non est; . . . arcus . . . si numquam cesses tendere, mollis erit*). The use of such a steamy quotation in the context of this martial letter is quite humorous.[16] The writer also evokes some celebrated avatars of military life, the "duke of Macedon" and the "Twelve Peers." The duke is Alexander the Great, as depicted in the *Alexandreis* (1170s), a widely read life of Alexander composed by Walter de Châtillon in Latin verse.[17] The Twelve Peers could be either the "paladins" of the epic cycle of Charlemagne or the twelve companions of Alexander the Great in Alexander of Paris's late twelfth-century epic *Roman d'Alexandre*.[18]

The writer's urgent plea for a rest, his blunt language, his ancestral and literary allusions, his sturdy enthusiasm, and his wry reference to gout in closing all bespeak a man of some age and elite education. In fact, they strongly recall the language of DOCUMENT 65 (1214 × 40), suggesting that this letter might be a follow-up to it. If so, the earl to whom DOCUMENT 66 is addressed is presumably the same earl "O." of DOCUMENT 65 with whom Warenne agreed to sponsor a tournament, and Warenne is now begging him to agree to a brief break.

The writer is clearly echoing the prevailing belief that knights required time—typically, two weeks—to recuperate between tournaments. Although the fictional hero Lancelot fought three tournaments on consecutive days in Chrétien's *Chevalier de la Charette*, the poet Jakemes, in his mid-thirteenth-century romance of the castellan of Couci, observed that it was customary for knights to have a two-week period of grace in which to rest between tournaments.[19] In the biography of William Marshal and the works of Philippe de Remy the two-week interval is also mentioned as customary.[20]

Despite its heartfelt request for a break, however, this letter reveals clearly the massive enthusiasm for the tournament that still energized the higher aristocracy in the early thirteenth century. The sponsors of the tournament in England were, as here, generally earls. Those of Gloucester, Pembroke, Salisbury, and Aumale were particular patrons, who called and sponsored tournaments in the reigns of John and the earlier part of the reign of Henry III.[21] The earl's blunt assertion in this letter that anyone who fears the financial costs or the physical risks of tourneying should stay at home makes it clear that this sport is only for those who are very fit, very brave, and very rich. It is also perhaps a defiant response to the strictures of preachers, who had long decried tournaments as wasteful, vainglorious, and sinful. Around 1187, for example, Ralph Niger, a former chaplain of the great tourneying hero the Young King Henry of England (d. 1183), declared that "Knights have long squandered their inheritances and energy in tournaments, and most of all their souls and lives in pursuit of empty praise and popular fame, and have wasted away military expertise in wickedness. For feuds causelessly become battle, and vanity, greed and foolishness are blended into a mixture of pure wickedness."[22]

NOTES

1   Fairfax 27, fol. 4v.

2   *arcum* in MS.

3   This line derives from Ovid's *Heroides*, 4:89–92: "quod caret alterna requie, durabile non est; haec reparat vires fessaque membra novat. arcus—et arma tuae tibi sunt imitanda Dianae—si numquam cesses tendere, mollis erit." In Ovid, *Heroides and Amores*, trans. Grant Showerman (Cambridge, Mass.: Harvard University Press, and London: William Heinemann, 1914, rpt. 1958), 50–51. See below.

4   *milicam* in MS.

5   *resumtis* in MS.

6   *predessorum* in MS.

7   *du* expunged in MS after *resistere*.

8   Word uncertain; *appi*[n] in MS.

9   *qem* in MS.

10   *tumiditas* in MS.

11   *retrait* in MS.

12   *traunt* in MS.

13   *perdere* in MS.

14   *et* in MS.

15   *exissat* in MS.

16   Horace used a similar expression in *Odes*, 2.10.18–20, in which the poet reminds his friend Licinius Murena that even Apollo let his bow relax sometimes ("*neque semper arcum tendit Apollo*"). For these and other classical references on this theme, see E. Kerr Borthwick, "'The Wise Man and the Bow' in Aristides Quintilianus," *Classical Quarterly*, new ser., 41, no. 1 (1991), 275–78. The quotation from Ovid's *Heroides* also appears in DOCUMENT 93. For the text, see Ovid, *Heroides and Amores*, trans. Showerman, 50–51.

17   *The Alexandreis: A Twelfth-Century Epic*, trans. David Townsend (Peterborough, Ontario: Broadview, 2007), 11–16.

18   See *The Medieval French "Roman d'Alexandre,"* vol. 7, *Version of Alexandre de Paris: Variants and Notes to Branch IV*, ed. Bateman Edwards and Alfred Foulet, Elliott Monographs, 41 (Princeton, N.J.: Princeton University Press, 1955).

19   *Le Roman du Castelain de Couci et de la Dame de Fayel*, ed. Maurice Delbouille (Paris: Société des anciens texts français, 1936), lines 3332–35.

20   See observations in Crouch, *Tournament*, 57–58.

21   Crouch, *Tournament*, 31.

22   Ralph Niger, *De re militari et triplici via peregrinationis Ierosolimitane*, ed. Ludwig Schmugge (Berlin: Gruyter, 1977), 114 (translation by David Crouch).

67

An Earl Asks a Baron to Send Him a Destrier
Equipped for a Tournament[1]

Comes baroni salutem. Ad illos in quibus amplius confidimus in necessitatis articulo confugimus, licet enim nulla merita [nostra][2] precesserint, de mera vestra libertate tamen confidentes,[3] vos rogamus quatinus, si placet, dextrarium vestrum [et][4] lenes et tenues coopertas ad torneandum aptas per armigerum vestrum proprium nobis mittere velitis. Scimus enim quod huiusmodi ludis[5] ad presens pretendere non potestis, cum pro terra vestra defendenda coram iusticiariis placitare debeatis. Dextrarium afforare faciatis, ut si de illo aliquod infortunium accidit, de precio vobis respondere valeamus.

An earl to a baron, greetings. We resort when needs must to the people in whom we have full confidence, for although our merits might not be outstanding,[6] trusting, nevertheless, in your pure generosity, we ask that, if you please, you might be willing to send us your destrier by your own squire, and soft and fine trappings suitable for tourneying. For we know that at present you cannot stretch to any sports of this sort, since you have to plead before the justices to defend your estate. Please make sure to have the destrier valued, so that if some misfortune should happen to it we would be able to recompense you for its price.

This letter is a glimpse of the relations between members of the upper tier of the aristocracy. The writer is clearly an earl of great power who has other, lesser magnates within his affinity. The request that he makes is politely expressed, but admits of no denial. In effect, it deprives the subordinate baron of a valuable warhorse, together with its finest trappings and a squire to deliver it, so that the earl may pursue his interest in the tournament. The baron is reminded that he cannot himself join the earl at the sport since he has to defend a lawsuit concerning his lands in the royal court. The entire tone of the letter is the assertion of power by a great magnate over a lesser one.

The medieval tournament generated something of a support industry among the armorers, saddlers, farriers and blacksmiths who attended the great staged tournaments. The herald Sarrazin described their appearance at the tournaments of northern France in the 1260s.[7] Many tradespeople also supplied the tournament circuit, including keepers of lodgings; sellers of food, drink, and horse fodder; and providers of various other commodities and services, including horse dealers. The ransoms that enriched successful tourneyers, and lured many knights to compete, were mostly levied from the horses and arms of the vanquished. Horse dealers were an essential means of converting horseflesh into portable cash, and both they and horse thieves are mentioned as frequenters of the tournament circuits.[8]

NOTES

1 Fairfax 27, fol. 4v.
2 Word inserted to preserve the sense of this passage.
3 See DOCUMENT 5 for very similar phrasing: *Quamvis merita nostra non exigant (vel non precesserint) tamen de libertate vestra confidimus* (etc.).
4 Word inserted to preserve the sense of the passage.
5 *ludᶦcis* in MS.
6 An earl uses a similar self-deprecating phrase in DOCUMENT 5.
7 See *Le Roman de Ham*, in Michel, ed., *Histoire des ducs de Normandie et des rois d'Angleterre*, 217.
8 Crouch, *Tournament*, 62–63.

--------------------------------------- 68 ---------------------------------------

The Baron Agrees to Lend His Destrier to the Earl, Because His Legal Affairs Will Prevent Him from Attending the Tournament Himself[1]

Comiti baro salutem. Preces vestras preceptum repute, nec in mea[2] quicquam habetur facultate, quod vestre voluntati non sit promtum et paratum. Dextrarium meum apreciare nolui,[3] sciens si de eo casus eveniat, per optime vos responsuros in [p]repreciori[4] valorem[?].[5] Ultra modum doleo, quod oportet me in placitis intendere, dum commilitones mei tornamentis et aliis negociis indulgent militantibus. Set cum deus[6] adversos casus sedaverit, exercicio[7] militari peterimus operam et diligenciam exibere.

To an earl, a baron [sends] greetings. Your requests I consider as a command, and there is nothing in my power that would not be prompt and ready [to serve] your will. I did [not] wish to put a price on my warhorse, knowing that if anything happened to him you would, in the kindest way, return his value in a much more precious form. I am sorry beyond measure that I have to go to court while my fellow-knights are enjoying tournaments and other knightly pastimes, but when God shall have settled these unfortunate lawsuits, we shall seek to employ our efforts and diligence in martial exercise.

This is clearly a response to DOCUMENT 67. The baron has gotten the message, and civilly complies by lending his horse to the earl. In doing so, however, he artfully uses the earl's own obligation to give largesse against him, by obliging the earl to guarantee a handsome replacement should the horse be injured or killed. This letter thus offers quite a subtle insight into the interplay of power relations between a magnate and his followers. Magnates who wanted to lead had to offer their followers substantial rewards in return for their compliance. A reputation for stinginess was a stigma that a leader had to avoid, as this baron knows well.

NOTES

1   Fairfax 27, fol. 4v.
2   *meam* in MS.
3   *volui* ("I wished") in the MS, but *nolui* ("I didn't wish") seems more likely in the context, and as a response to DOCUMENT 67.
4   *repreciori* in MS.
5   Word uncertain; it appears as *v*[iii] in MS.
6   *quid versus casus* expunged after *deus* in MS.
7   *exerccio* in MS.

CHAPTER 4

Family and Community

NEWS, GOSSIP, AND FAMILY

───────── 69 ─────────

A Serjeant Writes to His Master, a Knight, to Justify His Refusal to Obey the Orders of the Knight's Wife[1]

Militi, W. serviens suus salutem et fidele servicium.[2] Mirari non vero[3] sufficio, cauti tamque prudentis viri prudenciam, facta subieccione, circumveniri[4] posse, et quod de facili[tate][5] fidem adibetis pro suasionibus adul[a]torum,[6] qui discordia inter vos et fideles vestros homines seminare nituntur. Bonorum et leg[al]ium[7] virorum testimoniis iudicari desidero, et uti secundum quod oculum videtis, sive bonum sive malum; scilicet, quod merui michi redderetis. Exitus acta approbat,[8] et semper in fine patebit qualiter vobis servi[v]erim.[9] Vero quod secus egesserim[10] mea; me non remordet consciencia. Restat tamen [verum],[11] quod uxoris vestre domine mee preceptis et voluntati non adquievi, sed ad honorem vestrum conservandum. Me totum exibui quod, quicquid sum et quicquid possum, in fidelitate et bono servicio vestro totum expendetur. Valete.

To a knight, W. his serjeant [sends] greetings and faithful service. I cannot indeed be surprised that, when a deceit has been perpetrated, the foresight of a careful and prudent man can be circumvented, and that you rest your faith in good nature on the blandishments of flatterers who endeavor to sow discord between you and your faithful men. I wish to be judged by the evidence of upright and reliable men, and to be used according to what you see with your own eyes, be it good or bad; in other words, you should give me what I have deserved. The proof is in

Figure 11. Potiphar's wife fails to seduce Joseph, then shows his cloak to her husband as evidence that Joseph tried to rape her. From the Joseph window in Bourges Cathedral (*c.* 1210–15).

the pudding,[12] and it will always be apparent in the end how well I have served you. Indeed, were it otherwise I would have packed my bags; my conscience does not gnaw at me. Nevertheless, it is true that, in order to maintain your honor, I did not obey the commands and will of my lady your wife. I have fully demonstrated that whatever I am and whatever I can do will be entirely spent in good faith and good service to you. Farewell.

In the thirteenth century, the word "serjeant" (*serviens*) was used to refer to someone who "served"—for example, as an officer, servant, assistant, or manorial bailiff (see DOCUMENT 50). The serjeant in this letter serves in an unnamed knight's household, and he has gotten into trouble in the knight's absence for refusing to obey the orders of the knight's wife. Someone—either the lady herself, or another senior member of the household—evidently has complained about him to the knight, and now the serjeant sends the knight a very formal letter to defend his actions and to proclaim his entire loyalty to the knight's interests and service.

The exact circumstances of the dispute are not given, and the serjeant's claim that he refused to obey the lady's commands so as "to maintain your honor" is ambiguous. Did he thwart the lady's intentions, which would have brought the knight into disrepute if she had carried them out? Or did he in some manner challenge her to her face about her commands? Or, more scandalously, is the serjeant hinting that the lady, in the manner of Potiphar's wife toward Joseph (see DOCUMENT 70), made improper advances to him, which he, like Joseph, rejected? (Fig. 11). In this letter, the serjeant seems to imply that, like Joseph, he has been falsely charged with some sort of impropriety in retaliation for his refusal to obey the commands of his lord's wife. The appearance in a formulary of a model letter such as this suggests that situations of this kind were not uncommon, and that household officers and other senior servants, if accused of misbehavior, might well feel the need to justify their actions in writing to absent employers.

The indignant and self-righteous tone of this letter is very pronounced, but the serjeant is careful to avoid outright rudeness by seeming to excuse the knight's trust in the lies of flatterers on the grounds that he has been deceived by them. Note, however, the careful ambiguity of the sentence in question, which leaves it unclear whether the "careful and prudent man" who has been the victim of deception here is the knight or the writer himself.

NOTES

1 Add. 8167, fol. 129r.
2 For other examples of this salutation, see DOCUMENTS 60 and 99.
3 In the MS, this word is given as an "n" with a bar over it, usually an abbreviation for "*non*," but here probably a scribal error for the abbreviation for "*vero*." The same error occurs in DOCUMENT 40.
4 *circumventiri* in MS.
5 *facili* in MS.
6 *adultorum* in MS.
7 *legium* in MS.
8 This phrase occurs in Ovid's *Heroides* (2:85) as "*exitus acta probat*." Ovid, *Heroides and Amores*, trans. Grant Showerman (Cambridge, Mass.: Harvard University Press, and London: William Heinemann, 1914, rpt. 1958), 2:85 (pp. 26–27).
9 *servierim* in MS.
10 *egerim* in MS.
11 *vir'* in MS.
12 Literally, "a result reveals the acts that produced it," or, in effect, "the product provides proof of the process."

70

A Man Warns His Friend that He Has Seen the Latter's Wife Naked in Bed with Another Man, and Sends Her Girdle as Evidence

F. mandat G. quod vidit alienum cum uxore sua in talamo suo[1]

Dilecto amico suo A., B. salutem. Nisi credere[m][2] te offendere, ego quoddam revelarem quod nuper vidi. Set quia scelus est scelus celare,[3] malo ostendere quam celestis regni odium[4] habere. Vidi enim uxorem tuam in thalamo R., solam cum solo, nudam cum nudo; et ut hec negare non possit, cepi zonam eius in sign[o][5] quam tibi transmitto, et per visum factum connoscas. Tantum facias ut illa castigetur, et ille insimul. Valete.

F. tells G.[6] that he has seen another man in bed with G.'s wife

To his beloved friend A., B. sends greetings. Except that I believed it would offend you, I would reveal something that I lately saw. But because it is wicked to conceal wickedness, I prefer to disclose [it][7] rather than to have the odium of the heavenly realm. For I saw your wife in R.'s bed,[8] the two of them alone and naked together. And so that she cannot deny it, I took her girdle [*i.e., belt*] as a token, which I send to you, and the sight of it should serve you as evidence of this misdeed.[9] You should see to it that she is punished, together with him.[10] Farewell.

At first sight, this would seem to be an odd candidate for inclusion in a collection of model letters, since the compiler is unlikely to have assumed that there was a need for a form letter in which one friend notified another of the adultery of the latter's wife. It seems likely that this letter was included in the collection for somewhat different reasons. First, it may have been intended, at least in part, for the amusement of the business students and other male readers for whom the formulary was primarily designed. In a similar fashion John of Garlande included some smutty material in his *Dictionarius*, a contemporary treatise designed to teach Latin vocabulary but written primarily in the form of a walking tour of Paris.[11] Second, and more seriously, this letter may have been included to remind readers that, if they ever made a serious accusation against another person in writing, they had better have solid evidence— such as the wife's girdle, in this case—to support their allegation. A similar case can be found in DOCUMENT 50, in which a tenant writes to his lord to

Figure 12. A girdler's shop or stall, from the Life of St. Nicholas (III) window in the nave of Chartres Cathedral (*c.* 1210).

accuse the bailiff of the manor of corruption, and names three local men as witnesses. Adultery was a very serious charge; for its legal and social implications, see DOCUMENTS 71–73.

This letter, like DOCUMENT 69, may have been inspired in part by the biblical story of Joseph and Potiphar's wife (Genesis 39:6–20). Joseph was a Hebrew slave owned by the Egyptian Potiphar. Potiphar's wife attempted to seduce Joseph, but he rejected her advances and broke away, leaving his garment in her clutch. She then showed the garment to her husband as evidence that Joseph had tried to rape her, and Joseph was imprisoned. Articles of dress and accessories such as girdles were often distinctive personal items that would have been readily identifiable by the owner's intimate circle.

Girdles were long belts made of leather, linen, or silk, sometimes studded with silver or garnished with other decorations (Fig. 12). They were used by both women and men to cinch in their gowns at the waist and, in an age without pockets, to support a hanging purse, a knife, a small set of writing tablets, or similar items. Some girdles were so closely identified with their owners that they became heirlooms, prized for their personal associations as well as their intrinsic value. In 1399, for example, the widowed duchess of Gloucester bequeathed to her daughter Isabel, a Minoress nun, as a special keepsake ("with my blessing"), a black leather girdle with gold trappings that had belonged to Isabel's father, Thomas of Woodstock.[12]

NOTES

1   Add. 8167, fol. 101v. This letter also occurs, with some variations, in Gonville & Caius 205/111, p. 287, which in several places provides better readings than the text in Add. 8167: "Dilecto amico suo A. B. salutem. Nisi crederem te offendere; ego quedam tibi revelarem quod nuper vidi. set quia scelus est scelus celare malo te offendere; quam celestis regni odium habere. Scias enim quod uxorem tuam vidi in talamo .R. solam cum solo. nudam cum nudo. Et ut negare non possit; cepi zonam eius in intersigno quam tibi transmitto; ut videas et per visum facinus cognoscas. Et tantum inde facias ut illa castigetur; et ille longius amoveatur. Valete."

2   *credere* in MS; *crederem* in Gonville & Caius 205/111, p. 287.

3   *scelare* in MS; *celare* in Gonville & Caius 205/111, p. 287.

4   *hodium* in MS; *odium* in Gonville & Caius 205/111, p. 287.

5   *signe* in MS; *intersigno* in Gonville & Caius 205/111, p. 287.

6   In the body of the letter, however, the sender and recipient are called "B." and "A.," suggesting that, as in DOCUMENTS 10, 16, 33, 50, and 90, the compiler of the formulary copied this letter from another collection and neglected to revise the initials in the heading.

7   Gonville and Caius College, MS 205/111, p. 287, has a seemingly better reading here: "*malo te offendere*" ("I prefer to offend you"), in place of Add. 8167's "*malo ostendere*" ("I prefer to disclose"). However, the latter may have used *ostendere* here so as to avoid repetition of the phrase *te offendere*.

8   The Latin phrase "*in thalamo .R.*" can also mean "in the chamber of R." However, since the sender of this letter was able to spy on the lovers and furtively remove the lady's girdle without their being aware of him, it seems much more likely that the lovers were in a curtained bed rather than simply in a chamber together.

9   Gonville & Caius 205/111, p. 287, uses the stronger word "*facinus*" (deed, misdeed, outrage, or crime) here instead of "*factum*" (deed or misdeed).

10   Here Gonville & Caius 205/111, p. 287, suggests a different fate for the wife's lover: he should be banished or exiled far away ("*longius amoveatur*").

11   John of Garlande, an Englishman who taught Latin grammar in Paris, wrote the *Dictionarius* around 1218 and revised it *c.* 1230. See Martha Carlin, "Shops and Shopping in the Early Thirteenth Century: Three Texts," in *Money, Markets and Trade in Late Medieval Europe: Essays in Honour of John H. A. Munro*, ed. Lawrin Armstrong, Ivana Elbl, and Martin M. Elbl (Leiden: Brill, 2007), 491–92, 494–98, 508–17 (especially caps. 51 and 69, pp. 515 and 516).

12 Martha Carlin, "St Botolph Aldgate Gazetteer. Holy Trinity Minories (Abbey of St Clare, 1293/4–1539)," in *Historical Gazetteer of London Before the Great Fire*, ed. Derek Keene (London: Centre for Metropolitan History, 1987; unpub. typescript; available in the Institute of Historical Research, University of London), 40, citing John Nichols, ed., *A Collection of All the Wills, Now Known to Be Extant, of the Kings and Queens of England, Princes and Princesses of Wales, and Every Branch of the Blood Royal, from the Reign of William the Conqueror, to That of Henry the Seventh Exclusive* (London: J. Nichols, 1780), 183 (*Item un seinture de quire noir ove un bocle & pendant & xii roundes & plaines barres d'or quel feust a mon seignour & mari son piere le quele il usa mesmes meint avis & apres q'il feust on son darrein desaise, ove ma beneison*).

71

Bishop H[ugh] of C[arlisle] Orders His Archdeacon to Inquire About Adulterers in His Archdeaconry[1]

Episcopus mandat archidiacono su[o][2] ut faciat per archidiaconatum inquiri qui sin[t][3] adultores

H. dei gratia episcopus de C., karissimo archidiacono suo salutem. In virtute obediencie vobis iniungamus ut faciatis inquiri per archidiaconatum vestrum diligenter si aliqui possint ibi inveniri quos fama acusat adulterii. Si aliquos tales inveniritis, faciatis eos citari ut sint coram nobis in loco tali [n]obis[4] responsuri, et ill[um][5] qui famam sic eos inponit. Et si forte venire nolunt, vigore sentencie compellantur ad veniendum. Perventum enim est ad audienciam nostram quod in iurisdiccione multi sunt persone, quare error[6] nisi cicius obvietur tota provincia poterit corrumpi, quia modicum[7] fermenti totam massam corumpit.[8] Tantum ergo faciatis ne nos et vos per agnicionem similes illis efficiamur quia verum est. pacientes et agentes pari pena puniendi sunt. Valete.

A bishop sends word to his archdeacon to have an inquiry made in his archdeaconry as to who might be adulterers

H[ugh] by the grace of God, bishop of C[arlisle], to his beloved archdeacon, greetings. We order you, by virtue of your obedience, to diligently cause an inquiry to be made throughout your archdeaconry [to see] if anyone may be found there whom common report accuses of adultery. If you do find any such people, have them and the man who accuses them of this cited to appear before us in such-and-such a place to answer to us. And those who refuse to come should be forced to attend by threat of excommunication. For it has come to our attention that there are many such persons in [your] jurisdiction, so that the vice, if it is not quickly stopped, will be able to corrupt the entire diocese, just as a small amount of yeast permeates the whole lump of dough. So take care of it in such a way that we and you do not become like them through inaction, for it is true that those who condone [evil] and those who do it ought to receive the same punishment. Farewell.

This is the first of three ecclesiastical letters that deal with the vexed issue of sexuality. By the early thirteenth century, the Roman Church had been attempting to regulate sexual behavior for more than two hundred years.[9] The Church's original concern had been to impose celibacy on the clergy, but the agenda of reformers had increasingly included the laity as well. Much of the effort of the reform movement was focused on the regulation of sex through monogamous marriage. In England, the Church was well on its way to imposing its view of marriage, and its control over marital litigation, by the second half of the twelfth century (see DOCUMENT 44). Sex outside marriage was condemned as adultery, a sin identified with the mortal sin of "luxury" (sensual self-indulgence). It was also an offense that was actionable in church courts, and it was equated from early times with the serious offense of blasphemy, because it was sin against the body, which was the temple of the Lord. Originally the word "adultery" covered all sorts of sexual misconduct, but in the legalistic world of the twelfth century, adultery came to be defined more narrowly by canon lawyers, and by 1190 it meant sex between a single or married person and someone else's spouse of the opposite sex. Within this understanding of the offense there were certain qualifications. For instance, a married man who had sex with another male was not considered an adulterer, though he might be considered a sodomite. Also, since women were considered to be sexually voracious, and certain occupations, such as that of barmaid, exposed them to dangerous temptations, a husband who allowed his wife to work in a drinking-house was not permitted to press charges of adultery against her if she succumbed. Canon lawyers also ruled that a wife who had been raped could not be charged with adultery.[10]

Adultery could be a serious matter in medieval society, but only a deceived husband's interests were considered. Around 1215, Thomas of Chobham, a canon lawyer and subdean of Salisbury, summarized the legal recourse available to an outraged husband, as he understood it: "It is worth noting that secular law once allowed a man to kill an adulterer found with his wife. This is no longer permitted, but only for him to cut off the man's genitals so that he will never spawn another who will follow him in his vileness."[11] However, Thomas also noted that in such a case, a secular judge could instead order the offenders to be flogged through the streets. A wife whose husband committed adultery had no redress either in the secular law courts or through social sanction, but the Church's penalty for adulterers of either sex was a period of up to seven years' strict penance.[12]

Although the Church's positions on marriage and adultery were clear, and enforceable in church courts, medieval society harbored a much wider range of sexual practices and partnerships than the Church approved. This was at its most obvious in the extramarital relationships of kings and princes such as Henry II and John,[13] and of great nobles and other wealthy people whose lives were also closely observed and recorded. For example, Stephen of Blois, as count of Mortain and Boulogne in the late 1110s and 1120s, had a long relationship and at least two children with a woman he called "Damette" ("Little Lady").[14] The famous Anstey inheritance case of the late 1150s hinged on the fact that in the previous decade the Essex landowner William de Sackville, who was married to Alberada de Tresgots, nonetheless lived and had children with Adelicia, daughter of the sheriff of Essex.[15] John Marshal II (d. 1194) had a long affair with a woman called Alice de Colleville that produced at least one child, while both were apparently married to others.[16] Such behavior was naturally condemned by the clergy. Thomas of Chobham, for example, made a particular point of condemning husbands who condoned or forgave their wives' adultery, calling them no better than pimps.[17] Nonetheless, the romance literature of the period often celebrated extramarital affairs as the truest form of love. The relaxed attitude to extramarital sex that can be seen in many sources should not be taken as evidence of a universally tolerant society, but it is clear from this letter and from DOCUMENTS 72 and 73 that adultery was a common occurrence at all levels of society.

It is quite possible that this model letter is based on a genuine document. The identity of its sender is only lightly disguised. There was only one "H. bishop of C." in early thirteenth-century England, and that was Hugh de Beaulieu, bishop of Carlisle (1219–23) and a former Cistercian abbot. It seems very likely that letters such as this were sent out by bishops to their underlings. Thomas of Chobham criticized archdeacons and rural deans who failed to pursue cases of adulterers on the run, saying—just as this letter does—that the failure to weed out adultery among the laity was as much a sin as adultery itself.[18]

There is evidence of archdeacons carrying out general visitations of their archdeaconries as early as the 1150s,[19] and in the 1230s the statutes of the archdeaconry of London classified adulterers among those worthy of being excommunicated.[20] This letter, together with DOCUMENTS 72 and 73, provides a glimpse of the actual procedures that were used by the Church in England to identify and prosecute adulterers at the local level.[21]

Figure 13. King David commits adultery with Bathsheba, from the Maciejowski Bible (Paris, 1244–54), fol. 41v. The Pierpont Morgan Library, New York. MS M.638, fol. 41v. Purchased by J. P. Morgan (1867–1943) in 1916. Photograph courtesy the Pierpont Morgan Library, New York.

NOTES

1   Add. 8617, fol. 102r–v.
2   *su* in MS.
3   *sin* in MS.
4   *vobis* in MS.
5   *ille* in MS.

6   *errorum* in MS.

7   Fol. 102v commences here.

8   1 Corinthians 5:6.

9   See David d'Avray, *Medieval Marriage: Symbolism and Society* (Oxford: Oxford University Press, 2005), 169.

10 See the magisterial summary of canon law on adultery in James A. Brundage, *Law, Sex and Christian Society in Medieval Europe* (Chicago: University of Chicago Press, 1987), 385–89.

11 Thomas of Chobham, *Summa Confessorum*, ed. F. Broomfield, *Analecta Mediaevalia Namurcensia*, 25 (Louvain, 1968), 192. Thomas may have been recalling a recent case: the castration of William Wake for his adultery with the wife of Robert Butler of Candover (Hampshire) in 1212, which was noted in the Close Rolls of the English Chancery. Bartlett, *England Under the Norman and Angevin Kings*, 568.

12 Chobham, *Summa Confessorum*, 361, 368.

13 On kings and their mistresses and illegitimate offspring, see Chris Given-Wilson and Alice Curteis, *The Royal Bastards of Medieval England* (London: Routledge and Kegan Paul, 1984).

14 Henry Gerald Richardson and George Osborne Sayles, "Gervase of Blois, Abbot of Westminster," in idem, *The Governance of Medieval England* (Edinburgh: Edinburgh University Press, 1963), 413–21.

15 Patricia M. Barnes, "The Anstey Case," in *A Medieval Miscellany for Doris Mary Stenton*, ed. Patricia M. Barnes and Cecil F. Slade, Pipe Roll Society, new ser., 36 (London, 1962, for 1960), 1–24.

16 David Crouch, *William Marshal: Knighthood, War and Chivalry, 1147–1219*, 2nd ed. (London: Longman, 2002), 89–90 and n.

17 Chobham, *Summa Confessorum*, 366.

18 Chobham, *Summa Confessorum*, 367.

19 Brian Robert Kemp, ed., *Twelfth-Century Archidiaconal and Vice-Archidiaconal Acta*, Canterbury and York Society, 92 (London, 2001), 130.

20 The excommunications were to take place at the beginning of Advent and Lent, on Trinity Sunday (the Sunday after Pentecost), and on the Sunday following the feast of the Assumption (i.e., the Sunday following August 15). In 1240 the statutes of the diocese of Worcester enjoined archdeacons and their officials (legal deputies) to identify clergy who cohabited with women. *Councils and Synods*, 311–12, 332–33.

21 Cf. a letter written in 1289 by the official of the archdeacon of Ely to the sacrist of Bury St. Edmunds, Suffolk, notifying him of the reported presence of an adulterous couple in his jurisdiction, and requesting that the sacrist have them publicly denounced as excommunicates who were to be shunned by all until they had been absolved by the Church. Antonia Gransden, ed., *The Letter-Book of William of Hoo*, Suffolk Record Society, 5 (1963), nos. 48 and 79. For this reference we are grateful to Paul Hyams.

72

An Archdeacon Orders a Dean to Investigate the Alleged Bribing of a Chaplain by an Adulterer to Conceal His Affair[1]

Hoc est de fornicacione

> Archidiaconus decano salutem. Ad audienciam domini episcopi perventum est quod in parochia de C., T. cum uxore alterius viri longo tempore transacto C. mecatus,[2] sacerdote precio corupto ut celet eius adulterium. Quare tibi mando ex parte domini episcopi, quatinus capellanum predicte ville [et][3] adulterum prefatum, [T.][4] nomine, ut dictum, citari facias ut die lune proxima coram domino episcopo compareant, responsuri et iuri parituri de illis que eis obiciuntur. Et tantum faciatis ne illorum criminis particeps esse puteris. Vale.

This concerns fornication

> An archdeacon to a dean, greetings. It has come to the lord bishop's attention that, in the parish of C., T. has been committing adultery for a long time with another man's wife at C., having bribed the priest to conceal his adultery. So I order you on the lord bishop's behalf to have the chaplain of the village [and] the said adulterer, [T.] by name, as it is said, cited to appear before the lord bishop next Monday, there to answer and obey the law concerning the charges against them. And take care of this in such a way that you will not be considered an accomplice in their crime. Farewell.

Here, as in DOCUMENTS 71 and 73, ecclesiastical authorities are preoccupied with the problem of adultery in their jurisdiction. In this letter, collusion is suspected between "T." and his parish priest, whom T. allegedly has bribed to conceal his long-standing affair with another man's wife.

Archdeacons and deans had themselves been accused of similar corruption. In 1158, for example, Henry II complained that archdeacons and deans were extorting more money from his subjects with false allegations of adultery than the king himself was able to extract from them.[5] In 1170 the Inquest of Sheriffs, a royal inquiry into local corruption, had a clause (12) that required royal justices to inquire into payments that archdeacons and deans had demanded "unjustly and without judgement."[6] Denunciation for sexual irregularity entered an especially harsh phase in the mid-thirteenth century, when the intrusive power of the papacy reached its height in England and the Church attained a peak of influence over lay life. Matthew Paris reported that in 1246 Bishop Robert Grosseteste of Lincoln launched an inquiry into morals and behavior throughout his large diocese, inspired, it was said, by the Franciscans and Dominicans. The bishop went too far, however, by including the aristocracy in his enquiries and thus exposing a dangerous level of scandal among the powerful. The king was persuaded to intervene and to prohibit church officials from taking statements under oath about the behavior of people of rank.[7]

NOTES

1   Add. 8167, fol. 103r.
2   I.e., *moechatus*. We are grateful to Ruth Karras for this suggestion.
3   *et* missing in MS but required by the sense of the passage.
4   *c.* in MS.
5   William Fitz Stephen, *Vita sancti Thomae*, in James Craigie Robertson and Joseph Brigstocke Sheppard, eds., *Materials for the History of Thomas Becket.*, 7 vols., Rolls Series, no. 67 (London: Longman, 1872–85), 3:44.
6   *Select Charters*, 177.
7   Matthew Paris, *Matthæi Parisiensis, monachi Sancti Albani, Chronica Majora*, ed. Henry Richards Luard, 7 vols., Rolls Series, 57 (London: Longman, 1872–83), 4:579–80.

73

A Rural Dean Offers to Cover Up an Allegation Against a Chaplain of Adultery with the Wife of One of His Parishioners[1]

Incipit aliud de eodem

Decanus capellano salutem. Relicta[2] cuiusdam[3] parochiani vestri michi datur intelligi ovem propriam et viro desponsatam longo tempore transacto in aldulterio fedasti. Quod sive sit verum sive non, priusquam rumor vulgetur[4] in secretis ad me venias. Sciturus quod si hoc feceris et verum sit, veritatem extinguam; si falsum sit, ad nichilum faciam redigi. Si[c][5] ergo venias ut tibi prosit obieccio, et michi placeat tua presencia. Vale.

Here begins another letter about the same thing

A dean to a chaplain, greetings. The widow of a parishioner of yours has given me to understand that you have defiled in adultery one of your own flock, a woman long married. True or not, you should come to me in secrecy before it becomes common knowledge. You know that if you do as I say and it turns out to be true, I will suppress the truth; if it is false, I will make sure the affair comes to nothing. So make sure you come so that the charge might go well with you, and so that your presence will make me well disposed to you. Farewell.

This is the third of three letters by ecclesiastical administrators (see Documents 71 and 72) concerning allegations of adultery. This time the alleged adulterer is himself a clergyman. Clerics were supposed to be celibate, but medieval sources are full of incidents of sexual incontinence by clergy. In the 1190s, for example, Gerald of Wales, archdeacon of Brecon, was very critical of colleagues who were lax in punishing clerics who had sexual relations with women. He called it a "gross abuse" and regarded it as an extremely widespread offense among clergy.[6]

The correspondence of the distinguished Franciscan friar Adam Marsh reveals how easy it was in the mid-thirteenth century for a clergyman to avoid exposure and evade censure for sexual misbehavior for quite some while. Around 1251 the abbess of Godstow had nominated an apparently respectable priest to the bishop of Lincoln for institution as vicar of Bloxham in Oxfordshire. The priest was interviewed and approved by a panel appointed by the bishop. But Adam—who had been present at the interview—subsequently learned that the priest, "to the offence of God and to public scandal," had been carrying on a long-standing affair with a woman by whom he had already fathered a child. It was not until an enemy found a way of exposing him to Adam Marsh that the affair was revealed and the priest punished.[7]

The presence in a formulary of a model letter in which a church administrator offers to collude with a subordinate in concealing the latter's adultery seems odd indeed. Like DOCUMENT 70, this letter may have been included simply to amuse its male readers, or perhaps it was the author's own wry comment on the corruption of the times. Whatever the reason, it depicts all too clearly a seamy side of clerical behavior and patronage at the parochial level.

NOTES

1   Add. 8167, fol. 103r.
2   Corrected in MS from *relaicta*.
3   Corrected in MS from *cuidam*.
4   *wlgetur* in MS.
5   *Si* in MS.

6   Gerald of Wales, *Speculum Ecclesiae*, in *Giraldi Cambrensis Opera*, ed. John Sherren Brewer et al., 8 vols., Rolls Series, 21 (London: Longman, 1861–91), 4:329.

7   *Adae de Marisco Epistolae*, in *Monumenta Franciscana*, ed. John Sherren Brewer, 2 vols., Rolls Series, 4 (London: Longman, 1858–82), 2:108–9.

74

A Steward Writes to His Lord About a Gravely Ill Knight Whose Wife and Daughter Have Gone Elsewhere[1]

Reverendo domino suo W. de G., senescallus [suus][2] salutem. Noscat discrecio vestra dominum R. de B. grave morbo vexatum, unde ipsum melius extimamus mori quam vivere.[3] Preterea sciatis pro certo quod domina A. uxor sua, cum filia sua E. et cum quodam garcione, apud A. perendinavit. Unde placitum vestrum de mandato isto nobis mandetis. Valete.

To his respected lord W. de G., his steward [sends] greetings. Let Your Discretion know [that] Sir R. de B. is seriously ill, and I think he is more likely to die than to live. You should also know for certain that Lady A. his wife, with her daughter E. and a servant, has gone to stay at A. Therefore, send me word what your wishes are concerning that message. Farewell.

It was important for a lord to know the family affairs of his tenants, since his lordship over them gave him certain rights, including that of wardship. In this letter, therefore, the steward is not merely reporting local gossip; rather, the final sentence suggests that the sick knight was a tenant of the steward's lord, and thus the knight's expected death and the disposition of his widow and heir were matters of direct concern to him.

A sign of the importance of such information is that one of the earliest surviving surveys of the English royal administration was an inquisition, carried out in 1185, on widows and children who by rights ought to have been wards of the Crown. This resulted in the "Rolls of Ladies and Children" (*Rotuli de Dominabus et Pueris*).[4] The profits of wardship could be enormous, and the granting of wardships to favored subordinates, friends, or allies was a major act of patronage, one that King Henry II (1154–89) and his sons Richard I (1189–99) and John (1199–1216) exploited vigorously. Around 1185, for example, Henry gave William Marshal, one of his principal captains, the wardship of Heloise, the teenage heiress to the honor of Kendal in northern

England. Marshal might have married her and made her estates his own, but instead he decided to wait for an even grander heiress. In 1188 the king fulfilled his expectations by promising Marshal the noble heiress of the great French honor of Châteauroux in Berry in return for his military support. But the next year the king raised the stakes further by the promise of Countess Isabel, the heiress to the earldom of Pembroke. For this promise, Marshal had to give up Heloise of Lancaster to a fellow courtier. In the end the king died before he could fulfil the promise, but the new king, Richard the Lionheart, sanctioned the grant, and so William Marshal, after five years of hopeful negotiation, married the heiress of his dreams in London and took charge of her and her estates.[5]

The fate of widows, female heirs, and under-age wards was an abiding subject of gossip in medieval society. In 1250 the French baron Jean de Joinville was scandalized by a group of knights who were chatting and laughing through the funeral mass of one of their fellows, distracting the priest at the altar. Joinville told them to keep quiet, remarking that talking during mass was not the way a nobleman should behave. They just laughed and told him that they were arranging the marriage of the widow. The outraged Joinville observed with some satisfaction that all of them were subsequently killed in battle.[6]

The inclusion of a letter such as DOCUMENT 74 in a formulary indicates that such letters must have been common in a society in which timely news of the mortal illness and death of landowners was crucial in establishing rights of wardship over heirs and collecting reliefs (death duties) owed by incoming tenants. At least one genuine example of such a letter survives from this period. It was dashed off in October 1227 by a clerk of Earl William Marshal II of Pembroke to Bishop John of Bath and Wells to notify him of the death of a wealthy knight, Nicholas of Anstey: "William Marshal, earl of Pembroke, gives greeting and devout reverence to the venerable father in Christ and lord, J[ohn], by the grace of God, bishop of Bath. It was given to us to understand at Llant[risant, Gwent] in all truth on the Monday after the feast of St Lawrence [October 14] that Nicholas of Anstey has died."[7]

NOTES

1 Add. 8167, fol. 127r–v.

2 In MS, the phrase *reverendo W. de G.* is mistakenly repeated here, and the word *suus* is omitted.

3 Fol. 127v commences here.

4 See Susan M. Johns, *Noblewomen, Aristocracy and Power in the Twelfth-Century Anglo-Norman Realm* (Manchester: Manchester University Press, 2003), Chap. 9. Only the returns from several Midland counties survive.

5 David Crouch, *William Marshal: Knighthood, War and Chivalry, 1147–1219,* 2nd ed. (Harlow, Essex: Longman, 2002), 59–60, 65–71.

6   Jean de Joinville, *Vie de Saint Louis*, ed. and trans. Jacques Monfrin (Paris: Classiques Garnier, 1995), 146–48.
7   TNA, PRO: SC 1/2/19.

75

A Man of Property Writes Home to
His Wife, Niece, and Servants[1]

A. de G. dilectis sibi Iohanne uxori sue, et N. nepte sue. T. clerico, G. de Cestria, et ceteris fidelibus suis salutem. Noveritis me esse sanum et incolumum, et hoc idem de vobis scire desidero. Mitto vobis etiam .v. dolea vini, unde vobis, T. clerico et G. de Cestria, mando, quatinus quam cito poteritis per aliquam ydoneum nuncium, pro amore dei, quibus multum indigeo sicut alias vobis mandavi, michi mittatis. Per eundem vel per alium cicius intervenientem, michi rescribatis quod factum fuerit unde dominus rex multas accepit peticiones, et cum predictis statum et esse vestrum nec non terrarum mearum. Intim[a]ndum[2] michi studeatis. Valeat dileccio vestra.

A. de G. to his beloved wife Joan and his niece N., to T. the clerk and G. of Chester and his other faithful servants, greetings. You will know that I am well and safe, and I hope to hear the same of you. Also, I am sending you five tuns of wine, and I ask that you, T. the clerk and G. of Chester, send me by some honest messenger, as quickly as possible, for the love of God, the things that I need very much, as I have sent you word about elsewhere. Write back to me by the same man—or by another who will come quickly—what took place when the lord king received all those petitions, together with how you are and the state of my lands. Keep me fully informed. May your love flourish.[3]

This is an unusually circumstantial letter. We are given the full initials of the writer, as well as the name of his wife, the initials or partial names of two of his senior officers, and possibly the initial of his niece, although in her case the initial "N." more probably stands for *nomen* (name) or *nepta* (niece). In addition to the reference to the wine we are told that the writer is very anxious for news about his own lands and about an event at court. The writer is evidently a man of some wealth, since he has an estate and at least two household officers, and since he can afford to buy and transport wine in wholesale quantities. His anxiety for news of the court and of his lands suggests that he is far from home and has been for some time—for example, on business, or on a judicial circuit, a diplomatic mission, or a military campaign. The five tuns of wine that the writer is sending to his family may be an indication that he was taking part in the Gascon campaign of 1225–27.[4] All of these details suggest that this text may be based on a genuine letter, while the urgent request for news about "what took place when the lord king received all those petitions" may give a clue to its date and political context.

In January 1227 the nineteen-year-old Henry III announced that, on the advice of the archbishop of Canterbury and "our bishops, abbots, earls, barons and other magnates and *fideles* [faithful men]," he would thenceforth issue charters under his own seal. This announcement marked the young king's assumption of full regal powers, and the effective end of his minority, even though he was not yet twenty-one, the customary age of majority. It also marked a major change in national politics, since Henry III could now "dispense patronage on a permanent basis."[5] Petitions flooded in immediately,[6] and the king's response to these may well be the news that was so avidly sought by A. de G. in the letter above. If so, it was probably written in early 1227. This interpretation would also fit the possibility mentioned above that A. de G. was writing from the Gascon campaign.

The domestic content of this letter recalls letters written more than a century earlier by men who had joined the First Crusade to their wives and families back home. Two such letters survive from Count Stephen of Blois to his wife Adele, a daughter of William the Conqueror. In the second of these, dated March 29, 1098, Count Stephen wrote from Antioch as follows: "Count Stephen to Adele, his sweetest and most amiable wife, to his dear children, and to all his vassals of all ranks, his greeting and blessing. You may be very sure, dearest, that the messenger whom I sent to give you pleasure left me before Antioch safe and unharmed and, through God's grace, in the greatest prosperity." After giving a detailed account of the campaign to date, he closed by saying: "These which I write to you are only a few things, dearest, of the many which we have done; and because I am not able to tell you, dearest, what is in my mind, I charge you to do right, to watch carefully over your land, and to do your duty as you ought to your children and your vassals. You will certainly see me just as soon as I can possibly return to you. Farewell."[7]

An intriguing feature of A. de G.'s letter is the inclusion of his niece among the senior members of his household. Perhaps she was an orphaned ward of his, or perhaps she had been sent by her parents, who would have been of equal or lesser rank than A. de G., for training in his household. This was a common arrangement for the children of wealthy families, but it is recorded more commonly of boys than of girls. A few details for such an arrangement can be found, however, in a model custody agreement copied into the Oxford formulary dating from *c.* 1202–9 in the Walters Art Museum (MS W. 15). In this agreement, the children of a deceased man of property are committed to the care of two men. One takes the dead man's two sons, together with eleven acres of their father's land and his principal messuage,[8] and pledges to provide them with all their necessities until they are thirty years of age, when he will divide the property between them, as their father directed in his testament. The other takes the dead man's two daughters, together with seven acres of land and some stone buildings. He pledges to provide for the daughters' necessities until they are twenty years of age, or, when they have reached marriageable age, if they wish to marry, he will find them the best husbands he can, with the advice of their friends. If, instead, the daughters wish to become nuns or anchoresses, he will hand over their land to the next heirs, and the heirs will pay them ten marks (£6 13*s.* 4*d.*) in rent.[9] This letter and custody agreement offer some rare glimpses into the lives of well-born girls of this period.[10]

NOTES

1   Add. 8167, fol. 127v.

2   *Intimendum* in MS.

3   On this valedictory phrase, see Document 51.

4   We are grateful to Robert Stacey for this suggestion.

5   David A. Carpenter, *The Minority of Henry III* (London: Methuen, 1990), 389. This episode was also discussed by Kate Norgate in *The Minority of Henry the Third* (London: Macmillan, 1912), 265–68.

6   Robert Stacey commented on this episode that "[a]n unseemly scramble ensued in the early months of 1227 to secure as many of the newly available prizes as possible." Robert C. Stacey, *Politics, Policy, and Finance Under Henry III, 1216–1245* (Oxford: Clarendon, 1987), 35.

7   The entire letter is printed in Dana Carlton Munro, ed. and trans., *Translations and Reprints from the Original Sources of European History*, vol. 1, no. 4 (Philadelphia: Department of History of the University of Pennsylvania, 1900), 5–8. Count Stephen never returned home; he was killed at the battle of Ramla in 1102. Their son Stephen succeeded his uncle Henry I as king of England in 1135. On Adele, Stephen, and their relationship, see Kimberly A. LoPrete, *Adela of Blois: Countess and Lord, c. 1067–1137* (Dublin: Four Courts, 2007).

8   A messuage or tenement was a building plot with its buildings, if any; here it is evidently the father's house.

9   Walters MS W. 15, fol. 81r.

10   On the education and training of boys and girls sent away from home in this way, see Urban Tigner Holmes, Jr., *Daily Living in the Twelfth Century, Based on the Observations of Alexander Neckam in London and Paris* (Madison: University of Wisconsin Press, 1952), 177–79.

76

A Wife Writes to Her Absent Husband[1]

Karissimo domino suo et amico B., M. uxor sua salutem et amicicie medullam. Preces vestras precepta repeto, et quicquid michi preceperitis in continenti sine dilacione faciam, et quod michi per B. garciferum vestrum mandatum, complebitur valde velociter. Vos autem quam cicius poteritis ad me redeatis, ut de bonis nobis[2] a deo debitis perfrui simul et letari valeamus. Valete.

To her dearest lord and friend B., M. his wife sends greetings and deepest affection.[3] Your wishes I repeat as orders, and whatever you will order me [to do] I shall do immediately, without delay, and what you sent me word about through B., your servant, will be finished very rapidly. And you are to return to me as quickly as you can, so that together we may enjoy to the full the good things from God and take pleasure in the duties owed by us. Farewell.

Behind the fervent expressions of wifely obedience in this letter one can see that the husband has, as was common, left his wife in charge of his household in his absence. In turbulent times, wives even deputized for their husbands in supervising military operations. On May 29, 1267, for example, William de Valence, earl of Pembroke, wrote to his wife, addressing her as "his dear companion and friend" (*a sa chere conpaigne et amie*), to tell her that he was sending Sir Robert de Immer and two assistants to provision and defend Winchester Castle under her command. The earl concluded by formally granting his wife full powers to act as she thought best: "we give you power over them all and of them all, to ordain and arrange in all things according to that which you shall see to be best to do" (*vus donoms le poer sur eus tuz et de eus tuz, a ordener et a puruer en tute choses solom ceo que vus verrez que meuz fra a fere*).[4]

In the model letter above, the husband evidently has sent his wife instructions both in writing and by word of mouth through his servant. Such verbal instructions may have been reserved for sensitive personal, political, or military matters that the husband was unwilling to entrust to a letter for fear that it would fall into the wrong hands. This sort of arrangement is mentioned explicitly in a letter written about 1217 × 1219 by Isabelle of Angoulême, widow of King John, to her young son, Henry III. After the death of King John in 1216, Isabelle had returned to her own county of Angoulême in France. Now she was asking for assistance in defending her lands against the king of France, and she closed her letter by saying that her messengers would report certain confidential information verbally, since it was unsafe to send it in writing: "we are sending over to you Sir Geoffrey de Bodeville and Sir Waleran, entrusting to them many matters which cannot be set down in writing to you, and you can trust them in what they say to you on our behalf concerning the benefit to you and us."[5]

The last sentence in the model letter marks an abrupt shift from business to passion. Here the wife takes the upper hand, ordering—not begging—her husband to return to her as soon as possible so that together they can pay the marriage debt, a euphemism for marital sex. The Church taught that husband and wife were "one flesh," and that neither spouse could refuse the sexual demands of the other. There were, however, restrictions on marital sex: it had to be procreative (intended to result in conception) rather than carnal (undertaken simply for pleasure), and it had to occur in a permissible manner (only vaginal sex in the "missionary position" was acceptable) and at a permitted time (sex was forbidden, for example, during many religious holidays or while the wife was menstruating). Sex outside these restrictions was deemed sinful. Women were assumed to have sexual urges that were as strong as men's, or even stronger, and wives were not shy about demanding sex.[6] Anti-feminist writers, many of them clerics who considered even marital sex to be polluting, viewed such displays of female power with alarm and outrage. For example, the Anglo-Norman chronicler Orderic Vitalis (1075–c. 1142) alleged (improbably) that a number of the Norman barons and knights who had followed William the Conqueror to England in 1066 were summoned back to Normandy two years later by their wives who, "consumed by fierce lust, sent message after message to their husbands urging them to return at once, and adding that unless they did so with all speed they would take other husbands for themselves." The husbands, terrified at the threat of cuckoldry, "returned to Normandy to oblige their wanton wives," even though this meant forfeiting the English fiefs that they had obtained from the victorious William.[7] Similar accounts of female sexual demands can be found in the satirical literature of the period. In the anti-matrimonial poem *Lamenta* ("Laments"), for example, written in Latin around 1280–90 by Mathieu de Boulogne-sur-mer,[8] the narrator complains that a husband is tormented day and night by his wife's constant demands for sex.[9] And, he wails, when his own wife claims her conjugal rights but his advancing age makes him unable to perform, she rips out his hair.[10]

This breathless missive reads suspiciously like a man's notion of an ideal letter from a wife. However, in its extravagant declarations of obedience and open avowal of sexual frustration, it also recalls the dozens of passionate letters in meticulous Latin, believed to have been written in Paris, *c.* 1115–17, by the brilliant young Heloise (*c.* 1094?–1164) to her lover and teacher, the celebrated scholar Abelard (1079–1142), during their tempestuous affair and before their clandestine marriage: "Just how excruciating your long absence since you left has been for me is known only to the one who looks into the secrets of everyone's heart. . . . I cannot deny myself to you any more than Byblis could to Caunus, or Oenone to Paris, or Briseis to Achilles. . . . Do not delay in coming; the quicker you come, the quicker you will find cause for joy."[11] Years later, long after Abelard's castration, downfall, and retreat to monastic life, Heloise, who had become a nun at his command and was now an abbess, poured out her heart to him in similar fashion from her convent of the Paraclete near Troyes: "I have carried out all your orders so implicitly that when I was powerless to oppose you in anything, I found strength at your command to destroy myself. I did more, strange to say—my love rose to such heights of madness that it robbed itself of what it most desired beyond hope of recovery, when immediately at your bidding I changed my clothing along with my mind, in order to prove you the possessor of my body and my will alike." And, she continued:

> I carried out everything for your sake and continue up to the present moment in complete obedience to you. It was not any sense of vocation which brought me as a young girl to accept the austerities of the cloister, but your bidding alone. . . . I would have had no hesitation, God knows, in following you or going ahead at your bidding to the flames of Hell. My heart was not in me but with you, and now, even more, if it is not with you it is nowhere; truly, without you it cannot exist. . . . I have finally denied myself every pleasure in obedience to your will, kept nothing for myself except to prove that now, even more, I am yours.[12]

NOTES

1   Add. 8167, fol. 128v.

2   *vobis* in MS.

3   Literally, "the marrow of friendship."

4   Shirley, ed., *Letters*, vol. 2, 311 (Anglo-Norman text), 371 (English translation). This letter is now TNA: PRO, SC 1/11/101. On powers exercised by women in the absence of their husbands, see also Johns, *Noblewomen, Aristocracy and Power*, Chap. 3.

5   Anne Crawford, ed., *Letters of the Queens of England, 1100–1547* (Stroud, Gloucestershire: Sutton, 1994, rpt. 1997), 50–52. The Latin text of this letter can be found in Shirley, ed., *Letters*, vol. 1, 22–23; the original is TNA: PRO, SC 1/3/181. Shirley (p. 22n.) dates the letter to the period between Prince Louis's departure from England in September 1217 and Isabelle's second marriage in May 1220; perhaps in the spring or summer of 1219, "when war with France seemed imminent." Patricia Barnes dates the letter to 1217–19 in *PRO Lists and Indexes, No. XV: List of Ancient*

Correspondence of the Chancery and Exchequer, rev. ed. (New York: Kraus Reprint, 1968), p. 51 (no. 181).

6   Brundage, *Law, Sex, and Christian Society*, 278–88, 348–51, 358–60. We are grateful to Merry Wiesner-Hanks for this reference.

7   *The Ecclesiastical History of Orderic Vitalis*, ed. and trans. Marjorie Chibnall, 6 vols. (Oxford: Clarendon, 1968–80), 2:218–21.

8   Mathieu's Latin poem, also known as *Liber Lamentationum Matheoluli* (*The Book of Lamentations of Little Matthew*), was translated into French between 1380 and 1387 by Jean le Fèvre de Ressons, who wrote a response called *Le Livre de Leesce* (*The Book of Joy*). Renate Blumenfeld-Kosinski, "Jean le Fèvre's *Livre de Leesce*: Praise or Blame of Women?," *Speculum*, 69 (1994), 705 and n. 4. The texts of Mathieu's Latin poem and Le Fèvre's French translation can be found in Jean le Fèvre, *Les Lamentations de Matheolus et le Livre de Leesce*, ed. Anton-Gérard van Hamel, 2 vols., Bibliothèque de l'École des Hautes Études, Sciences philologiques et historiques (Paris, 1892–1905), fasc. 95–96. For the Latin title, *Lamenta*, see Book I, p. 2 (Latin text, line 9). The poems are discussed in Charles Victor Langlois, *La Vie en France au Moyen Âge, de la fin du XIIᵉ au milieu du XIVᵉ siècle, d'après des moralistes du temps*, nouv. éd., 4 vols. (Paris, 1924–28), 2:241–90. On the date and authorship of the *Lamenta*, see also Jean Batany, "Un Drôle de métier: le 'Status conjugatorum,'" in *Femmes, mariages-lignages: XIIe–XVIe siècles: mélanges offerts à Georges Duby*, ed. Jean Dufournet, André Joris, and Pierre Toubert, Bibliothèque du Moyen Âge, 1 (Brussels: De Boeck Université, 1992), 36.

9   (In Latin): "*Nulla viro requies, cum nocte dieque legatur/Passio quindecies illi, semper cruciatur.*" (In French): "*Quinze fois de nuit et de jour/Avra passion sans sejour/Et sera tormentés forments.*" (She'll demand it fifteen times a day, sex without remission, it'll be pure hell.) See le Fèvre, *Lamentations*, ed. van Hamel, Book I, p. 24, lines 759–61 (French text) and 341–42 (Latin text).

10 See le Fèvre, *Lamentations*, ed. van Hamel, Book I, pp. 40–41, lines 1307–56 (French text) and 560–87 (Latin text). In Book I, p. 4 (French text, lines 154–57; Latin text, line 29) the narrator explains that he has married a widow who turned out to be a virago.

11 Constant J. Mews, *The Lost Letters of Heloise and Abelard: Perceptions of Dialogue in Twelfth-Century France*, with a translation by Neville Chiavaroli and Constant J. Mews (New York: St. Martin's Press, 1999), Letter 45, pp. 224–25. On the dates of the correspondence and the affair, see p. 146; on the date of Heloise's birth, see p. 32; on the deaths of Abelard and Heloise, see pp. 174–75. The attribution of the letters in this volume to Heloise and Abelard remains the subject of debate.

12 *The Letters of Abelard and Heloise*, trans. Betty Radice (Harmondsworth, Middlesex: Penguin Books, 1974), Letter 1 (Heloise to Abelard), 109–18 (these excerpts are from pp. 113, 115–16).

77

A Knight in the Queen's Service Asks His Wife to Send Him Linen Cloth and Sheets[1]

Miles uxori sue salutem. Quicumque alii deficiant,[2] suo viro non debet deficere ubi precipue desid[erio?][3] non deficit m[oneta?].[4] Bene nosci quod diu iam regina meum[5] detinuit servicium. Lineos pannos et lincea-mina[6] consumpsi, et ideo, quam cicius poteritis, defectum illum emend-are satagas,[7] et in hiis et in aliis que presensium lator dixerit tibi. Michi subvenias ut cum ad te rediero tibi grates referre valeam.

A knight to his wife, greetings. Whatever other things one's husband may lack, he should certainly not go short where there is no want of money (*moneta*) for what he desires (*desiderio*). You know well that for a long time now the queen has engaged my service. I have used up my linen cloth and sheets, and therefore, as quickly as you can, busy yourself with repairing that loss, both in these things and in others that the bearer of this present letter will tell you about. Please help me in this, and when I return to you I shall be duly grateful.

This document sheds interesting light on the conditions of royal service in early thirteenth-century England. The queen in this letter is presumably intended to be Eleanor of Provence, who married Henry III on January 14, 1236. Members of her entourage would have been provided each year with liveries of one or more suits of woolen outer clothing; shoes and woolen hose were sometimes included as well. Such liveries varied in quality, quantity, and value according to the rank or office of the recipients, and formed a substantial portion of their annual retainer or wage.[8] The letter above makes it clear, however, that a knight of the queen's household was expected to provide his own linens in the form of underclothing (shirts and drawers), bedding (sheets and pillow-covers), and towels.

Linen cloth of various kinds was widely used in medieval Europe. In addi-tion to underwear, bedding, and toweling, its domestic uses included wall hangings, tablecloths, napkins, aprons, cleaning cloths, head coverings (veil-ing, kerchiefs, and coifs), girdles (belts), and baby linens. In well-to-do house-holds it was customary to buy linen cloth in quantity, or to have it woven from the raw flax, and then to make it up into various articles as needed. For example, at her death in 1267 Cecily Heosey or Huse bequeathed all her towels and table linens "that are now made or to be made" to be divided among her husband and daughters. A post-mortem inventory of her possessions found that her household belongings at the manor of "Tephonte" (Teffont Evias, Wiltshire) included thirty-nine ells (44.577 meters) of linen cloth, and that she had died owing 12*d.* and 26*d.*, respectively, to two women for weaving linen cloth.[9]

It is interesting to note that in this letter the knight writes home for fresh supplies of linen and sheets rather than buying them for himself. His motive seems likely to have been economic: if his household commissioned its linens from local weavers or purchased them in bulk at local fairs, it may well have been cheaper for the knight to have these goods sent to him from home than to buy them in London (or wherever the court was at the time). This letter thus also provides an intriguing glimpse into the domestic economy of a knight's household.

NOTES

1   Add. 8167, fol. 128v.

2   *deficiat* in MS.

3   *defidi* in MS. The proper reading here is uncertain; *desiderio* seems to best suit the context.

4   This word is uncertain; in the MS, it is given in abbreviated form as M^a. The same abbreviation occurs in DOCUMENT 84, where, however, it seems most likely to stand for *miseria*.

5   *me* in MS.

6   Corrected in MS from *linceamena*.

7   Corrected in MS from *satagare*.

8   Margaret Wade Labarge, *A Baronial Household of the Thirteenth Century* (London: Eyre and Spottiswoode, 1965; rpt. New York: Barnes and Noble, 1966), 130–31; see also Frédérique Lachaud, "Liveries of Robes in England, *c.* 1200–1330," *English Historical Review*, 111, no. 441 (April 1996), especially pp. 281–83, 290. Eleanor de Montfort provided shoes and hose for at least some of her servants. See, e.g., Thomas Hudson Turner, ed., *Manners and Household Expenses of England in the Thirteenth and Fifteenth Centuries*. Roxburghe Club Publications, no. 57 (London, 1841), 31. For livery robes, see also DOCUMENTS 5 and 6.

9   *mappe et manutergia que nunc sunt facta vel facienda.* TNA: PRO, E 210/291 (testament); E 154/1/2 (inventory). Cecily and her husband Geoffrey had acquired a quarter of a knight's fee in Teffont Evias before 1242–43. *Victoria History of the Counties of England, Wiltshire*, vol. 13, *South-West Wiltshire: Chalk and Dunworth Hundreds*, ed. D. A. Crowley (Oxford: Oxford University Press, for the Institute of Historical Research, 1987), 188. On knight's fees, see DOCUMENT 34, note 9.

78

A Man Asks a Friend to Take His Son into His Service[1]

A. B. salutem. Quoniam de vestra quamplurimum confidimus amicicia, dilectum filium nostrum vobis transmittimus,[2] suplicantes quatinus, pro amore meo et servicio, illum in servicio vestro recipiatis. Scientes[3] pro certo quod morigeratus est, et ad omne servicium promtus et paratus et fidelis. Et eciam in omnibus eum talem promittamus, et si de illo fideiussores vel securitatem velitis habere, pro illo fideiubemus[4] ut manucapiamus illius fidelitatem. Tantum ergo pro nostra peticione faciatis, ut preces nostras presens penes vos senciat profuisse. Valete.

To A., B. [sends] greetings. Since we have the greatest confidence in your friendship, we send our beloved son to you, asking that, for my love and service, you receive him into your service, knowing for certain that he is of good character, and prompt, ready, and loyal for every [kind of] service. And we also promise that he is such in all things, and if you wish to have guarantors and security for him, we stand surety for him, so we may guarantee his trustworthiness. Therefore, please act in such a way, for the sake of our request, that the bearer may think that our wishes have found favor with you. Farewell.

Obtaining employment in the medieval world was often a matter of whom one knew, and the use of unabashed patronage or nepotism by a lord or lady was considered a proper—indeed, an essential—demonstration of personal power. Offering or soliciting employment or similar favors for relations, friends, and dependents was an important aspect of lordship, one to be practiced openly and publicly, rather than a corrupt act to be practiced furtively or revealed only to intimates. Shame lay not in offering such patronage, but in failing to provide it, which is why men and women of the highest standing were constantly sending and receiving letters of this kind (cf. Documents 86–87 and 92). Examples can be found in the correspondence of Queen Dowager Eleanor of Provence (d. 1291) and of her daughter-in-law, Queen Eleanor of Castile (d. 1290), both of whom wrote to the senior royal administrator John de Kirkby to request assistance for various dependents.[5]

The language of this model letter clearly reflected contemporary usage. For example, Peter de Maulay, who from 1215 to 1220 had custody of Richard of Cornwall, the king's younger brother, wrote to the justiciar Hubert de Burgh about 1219 × 1221 on behalf of Richard's tutor Roger of Acaster, and his letter employs very similar expressions. De Maulay asked de Burgh to assist Roger "for my love" (*pro amore meo*), and concluded: "please act in such a way concerning my wishes that I shall be deeply indebted to you, and that he [*i.e., Roger*] may feel that my request was useful to him" (*super his tantum ad preces meas facientes, quod vobis ad multiplices tener gratiarum actiones, et quod preces meas sibi sentiat fructuosas*).[6]

NOTES

1 Fairfax 27, fol. 6r.
2 *tranmittimus* in MS.
3 *Sientes* in MS.
4 *fideiudebemus* in MS.
5 TNA: PRO, SC 1/10/47 (1274 x 86), SC 1/10/51 (1283), SC 1/10/132 (1287 × 90). On Kirkby, see *Oxford DNB*, s.n. "Kirkby, John (*d.* 1290)."

6 Shirley, ed., *Letters*, vol. 1., 179–80 (no. 156). This letter is now TNA: PRO, SC 1/1/ 153. It was dated by Shirley to *c.* 1221, and by Patricia M. Barnes to 1219–21 (see PRO, *Lists and Indexes, No. XV, List of Ancient Correspondence*, rev. ed., p. 13 [vol. 1, no. 153]). On de Maulay, see *Oxford DNB*, s.n. "Maulay, Peter (I) de (*d.* 1241)."

STUDENT LIFE

79

A Student Tells His Friends that He Is Going to Become a Monk[1]

Siquis debeat in religionem convertere et habeat socios quibus velit mittere salutes, [?exemplum][2] habeat huiusmodi

Scolaris sociis salutem. Consilio amicorum m[e]orum[3] et fructu divino, spero [quod][4] habitum die proxima induam monachalem, quare vobis omnibus humiles effundo preces, affectuose expostulans quatinus, divine caritatis respectu uniuscuiusque, vestr[as][5] pro me dignetis oraciones effundere. [et quod][6] rogaturi ut quod intuitu p[u]ericie[7] minus egi perite, ante vesperam vite michi liceat illud corrigere. [Sciatis quod, me vivente, vestri immemor esse non potero, set ante meos oculos vestra imago tanquam presens habebitur.][8] Quare tantum faciatis ut oracionibus nostris[9] memores efficiamini. Valete.

If a man feels compelled to enter a monastery and has fellow-students to whom he might wish to send regards, let him have a [?model letter] of this sort

A student to his fellow-students, greetings. By my friends' advice and the working of God's plan, I hope to assume the monastic habit tomorrow, and so I pour out my humble prayers to you all, tearfully requesting that, in consideration of God's love of every person, you feel moved to pour out your prayers for me, [and that] you will ask that what, by the prompting of youth, I have done with little skill, it shall be vouchsafed to me to correct before the evening of life. [You should know that, while I am living, I shall never be able to be unmindful of you, but your image will always be before my eyes just as if you were present.] Therefore, I hope that you will act in such a way that you will be held as fond memories in our prayers. Farewell.

This letter, despite its many flaws in composition or copying, illustrates an important facet of medieval spiritual life. Renunciation of the world's vanities was a prominent theme in twelfth- and thirteenth-century spirituality, and entry into the monastic life was the ultimate form of renunciation since, upon their profession, cloistered monks and nuns were supposed to have died to the world.

In the early thirteenth century, the emerging universities often served as recruiting grounds for the religious orders, although students were more likely to be drawn to the popular new mendicant orders of Franciscan and Dominican friars than, as here, to one of the older monastic orders. In the 1220s, hundreds of teachers, graduates, and undergraduates of Padua, Paris, and Oxford joined the Dominicans in what amounted to a deliberate mission to the universities.[10]

In this letter, the student apparently has had an intense conversion experience that has led him to leave his studies and renounce the world, including his family and friends, in order to become a monk. St. Bernard of Clairvaux (1090–1153), the celebrated Cistercian abbot, wrote an eloquent letter to a young scholar, Master Walter of Chaumont, who was contemplating a similar move. Bernard urged the eternal benefits of the spiritual life over the temporal joys of scholarship:

> I am filled with sadness for you, my dear Walter, when I think of the flower of your youth, the brightness of your intelligence, the ornaments of your knowledge and scholarship and, what more becomes a Christian than all these, your noble bearing, all being wasted in futile studies and the pursuit of what is merely passing, when they would be so much better used in the service of Christ. God forbid that a sudden death should snatch them from you, that all should suddenly wither like grass in the fury of a burning wind, fall from you like leaves from autumn trees. What fruit will you have then of all your labours upon earth? What return will you be able to make to God for all he has given you? What will you have to show for all the talents he has entrusted to you? What will happen to you, if with empty hands you stand before him who, although he willingly gave you all your gifts, will nevertheless exact a strict account of how you have used them? He will come, he will soon come, who will demand back with increase what was his own. He will take away all those gifts which have earned you such spectacular, but such treacherous, applause in your own country. Noble birth, a lithe body, a comely appearance, a distinguished bearing, are great acquisitions, but the credit of them belongs to him who gave them. You may use them for your own advantage, but there is one who will enquire into it and judge if you do.[11]

NOTES

1   Add. 8167, fol. 104r.
2   Word supplied to preserve the sense of the passage.
3   *morum* in MS.
4   Word supplied to preserve the sense of the passage.
5   *vestrum* in MS.
6   Words supplied to preserve the sense of the passage.
7   *pericie* in MS.
8   The text in square brackets comes from a more accurate version of the same letter, in CCCC 297, fol. 114v. It was printed by H. G. Richardson in H. E. Salter, W. A. Pantin, and H. G. Richardson, eds., *Formularies Which Bear on the History of Oxford, c. 1204–1420*, 2 vols., Oxford Historical Society, 2nd ser., 4–5 (1939–42), 2:347. In Add. 8167, fol. 104r, this passage is so garbled as to be incomprehensible: *Sciatis quod in iuventute iuvenior esse non potero. set ante meos oculos ymago vestra tanquam presens habituri.*
9   Corrected in MS from *vestris*.
10 Clifford Hugh Lawrence, *Medieval Monasticism*, 3rd ed. (Harlow, Essex: Longman: 2001), 261–62.
11 *The Letters of Bernard of Clairvaux*, trans. B. S. James (Stroud, Gloucestershire: Sutton, 1998), 152.

80

A Student at Paris Writes to His Father for Money[1]

Proles parisius scolam excercens mandat patri ut indiget auxilio[2] suo

Venerabili domino suo et patri A., B. suus proles et alumpnus salutem. Ad consilium et preceptum iter arripui parisius ut, adversans paupertatem, pacior multimodam. Hinc enim fames, hinc enim frigus, hinc laboris assiduitas de labore. Tamen non conqueror, quia non debet esse alienus. Set cetera incommoda defleo, quia laborem non fit in actum procedere. Esuriens enim et languens, vix possum opera operi inpendere. Quare paternitati vestre pias preces porrigo, petens attencius quatinus divine pietatis intuitu paupertatem meam oculo respicias clemencie. Et tantum faciatis ne[3] compulsus ab honesto proposito redire compellar. Valete.

A son studying at a school in Paris sends word to his father that he needs his aid

To his venerable lord and father A., B. his son and student sends greetings. I have eagerly embraced the path to wisdom and instruction at

Paris so that, encountering poverty, I might be capable of enduring many forms of it. For on this side [is] hunger, on that side cold, and on the other side the exhaustion of labor. Nevertheless, I do not complain, because this should not be unfamiliar [to me]. But I do bewail certain other misfortunes, because it makes it impossible for my work to advance in performance. For, starving and languishing, I can scarcely pour out works on top of work. Therefore, I send pious prayers to Your Paternity, seeking anxiously that, by the prompting of holy charity, you look on my poverty with the eye of clemency. And I hope that you will act in such a way that I will not be compelled to withdraw from my honest design. Farewell.

The four student letters included in this volume (DOCUMENTS 80–83) are typical examples of a genre that became popular throughout medieval Europe. Such letters were sent not only to parents, but also to anyone else who might be willing to provide financial assistance, such as guardians, brothers, sisters, uncles, cousins, and patrons.[4] The theme of these letters, exemplified in the letter above, was universal: the writer is working diligently, but suffers greatly for want of money, and if it is not forthcoming he will have to pawn his belongings, give up his studies—or perish of cold and hunger. As a father in an Italian formulary letter sighed, "a student's first song is a demand for money, and there will never be a letter which does not ask for cash."[5] Such letters, while sometimes adapted to include circumstantial details particular to the correspondents, were for the most part purely rhetorical exercises. To demonstrate the writer's scholarly attainments, the text was often garnished with classical or biblical quotations or allusions, or elaborate metaphors drawn from the natural world, while to ingratiate the sender with the recipient, it was sprinkled with expressions of respect for the latter, mingled with suggestive reminders of the obligations of Christian charity.

Some historians have seen the routine resort to model letters by medieval students as evidence that they were not especially proficient themselves at composition and rhetoric.[6] Others have argued more charitably that students naturally turned to model letters, not because they were unable to compose letters themselves, but because they wished to make use of the advanced rhetorical skills of the professional *dictatores*.[7] A notable feature of many such letters is their singleness of purpose: the writer speaks only of his own situation and does not inquire about the health or circumstances of the recipient, even in a cursory way. These missives, written in the classic four- or five-part structure of the formal letter,[8] thus were intended to serve not as personal correspondence, but rather as a genteel form of bill.

NOTES

1   Add. 8167, fol. 104r.

2   Corrected in MS from *aluxilio*.

3   *ut* in MS.

4   See Alan Cobban, *English University Life in the Middle Ages* (London: UCL Press, 1999), 22, 35–36; Charles Homer Haskins, "The Life of Medieval Students as Illustrated by Their Letters," *American Historical Review*, 3, no. 2 (January 1898), 203–29, revised and expanded in idem, *Studies in Mediaeval Culture* (Oxford: Clarendon, 1929), Chap. 1; and Salter, Pantin, and Richardson, eds., *Formularies*, vol. 2, 331–450.

5   *Primum carmen scolarium est petitio expensarum, nec umquam erit epistola que non requirit argentum.* Boncompagno (or Buoncompagno), *Rhetorica antiqua* (composed at Bologna in 1215), quoted in Haskins, "Life of Medieval Students," 208–9; see also 207, n. 3 (last paragraph); idem, *Studies in Mediaeval Culture*, 7–8 ; see also 6, n. 2 (last paragraph, extending to p. 7). There is one known English copy of Boncompagno's *Rhetorica antiqua*, in BL, Cott. MS Vitellius C. VIII, fols. 91r–130v. See also Martin Camargo, "The English Manuscripts of Bernard of Meung's *Flores Dictaminum*," *Viator*, 12 (1981), 208–9.

6   See, e.g., Haskins, "Life of Medieval Students," 203–4, and idem, *Studies in Mediaeval Culture*, 2.

7   See, e.g., Cobban, *English University Life*, 22, 35.

8   For a model student letter that is broken down into its four main component parts (proverbial *exordium*, *narratio*, *petitio*, and proverbial *conclusio*), see Haskins, "Life of Medieval Students," 209, n. 2, and idem, *Studies in Mediaeval Culture*, 9, n. 2 (quoting BL, Additional MS 18322, fol. 59).

81

A Student at Oxford Writes to His Father for Money[1]

Alie de eodem

Venerabili domino suo. A., B. salutem. Noverit universitas vestra quod ego Oxonie studeo cum summa diligencia, set moneta[2] promocionem meam multum impedit. Iam enim due mense transacte sunt ex[3] quos michi misisti expendidi. Villa enim cara est et multa exigit; oportet hospicium conducere et utensilia emere, et de multis aliis extra predicta que ad presens non possum nominare. Quare paterni[tati][4] vestre pie suplico quatinus, divine pietatis intuitu, michi succuratis ut possim [con]cludere[5] quod bene incoavi. Sciatis quod sine Cerere et [Baccho][6] [f]rigescit[7] Apollo.[8] Quare tantum faciatis ut vobis mediantibus incoatum bene possim terminare. Valete.

Another letter of the same type[9]

B. to his venerable master A., greeting. This is to inform you that I am studying at Oxford with the greatest diligence, but the matter of money stands greatly in the way of my promotion, as it is now two months since I spent the last of what you sent me. The city is expensive and makes many demands; I have to rent lodgings, buy necessaries, and provide for many other things which I cannot now specify. Wherefore I respectfully beg Your Paternity that by the promptings of divine pity you may assist me, so that I may be able to complete what I have well begun. For you must know that without Ceres and Bacchus Apollo grows cold. Therefore, I hope that you will act in such a way that, by your intercession, I may finish what I have well begun.[10] Farewell.

In this letter the sender claims to have been without funds for the past two months. He begs his father's aid on the grounds of his own zealous work and his father's natural obedience to God's will, and ends with a flourish of allusion to classical mythology and literature as both a demonstration of his attainments and a graceful reminder of what is needed. Another student letter in the same collection begins, "To my father, his son sends greetings and his entire self. [Know that] he is giving himself completely to his studies and to preserving the flower of his chastity untouched."[11]

The frequent references in letters such as these to the impoverished writer's diligence, obedience, and chastity would have been inspired, at least in part, by the biblical story of the Prodigal Son (Luke 15:11–32), in which a younger son demanded his inheritance from his father and then left home and squandered it all, so that he was forced to return in abject poverty and beg once more for his father's assistance. The point of this parable (that God, like a good parent, rejoices in welcoming home the child that was lost and now is found) was driven home by medieval commentators and illustrators, who portrayed the Prodigal Son as having lost his inheritance not through simple misfortune, but through his own sinful behavior—indolence, wine, sex, and gambling. The *dictatores* who composed model letters, therefore, were careful to reassure anxious (or skeptical) parents and other sponsors that the writer was hardworking and of upright character, and not a wastrel, spendthrift Prodigal Son.[12]

The student in this letter is studying at Oxford. He may be enrolled with a master at the university, then in its early years of development, or he may be taking a business course with a private instructor of *dictamen* (the art of letter-writing) and other subjects related to estate-management. It was for the latter sort of student that formularies such as those represented in this volume were compiled.[13]

NOTES

1   Add. 8167, fol. 104r–v.
2   Fol. 104v commences here.

3   *Sic.*

4   *patrui* or *paterni* in MS.

5   *includere* in MS.

6   *bacone* in MS.

7   *strigescit* in MS.

8   This tag derives from a line in *Eunuchus* (*The Eunuch*), a comedy by Terence (d. 159 B.C.), Act IV, Scene 5, line 732: *Sine Cerere et Libero* [another name for Bacchus] *friget Venus* ("Without Ceres [*bread*] and Bacchus [*wine*], Venus [*love itself*] grows cold"). In Terence, *The Eunuch*, ed. and trans. A. J. Brothers (Warminster, Wiltshire: Aris and Phillips, 2000), 118–19, where this line is translated as, "No food and drink, and love's out in the cold."

9   This letter was printed (with silent emendations to the Latin) and translated by Haskins in "Life of Medieval Students," 210, and again in *Studies in Mediaeval Culture*, 10. The translation given here, as far as the word "Apollo," is by Haskins. In his translation, Haskins omitted the final sentence and the valediction.

10 This sentence largely re-states an earlier one, which may be why Haskins omitted it from his translation.

11 BL, Add. MS 8167, fol. 125v: *Patri filius salutem et se totum fundere in scolis sue que castitatis florem illesum conservare.* The letter breaks off immediately after this opening.

12 For additional student letters, see DOCUMENTS 80, 82, and 83.

13 On Oxford University in the first half of the thirteenth century, see INTRODUCTION, pp. 12–13. On the private instruction of *dictamen* and estate-management there, see Camargo, "English Manuscripts of Bernard of Meung's 'Flores Dictaminum,'" 205; Henry Gerald Richardson, "The Oxford Law School Under John," *Law Quarterly Review*, 57 (1941), 319–38; and Richardson and and George Osborne Sayles, "Early Coronation Records [Part I]," *Bulletin of the Institute of Historical Research*, 13 (1935–36), 134–38; Cobban, *English University Life*, 146–48.

82

A Student at Oxford Writes to His Mother for Money[1]

Alu[m]pnus[2] mandat matri

Karissime matri sue A., B. suus alumpnus salutem. Maternus affectus erga prolem promptus et propicius tenetur, sin[3] mores maternas mutat vidua[4] erit crudelior noverca. Vos autem hactenus[5] tam opere quam verbo maternam pietatem michi exibuistis. Si indigentem aliqua muneris largicione in opere refocillastis [*sic*], ut mens pristina[6] vobis maneat, ut vos talem inveniam[7] qualem solebam invenire—et inveniam, deo volente, quia nunquam offendi nec offendam in tota vita mea. Noveritis autem quod sanus sum Oxonie et illaris [*sic*] tantum quantum esse possum, set longo tempore nudus sum et famem sustineo quia monetam non habeo, unde sitim malo[8] sedare[9] aud [*sic*] famem. Quare materni-tati[10] vestre pias preces effundo, petens attencius quatinus filium ves-trum, in lacu miserie iacentem, dextra largitatis [eum turpitior[11] mori quam oneste][12] hactenus[13] educatis.[14] Et[15] sic eum ad presens consulatis ut vos possit visitare in statu meliori et manere[16] diutius.[17] Valete.

A student sends an appeal to his mother

To his dearest mother A., B. her son sends greetings. A mother's love for her child is bound to be strong and gracious, but if a widow changes her maternal habits she will be crueler than a stepmother. For until now, both in deed and in word, you showed me maternal piety. If you relieved my want through some lavishing of favor, would that your former feelings might endure in you, so that I might find you as I used to find you—and as I *shall* find you, God willing, because I have never offended nor shall I offend [you] in all my life. You will know, moreover, that I am well at Oxford, and as happy as possible, but I have been bare of clothing for a long time, and I am hungry because I have no money with which I may choose to allay thirst or hunger. And so I pour out pious prayers to Your Maternity, seeking anxiously that, with the right hand of largesse, you raise up your son, who has been lying until now in a lake of misery, in a manner more shameful than honorable. And thus, may you look to his immediate welfare, so that he might visit you in a better state and stay for a longer time. Farewell.

The cruelty of stepmothers, so familiar today from fairy and folk tales such as *Cinderella* and *Hansel and Gretel,* was proverbial in medieval Europe as well. Charles Homer Haskins quoted a model student letter similar to that above, in which the *exordium* (the proverbial expression or scriptural quotation used to open the letter and to establish its theme and tone) declares sternly that "a mother who does not relieve the poverty of her son has the smell of a stepmother about her."[18]

Here the writer also draws on Psalm 39 to evoke the "lake of misery" in which his poverty has forced him to lie, while beseeching his widowed mother to emulate, by implication, the generosity of St Nicholas in extending to him the "right hand of largesse." The exaggerated description of the writer's wretchedness may be especially designed to appeal to a mother's tender heart; another letter in this collection from a son to a father merely states, rather gruffly, "If you want to know about my situation, I shall tell you briefly: I am alive, and shall be fine if I have the things I need for school."[19]

NOTES

1   Add. 8167, fol. 105r.
2   *Alupnus* in MS.

3 *sine* in MS.
4 *vedua* in MS.
5 *actenus* in MS.
6 *pristena* in MS.
7 *qualem* expunged here in MS.
8 *malleo* in MS.
9 Richardson printed this single sentence from this letter, in which he mistranscribed these three words as "*sitium malleo sedere.*" He then corrected them to "*sitium malleum sedem,*" while noting that "[t]he scribe has so bungled the letter to the student's mother . . . that it is difficult to make sense of it." Salter, Pantin, and Richardson, eds., *Formularies*, vol. 2, 347.
10 *mrnitati* in MS.
11 *turpiter* in MS.
12 The phrase in square brackets was inserted in the margin in the same hand as the main text.
13 *actenus* in MS.
14 Cf. Psalms 39:3: *eduxit me de lacu miseriae* ("He has led me from a lake of misery"). This sentence also recalls a twelfth-century hymn to St Nicholas ("*Cantu miro summa laude*"), of English provenance, which extolled the saint's *dextra largitatis* ("right hand of largesse"). See John Stevens, *The Later Cambridge Songs: An English Song Collection of the Twelfth Century* (Oxford: Oxford University Press, 2005), 119 (line 1b).
15 *set* in MS.
16 *mentere* in MS.
17 *diociori* in MS.
18 *Assumendum est proverbium in hunc modum: Mater moribus redolet novercam que filii non sublevat egestatem.* Haskins, "Life of Medieval Students," 209, n. 2, repeated in idem, *Studies in Mediaeval Culture*, 9, n. 2, quoting from an anonymous treatise in BL, Add. MS 18322, fol. 59.
19 BL, Add. MS 8167, fols. 104v–105r: *de statu meo si queritis breviter expediam vivo et valebo si necessaria in scolis habuero.* The Latin text of this letter was printed by H. G. Richardson in Salter, Pantin, and Richardson, eds., *Formularies*, vol. 2, 347. For additional student letters, see DOCUMENTS 80, 81, and 83.

83

A Son Responds to a Letter from His Father[1]

Patri filius salutem. Scolari, pie paternitas, affectum semper et habundanter effluere [?faciatis].[2] Nature linea penitus obliquatur et equitatis iura violari vide[n]tur[3] in patre filio dificiente.[4] Saneque[5] pietas in homine[6] qui vi[s]cerum[7] suorum obli vi[s]citur[8] Leones et tigri def[endunt][9] catulos suo donec naturali feritate vigeant, et sui compotes effectu[10] educare videntur illis victui neccessaria subministrantes.[11] Feris ergo ferocior est qui de se genito deficit filio, precipue cuius intencio talis est ut honestate vivat et honeste vivendo simul deo et parentibus suis acceptus existat. Ve[st]re[12] paternitatis litteras suscepi quibus verbotenus affectum nos[13] habere paternum ostendistis,[14] set, [ne][15] affectum literatorie tantum modo[16] sit expressum, aliquis effectus in necessariorum tran[s]missione[17] licet fere subsequeretur, [ne][18] vestre paternitatis auxilium aliter[19] nullam habeam ([*vel*] *sentiam*)[20] valorem. Valet[e].[21]

To his father, his son sends greetings. Upon your scholar, O Pious Paternity, [may you cause] your affection to flow always—and abundantly. The course of nature is seriously distorted, and the laws of equity seem violated, in a father who does less than he might for his son. And, for God's sake! (*saneque*) what sort of goodness is there in a man who is oblivious of his own offspring? Lions and tigers defend their young until they can thrive by their own natural fierceness, and are seen to teach their skills (*compotes*) by demonstration (*effectu*) while providing the necessities for life for them. More savage, therefore, than savage beasts is he who fails to come to the aid of his own son, especially one whose intention is to live honestly and, by living honestly, to be acceptable both to God and to his parents. I have received Your Paternity's letter by which you showed, so far as words go, that you hold us in tender paternal affection but, so that your affection is not expressed only in a literary form, some practical performance in the sending of necessities should generally follow it up, [lest] otherwise I regard ([*or*] *consider*) your paternity's assistance as valueless. Farewell.

In the three previous student letters in this volume (DOCUMENTS 80–82) the student writes humbly to request financial assistance from his father or mother. The student in this letter, however, writes in a much sharper tone in responding to a letter from his father in which the latter evidently professed paternal affection for his son, but did not send any practical demonstration of it in the form of cash or supplies. The student is aggrieved; he considers that his father has let him down—after all, he argues, even wild animals provide for their young until they are able to fend for themselves. A father who fails to do likewise is therefore worse than a savage beast; a father who neglects the support of his son—especially an honest and diligent son!—contravenes the laws of both nature and justice.

In another letter in the same collection, a son similarly argues that Nature as well as God demands that a father support his hardworking and obedient son: "The wild birds of the sky bring up their chicks until they can fly; the beasts of the forest nurse their young until they can feed themselves; the ewe does not desert her lamb until it can satisfy itself with grass . . . you should do [the same] for your son who is not yet able to support himself; for your son who is obedient in all things; for your son who is working hard at honest study. . . . Therefore, I earnestly request that you behave towards me as Nature would tell [you]; as the Creator has ordained."[22] There may be a hint of legalism in the appeal to the laws of nature, God, and equity that figure so strikingly in these two demands for paternal assistance; perhaps these model letters were especially designed for students who were studying law.

NOTES

1   Add. 8167, fols. 125v–126r.
2   This or a similar verb in the hortatory subjunctive appears to be missing here, meaning something like "may you cause." The Latinity throughout this letter is especially problematic; we are very grateful to the late John Barron for his kind help with it.
3   *videtur* in MS.
4   *difi*ce in MS.
5   *sane que* in MS.
6   Fol. 126r commences here.
7   *vicerum* in MS.
8   *oblivicitur* in MS.
9   *des* in MS.
10   *eff*co in MS.
11   *subministrantis* in MS.
12   *vere* in MS.
13   *vos* in MS.
14   *offendistis* in MS.
15   *ut* in MS, but the sense appears to require a negative here.
16   *m*9 in MS.
17   *tranmissione* in MS.
18   *et* in MS.
19   *aliunde* in MS.
20   In MS, "*sentire*" alone, without the preceding "*vel*," but the sense here suggests a variant phrase for "*habeam*."
21   *valet* in MS.
22   BL, Add. MS 8167, fol. 104v: *volucres celi pullos educant donec possint volare. bestie silve fetus suos lactant dum possint sustentare. Ovis agnum non deserit donec possit herba saturari . . . agere debeatis erga filium vestrum non dum sibi sufficientem. erga filium vestrum per omnia parentem erga filium honesto studio invigilantem . . . ergo postulo attentissime quatinus erga me faciatis sicut natura dixerit. sicut creator induxit.*

84

A Master Tells His Student to Stop Wasting Time[1]

Magister scolari[2] salutem. Decenti sedulitas totum[3] exigit discipulum ut magister paciatur ociis indulgere. Vero vagi[4] vanitas discipuli defectum discendi non admittit si[5] sui monitoris exercitium[6] interrumpit, et sic uterque[7] desidie miseria[8] gravitur. Set ne tuum tempus admittas, ne tuorum parentum et amicorum facultates tibi transmissas in cassum consumeri,[9] videaris a tuo debili principio vitupera[bi]lique[10] propositum tuum animum[que][11] retrahere;[12] satagas bene discencium emitando vestigia, ne pro defectu tuo[13] tarditas[14] mee possit imputari pigricie—que non in medico semper relevetur,[15] nec in doctrina[16] quam auditor bene discat. Valete.

A master to his student, greetings. Zeal for what is fitting requires that a master allow a dedicated student to enjoy some free time. However, the fecklessness of a wandering student cares nothing for the harm to his studies if he breaks the training of his instructor, and thus each of them is burdened with the misery of idleness. But, lest you allow your own time, and the resources of your parents and friends that were sent to you, to be wasted in vain, you should show that you are changing your attitude and intention from their feeble and blameworthy beginning, and repay [your benefactors] by following in the footsteps of those who learn well, lest through your own fault your slow progress—which cannot always be cured by the physician, nor by the instruction that the auditor might learn well—be imputed to indolence on my part. Farewell.

In this classic example of professorial exasperation, a teacher upbraids his student for wandering off instead of attending to his studies. This, the teacher scolds, results in a waste of his own time as well as the student's, and also wastes the funds sent to the student by his parents and friends. He advises the student sternly to shape up and to become a credit to his benefactors by modeling himself on successful students. In closing, however, the teacher makes it clear that he is concerned not only for the student's welfare but also for his own reputation, which would be damaged if the student's lack of progress were imputed to the teacher's laziness rather than to the student's indolence or inability.

In the early thirteenth century, a master's concern for his reputation was not merely a matter of professional pride, but of money. Teachers at Paris, Oxford, and similar centers of learning were not paid a salary by the nascent universities; instead, they obtained much or all of their income from fees paid directly to them by their pupils.[17] A master who developed a reputation, however undeserved, for poor teaching would be unable to attract new students and would lose his livelihood.

It is ironic that the letter above, whose tone is one of outrage and alarm at a student's poor academic performance, is itself so peppered with errors in its

Latinity. This may have been the result of poor drafting by the original author (possibly a student himself), or of poor editing and copying by a later compiler and copyist. Perhaps, however, as is also suggested in the case of DOCUMENT 93, the flawed Latin grammar of this letter was intentional; in this case, as a deliberate burlesque of the genre of admonitions by teachers to students, intended as much to amuse as to instruct.

NOTES

1   Add. 8167, fols. 128v–129r.
2   *scolaribus* in MS, but (with the exception of *tui tardatis*, for which see below) the sender subsequently addresses the recipient using verbs and pronouns in the second person singular, not plural, so evidently the addressee is really a single student, not a group.
3   The meaning of "*totum*" here ought to be something like "absorbed," suggesting that an accompanying phrase such as "in his work" is missing. It is translated below as "dedicated."
4   *vagii* in MS.
5   *set* in MS.
6   *excercitum* in MS.
7   *utrique* in MS.
8   This word is uncertain; in the MS, it is given in abbreviated form as M^a. The same abbreviation occurs in DOCUMENT 77.
9   *consumere* in MS. Fol. 129r commences here.
10 *vituperalique* in MS.
11 *animum* in MS.
12 *Retraere* in MS.
13 *tui* in MS.
14 *tardatis* in MS.
15 This line recalls Ovid's *Epistulae ex Ponto*, 1:3 (to Rufinus), lines 17–18: *Non est in medico semper relevetur ut aeger:/ interdum docta plus valet arte malum* ("No doctor can always ensure that the patient recovers—/ sometimes the disease will win despite (or because of) his skill"). Latin text in *P. Ovidi Nasonis, Tristium libri quinque; Ibis; Ex ponto libri quattuor; Halieutica fragmenta*, ed. S. G. Owen (Oxford: Clarendon, 1915; rpt. 1946); English translation in Ovid, *The Poems of Exile: Tristia and the Black Sea Letters*, trans. Peter Green (Berkeley: University of California Press, 2005).
16 *doctrine* in MS.
17 Cobban, *English University Life*, 7–10, 58–59.

NEIGHBORLINESS AND COMMUNITY

——————————— 85 ———————————

An Angry Letter of Refusal[1]

Adhuc de huiusmodi literis dicemus

A. B. salutem. Obsequium aliud exigit, et subtraccio exigit subtraccionem. Pecii nuper ut michi succureres de tignis et trabibus quorum copia penes te est. Tu autem surdas aures peticioni mee prebuisti, et ideo non mireris[2] si preces tuas presentes audire recusem. Nolo enim, [nec][3] velle debeo, tibi de meo succurere, quoniam [quando][4] de rebus vestris unum pecii, dedignatus fuisti michi subvenire. Et ideo ut de cetero amicum h[ab]eas,[5] amicu[s][6] inveniaris. Vale.

Again we speak of letters of the same type

A. to B., greetings. One consent demands another, and a refusal demands a refusal. Lately I asked you to help me out with some boards and beams, of which you have plenty at your place. But you turned deaf ears to my petition, and therefore you will not be surprised if I refuse to listen to your own present requests. For I do not wish, [nor] ought I to wish, to aid you from my stock (*de meo*), since, [?when] I sought one thing of yours, you disdained to come to my aid. And so, in future, if you want to have a friend, you will need to behave as a friend. Farewell.

This is a classic rejection letter, one designed according to the standard dictaminal model (described above in the INTRODUCTION, p. 17) of *salutatio*, *exordium*, *narratio*, and *conclusio*, rather than to the somewhat looser instructions given in DOCUMENT 7. The writer begins by asserting a general principle—that one good or ill turn deserves another—and then proceeds to apply it. Recently, he says, the man who has just petitioned him for a favor unreasonably refused his own similar request. As a result, he now duly rejects the other man's petition. He concludes his letter with another general statement of principle, a variation on the golden rule, expressed in the form of a rather patronizing recommendation to the unsuccessful petitioner that, if he wishes to have a friend, he needs to act like a friend himself.

The writer's language here is markedly curt and blunt, suggesting that he is writing to someone, such as a fellow merchant, who is his equal or inferior in rank and power, to whom he uses the familiar *"tu"* rather than the respectful *"vos,"* and whom he is willing to offend and unafraid to anger. His opening *exordium* and closing *conclusio*, however, are couched in lofty proverbial terms. The opening recalls the Roman expression *"manus manum lavat"* ("one hand washes the other"), which at least one modern translator has rendered as "one good turn deserves another,"[7] while the conclusion echoes a number of Roman sayings on friendship, including Ovid's *"ut ameris, amabilis esto"* ("if you would be loved, be lovable"),[8] Seneca's *"Si vis amari, ama"* ("If you wish to be loved, love"),[9] and Pliny the Younger's *"habes amicos, quia amicus ipse es"* ("you have friends, because you yourself are a friend").[10]

NOTES

1 Add. 8167, fol. 98r.
2 Corrected in MS from *mirereis*.
3 The sense of this phrase requires a negative here; it may have been inadvertently dropped because its abbreviation resembled that of the preceding "*enim.*"
4 The sense of this phrase requires some such word as "*quando*" ("when") here. It may have been skipped because its abbreviation resembled that of the preceding "*quoniam.*"
5 *heas* in MS.
6 *amicum* in MS.
7 Petronius, *The Satyricon*, trans. Alfred R. Allinson (New York: Panurge, 1930), Chap. 7, p. 45. The same expression was used by Seneca in *Apocolocyntosis Divi Claudii*, cap. 9:6, edited by Allan P. Ball in *Selected Essays of Seneca, and the Satire on the Deification of Claudius* (New York: Macmillan, 1908), 32.
8 *P. Ovidi Nasonis de arte amatoria libri tres*, ed. Paul Brandt, vol. 2 (Hildesheim: Georg Olms, 1963), 107.
9 *L. Annaei Senecae: Ad Lucilium Epistulae Morales*, ed. L. D. Reynolds, 2 vols. (Oxford: Oxford Universty Press, 1965), Lib. I, 9:6. This dictum of Seneca's was quoted by Albertano of Brescia in *De amore et dilectione Dei et proximi et aliarum rerum et de forma vitae* (1238), cap. 12, ed. Sharon Hiltz Romino (unpub. doctoral dissertation, University of Pennsylvania, 1980), available online at http://www.intratext.com/IXT/LAT0673/_PL.HTM#$G0 [seen January 10, 2008].
10 *Epistularum libri novem; Epistularum ad Traianum liber panegyricus*, ed. R. C. Kukula (Leipzig: Teubner, 1908), *Panegyricus*, 85:3, p. 395.

86

A Friend Requests Assistance for a Kinsman[1]

Pro parente fiant huiusmodi litere

Karissimo amico suo A., B. salutem. Pro honore et obsequio G. connato meo a vobis collato, et adhuc si placet conferendo, multiplices grates reffero vobis et relaturus sum omnibus diebus vite mee. Set quia, cum dicitur, "Nil nocet amisso subdere calcar equo," ideo pro eo preces precibus acumulo, petens attencius quatinus, divine pietatis intuitu, opus in ipso incoatum bene terminetis. Sciturus quod si deus vitam et salutem michi annuerit, ego vobis et vestris cum videro opus ingruere persolvam, nec magis deero vestre necessitati quam proprie commoditati mee.[2] Quare tantum faciatis predicto G. ut preces meas penes vos sibi senciat profuisse. Valete.

For a kinsman, let there be a letter of this type

To his dearest friend A., B. sends greetings. For the honor and courtesy that you have previously shown and, if it pleases you, will confer in future, to my kinsman G., I send you thanks again and again, and I shall be bound to you all the days of my life. But because, as it is said, "it does no harm to set spur to a galloping horse,"[3] therefore on his behalf I pile up prayers upon prayers, seeking earnestly that, by the prompting of holy charity, you complete the work that you have begun well on his behalf. For you know that, as long as God grants me life and health, when I shall see need threaten you and yours, I shall repay the debt in full, nor shall I be more neglectful of your need than I am of my own advantage. So I hope that you will treat the said G. in such a way that he may know that my prayers to you were of service to him. Farewell.

Soliciting favors on behalf of family, friends, and dependents was a commonplace in the medieval world, and the intricate networks of reciprocal obligations that resulted from such arrangements must have underlain friendships and alliances at all levels of society. Here the writer asks a friend to assist the writer's kinsman, whom the friend has already helped. The writer promises to offer reciprocal assistance to his friend, should the latter ever require it, and he closes with the revealing request that not only should the friend offer the kinsman assistance, but that the kinsman should know that he owed this assistance to the writer's petition. A similar request can be found in DOCUMENT 45.

Genuine examples of such letters survive. In one, sent by William Wickwane, chancellor of York, between 1266 and 1268, Wickwane writes that he is compelled by the wretchedness of a friend, and emboldened by the generosity of the addressee, to request assistance for the friend, who is also the bearer of the letter. He closes, like the letter above, by asking that the friend know that Wickwane's request on his behalf has proved fruitful.[4] While many such petitions were successful, sometimes they ended unhappily, with the rejection of the request or the ungrateful behavior of the recipient of the favor. Examples of such outcomes can be seen below in DOCUMENTS 87 and 88.

NOTES

1   Add. 8167, fol. 99r.

2   *me* in MS.

3   This Latin tag comes from Ovid's *Epistulae ex Ponto*, 2:6 (to Graecinus), line 38 (final line): *nec nocet admisso subdere calcar equo* (printed in *P. Ovidi Nasonis, Tristium libri quinque; Ibis; Ex ponto libri quattuor; Halieutica fragmenta*, ed. Owen). In 1242 it was quoted by Robert Grosseteste, Bishop of Lincoln, in a letter to the Dean and Chapter of Lincoln. *Roberti Grosseteste quondam episcopi Lincolniensis epistolae*, ed. Henry Richards Luard, Rolls Series, 26 (London: Longman, 1861), Letter 95, pp. 296–297. It was later quoted by Pope Clement IV in a letter of January 25, 1268, to Amatus de

Amatis, Podestà of the Mercanzia of Cremona. *Epistole et dictamina Clementis pape quarti*, ed. Matthias Thumser, no. 431, pp. 235–36, available online as a PDF file at http://userpage.fu-berlin.de/~sekrethu/clemens/index.htm [seen July 13, 2010].

4   Christopher R. Cheney, "Letters of William Wickwane, Chancellor of York, 1266–1268," *EHR*, 47 (1932), 188 (October 1932), 626–42, Letter XIV ("pro amico," p. 635).

87

A Man Who Assisted His Friend's Kinsman Requests Reimbursement for His Expenses[1]

Litere responsales

Karissimo amico suo A., B. salutem. Preces vestras pro G. cognato vestro effusas nuper accepi, quas preces pro posse duxi ad effectum. Ex quo enim illum vidi in partibus nostris, suscepi eum in domo mea, susceptum procreavi, et de substancia mea acomodavi ad negocium suum prosequendum. Set nec ille nec aliquis pro eo me respecsit.[2] Quare vos precor ut, sicut pro eo promisistis, ita michi reddatis meas expensas et peccuniam [*sic*] quam illi commisi. Et tantum faciatis ut alias vobis fiam obnoxius. Valete.

A letter of response

To his dearest friend A., B. sends greetings. I lately received your request concerning your kinsman, G., which I carried out to the best of my ability. For, as a result of it, I met with him here, I took him into my home, I got his enterprise off the ground (*susceptum procreavi*), [and] I made him a loan from my own assets to carry out his business. But neither he, nor anyone else on his behalf, has shown any concern for me. So I pray you that, as you promised, you reimburse me for my expenses and for the money that I lent him. And take care of this in such a way that I may [be willing to] come to your assistance on another occasion. Farewell.

The exchange of favors was a mainstay of medieval life at all levels of society and (as discussed in DOCUMENT 86) frequently served to initiate and bind friendships and alliances among powerful people and their dependents. When someone failed to reciprocate a favor or reneged on an obligation to a person of rank, however, this was viewed as far worse than a mere social or financial slip. It was a personal affront, a loss of face that people of standing could not tolerate, since it represented a challenge to their prestige and reputation. The consequences of such a lapse, therefore, could be grave, ranging from social coldness and financial embarassment all the way to mortal enmity (see Docu- MENT 48).

In this letter, a man writes to a friend that he has put himself to consider- able trouble and expense to assist the latter's kinsman, but the friend has so far failed to make good his promise to reimburse his expenses. The sender reminds his friend quite civilly of his obligations, but ends on a more threaten- ing note with a warning that a continued failure to pay up will make him reluctant to respond to any future requests for assistance.

NOTES

1   Add. 8167, fol. 100r.
2   Corrected in MS from *respeccit*.

88

A Man Refuses to Aid His Friend's Shiftless Kinsman and Warns Against Lending Him Further Funds[1]

Litere responsales et quesitive

Karissimo amico suo A., B salutem. Peticionem vestram nuper accepi, ut G. cognatum vestrum in partibus nostris mantinerem,[2] et si opus haberet de denariis meis illi acomodarem, quantum opus haberet, vobis in manucapientibus omnia nos esse reddituros pro illo que ipse non redderet. Set volo ut scias nec volo nec possum illi aliquid de meo aco- modare, quia aleator[3] est fortis et omnia perdidit que lucratur. Quare neuter vestrum tutum est aliquid illi acomodare dum vicio tali laborat, quia[4] sortem idem dedit intelligi quod ex animo malivolo denarios pet- itos illos denegaret. Set illi qui cum eo erant[5] in taberna quando[6] .x. perdidit. et vadia sua profuit usque ad extremas braccas. Quare tantum faciatis ne peccuniam [*sic*] propriam de me promptam ei amplius trade- tis, et perdere in eo quod reddere debetis. Valete.[7]

A letter of response and [advice][8]

To his dearest friend A., B. sends greetings. I lately received your request that I maintain your kinsman G. here and, if he should have need, lend him my own money as his need should require, with you standing surety for him to repay anything that he does not repay himself. But I want you to know that I do not wish, nor am I able, to lend him anything of mine, for he is an inveterate dice-player and he loses everything that he gambles. Nor is it prudent to lend anything to him of yours while he labors under such a vice, since he has made it quite clear that, because of his malevolent spirit, he will repudiate his debts. But as for those who were with him in the tavern when he lost "x" [*perhaps ten shillings, marks, or pounds*] and his pledges—they gained everything, right down to his drawers. So take care that you refrain from handing over any more of your own money—which you borrowed from me—and so lose on him what you ought to repay me. Farewell.

This letter was evidently designed as a variant to DOCUMENT 87. Here the sender, instead of aiding his friend's kinsman G. and then asking the friend to reimburse his expenses, declines outright to give G. any assistance at all on the grounds that his reckless addiction to gambling makes him an impossible credit risk.

Gambling with dice was a common pastime, much decried by moralists.[9] The French preacher Jacques de Vitry (d. 1240), for example, told of a man who lost his entire inheritance at dice and was reduced to rags, much like the reprobate in this letter.[10] In similar fashion, the early thirteenth-century windows of Chartres and Bourges cathedrals show the Prodigal Son losing his clothes at dice (Fig. 14).[11] An especially vivid depiction of the kind of tavern gambling described in this letter can be found in the *Play of St. Nicholas*, the earliest French miracle play, written around 1200 by Jean Bodel of Arras. In several lively scenes a courier and three thieves gamble in a tavern at two different games, Highest Points (*plus poins*) and Hazard, each played with three dice on a dicing board or table, as in Fig. 14. The players do not have their own dice, but one of the thieves hires some from the tavern-keeper, who charges a penny, and the barman lends a set of dice of his own, which he claims are "square cut, regular, and standard size," and which he has had "officially tested."[12]

The popularity of such games is reflected in a contemporary Latin poem that contains probability calculations on the throw of three dice. This poem, called *De vetula*, written in France about 1250, provides the earliest evidence for the establishment of an elementary probability calculus. After reviewing the odds, the author concludes wryly, "If you play honestly, you won't win much" (*Si recte iacias, modicum valet*).[13]

Compulsive gambling of the kind described in this letter was generally viewed as a male vice. One reason for this was that women rarely controlled the amount of cash or credit that compulsive gambling required. In addition,

Figure 14. The Prodigal Son loses his clothing at dice, from the Prodigal Son window of Bourges Cathedral (*c.* 1215).

such gambling was commonly associated with heavy drinking and with public displays of competitiveness, trickery, anger, and aggression, sometimes leading to nudity or violence.[14] These behaviors were considered acceptable (if regrettable) in men but not in women, and strong social sanctions prevented most women from engaging in them.[15] Such a depiction of male gambling appears in the *Roman de Brut* (1155), an Anglo-Norman verse expansion of Geoffrey of Monmouth's Latin *History of the Kings of Britain* (*c.* 1138). The writer, a Norman canon of Bayeux named Wace, elaborated Geoffrey's account of the coronation of King Arthur.[16] In Wace's version, the after-dinner entertainments enjoyed by Arthur's guests included dice games at which the men played in pairs. Like the ne'er-do-well in the letter above, those who ran out of cash or credit ended up gambling their clothing on the outcome:

> Two by two they were joined in the game, some losing, some winning; some envied those who made the most throws, or they told others how to move. They borrowed money in exchange for pledges, quite willing only to get eleven to the dozen on the loan; they gave pledges, they seized pledges, they took them, they promised them, often swearing, often protesting their good intentions,

often cheating and often tricking. They got argumentative and angry, often miscounting and grousing. They threw twos, and then fours, two aces, a third one, and threes, sometimes fives, sometimes sixes. Six, five, four, three, two, and ace—these stripped many of their clothes. Those holding the dice were in high hopes; when their friends had them, they made a racket. Very often they shouted and cried out, one saying to the other: "You're cheating me, throw them out, shake your hand, scatter the dice! I'm raising the bid before you throw! If you're looking for money, put some down, like me!" The man who sat down to play clothed might rise naked at close of play.[17]

NOTES

1   Add. 8167, fol. 100r–v.
2   *maniterem* in MS.
3   *alliator* in MS.
4   *et* in MS.
5   *orant* in MS.
6   Fol. 100v commences here.
7   *Walete* in MS.
8   "inquiry" (*quesitive*) in MS, but this is clearly a letter of advice, not inquiry.
9   Playing cards are not recorded in Europe until the fourteenth century. On dicing, see Rhiannon Purdie, "Dice-Games and the Blasphemy of Prediction," in *Medieval Futures: Attitudes to the Future in the Middle Ages*, ed. J. A. Burrow and Ian P. Wei (Woodbridge, Suffolk: Boydell, 2000), 167–68.
10 Vitry, *Exempla*, ed. Crane, no. 296, pp. 124–25, 263–64.
11 For the New Testament story of the Prodigal Son, see Luke 15:11–32. On the Prodigal Son windows from Chartres and Bourges, see Wolfgang Kemp, *The Narratives of Gothic Stained Glass* (Cambridge: Cambridge University Press, 1997), 22–41. The scene from Chartres Cathedral is available online at http://fits.depauw.edu/aharris/Courses/Gothic/TopicImages/ProdigalSonFS.jpg [seen October 17, 2007].
12 *Le jeu de saint Nicolas*, in *French Medieval Plays*, trans. Richard Axton and John Stevens (Oxford: Basil Blackwell, 1971), lines 300–309, 813, 827–940, 1055–1141. For the original Old French text with a translation into modern French, see *Le jeu de saint Nicolas de Jehan Bodel*, ed. and trans. Albert Henry, Université Libre de Bruxelles, Travaux de la Faculté de Philosophie et Lettres, Tome XXI (Brussels: Presses Universitaires de Bruxelles, and Paris: Presses Universitaires de France, 1962). For a discussion of the dice games in this play, see Purdie, "Dice-Games," 170–71.
13 D. R. Bellhouse, "*De Vetula*: A Medieval Manuscript Containing Probability Calculations," *International Statistical Review*, 68, no. 2 (August 2000), 123–36. The author of *De vetula* (which was fictitiously ascribed to the Roman poet Ovid) may have been the mathematician and scientist Richard de Fournival (1201–60), son of the French king Philip Augustus's personal physician. The poem circulated widely; an early reader was the English scientist Roger Bacon, who quoted it in his *Opus Maius* (1266 × 69). On the authorship, circulation, and Latin text of *De Vetula*, see Dorothy M.

Robathan, *The Pseudo-Ovidian De Vetula* (Amsterdam: Adolf M. Hakkert, 1968), 1–10 (authorship), and Book I, lines 428–95 (dicing and probability calculations). About 960, Bishop Wibolf of Cambrai calculated all fifty-six possible throws with three dice but not, apparently, the odds of casting them. F. N. David, *Games, Gods and Gambling: The Origins and History of Probability and Statistical Ideas from the Earliest Times to the Newtonian Era* (New York: Hafner, 1962), 31–33; http://dspace.ucalgary.ca/bitstream/1880/41346/1/aih.pdf [seen January 4, 2009].

14 Purdie, "Dice-Games," 167, 171.

15 At Acre in 1250 Count Alphonse of Poitiers, brother of Louis IX, "courteously" (*courtoisement*) invited both noblemen and ladies (*gentilz homes et les gentil femmes*) into the hall of his residence where he was playing dice, and they all apparently joined in the gambling at his invitation. However, the ladies' gentility was not threatened on this occasion, because Count Alphonse provided the stakes and made up the losses. Jean, sieur de Joinville, *Vie de saint Louis*, ed. Jacques Monfrin, 2nd ed. (Paris: Classiques Garnier, 1998), 206.

16 On Wace and his text (which was based on a revised version of Geoffrey of Monmouth's work), see *Wace's Roman de Brut: A History of the British, Text and Translation*, ed. and trans. Judith Weiss (Exeter: University of Exeter Press, 1999), xi–xxix.

17 *Wace's Brut*, ed. Weiss, 264–67, lines 10561–88.

89

A Man Thanks His Friend for a Loan and Promises to Repay It with Grain After the Harvest[1]

Litere grates reddentes

Karissimo amico suo A., B. salutem. Quia pro me et meis multa fecisti, cum merces vestras acomodando, [t]um[2] denarios vestros michi dando, ideo si tantam habere facultatem quantam habeo voluntatem vobis honore respiciendi, ego domum vestram opibus cumularem. Set qui facit quod potest non est culpandus, quia eciam voluntas pro facto reputetur.[3] Ego constanter promitto quod [ad][4] messem novam vobis dabo de omni genere bladi duo quarteria ad minus. Precor ergo ut in principio augusti tri[t]uratores[5] perquiratis qui in [horreo][6] meo prefatum bladum triturent et tri[t]urato[7] vano mundant ad vos deducant. Sciatis quod homines non habeo qui hoc facere possint. Et ideo tantum faciatis ne commoditas vestra differatur.

Letter bearing thanks

To his dearest friend A., B. sends greetings. Because you have done many things for me and my people, not only by lending your own goods, but also by giving me your own money, therefore, if I had as great means as

Figure 15. Threshing and winnowing grain, from the Maciejowski Bible (Paris, 1244–54), fol. 18r. The Pierpont Morgan Library, New York. MS M.638, fol. 18r. Purchased by J. P. Morgan (1867–1943) in 1916. Photograph courtesy the Pierpont Morgan Library, New York.

I have the desire to provide for you with honor, I would heap your house with wealth. But he who does what he can, cannot be faulted, since the will is taken for the deed. I firmly promise that at the new harvest I shall give you at least two quarters[8] of every kind of grain. Therefore I pray that at the beginning of August you find threshers to thresh the grain in my barn (*horreo*), and to winnow the threshed grain,[9] [and] then carry it to you. You should know that I do not have men who can do this. And therefore, take care of this matter in such a way as to serve your best interests.

Edible grains are the seeds of certain grasses, such as wheat, barley, oats, and rye. In medieval England, the stalks of ripened grain were reaped (cut) in the autumn by hand, bound into sheaves (bunches), and stooked (stacked) in a barn or sheltered place to dry. The dry stalks were threshed (thrashed or beaten) with a flail, to crack off the clusters of seeds from their heads and to loosen the chaff (papery husk) that surrounded the grain. Then the grain was scooped into a winnowing fan (a broad, shallow basket) and tossed in a breezy spot to blow away the chaff (Fig. 15). The cleansed grain, much heavier than the chaff, fell back into into the basket, and was stored for later use in baking, cooking, or brewing. The straw (threshed grain stalks) was used for animal litter, for filling mattresses, and for many other purposes.

Repaying a loan after the autumn harvest was a common arrangement. Sometime between 1224 and 1226 the precentor of Chichester Cathedral, who had fled Chichester because he was unable to pay his debts, wrote to his bishop, Ralph de Neville, to thank Neville for offering to lend him some grain until Michaelmas (September 29). However, he says that he has so many other debts due at that time that he will have to sell most of his own grain to satisfy them, and so will not be in a position to repay the bishop's loan.[10]

NOTES

1   Add. 8167, fol. 101r.
2   *cum* in MS.
3   Cf. the gloss *"voluntas reputatur pro facto"* in the *Glossa Ordinaria* to the *Liber Extra* (Decretals of Pope Gregory IX, 1234), in *Corpus juris canonici emendatum et notis illustratum, Gregorii XIII. pont. max. iussu editum* (Rome: In aedibus Populi Romani, 1582), Part 2: *Decretales d. Gregorii papae IX,* Lib. 2, Tit. 15, Cap. 1, Col. 666, s.v. *"voluntatem,"* between lines 20 and 30; available in an electronic edition at UCLA Digital Library Program, *Corpus Juris Canonici* (1582); http://digital.library.ucla.edu/ canonlaw [seen July 7, 2009].
4   Word missing in MS.
5   *tricuratores* in MS.
6   *ortu* (i.e., *hortu,* garden) in MS, probably in mistake for *horreo* (barn).
7   In MS, *tricurato.*
8   A quarter was eight bushels, or 281.92 liters.
9   Literally, "cleanse the threshed grain with a winnowing fan." See below.
10   Shirley, ed., *Letters,* vol. 1, 283–84, no. 235. This letter is now TNA: PRO, SC 1/6/51 (April 21, 1224 × June 28, 1226).

90

A Neighbor Requests the Loan of a Plow and Plowshare Until He Can Get Some Iron to Have a Plowshare Made for His Own Plow[1]

E. mandat F.[2] ut comodat sibi aratrum ad arrandum terram[3] suam

Karissimo amico suo A., B. salutem. Vicinus non debet deesse vicino. Vicinitatem tuam exoro ut aratrum tuum et vomerem et unum iugum michi acomodetis. Sciatis quod aratrum michi emi, set[4] non habeo ferrum ad vomerem faciendam. Tantum ergo faciatis ne terra mea iaceat inculta. Sciturus quod ea diucius non peto quam ferrum inveniam ad emendum. Valete.[5]

E. sends word to F. to lend him a plow to plow his land

To his dearest friend A., B. sends greetings. A neighbor should not fail to aid a neighbor. I beg your neighborliness to lend me your plow and plowshare and a yoke. You should know that I bought myself a plow, but I do not have the iron for making a plowshare. Therefore, I hope that you will act in such a way that my land does not lie untilled. Rest assured that I do not seek to borrow them for longer than it will take me to find some iron to buy. Farewell.

Many of the letters in this collection make an appeal to neighborly generosity, and this letter is a reminder that such mutual dependence was not restricted to the poor. The scarcity and costliness of iron and steel meant that many common agricultural tools, such as rakes and pitchforks, were made entirely of wood, while others, such as spades and plows, were made primarily of wood with a minimum of metal. Only the front edge of spades and shovels was reinforced with a strip of iron; the rest was made of wood. Plows had a wooden frame, often wheeled, with an iron or steel knife called a coulter that sliced the soil vertically, and a thick, sharpened, iron bar or tip called a "share" that sliced under the sod horizontally, enabling the wooden moldboard to turn over the furrow (the entire strip of sod).[6] A letter written between 1214 and 1222 by Ralph de Neville, dean of Lichfield (later bishop of Chichester and chancellor of England), reflects a concern similar to that in DOCUMENT 90 about the availability of iron for plows. Nevill was writing to his steward or agent G. Salvage about the sale of wheat and other matters, and mentions that he has spoken to Sir Richard Duket, who is to supply him with herring, wax, a fur lining, and "iron and steel for my plows" (*de ferro et ascero ad carucas meas*). Evidently anxious to secure these supplies, Nevill told Salvage to meet with Duket as soon as possible.[7]

NOTES

1   Add. 8167, fol. 101v.
2   As in DOCUMENTS 10, 16, 33, 50, and 70, this letter was evidently copied from another collection, and the initials in the body of the letter were revised, but not those in the heading.
3   Corrected in MS from *terrram*.
4   *terra mea* expunged in MS following *set*.
5   Or *Vale* (*Val'* in MS); the sender addresses the recipient using a mixture of singular (familiar) and plural (polite) verbs, and singular pronouns.
6   John M. Steane, *The Archaeology of Medieval England and Wales* (Athens: University of Georgia Press, 1985), 155–56 and Fig. 5.4; London Museum, *Medieval Catalogue* (London: H. M. Stationery Office, 1940), 123–24 and Pl. XXII. For a late thirteenth-century sketch of a nonwheeled plow from the cartulary of Nun Cotham or Coton

Priory, Lincs., with the parts labeled in Latin, see Howard M. Colvin, "A Medieval Drawing of a Plough," *Antiquity*, 27, no. 107 (September 1953), 165–67. This sketch is now Bodleian Library, MS. Top. Lincs. D.1, fol. 53.

7   W. H. Blaauw, "Letters to Ralph Neville," *Sussex Archaeological Collections*, 3 (1850), 41; also in Shirley, ed., *Letters*, vol. 1, 190–91 (no. 165). This letter is now TNA: PRO, SC 1/6/3. The accounts of a prebendary of St Paul's cathedral included 7¹/₂*d.* for the final payment for iron for a plow (*In ferro caruce acquietando*), and 6*d.* for iron and steel for a plow. Christopher M. Woolgar, ed., *Household Accounts from Medieval England*, vol. 1, British Academy, Records of Social and Economic History, new ser., 17–18 (Oxford: Oxford University Press, for the British Academy, 1992–93), 119–20, 124. These accounts date from the early thirteenth century (probably 1219 or 1224; or possibly 1213).

91

A Neighbor Requests Financial Assistance Following a Burglary[1]

Vicinus mandat vicino ut subveniat ei

Vicinus vicino salutem. Vicinus non debet deesse vicino, si tamen deus dederit ei unde vicino possit succurrere. De vobis reperto magnam[2] fiduciam, et de vestra liberalitate[3] spem habeo certissimam. Si quo modo potestis, michi subveniaris? Latrones enim nocturno tempore domum meam pridie fregerunt, omnia bona que possidebam asportaverunt, et me letaliter vulneraverunt;[4] me semimortuo relicto abierunt. Curata[5] iam deo dante vulnera[6] mea, set rerum mearum detrimentum nondum est restauratum. Et ideo vos precor quatinus in denariis meam miseriam relevare[7] velitis, et de bonis vestris meum supplere defectum, pro certo scientes quod in articulo consimili pro posse meo vobis [non][8] deficerim. Valete.

A man sends word to his neighbor to come to his aid

A neighbor to his neighbor, greetings. A neighbor should not fail to assist a neighbor if God should give him the means whereby he can aid him. I place great confidence in what I have heard of you, and I have the firmest hope of your generosity. If you can in some way, would you help me out? For yesterday thieves came at night, broke into my house, carried off all the goods that I possessed, wounded me gravely, and left me half-dead. My wound has been treated, thank God, but the loss of all my possessions has not been made good, and therefore I pray that you might be willing to relieve my misery with money and to supply my want with your own goods, knowing for certain that in a similar situation I would [not] let you down, to the best of my ability. Farewell.

The unfortunate sender of this letter (apparently a victim of the criminal gang described in Document 40) has been burglarized, injured, and robbed of all his possessions. Evidently lacking family and friends of his own who might aid him in his distress, he appeals to a wealthy and generous neighbor for cash and goods to make up his losses, pledging himself to reciprocate if the neighbor should ever find himself in a similar plight.

Although this is clearly a fictitious model letter (one in which the author seems to have enjoyed dreaming up a worst-case scenario), it nevertheless neatly sums up some of the very real everyday dangers of the medieval world, in which the threat of armed violence was ever present, police and emergency services were minimal at best, and insurance did not exist. When disaster struck, there were no relief agencies or legal or social services to aid the victims, and it is striking that none of the appeals for emergency assistance in this collection is addressed to a member of the clergy or to an ecclesiastical institution. Instead, the victims' recourse was to beg for assistance from family, friends, and neighbors. It is not surprising, therefore, that so many of the letters, including the one above, resort to invoking the claims of kinship, friendship, neighborliness, piety, and charity in their anxious attempt at securing aid.

In another letter on the same theme in this formulary, a knight begs a neighboring freeman for assistance by similarly invoking the duties of good neighborliness: "A knight to a free man, greetings. Good neighbors mean a good night's rest.[9] For the law of neighborliness demands that the good things that the lord might grant to one of them, be granted to the other to have as his own, since the more every good thing is brought into common use, the more fragrant it seems and the more sweetness it has." The knight explains that necessity compels him to seek relief from his friends and neighbors, and begs his neighbor to assist him, and concludes: "And because I [have] trust in you as in a special friend, and because I wish to make this request to you first, and to your benevolence, I earnestly beg you to help me if you will. Farewell."[10]

NOTES

1 Add. 8167, fol. 107r.
2 *magnan* in MS.
3 *libertate* in MS.
4 *wlneraverunt* in MS.
5 Corrected in MS from *curanta*.

6   *wlnera* in MS.

7   *revelare* in MS.

8   Word supplied to preserve the sense of the passage.

9   Literally, "He who has a good neighbor has a good morning." This is the inverse of an otherwise-unknown proverb quoted *c.* 1108 by Fulcher of Chartres: "In country proverbs is written: 'He who has a bad neighbor has a bad morning'"—that is, a bad night's sleep (*qui habet malum vicinum habet malum matutinum*). Jacques-Paul Migne, ed., *Patrologiae cursus completus: series Latina*, 221 vols. (Paris: Garnier, 1844--64), vol. 155, col. 937. See also Fulcher of Chartres, *A History of the Expedition to Jerusalem, 1095–1107*, trans. Frances Rita Ryan, ed. Harold S. Fink (Knoxville: University of Tennessee Press, 1969), 297; and Arpad Steiner, "The Vernacular Proverb in Mediaeval Latin Prose," *American Journal of Philology*, 65: 1 (1944), 37–68.

10 Add. 8167, fol. 106v. *Miles libero homini salutem. Qui bonum habet vicinum bonum habet matutinum. Ius enim vicinitatis exigit ut bona que dominus eorum alteri concessit alteri tanquam propria possidente concedantur, siquidem omne bonum in commune deductum plus sapit plus et dulcedinis habere videtur . . . et quia de vobis [?habeo] tanquam speciali amico fiduciam et quia vos primum et vestram benevolenciam volo exortari, vos diligenter exoro michi si placet succurratis. Valete.* The freeman's response is discussed under DOCUMENT 92.

92

The Burglary Victim's Neighbor Agrees to Assist Him[1]

Concessio ad peticionem predictam

Vicino vicinus salutem. Iustum est et equitati consocium[2] ut a vicino vicini penuria relevetur,[3] si tamen vicinus habeat unde vicino suo remedium faciat (*vel conferre valeat*).[4] Literas vestras accepi vestrum narrantes[5] infortunium, et tam corporis vestri quam rerum vestrarum[6] detrimentum et dispendium ultra modum doleo. Deum testor[7] quod vobis factum est michi factum, reputans de mea vobis substancia quantum michi facultas suppeditat.[8] Libentissime subveniam, scientes potero; quod sicut literis vestris michi significastis in casu consimili nullo modo defeceritis. Hoc enim quod per latorem presencium vobis transmitto accipiatis, ac si preciosiora vobis destinassem. Valete.

Agreement to the aforesaid request

To his neighbor, a neighbor sends greetings. It is right and fitting that the poverty of a neighbor should be relieved by his neighbor. If a neighbor has the means (*or, is in a condition to do so*), he should give aid to his neighbor. I received your letter describing your misfortune, both the harm to your body and to your goods, and I mourn your loss beyond measure. I call God as my witness that your problems are mine, and I consider that my means can provide from my resources for you as well as for me. I shall come to your aid with great pleasure, knowing that I shall be able to do so; as you signified in your letter to me, in a similar situation you would in no way fail [me]. Therefore, please accept this, which I send to you by the bearer of this present letter, since indeed if it were even more precious I would have intended it for you. Farewell.

This high-minded response to the request for aid in DOCUMENT 91 is a fine example of the rhetorical skill of the master or student of *dictamen* (the art of letter-writing) who composed it. Conforming to the classic four-part structure of a formal letter, it begins with a brief *salutatio* (greeting), and then introduces the theme of the letter with a proverbial *exordium* (introduction) on the duties of neighborliness that also recalls St. Paul's epistle to the Colossians. The *narratio* (body of the letter) rehearses the sad events described in the addressee's original petition (DOCUMENT 91) and proclaims that the sender will be happy to come to his aid, since he has the means to do so. Finally, the *conclusio* implicitly sums up the major premise of the *exordium* (that neighbors should assist one another) and the minor premise of the *narratio* (that the sender has the means to help, and knows that the addressee would aid him if their positions were reversed), and ends with additional expressions of courtesy and a brief valediction (farewell).

The underlying moral of this letter—the importance of observing the Golden Rule—has a suggestion of sermon literature about it (cf. Matthew 7:12), but suits its secular subject equally well. The writer here displays the same magnificently disinterested generosity as the neighbor in DOCUMENT 11. In the same fashion, the freeman to whom a neighboring knight has appealed for assistance (discussed under DOCUMENT 91) sends the following encouraging response:

> To a knight, a free man [sends] greetings and expressions of friendship. I grieve beyond measure and in many ways over your difficulties. You may count harm done to you as to me, and because you have considered me first among your friends, I want you to know [*i.e., that you will have*] aid and counsel quickly with me. I send you an ox for improving your land, and two measures of each kind of grain for eliminating the barrenness of your lands, and to satisfy the requirement of your legal pleas I shall appear in person whenever and wherever you wish. In this way I very much want

your other kinsmen and friends to take me as an example of how to assist you.[9]

While all three of these positive responses to requests may be idealized, they reflect the frequency with which petitions of this kind must have been presented to people of wealth, and the need to provide ready models for responding to them.

NOTES

1   Add. 8167, fol. 107r.
2   Cf. Colossians 4:1: *Domini, quod justum est et æquum, servis præstate: scientes quod et vos Dominum habetis in cælo* ("Masters, give what is just and fair to your servants, knowing that you, too, have a Master in heaven").
3   *reveletur* in MS.
4   Here, as in Documents 5, 24, 32, 44, 46, 47, and 62, the parenthetical phrase represents an alternate phrasing provided in the model letter.
5   Following *narrantes*, the word *officium* is expunged in MS.
6   *mearum* in MS.
7   *testes* in MS.
8   *suspediat* in MS.
9   Add. 8167, fol. 106v. *Responsio ad peticionem predictam. Militi liber homo salutem et amicicias. De gravamine vestro multipliciter ultra modum doleo. Nocumentum vestrum meum reputaris et quia me primum inter ceteros amicos vestros reputastis, volo quod mecum indilate sencias consilium et auxilium. Ad culturam terre vestre meliorandam, mitto vobis .i. bovem, et ad sterilitatem terrarum [corrected in MS from terrrarum] vestrarum amovendam, duas summas uniuscuiusque bladi, et ad inportunitatem placitorum vestrorum solvendam, quandocumque et quocumque volueritis propriam personam exibeo. Multum sic desidero ut ceteri parentes et amici vestri de me capiant exemplum vobis benefaciendi.*

93

A Peasant Writes to Another About His Adversities[1]

Rusticus rustico salutem. Plurimum humani generis viciavit condicioni qui peccatis suis exigentibus emergere fecit[2] servitutem. Quia res in estimabilis est libertas;[3] servitus suus [*sic*] honerosa [*sic*] poscessionibus [*sic*] existit. Bene vidisti quod durum habemus dominum, hastutum [*sic*] servientem, propositum [*sic*] iniquissimum, terram fere sterilem, et hec omnia ultra modum adversantur. Requie penitus alterna caremus, et[4] quod caret alterna requie durabile non est, [ut][5] arcum incesses tendere lentus erit,[6] nec est in mundo quicquam dum vivimus quod nostras refocillat animas. A te consilium expeto cum racione rusticitatis; michi

non deesse debeas. Libere siquidem condicionis et homines non tanquam et habitos et publicos[7] abhorrent,[8] nisi racionabiles nobis[9] essent[10]
anime, tanquam rabidi cani[11] inter illos haberemur. In hiis autem nobis
neccessaria est paciencia, quia si murmurantes repungnabimus nostra
miseria nobis apocopabitur. Illud unicum solacium habemus: quod[12]
moriemur, et in morte nostra servitus terminentur. Valete.

A peasant to a peasant, greetings. Most of the human race has degener-
ated to the point that, for its sins, it has caused slavery to emerge. For
freedom is an inestimable thing; their slavery is burdensome to those
who are property. You have seen well that we have a harsh lord, a sly
serjeant, a wicked reeve, and almost barren land, and all these are
adverse beyond measure. We almost entirely lack intervals of rest, and
that which lacks daily rest cannot endure, just as a bow that you do not
cease to bend will grow slack, nor is there on earth anything while we
live that revives our spirits. I need advice with rustic wisdom from you;
you must not fail me. And since men of free condition abhor both common manners and common people,[13] were it not for our rational souls[14]
we would be held but as rabid dogs (*rabidi cani*) among them. In these
things the ability to endure hardship (*paciencia*) is necessary for us,
because if, complaining, we resist, our misery will be cut short[15] for us.
We have but one solace: we shall die, and at our death our servitudes
will end.

This anguished account of the miseries of villeinage, sprinkled (despite its
flawed Latinity) with quotations from Ovid and Justinian's *Digest* and an allusion to contemporary scholastic debate on the nature of the soul, obviously
cannot have represented a genuine letter by a genuine villein. It reads instead,
like the letter ostensibly written by a villein in DOCUMENT 49, much more like
a classroom exercise in composition, but one that echoes, in its sympathetic
depiction of the villein's hard life, a much earlier school text. This was the
Latin dialogue on daily life known as the *Colloquy*, written about 998 by Ælfric
(*c.* 950–*c.* 1010), a monk at Cerne Abbas in Dorset and later (1005) abbot of
Eynsham.[16] In the *Colloquy*, which Ælfric wrote in the form of a dialogue to
teach Latin to his students, a villein describes the wretchedness of his unfree
condition, though in much less dramatic terms than those in the letter above:

MASTER: What do you say, plough boy, how do you do your work?
PLOUGH BOY: Oh, sir, I work very hard. I go out at dawn to drive the
oxen to the field, and yoke them to the plough; however

hard the winter I dare not stay at home for fear of my master; and having yoked the oxen and made the plough-share and the coulter fast to the plough, every day I have to plough a whole acre or more.

MASTER: Have you anyone with you?

PLOUGH BOY: I have a boy to drive the oxen with a goad, and he is now hoarse with cold and shouting.

MASTER: What more do you do in the day?

PLOUGH BOY: A great deal more. I have to fill the oxen's bins with hay, and give them water, and carry the dung outside.

MASTER: Oh, it is hard work.

PLOUGH BOY: Yes, it is hard work, because I am not free.[17]

The text of the letter above, ostensibly written by an unnamed villein, is so riddled with misspellings and grammatical errors that it seems possible that these were intended by the author to represent a peasant's uneducated speech and accent. Here the writer may have been drawing upon a classical model, a poem by the celebrated Roman poet Catullus. In this letter, the addition of an aspirate "h" to words such as *(h)onorosa* and *(h)astutum* recalls Catullus's lampooning of a man called Arrius for inserting inappropriate aspirates, such as saying *chommodas* for *commodas*, and *hinsidias* for *insidias*, and calling the Ionian Sea the "Hionian."[18]

NOTES

1 Add. 8167, fol. 128r–v.
2 *fecerit* in MS.
3 This phrase derives from the line *"Libertas inaestimabilis res est"* in the *Digest* (50.17.106), a collection and abridgement of Roman juristic writing, produced in AD 530–533 under the Byzantine emperor Justinian. The *Digest* was the first and most important part of Justinian's *Corpus Iuris Civilis*, which had a profound effect on the development of law and legal studies in medieval Europe. For this reference we are grateful to Paul Hyams.
4 A second *et* is expunged here in MS.
5 *et* in MS.
6 These lines derive from Ovid's *Heroides*, 4:89–92: *"quod caret alterna requie, durabile non est; . . . arcus . . . si numquam cesses tendere, mollis erit"* ("that which lacks alternations of repose will not endure; . . . the bow . . . if you never cease to bend it, will become slack"). The same quotation, together with a discussion of its context, appears in DOCUMENT 66.
7 *puplicanos* in MS.
8 *abornant* in MS.
9 *vobis* in MS.
10 *esset* in MS.

11 *rabilicanos* in MS.

12 Fol. 128v commences here.

13 This appears to be the sense of the emended phrase *libere siquidem condicionis et homines non tanquam et habitos et publicos abhorrent.*

14 This appears to be the sense of the emended phrase *nisi racionabiles nobis essent anime.* There was a major scholastic debate in the twelfth and thirteenth centuries on the nature of the soul; see Richard C. Dales, *The Problem of the Rational Soul in the Thirteenth Century* (Leiden: E. J. Brill, 1995).

15 See *Oxford Dictionary of Medieval Latin from British Sources*, s.v. "apocopare."

16 *Oxford DNB*, s.n. "Ælfric of Eynsham."

17 Excerpt from A. F. Leach, *Educational Charters and Documents* (Cambridge: Cambridge University Press, 1911), 37–41, quoted in *Educational Documents*, vol. 1, *England and Wales, 800–1816*, comp. David William Sylvester (London: Methuen, 1970), 7.

18 *The Poems of Catullus: A Bilingual Edition*, translated, with commentary by Peter Green (Berkeley: University of California Press, 2005), Poem 84, pp. 190–91 (commentary, pp. 260–61): *Chommoda dicebat, si quando commoda uellet/ dicere, et insidias Arrius hinsidias,/ et tum mirifice sperabat se esse locutum,/ cum quantum poterat dixerat hinsidias./ credo, sic mater, sic liber auunculus eius,/ sic maternus auus dixerat atque auia./ hoc misso in Syriam requierant omnibus aures:/ audibant eadem haec leniter et leuiter, / nec sibi postilla metuebant talia uerba,/ cum subito affertur nuntius horribilis:/ Ionios fluctus, postquam illuc Arrius isset,/ iam non Ionios esse sed Hionios.* ("Arrius aspirates: 'chommodore' when trying to articulate/ 'commodore,' while 'insidious' came out '*h*insidious'—/ imagining that he'd spoken up with wondrous impact/ by delivering 'hinsidious' full force./ His mother, I gather, as well as his (free-born) uncle/ and both maternal grandparents talked that way./ When he was posted to Syria, our ears all got a respite,/ heard these same words smoothly and lightly pronounced,/ without any lingering fear of such verbal mishandlings—/ then, suddenly, there arrived the horrible news:/ the Ionian sea, after Arrius had arrived, was/ Ionian no longer, but *C*hionian.")

CHAPTER 5

A Knight's Correspondence:
Building a Barn and a Windmill

94
A Knight Informs His Friend, a Royal Forester,
that the King Has Granted Him Four Oak Trees
with Which to Build a Windmill[1]

Karissimo amico suo tali forestario, talis miles salutem. A regia munifi-
cencia concesse sunt quatuor michi[2] quercus in foresta illa cuius ad vos
spectat custodia, quas ad quoddam molendinum ventericium ab ipso
rege postulavi.[3] Litteras eciam illius ad nos super hoc inpetravi, quarum
tenore, si placet, supplico[4] meis hominibus, quos ad istud negocium exe-
quendum ad vos mitto, quercus illas assignare velitis, donum regale in
quantum poteritis, salva vestra fidelitate, aumentantes.

To his dearest friend such-and-such a forester, such-and-such a knight
[sends] greetings. By the king's munificence, four oaks in the forest of
which the custody belongs to you have been granted to me, which I
asked for from the king for a certain windmill. I have succeeded in
obtaining his letter to us on this matter, by the tenor of which, if it please
you, I humbly beg that you will assign those oaks to my men, whom I
send to you to carry out this business, increasing the royal gift as much
as you can without betraying the king's trust.[5]

This is the first of a collection of seven model letters (DOCUMENTS 94–100)
included in the formulary in Fairfax MS 27 (c. 1230). They all concern the
proposed construction of a windmill, and also discuss various other administrative, professional, and personal matters. The correspondents are a knight of

| 278 |

the king's household, a royal forester, the forester's serjeants (assistants), a carpenter, the knight's manorial serjeant (bailiff), and the knight's wife. No original collection of correspondence of this kind among such a group of ordinary people of widely varying status has survived for this period, but the character of the letters in this formulary collection makes it clear that such communications must have been routine.

The windmill or "post" mill was the most important invention, in terms of power technology, of the later medieval world.[6] It first appeared in northwestern Europe, probably in Flanders or eastern England (especially East Anglia), where a lack of good watercourses made watermills scarce. Windmills are first mentioned in Flemish and English sources in the 1180s, and within a few years were common enough for Pope Celestine III (1191–98) to declare them liable for tithe.[7] In England, the building of windmills seems to have been modest until the 1230s and later, when there was a surge of construction in the eastern counties.[8] The proposed windmill construction that is the focus of this small collection of letters thus dates from the eve of the biggest growth of such construction in England.

In this letter, the knight writes to the officer in charge of a royal forest, a man of considerable standing and authority, to let him know that he has obtained a grant from the king of four oaks with which to build a windmill. The knight respectfully asks the forester to release the trees to the men whom he has sent to take charge of them, and he concludes with a delicately worded request that the forester increase the royal gift as much as he can without breaching the responsibilities of his office. The importance of the king's gift and the reason for the knight's desire to increase it was that oaks were valuable assets. A specimen manorial account of 1258–59 reports the receipt of 2*s.* from the sale of one oak; the same account lists payments to laborers at the rate of $\frac{1}{2}d.$ per day, and to artisans at 3*d.* per day. At these rates, the price of a single oak represented eight days' wages for an artisan, and forty-eight days' wages for a laborer.[9]

NOTES

1   Fairfax 27, fol. 5r–v.
2   Inserted above line in MS.
3   Fol. 5v commences here.
4   *suspecto* in MS.
5   Literally, "saving your fidelity."
6   Joel Mokyr, *The Lever of Riches: Technological Creativity and Economic Progress* (New York: Oxford University Press, 1990), 44.
7   Richard Holt, *The Mills of Medieval England* (Oxford: Blackwell, 1988), 20–22, 171–75. Holt discounts as incorrect or untrustworthy a number of citations by Edward J.

Kealey, in *Harvesting the Air: Windmill Pioneers in Twelfth-Century England* (Berkeley: University of California Press, 1987), of earlier references to mills in the twelfth century.

8   Holt, *Mills of Medieval England*, 21–35.
9   Bodleian Library, Oxford, Rawlinson MS C. 775, pp. 119, 120.

95

The Royal Forester Responds with an Offer of Assistance[1]

Tali militi, talis forestarius salutem. Dono domini regis in litteris eius contento nec volo nec debeo resistere, maxime cum tale sit concessum cui vellem ut triplicaretur. Regii doni numerus[2] deo dante non minuetur, immo pocius ad commodum vestrum, vestris viris videntibus, augebitur. Summitates eciam arborum et omnia que forestario inde competunt vobis concedimus ad focum vestrum; carpentariis et hominibus vestris in quantum poterimus ausiliabimur, nec aliam querimus remuneracionem quam vestram benevolenciam.

To such-and-such a knight, such-and-such a forester [sends] greetings. I neither wish to stand in the way of the gift of the lord king as contained in his letter, nor ought I to do so, especially since it is granted to one to whom I would wish it were tripled. The measure of the king's gift shall not, God granting, be reduced, but rather—as your men shall see—increased, to your advantage. The crowns of the trees, and everything that belongs to the forester's office, we grant to you, for your hearth; to your carpenters and men we shall give as much assistance as we can, nor do we seek any other recompense than your goodwill.

In this, the second letter of seven in this correspondence (see DOCUMENT 94), the royal forester replies graciously to the knight that he has no intention of blocking the king's gift of oak trees. Rather, he augments the gift with his own perquisite (his benefit or entitlement) of the crowns of the trees, for firewood, and promises to assist the knight's men who come to collect the trees, asking nothing in return but the knight's goodwill.

This is a fine example of the importance of favors and obligation in medieval society. By providing favors to the knight of the kind described above, the forester is placing him under an obligation and creating or reinforcing bonds of mutual friendship and cooperation (cf. DOCUMENT 86). Such ties could be crucial in a world in which enmities, such as the threat of mortal enmity used to intimidate a rival in DOCUMENT 48, were ever-present dangers.

NOTES

1   Fairfax 27, fol. 5v.
2   *num[er]us* or *munus* in MS; *numerus* seems to better fit the sense of this sentence.

96
The Royal Forester Orders His Serjeants
to Assist the Knight[1]

Forestarius sibi servientibus subditis salutem. Ex dono domini regis concesse sunt quatuor quercus tali militi in foresta illa quam vos custoditis, et ideo vobis mandamus quatinus, in competenti loco ad commodum illius, illas quercus et quintam ex dono nostro suis hominibus assignatis. Concessimus enim eidem[2] quicquid ad nos de predictis arboribus pertinet, et vobis precipimus quatinus de villis circumadiacentibus ausilium ad traendum et cariandum merinium eidem faciatis habere, non minus negociis illius in hac parte quam propriis meis intendentes.

A forester to the serjeants under his authority, greetings. Four oak trees in the forest that you guard have been granted by gift of the lord king to such-and-such a knight. And so we order you that, in a suitable place, at his convenience, you hand over those oaks, and a fifth one of our own gift, to his men, for we have granted him whatever pertains to us from those trees. And we order you to obtain assistance from the surrounding vills in hauling and carting the timber to him, and to consider his interests in this matter no less than my own.

This letter, the third in the collection of seven letters that begins with Docu-MENT 94, sheds some interesting light on the powers of royal foresters and the ways in which they used their authority.[3] Here the forester writes to his assistants to tell them to hand five trees over to the knight's men, and to summon men from the neighboring vills (villages or towns) to assist in transporting the trees to the knight's manor.

    In the preceding letter in this collection (DOCUMENT 95), the forester wrote that he was making the knight a gift of the crowns of the four oak trees granted by the king. These crowns would normally have been taken by the forester as a perquisite (benefit or entitlement) of his office. Here, however, the forester writes that he is giving the knight an entire tree as his own gift. Evidently he has the right to dispose of a number of the oaks in his custody.[4] Such a valuable gift represents another example of the use of favors to create obligations and reinforce strategic friendships among the landholding and office-holding classes, as discussed under DOCUMENTS 86 and 95.

The forester's perquisite of the crowns of felled trees provides an early example of the use of perquisites in kind (rather than in cash) to supplement money wages for officeholders, servants, and other employees at all levels of society. In the cash-poor economy of early thirteenth-century England, salaries of long-term employees were often modest and paid only at long intervals, such as once or twice a year. Cash wages were frequently supplemented with annual or semi-annual gifts of clothing ("livery robes," discussed under DOCUMENTS 5, 6, and 77), and these are listed in surviving financial accounts. DOCUMENT 96 shows that wages might also be supplemented at this time, as they were in later periods, with perquisites of a more irregular or nebulous character. Such in-kind supplements seldom appear in financial records, however, because they were "off-budget"—they represented leftover, surplus, or reused items that did not need to be accounted for separately under receipts, and thus never had to be accounted for under expenditures. In later years such perquisites are reflected, at least by implication, in manorial and household regulations. For example, the unknown author of *Fleta* (*c.* 1290) specified that the household steward was to have each day's allowance of flesh and fish cut up into portions in his presence and counted as they were delivered to the cook, but did not say what was to be done with unwanted off-cuts and leftovers, such as the heads and lower legs of meat-animals, feathers, fat, and empty barrels.[5] Some later regulations, however (such as the ordinances made in 1468 for the household of George, duke of Clarence, and in 1473 for the household of Edward, prince of Wales), stated explicitly that certain remains of this kind were to be the perquisites or "fees" of the servants who handled them.[6] The evidence from DOCUMENT 96 suggests that there may have been a similar arrangement in the early thirteenth century as well. Outside vendors also sometimes claimed perquisites; *Fleta* provides a glimpse of this in noting that the legitimate profits of a commercial baker included the bran sieved from the customer's flour.[7]

NOTES

1   Fairfax 27, fol. 5v.

2   In MS, the word "*quod*" ("that") occurs between "*eidem*" and "*quiquid,*" but it does not fit the sense of the passage and ought to have been expunged from the text.

3   On the royal forests and their administration, see Charles Young, *The Royal Forests of Medieval England* (Philadelphia: University of Pennsylvania Press, 1979), passim; for abuses by the foresters, see especially 26–27, 61, 81–83.

4   Such perquisites were subject to abuse: one forester allegedly cut down 600 oaks and tried to conceal the theft by covering the stumps with turf. Young, *Royal Forests*, 82.

5   Henry Gerald Richardson and George Osborne Sayles, eds. and trans., *Fleta*, Selden Society, 72 (1955), 2:243.

6   [Society of Antiquaries], *A Collection of Ordinances and Regulations for the Government of the Royal Household* (London: Society of Antiquaries, 1790), p. *32 [*sic*] (Prince Edward), pp. 95–96 (Clarence).

7   Richardson and Sayles, eds. and trans., *Fleta*, 2:118.

97

The Knight Hires a Carpenter to Finish the Windmill and Build a Barn[1]

Miles carpentario salutem. Relatu plurimorum didici te subtilem esse et ingeniosum, et ideo quam cito poteris ad nos venire non differas, ut [ad][2] perticam [?perducendam][3] de molendino ventericio quod facere proposui opus incoatum procedat, et ad perfeccionem perducatur. Operarios enim siquos in partibus vestris ad hoc ydoneos inveneritis tecum adducere non omittas. Nos autem et illorum sedulitatem et laborem vestrum digna mercede remunerabimus, unius enim nove grangie facturam [tibi][4] simul et carpentariis quos tecum adducceris committere volumus, cuius longitudinem, latitudinem et altitudinem[5] secundum tuam fieri volumus disposicionem.

A knight to a carpenter, greetings. I have learned from many people that you are meticulous and talented, and therefore do not delay coming to us as quickly as you can, so that the incomplete work on the [?unfinished] pole of a windmill that I have planned to build can proceed and be brought to completion. Do not neglect to find some honest workmen for this in your neighborhood to bring with you. We shall reward their zeal and your labor with an appropriate recompense, for we also wish to entrust [to you] and to the carpenters whom you will bring with you the making of a new barn, of which we wish the length, breadth, and height to be made according to your disposition.

DOCUMENT 97, written in the form of a letter of offer from a knight to a carpenter, anticipates by more than two decades the earliest references to building contracts in medieval England, and it is three-quarters of a century earlier than the earliest surviving texts. Nevertheless, despite the letter's generic language and lack of detail (suitable for a model document), it embodies the essential features of such a contract. These were: a firm offer of employment; a description of the project (completion of a windmill, and design and construction of a barn); a specification of what the contractor is to supply (carpentry and design, and a crew of skilled workmen); a proposed commencement date (as soon as possible); and a stated fee ("appropriate" compensation for both contractor and crew). As a letter rather than a contract, however, DOCUMENT 97 does not include the carpenter's acceptance of these conditions. It may well be that no standard form for building contracts existed in England at this time, since the early formularies do not include examples of them. In that case, this document may represent, in effect, medieval England's earliest known building contract.[6]

DOCUMENT 97 is also the fourth in the collection of seven letters (beginning with DOCUMENT 94) that concern a knight and his construction projects. Here the knight writes to hire a carpenter whom he has selected after obtaining numerous positive referrals. From other letters in this collection (DOCUMENTS 94–96 and 98) we learn that the timbers for the knight's mill will come from five oak trees from a nearby royal forest, and that the knight expects that both the windmill and the barn will be completed in the course of the summer.[7]

The pole (pertica) of the windmill on which the knight is so impatient for work to resume evidently is the tail pole, which is prominently depicted in the two earliest known illustrations of windmills, both of them from England and both dating from the third quarter of the thirteenth century (Fig. 16).[8] The design of windmills was based on their use of large, latticed sails covered with canvas or board to catch the wind, which provided the power for turning a heavy millstone. Windmills had to be turnable so that their sails could always face into the wind. The solution to this requirement was to balance a revolving millhouse (called a cabin or "buck") atop a single, massive, vertical post (postis in Latin).[9] The cabin was built of lightweight planking and was suspended on the post by a strong transverse beam called a crown tree. The post, which was stationary, had to be strong enough not only to support the weight of the cabin and its sails, but also to withstand the vibration of the vertically turning sails, the horizontal rotation of the cabin, and the grinding of the two horizontal millstones (a rotating upper stone and a fixed lower stone), which weighed about a ton apiece. Additional heavy timbers were needed to brace the vertical post and to provide sturdy foundations. The door to the cabin was reached from ground level by means of a plank, ladder, or lightweight set of stairs, and the long tail pole was pushed like a capstan bar to rotate the cabin so that its sails faced into the wind.[10] The necessity, when building a windmill, of obtaining very large and heavy posts and timbers explains the importance of the

Figure 16. A windmill with its tail pole, from Cambridge University Library, MS Ee. 2. 31, fol. 130 (*c.* 1255–60).

king's and the royal forester's gift to the knight of five oak trees for this purpose in Documents 94 and 96.

Throughout most of this letter the knight addresses the carpenter with the familiar "*tu*," but occasionally he slips instead into the respectful "*vos*." This probably represents careless drafting on the part of the unknown author, but just possibly it reflects the knight's anxiety to obtain the services of this particular carpenter, causing him to address the latter at times as an equal (*vos*) rather than as an inferior (*tu*).

NOTES

1   Fairfax 27, fol. 5v.
2   A preposition such as *ad* that takes the accusative case appears to be wanting here.

3   Word uncertain; in the MS, it appears as *prudenciam*, which does not fit the sense of the sentence.
4   Word supplied to preserve the sense of the sentence.
5   Corrected in MS from *ltitudinem*.
6   There is no example of a building contract in Fairfax 27, Add. 8167, or Walters MS. W. 15.
7   In the only other extant contract for a windmill from medieval England, which dates from 1434, the abbot of Bury St. Edmunds hired a carpenter to build a windmill at Tivetshall, Norfolk, in the space of four months. Louis F. Salzman, *Building in England Down to 1540* (Oxford: Clarendon, 1952; rpt. with corrections and additions, 1967), 505, no. 65.
8   For the earliest illustrations of windmills, see Kealey, *Harvesting the Air*, 14–23, Frontispiece (BL, MS Harley 3487, fol. 161r) and Fig. 5 (Cambridge University Library, MS Ee. 2. 31, fol. 130). According to Nigel Morgan, both manuscripts were illustrated by the same workshop, probably in Oxford. Morgan dates CUL, Ee. 2. 31, to *c.* 1255–60, and BL, Harley 3487, to *c.* 1265–70. Nigel Morgan, *Early Gothic Manuscripts*, in *A Survey of Manuscripts Illuminated in the British Isles*, 4 (London: Harvey Miller, 1982–87), vol. 2, *1250–1285,* nos. 140, 142, pp. 125–27 (Cambridge University Library, MS Ee. 2. 31), and no. 145 (BL, MS Harley 3487).
9   See *Dictionary of Medieval Latin from British Sources*, s.v. "postis," 1(d) (1259).
10 On the design of windmills, see Kealey, *Harvesting the Air*, 14–21; and Holt, *Mills of Medieval England*, 139–44.

98

The Knight Orders the Bailiff of His Manor to Attend to Various Tasks, to Organize the Delivery of the Timber for the New Windmill and Barn, and to Prepare Provisions for the Forthcoming Visit of the Knight and His Household[1]

Talis miles servienti de illo manerio salutem. Manerium meum et res meas tue fidelitati[2] custodiendas commisi, de vestra fidilitate [*sic*] confidens et prudencia. Providias ut terra mea bene colatur, et segetes mee tribulis et aliis immundiciis emundantur, horrea mea bene cooperantur [et][3] sepibus[4] claudantur, et de omnibus aliis rebus meis prout michi melius expedire videris ordinentur. Precipue[5] quantam poteris diligenciam adhibeas ad perquirendum[6] michi [. . .][7] michi in foresta illa vicinorum et rusticorum meorum ausilium perquiras, ut in hac estate molendinum meum ventericium et grangia nova perfici valeant. Providias quoque de brasio faciendo [ad][8] servisiam, et bladum tritulare facias ad panem, et tres vaccas, et decem multones, et lx. aucas impinguari, quam ab inchoacione operis usque ad perfeccionem in illis partibus cum tota familia mea perhendinabo.

Such-and-such a knight to the bailiff[9] of that manor, greetings. I have committed the custody of my manor and my affairs to your loyalty, trusting in your fidelity and good judgment. See to it that my land is well cultivated, and my fields cleared of thorns and other rubbish, my barns well roofed [and] enclosed with fences,[10] and that all of my affairs are put in order for me as you shall think best. And especially, as much as you can, you are also to turn your diligence to seeking out for me ([?*or, to obtaining*] *for me*)[11] in that forest the assistance of my neighbors and villeins, so that this summer my windmill and new barn may be completed. You are also to arrange for the making of malt for ale, and to have wheat threshed for bread, and to have three cows and ten sheep and sixty geese fattened, since I shall be staying in those parts with my entire household from the beginning of that work [*i.e., construction*] until it is completed.

This letter provides a checklist of typical duties expected of a bailiff of a manor: overseeing farm-work, attending to the proper maintenance of buildings and enclosures, taking care of finances, and stocking up on provisions when the lord planned a visit. Another letter from a knight to a manorial bailiff about the performance of routine tasks can be found in DOCUMENT 53, and similar letters ordering the stocking of foodstuffs in anticipation of a visit can be found in DOCUMENTS 17, 18, and 64.

In this letter, the bailiff is also charged with obtaining local assistance to help complete the knight's new barn and windmill during the coming summer. That would make the barn and mill available by the time of the autumn harvest for storing the lord's crops and for grinding the grain of the lord and his tenants.

NOTES

1   Fairfax 27, fol. 5v.
2   *fideliti* in MS.
3   Word supplied to preserve the sense of the passage.
4   *sepes* in MS.
5   Abbreviated word unclear in MS: $p^a p$ or $p^{cc} p$ or $p^{ci} p$.
6   In MS, the "*per-*" here was inserted above the line.
7   There is a blank space here in the text about 1.6 inches (4 cm) long. The exemplar from which this text was copied may have contained a variant phrasing here, beginning with "*vel*" ("or") and ending with "*michi*" ("for me"), such as *vel, ad impetrandum michi* ("or, to obtaining for me"). On variant phrasings such as this, see DOCUMENTS 5, 24, 32, 44, 46, 47, and 62.
8   Word supplied to preserve the sense of this clause.
9   On the translation of *serviens* as "bailiff," see DOCUMENT 50.

10 The word *sepibus* here could also mean "hedges," but "fences" seems more likely in this context since it took much longer to grow a hedge than to build a fence.

11 On this suggested variant phrase, see note 7, above.

99

The Bailiff[1] Reports to the Knight that He Has Taken Care of Everything, and that He Has Borrowed Money on the Knight's Behalf to Cover the Expenses[2]

Tali militi, talis serviens salutem et fidele servicium.[3] Res vestras bonaque mee tutele commissa bene custodivi, nec aliam quero remuneracionem quam fideles vestri michi voluerint iudicare. Merenium vobis datum per ausilium vicinorum et rusticorum iam[4] extractum[5] est, et ad situm molendini perductum est, et de wa[r]nestura[6] de qua michi mandastis nihil omnino deficit. Sciatis[7] quod a creditoribus mutuo denarios ad hoc accepi, de quibus oportet ut de camera vestra vel de blado vestro cum veneritis satisfaciatis. Restat igitur sicut[8] mandastis veniatis, quia presencia vestra super carpentarios et operarios valde poterit esse neccessaria. Valete.

To such-and-such a knight, his bailiff [sends] greetings and faithful service. I have taken good care of your affairs and goods, which you committed to my keeping, and I seek no other remuneration than your loyal men would wish to accord me. The timber given to you has now been delivered by the aid of your neighbors and villeins and taken to the site of your mill, and concerning the provisioning (*warnestura*) of which you sent me word, nothing at all is lacking. You should know that I have received cash for this through a loan from your creditors. Concerning which, it would be a good idea (*oportet*), when you come, if you were to satisfy that debt from your chamber or your grain. As things stand, therefore, you should come as you sent word [you would], since your presence could be very necessary [for keeping an eye] on the carpenters and laborers. Farewell.

In this letter, written in response to DOCUMENT 98, the bailiff reports back to the knight to confirm that the manor is in good order, and that he has taken care of the tasks specified in the knight's letter—namely, organizing the delivery of timber for the knight's planned windmill, and provisioning the manor with foodstuffs against the arrival of the knight and his wife and household.

The bailiff also reports that he has taken it upon himself to obtain a loan on the knight's behalf to pay for the provisions. Clearly the bailiff had little or no cash at hand with which to make these purchases—yet another indication of the limitations of the cash supply. The lack of ready cash was a problem that is mentioned in many of the letters in this volume (see, e.g., DOCUMENTS 3, 11, and 13). Here the bailiff's solution (like that of the agent in DOCUMENT 13) was to obtain a loan in his master's name; in this case, from the knight's unnamed "creditors." These lenders evidently knew and trusted the bailiff as well as the knight and were prepared to extend additional credit to the knight for this purpose. However, the bailiff's delicately worded warning that the knight should repay this debt upon his arrival, either with cash from his "chamber" (his treasury, housed in his private bedchamber or suite) or grain from his stores, suggests that the loan in question was strictly for the short term.

NOTES

1 On the translation of *serviens* as "bailiff," see DOCUMENT 50.
2 Fairfax 27, fol. 5v.
3 For other examples of this salutation, see DOCUMENTS 60 and 69.
4 *per* struck through here in MS.
5 *extractatum* in MS.
6 *wanestura* in MS. Cf. *Dictionary of Medieval Latin from British Sources*, s.v. "garnestura." For this identification we are grateful to Richard Sharpe.
7 *siatis* in MS.
8 *sicut ut* in MS.

100

The Knight Asks His Wife to Join Him at the Manor Where the Mill and Barn Are Under Construction, and to Stay on After His Return to Court[1]

Talis miles uxori sue salutem, et amoris fedus indissoluibile. A curia recedens[2] apud illum manerium perhendinare proposui. Quare tibi mitto palefridum meum proprium et sumerium, et alios equos meos et homines, ut illuc ad me venias, et mecum ibidem perhendinas, donec molendinum meum et nova grangia perficiantur, per tantum enim tempus a domino rege licenciam optinui pro factis [*sic*] vero molendini et horrei. Cum ad curiam rediero, iocundius ibidem perhendinare cum familia tua poteris et morari. Valete.

Such-and-such a knight to his wife, greetings, and indissoluble bond of love. I am withdrawing from the court and have planned to stay at that manor. So I am sending you my own palfrey and sumpter, and my other horses and men, so that you can come to me there and stay with me until my mill and new barn are finished, for I have obtained leave from the lord king for the amount of time [needed] for the making of my mill and barn. When I return to court, you will be able to stay on and live there more pleasantly with your household. Farewell.

In addition to this letter, the two formularies represented in this volume include two other letters from husbands to wives (DOCUMENTS 75 and 77) and one letter from a wife to a husband (DOCUMENT 76). All four letters include strong expressions of conjugal affection, but combine this with a very matter-of-fact tone and content, providing an implicit demonstration that such letters between spouses were routine affairs in this period.

Regular correspondence between husbands and wives would have been necessary in many elite households because, while some married couples sometimes traveled together (as in DOCUMENT 15), important men often spent extended periods away from their families. Some traveled for official or business purposes, such as attending courts and councils, visiting scattered estates, and making buying trips to fairs (see, e.g., DOCUMENTS 10, 46, and 98). Others were summoned to war, or traveled for pleasure or for sport (as in DOCUMENTS 24, 25, 61, and 63), and some spent time in custody, such as the unfortunate knights in DOCUMENTS 27 and 28. Still others, like the knights in this letter and in DOCUMENT 77, were in royal service and lived much of the time at court. As this letter shows, royal household knights, like other members of the royal court, had to obtain formal permission in order to leave the court to visit their families, or for any other reason.[3]

The knight writes that he has sent his own palfrey (riding horse) and sumpter (packhorse) for his wife, together with men and additional horses, to convey her and her household to their manor.[4] This suggests that the knight and his wife are of rather modest means, since the knight's wife evidently has no riding horse or packhorse of her own. It seems likely that she has been staying with family or friends rather than in her own establishment, since her belongings do not require even a single cart to transport them to the manor. Now, however, she will be spending the summer with her husband in their own house, and after he returns to court she will be able to stay on there, to superintend the estate during the harvest season and take full advantage of the new barn and windmill.

It is interesting to note that in the opening salutation the knight puts himself first, a sign of superiority, while relegating his wife to the inferior secondary position. Throughout the text, however, he uses the familiar *ego/tu* (I/

thou) rather than the formal *nos/vos* (we/you), a sign of informality and intimacy.

NOTES

1   Fairfax 27, fol. 5v.
2   *residens* in MS.
3   See S. D. B. Brown, "Leavetaking: Lordship and Mobility in England and Normandy in the Twelfth Century," *History*, 79, no. 256 (June 1994), 199–215, especially 205 and 208.
4   On palfreys, see DOCUMENT 47.

BIBLIOGRAPHY

MANUSCRIPT SOURCES

UNITED KINGDOM

Cambridge
Cambridge University Library, MS Mm. I. 27
Corpus Christi College, MS 297
Gonville and Caius College, MS 205/111

London
British Library
    Additional MS 8167
    Additional MS 41201
Lambeth Palace Library, MS 105
The National Archives, Public Record Office
    C 47/3/33
    E 101/513/12
    E 154/1/2
    E 210/291
    JUST 1/-
       2, 777
    SC 1/-
       1/52, 1/153, 1/214, 2/19, 2/93, 3/181, 4/74, 6/3, 6/6, 6/46, 6/51, 6/134, 6/141, 6/149, 8/42, 8/72, 10/47, 10/51, 10/132, 10/137, 11/36, 11/101

Oxford
Bodleian Library
    Fairfax MS 27
    Rawlinson MS C. 775

UNITED STATES

Baltimore, Maryland
Walters Art Museum, MS W. 15

UNPUBLISHED MODERN WORKS

Albertano of Brescia. *De amore et dilectione Dei et proximi et aliarum rerum et de forma vitae* (1238). Ed. Sharon Hiltz Romino in unpub. doctoral dissertation, University of Pennsylvania, 1980. Available at http://www.intratext.com/IXT/LAT0673/_PL.HTM#$G0 [seen January 10, 2008].

Carlin, Martha. "St. Botolph Aldgate Gazetteer. Holy Trinity Minories (Abbey of St. Clare, 1293/4–1539)." In *Historical Gazetteer of London before the Great Fire*. Ed. Derek Keene. London: Centre for Metropolitan History, 1987. Unpub. typescript available in the Institute of Historical Research, University of London.

Clement IV, Pope. *Epistole et dictamina Clementis pape quarti*. Ed. Matthias Thumser. Available at http://userpage.fu-berlin.de/~sekrethu/clemens/index.htm [seen July 13, 2010].

Kleineke, Hannes. "William FitzStephen's 'Description of London': A New Edition." M.A. dissertation, Royal Holloway and Bedford New College, University of London, 1994.

Munro, John H. A. "Industrial Change in the Fifteenth- and Sixteenth-Century Low Countries: The Arrival of Spanish Merino Wools and the Expansion of the '*Nouvelles Draperies*.'" Working Paper No. 18. July 17, 2002. Available at http://www.chass.utoronto.ca/ecipa/archive/UT-ECIPA-MUNRO-02–03.pdf [seen October 31, 2007].

REFERENCE WORKS

Barnes, Patricia. *PRO Lists and Indexes, No. XV: List of Ancient Correspondence of the Chancery and Exchequer*. Revised edition. New York: Kraus Reprint, 1968. With two-volume index in *Lists and Indexes, Supplementary Series, No. 15, Index to Ancient Correspondence of the Chancery and Exchequer*. New York: Kraus Reprint, 1969.

[Bodleian Library.] *A Summary Catalogue of Western Manuscripts in the Bodleian Library at Oxford*. 7 vols. in 9. Oxford: Clarendon, 1895–1953.

British Library. *Catalogue of Additional Manuscripts*. Available at http://www.bl.uk/catalogues/manuscripts/INDX0095.ASP?Type = D.

Cheney, Christopher R., ed. *A Handbook of Dates for Students of British History*. New edition, revised by Michael Jones. Royal Historical Society Guides and Handbooks, no. 4. Cambridge: Cambridge University Press, 2000.

Cokayne, George Edward. *The Complete Peerage of England, Scotland, Ireland and Great Britain*. New edition, ed. Vicary Gibbs. 13 vols. in 14. London: St. Catherine Press, 1910–59.

Dictionary of Medieval Latin from British Sources. Prepared by Ronald E. Latham and David R. Howlett, under the direction of a committee appointed by the British Academy. In progress. Oxford: Oxford University Press, for the British Academy, 1975– .

Fryde, Edmund Boleslaw, Diana E. Greenway, S. Porter, and Ian Roy, eds. *Handbook of British Chronology*. Royal Historical Society, Guides and Handbooks, 2. 3rd ed., London, 1986.

Harvey, Paul D. A., and Andrew McGuinness. *A Guide to British Medieval Seals.* London: British Library and Public Record Office, 1996.

Hughes, A. *List of Sheriffs for England and Wales from the Earliest Times to A.D. 1831.* Public Record Office, London, Lists and Indexes, 9 (1898). Rpt. with additions, New York: Kraus Reprint, 1963.

James, Montague Rhodes. *A Descriptive Catalogue of the Manuscripts in the Library of Corpus Christi College, Cambridge.* 2 vols. Cambridge: Cambridge University Press, 1912.

———. *A Descriptive Catalogue of the Manuscripts in the Library of Gonville and Caius College, Cambridge.* 2 vols. Cambridge: Cambridge University Press, 1907–8.

Jenkinson, Hilary. *A Guide to Seals in the Public Record Office.* London: H. M. Stationery Office, 1968.

Latham, Ronald E. *Revised Medieval Latin Word-List from British and Irish Sources.* London: Oxford University Press, for the British Academy, 1965.

London Museum. *Medieval Catalogue.* London: H. M. Stationery Office, 1940.

Matthew, Henry Colin Gray, and Brian Howard Harrison, eds. *Oxford Dictionary of National Biography.* Oxford: Oxford University Press, 2004 (printed edition); 2004– (online edition).

Metcalf, D. M. *Sylloge of Coins of the British Isles,* 12, *Ashmolean Museum Oxford,* Part 2, *English Coins, 1066–1279.* London: Oxford University Press, for the British Academy, 1969.

Pearce, Ernest Harold [Bishop of Worcester]. *The Monks of Westminster. Being a Register of the Brethren of the Convent from the Time of the Confessor to the Dissolution, with Lists of the Obedientiaries and an Introduction.* Cambridge: Cambridge University Press, 1916.

Robinson, Pamela R. *Catalogue of Dated and Datable Manuscripts c. 737–1600 in Cambridge Libraries.* 2 vols. Cambridge, 1988.

Strayer, Joseph R., ed. *Dictionary of the Middle Ages.* 13 vols. New York: Charles Scribner's Sons, 1982–89.

Worstbrock, Franz Josef, Monika Klaes, and Jutta Lütten, eds. *Repertorium der Artes Dictandi des Mittelalters,* vol. 1, *Von den Anfängen bis um 1200.* München: Wilhelm Fink Verlag, 1992.

Zupko, Ronald Edward. *A Dictionary of English Weights and Measures, from Anglo-Saxon Times to the Nineteenth Century.* Madison: University of Wisconsin Press, 1968.

———. *A Dictionary of Weights and Measures for the British Isles: The Middle Ages to the Twentieth Century.* Philadelphia: American Philosophical Society, 1985.

———. "Weights and Measures, Western European." In *Dictionary of the Middle Ages,* ed. Joseph E. Strayer, vol. 12. New York: Charles Scribner's Sons, 1982–99, 582–91.

PRIMARY SOURCES

Alexander of Paris. *The Medieval French "Roman d'Alexandre,"* vol. 7, *Version of Alexandre de Paris: Variants and Notes to Branch IV.* Ed. Bateman Edwards and

Alfred Foulet. Elliott Monographs, 41. Princeton, N.J.: Princeton University Press, 1955.

Auvray, Lucien. "Documents Orléanais du xiie et du xiiie siècle extraits du formulaire de Bernard de Meung," *Mémoires de la Société archéologique et historique de l'Orléanais*, 23 (1892), 393–413.

Bailey, Mark, trans. and ed. *The English Manor c. 1200–c. 1500.* Manchester: Manchester University Press, 2002.

Barraclough, Geoffrey, ed. *The Charters of the Anglo-Norman Earls of Chester.* Record Society of Lancashire and Cheshire, 126 (1988).

Bartholomæus Anglicus. *On the Properties of Things: John Trevisa's Translation of Bartholomæus Anglicus, De Proprietatibus Rerum. A Critical Text.* Ed. Michael Charles Seymour et al. 3 vols. Oxford: Clarendon, 1975–88.

Bates, David, ed. *Regesta Regum Anglo-Normannorum: The Acta of William I (1066–1087).* Oxford: Clarendon, 1998.

Bernard of Clairvaux. *The Letters of Bernard of Clairvaux.* Trans. B. S. James. Stroud, Gloucestershire: Sutton, 1998.

Besalú, Raimon Vidal de. *"Abril issi'e."* In *Nouvelles occitanes du moyen age.* Ed. and trans. Jean-Charles Huchet. Paris: Flammarion, 1992, 38–139.

Bibbesworth, Walter de. *Le Tretiz.* Ed. William Rothwell. Anglo-Norman Text Society, Plain Texts Series, 6. London, 1990.

Blaauw, W. H. "Letters to Ralph Neville," *Sussex Archaeological Collections*, 3 (1850), 35–76.

Bodel, Jean. *Le jeu de saint Nicolas.* In *French Medieval Plays.* Trans. Richard Axton and John Stevens. Oxford: Basil Blackwell, 1971.

———. *Le jeu de saint Nicolas de Jehan Bodel.* Ed. and trans. Albert Henry. Université Libre de Bruxelles, Travaux de la Faculté de Philosophie et Lettres, Tome XXI. Brussels: Presses Universitaires de Bruxelles, and Paris: Presses Universitaires de France, 1962.

Born, Bertran de. *Poésies complètes de Bertran de Born.* Ed. André Antoine Thomas. Bibliothèque meridionale, première ser., 1. Toulouse, 1888.

Brandin, Louis, ed. *La Chanson d'Aspremont, chanson de geste du XIIe siècle. Texte du manuscrit de Wollaton Hall.* 2 vols. Classiques français du moyen âge, 19, 25. Paris: Champion, 1919–21.

Busby, Keith, ed. *Le Roman des Eles.* Amsterdam: John Benjamins Publishing, 1983.

Caenegem, Raoul C. van, ed. *English Lawsuits from William I to Richard I*, vol. 2, *Henry II and Richard I.* Selden Society, 107. London, 1991.

Calendar of Inquisitions Miscellaneous Preserved in the Public Record Office. 8 vols. London: H. M. Stationery Office, 1916–2003.

Calendar of the Patent Rolls Preserved in the Public Record Office: Henry III. 6 vols. London: H. M. Stationery Office, 1901–13.

Catullus. *The Poems of Catullus: A Bilingual Edition.* Translated, with commentary by Peter Green. Berkeley: University of California Press, 2005.

Châtillon, Walter de. *The Alexandreis: A Twelfth-Century Epic.* Trans. David Townsend. Peterborough, Ontario: Broadview, 2007.

Cheney, Christopher R. "Letters of William Wickwane, Chancellor of York, 1266–1268," *EHR*, 47 (1932), 626–42.

Chew, Helena M., and William Kellaway, eds. *London Assize of Nuisance, 1301–1431: A Calendar*, vol. 10. London Record Society, 1973.

Church, Stephen D., ed. and trans. *Constitutio Domus Regis: Disposition of the King's Household*. Oxford: Clarendon, 2007.

Close Rolls of the Reign of Henry III, 14 vols. London: H. M. Stationery Office, 1902–38.

Colvin, Howard M., ed. *Building Accounts of King Henry III*. Oxford: Clarendon, 1971.

Corpus juris canonici emendatum et notis illustratum, Gregorii XIII. pont. max. iussu editum. 3 parts in 4 vols. Rome: In aedibus Populi Romani, 1582. Available in an electronic edition at UCLA Digital Library Program, *Corpus Juris Canonici* (1582), http://digital.library.ucla.edu/canonlaw [seen July 7, 2009].

Coss, Peter R., ed. *The Langley Cartulary*. Dugdale Society, 32 (Stratford-upon-Avon, 1980).

Crawford, Anne, ed. *Letters of the Queens of England, 1100–1547*. Stroud, Gloucestershire: Sutton, 1994, rpt. 1997.

Curia Regis Rolls Preserved in the Public Record Office. 20 vols. London: H. M. Stationery Office, 1922–2007.

d'Andeli, Henri. *Les Dits d'Henri d'Andeli*. Ed. Alain Corbellari. Classiques français du Moyen Âge, 146. Paris: Champion, 2003.

Daniel of Beccles. *Urbanus Magnus Danielis Becclesiensis*. Ed. Josiah Gilbart Smyly. Dublin: Hodges, Figgis & Co., 1939.

Delisle, Léopold. *Notice sur une Summa Dictaminis jadis conservée à Beauvais*. Paris: Imprimerie nationale, 1898, 171–205.

Diceto, Ralph de. *Radulfi de Diceto decani Lundoniensis opera historica*. Ed. William Stubbs. 2 vols. Rolls Series, 68. London: Longman, 1876.

Douglas, David C., and George W. Greenaway, eds. *English Historical Documents, II, 1042–1189*. London: Eyre and Spottiswoode, 1953.

Elvey, Gerald Ranking, ed. *Luffield Priory Charters*. 2 vols. Northamptonshire Record Society, 22, 26 (Northampton, 1968–75).

Fantosme, Jordan. *Jordan Fantosme's Chronicle*. Ed. and trans. Ronald C. Johnston. Oxford: Clarendon, 1981.

Farley, Abraham, et al., eds. *Domesday Book seu Liber Censualis Willelmi primi regis Angli;ae*. 4 vols. London: Record Commission, 1783–1816.

Farrer, William, and Charles T. Clay, eds. *Early Yorkshire Charters*. 10 vols. Yorkshire Archaeological Society. Leeds, 1914–65.

Frederick II, Emperor of Germany. *The Art of Falconry, Being the* De arte venandi cum avibus *of Frederick II of Hohenstaufen*. Trans. and ed. Casey A. Wood and F. Marjorie Fyfe. Stanford, Calif.: Stanford University Press, and London: Oxford University Press, 1943.

Fulcher of Chartres. *A History of the Expedition to Jerusalem, 1095–1107*. Trans. Frances Rita Ryan; ed. Harold S. Fink. Knoxville: University of Tennessee Press, 1969.

Furnivall, Frederick J., ed. *The Babees Book*. Early English Text Society, original ser., 32, 1868.

Gaimar, Geoffrey. *L'Estoire des Engleis*. Ed. Alexander Bell. 3 vols. Anglo-Norman Text Society, 14–16 (1960).

Geoffrey of Monmouth. *The Historia Regum Britanniae of Geoffrey of Monmouth*, vol. 1, *Bern, Burgerbibliotehek, MS 568*. Ed. Neil Wright. Cambridge: D. S. Brewer, 1984.

Gerald of Wales. *De rebus a se gestis*; *Itinerarium Kambriae*; and *Speculum Ecclesiae*. In *Giraldi Cambrensis Opera*. Ed. John Sherren Brewer, James Francis Dimock, and George F. Warner. 8 vols. Rolls Series, 21. London: Longman, 1861–91.

———. *The Autobiography of Gerald of Wales*. Ed. and trans. Harold Edgeworth Butler. London: Cape, 1937; rpt. Woodbridge, Suffolk: Boydell, 2005.

Gervase of Canterbury. *The Historical Works of Gervase of Canterbury*. Ed. William Stubbs. 2 vols. Rolls Series, 73. London: Longman, 1879–80.

Giuseppi, Montague Spencer. "The Wardrobe and Household Accounts of Bogo de Clare, A.D. 1284–6," *Archaeologia*, 70 (1918–20), 1–56.

Goscelin of Canterbury. *Historia translationis sancti Augustini episcopi*. In Jacques-Paul Migne, ed. *Patrologiae cursus completus: series Latina*. 221 vols. Paris: Garnier, 1844–64, vol. 155.

Gransden, Antonia, ed. *The Letter Book of William of Hoo*. Suffolk Record Society, 5 (1963).

Grosseteste, Robert. *Roberti Grosseteste quondam episcopi Lincolniensis epistolae*. Ed. Henry Richards Luard. Rolls Series, 26. London: Longman, 1861.

Guillaume de Lorris and Jean de Meun. *The Romance of the Rose*. Trans. Harry W. Robbins, ed. Charles W. Dunn. New York: E. P. Dutton, 1962.

Guy, John A., and H. G. Beale, eds. *Law and Social Change in British History*. Royal Historical Society Studies in History, 40 (London, 1984).

Gysseling, Maurits. *Corpus van Middelnederlandse Teksten (tot en met het jaar 1300)*, series 2, vol. 1. The Hague: Nijhoff, 1977.

Hall, George Derek Gordon, ed. *The Treatise on the Laws and Customs of the Realm of England Commonly Called Glanvill*. London: Thomas Nelson & Son, 1965.

Hardy, Thomas Duffus, ed. *Rotuli de oblatis et finibus in Turri Londinensi asservati*. London: Record Commission, 1835.

———, ed. *Rotuli litterarum clausarum*, vol. 1, *1204–1224*. London: Record Commission, 1833.

———, ed. *Rotuli litterarum patentium in Turri londinensi asservati*, vol. 1, pt. 1. London: Record Commission, 1835.

Hassall, William Owen, ed. *Cartulary of St. Mary Clerkenwell*. Camden Third Series, 71. London: Royal Historical Society, 1949.

Hathaway, Ernest Jackson, et al., eds. *Fouke le Fitz Waryn*. Anglo-Norman Text Society, 26–28 (1975, for 1968–70).

[Henri de Laon.] A. Långfors. "Le dit des hérauts par Henri de Laon," *Romania*, 44 (1914), 216–25.

Hill, Rosalind, ed. *Ecclesiastical Letter Books of the Thirteenth Century*. Oxford: privately printed, 1936.

Holden, Anthony J., and David Crouch, eds.; Stewart Gregory, trans. *History of William Marshal*. 3 vols. Anglo-Norman Text Society, Occasional Publications Series, 4–6. London, 2002–7.

Iker-Gittleman, Anne, ed. *Garin le Loherenc*. 3 vols. Classiques français du moyen âge, 117–19. Paris: Champion, 1996–97.

Illingworth, William, ed. *Rotuli Hundredorum*. 2 vols. London: Record Commission, 1812–18.

Jakemes. *Le Roman du Castelain de Couci et de la Dame de Fayel*. Ed. Maurice Delbouille. Paris: Société des anciens texts français, 1936.

Jean le Fèvre. *Les Lamentations de Matheolus et le Livre de Leesce*. Ed. Anton-Gérard van Hamel. 2 vols. Bibliothèque de l'École des Hautes Études, Sciences philologiques et historiques, fasc. 95–96. Paris, 1892–1905.

Joinville, Jean, sieur de. *Vie de Saint Louis*. Ed. and trans. Jacques Monfrin. Paris: Classiques Garnier, 1995; 2nd ed., 1998.

Jones, Thomas, ed. *Brut y Tywysogyon; or, The Chronicle of the Princes. Red Book of Hergest Version*. Cardiff: University of Wales Press, 1955.

Joscelin of Brakelond. *The Chronicle of Joscelin of Brakelond*. Ed. H. E. Butler. London: Nelson, 1949.

Justinian, Emperor. *Digesta Iustiniani augusti*. Ed. Theodor Mommsen, with Paul Krueger. Berlin: Weidmann, 1870.

Kay, Sarah, ed. and trans. *Raoul de Cambrai*. Oxford: Clarendon, 1996.

Kemp, Brian Robert, ed. *Twelfth-Century Archidiaconal and Vice-Archidiaconal Acta*. Canterbury and York Society, 92. London, 2001.

Langlois, Ernest, ed. *Le Couronnement de Louis*. Classiques français du moyen âge, 22. Paris: Champion, 1984.

Lee, Geoffrey Alan. "The Oldest European Account Book: A Florentine Bank Ledger of 1211." In *Accounting History: Some British Contributions*. Ed. Robert Henry Parker and Basil S. Yamey. Oxford: Clarendon, 1994, 160–96.

Lodge, R. Anthony, ed. *Le Livre des manières*. Geneva: Droz, 1979.

Loey, Alphonse van. *Middelnederlands Leerboek*. Antwerp: De Sikkel, 1947.

Logan, F. Donald. "An Early Thirteenth-Century Papal Judge-Delegate Formulary of English Origin," *Studia Gratiana*, 14, Collectanea Stephan Kuttner, vol. 4. Bologna, 1967, 73–87.

Map, Walter. *De Nugis Curialium*. Ed. and trans. Montague Rhodes James, Christopher N. L. Brooke and Roger A. B. Mynors. Oxford: Oxford University Press, 1983.

Marsan, Arnaut-Guilhem de. *L'Ensenhamen d'Arnaut-Guilhem de Marsan, ou, Code du parfait chevalier*. Ed. Jacques de Cauna, with French trans. by Gérard Gouiran. Mounenh-en-Biarn [Monein]: Pyrémonde, 2007.

Marsh, Adam. *Adae de Marisco Epistolae*. In *Monumenta Franciscana*. Ed. John Sherren Brewer. 2 vols. Rolls Series, 4. London: Longman, 1858–82.

Mason, Emma, ed. *The Beauchamp Cartulary*. Pipe Roll Society, new ser., 44. London, 1980.

Mews, Constant J. *The Lost Letters of Heloise and Abelard: Perceptions of Dialogue in Twelfth-Century France*. With a translation by Neville Chiavaroli and Constant J. Mews. New York: St. Martin's Press, 1999.

Michel, Francisque, ed. *Histoire des ducs de Normandie et des rois d'Angleterre*. Paris: Société de l'histoire de France, 1840.

Migne, Jacques-Paul, ed. *Patrologiae cursus completus: series Latina*. 221 vols. Paris: Garnier, 1844–64.

Mooney, Linne R. "Diet and Bloodletting: A Monthly Regimen." In *Popular and Practical Science of Medieval England*. Ed. Lister M. Matheson. East Lansing, Mich.: Colleagues Press, 1994, 245–61.

Mora-Lebrun, Francine, ed. *Le Roman de Thèbes*. Paris: Lettres Gothiques, 1995.

Mullally, Evelyn, ed. and trans. *La Geste des Engleis en Yrlande*. Dublin: Four Courts Press, 2002.

Munro, Dana Carlton, ed. and trans. *Translations and Reprints from the Original Sources of European History*, vol. 1. Philadelphia: Department of History of the University of Pennsylvania, 1900.

Neckam, Alexander. *De naturis rerum*. Ed. Thomas Wright. Rolls Series, 34. London: Longman, 1863.

Nichols, John, ed. *A Collection of All the Wills, Now Known to Be Extant, of the Kings and Queens of England, Princes and Princesses of Wales, and Every Branch of the Blood Royal, from the Reign of William the Conqueror, to That of Henry the Seventh Exclusive*. London: J. Nichols, 1780.

O'Brien, Bruce R. *God's Peace and King's Peace: The Laws of Edward the Confessor*. Philadelphia: Pennsylvania University Press, 1999.

Orderic Vitalis. *The Ecclesiastical History of Orderic Vitalis*. Ed. and trans. Marjorie Chibnall. 6 vols. Oxford: Clarendon, 1968–80.

Oschinsky, Dorothea. *Walter of Henley and Other Treatises on Estate Management and Accounting*. Oxford: Clarendon, 1971.

Ovid. *Heroides and Amores*. Trans. Grant Showerman. Cambridge, Mass.: Harvard University Press, and London: William Heinemann, 1914, rpt. 1958.

———. *The Poems of Exile: Tristia and the Black Sea Letters*. Trans. Peter Green. Berkeley: University of California Press, 2005.

———. *P. Ovidi Nasonis De Arte Amatoria Libri Tres*. Ed. Paul Brandt. Hildesheim: Georg Olms, 1963.

———. *P. Ovidi Nasonis Tristium libri quinque; Ibis; Ex ponto libri quattuor; Halieutica fragmenta*. Ed. S. G. Owen. Oxford: Clarendon, 1915, rpt. 1946.

Palgrave, Francis, ed. *The Parliamentary Writs and Writs of Military Summons*. 2 vols. in 4. London: Records Commission, 1827–34.

Paris, Matthew. *Matthæi Parisiensis, monachi Sancti Albani, Chronica Majora*. Ed. Henry Richards Luard. 7 vols. Rolls Series, 57. London: Longman, 1872–83.

———. *Matthæi Parisiensis, monachi Sancti Albani, Historia Anglorum, sive, ut vulgo dicitur, Historia Minor; item, ejusdem abbreviatio chronicorum Angli;ae*. Ed. Sir Frederic Madden. 3 vols. Rolls Series, 44. London, 1866–69.

————. *Matthew Paris's English History*. Trans. J. A. Giles, 3 vols. London: H. G. Bohn, 1852–54.

Patterson, Robert B., ed. *Earldom of Gloucester Charters: The Charters and Scribes of the Earls and Countesses of Gloucester to A.D. 1217*. Oxford: Clarendon, 1973.

Petronius. *The Satyricon*. Trans. Alfred R. Allinson. New York: Panurge, 1930.

Phillimore, William P. W., ed. *Rotuli Hugonis de Welles episcopi Lincolniensis*. 2 vols. Lincoln Record Society, 3 and 6. Lincoln, 1912–13.

Pipe Rolls. Publications of the Pipe Roll Society (1884–).

Pliny the Younger. *Epistularum libri novem; Epistularum ad Traianum liber panegyricus*. Ed. R. C. Kukula. Leipzig: Teubner, 1908.

Potter, Kenneth R., and Ralph Henry Carless Davis, ed. and trans. *Gesta Stephani*. Oxford: Oxford University Press, 1976.

Powicke, Frederic Maurice, and Christopher R. Cheney, eds. *Councils and Synods, with Other Documents Relating to the English Church*, vol. 2, *A.D. 1205–1313*. Oxford: Clarendon, 1964.

Pryce, Huw, ed. *The Acts of the Welsh Rulers, 1120–1283*. Cardiff: University of Wales Press, 2005.

Radice, Betty, trans. *The Letters of Abelard and Heloise*. Harmondsworth, Middlesex: Penguin Books, 1974.

Ralph Niger. *De re militari et triplici via peregrinationis Ierosolimitane*. Ed. Ludwig Schmugge. Berlin: Gruyter, 1977.

Richardson, Henry Gerald, and George Osborne Sayles, eds. and trans. *Fleta*. Vols. 2–4 (vol. 1 never published). Selden Society, 72, 89, 99 (1955–84, for the years 1953, 1972, 1983).

Rickert, Edith. *The Babees' Book: Medieval Manners for the Young: Done into Modern English From Dr. Furnivall's Texts*. London: Chatto and Windus, New York: Duffield and Co., 1908.

Riley, Henry Thomas, ed. *Liber Custumarum*. In *Munimenta Gildhallae Londoniensis: Liber Albus, Liber Custumarum, et Liber Horn*. 3 vols. in 4. Rolls Series, 12. London: Longman, 1859–62 vol. 2 (parts 1–2).

————, ed. *Memorials of London and London Life in the XIIIth, XIVth, and XVth Centuries*. London: Longman, 1868.

Rio, Alice, ed. *The Formularies of Angers and Marculf: Two Merovingian Legal Handbooks*. Liverpool: Liverpool University Press, 2008.

Robathan, Dorothy M. *The Pseudo-Ovidian De Vetula*. Amsterdam: Adolf M. Hakkert, 1968.

Robertson, James Craigie, and Joseph Brigstocke Sheppard, eds. *Materials for the History of Thomas Becket*. 7 vols. Rolls Series, no. 67. London: Longman, 1872–85.

Rodes, Robert E., Jr. *Ecclesiastical Administration in Medieval England, the Anglo-Saxons to the Reformation*. Notre Dame, Ind.: Notre Dame University Press, 1977.

Roger of Wendover. *Flores Historiarum*. Ed. Henry G. Hewlett. 3 vols. Rolls Series, 84. London: Eyre and Spottiswood, 1886–89.

Roteland, Hue de. *Protheselaus*. Ed. A. J. Holden. 3 vols. Anglo-Norman Text Society, 47–49. London, 1989–93.

Rothwell, Harry, ed. *English Historical Documents, III, 1189–1327.* London: Eyre and Spottiswoode, 1975.

Russell, John. *The Book of Nurture (c. 1460).* In Frederick J. Furnivall, ed., *The Babees Book,* Early English Text Society, original ser., 32 (1868), 115–239.

Rymer, Thomas. *Fœdera conventiones litteræ et acta publica.* Ed. Adam Clarke and Frederick Holbrooke. 4 vols. in 7. London: Record Commission, 1816–69.

Salter, Herbert Edward, William Abel Pantin, and Henry Gerald Richardson, eds. *Formularies Which Bear on the History of Oxford, c. 1204–1420.* 2 vols. Oxford Historical Society, 1942.

Sayers, Jane E. "A Judge Delegate Formulary from Canterbury." In eadem, *Law and Records in Medieval England: Studies on the Medieval Papacy, Monasteries and Records.* London: Variorum, 1988, 198–211.

Seneca. *L. Annaei Senecae: Ad Lucilium Epistulae Morales.* Ed. L. D. Reynolds. 2 vols. Oxford: Oxford University Press, 1965.

———. *Selected Essays of Seneca, and the Satire on the Deification of Claudius.* Ed. Allan P. Ball. New York: Macmillan, 1908.

Shirley, Walter W., ed. *Royal and Other Historical Letters Illustrative of the Reign of Henry III. from the Originals in the Public Record Office.* 2 vols. Rolls Series, 27. London: Longman, 1862–66.

Smith, David M., ed. *English Episcopal Acta IV: Lincoln 1186–1206.* London: Oxford University Press, for the British Academy, 1986.

———. *The Acta of Hugh of Wells, Bishop of Lincoln, 1209–1235.* Lincoln Record Society, 88. Lincoln, 2000.

[Society of Antiquaries.] *A Collection of Ordinances and Regulations for the Government of the Royal Household.* London: Society of Antiquaries, 1790.

Stenton, Doris Mary, ed. *Pleas Before the King or His Justices, 1198–1202.* 4 vols. Selden Society, 67, 68, 83, 84. London, 1948–67.

Stevens, John. *The Later Cambridge Songs: An English Song Collection of the Twelfth Century.* Oxford: Oxford University Press, 2005.

Stubbs, William, ed. *Gesta Henrici Secundi.* Rolls Series, 2 vols. London: Longman, 1867.

———. *Select Charters and Other Illustrations of English Constitutional History.* Ed. Henry William Carless Davis. 9th ed. Oxford: Oxford University Press, 1913.

Sylvester, David William, comp. *Educational Documents, 1: England and Wales, 800–1816.* London: Methuen, 1970.

Taylor, Arnold J., ed. *Records of the Barony and Honour of the Rape of Lewes.* Sussex Record Society, 44 (1939).

Terence. *The Eunuch.* Ed. and trans. A. J. Brothers. Warminster, Wiltshire: Aris and Phillips, 2000.

Thomas of Chobham. *Summa Confessorum.* Ed. F. Broomfield. *Analecta Mediaevalia Namurcensia,* 25. Louvain, 1968.

Thomas of Kent. *Le Roman de toute chevalerie.* Ed. Brian Foster. 2 vols. Anglo-Norman Text Society, 29 and 33. London, 1976–77.

Thompson, Edward Maunde, ed. *Customary of the Benedictine Monastery of St. Peter, Westminster.* Henry Bradshaw Society, 28 (1904), 1–247.

Timson, Reginald Thomas, ed. *Blyth Priory Cartulary*. 2 vols. Thoroton Society, 27, 28. Nottingham, 1973.

Torigny, Robert de. *Chronica*, in *Chronicles of the Reigns of Stephen, Henry II and Richard I*, ed. Richard Howlett, Rolls Series, 4 vols. London: Longman, 1886–89.

Transmundus. *Introductiones dictandi*. Ed. and trans. Anne Dalzell. Studies and Texts, 123. Toronto: Pontifical Institute of Medieval Studies, 1995.

Treharne, Reginald F., and Ivor J. Sanders, eds. *Documents of the Baronial Movement of Reform and Rebellion, 1258–1267*. Oxford: Oxford University Press, 1973.

Troyes, Chrétien de. *Erec et Enide*. Ed. Mario Roques, Classiques français du moyen âge, 80. Paris: Champion, 1952.

Tuczek, Suzanne. *Die Kampanische Briefsammlung (Paris Lat. 11867). Monumenta Germaniae Historica: Briefe des späteren Mittelalters*. Hanover: Hahnsche Buchhandlung, 2010.

Türlin, Heinrich von dem. *Diu Crône von Heinrich von dem Türlin*. Ed. Gottlob Heinrich Friedrich Scholl. Stuttgart, 1852.

———. *The Crown: A Tale of Sir Gawein and King Arthur's Court by Heinrich von dem Türlin*. Trans. J. W. Thomas. Lincoln: University of Nebraska Press, 1989.

Turner, George James, ed. *Select Pleas of the Forest*. Selden Society, 13. London, 1899.

Turner, Thomas Hudson, ed. *Manners and Household Expenses of England in the Thirteenth and Fifteenth Centuries*. Roxburghe Club Publications, no. 57. London, 1841.

———. "Original Documents," *Archaeological Journal*, 4 (1847), 142–44.

Varro. *Rerum Rusticarum*. In *Marcus Porcius Cato, On Agriculture; Marcus Terentius Varro, On Agriculture*. Trans. William Davis Hooper, revised by Harrison Boyd Ash. Cambridge, Mass.: Harvard University Press, and London: William Heinemann, 1935, rpt. 1960.

Virgil. *The Georgics*. Trans. Lancelot Patrick Wilkinson. Harmondsworth, Middlesex: Penguin, 1982.

Vitry, Jacques de. *The Exempla, or Illustrative Stories from the Sermones Vulgares of Jacques de Vitry*. Ed. Thomas Frederick Crane. London: Folk Lore Society, 1890; rpt. New York: Burt Franklin, 1971.

Wace. *Wace's Roman de Brut: A History of the British, Text and Translation*. Ed. and trans. Judith Weiss. Exeter: University of Exeter Press, 1999.

———. *Le Roman de Rou*. Ed. Anthony J. Holden. 3 vols. Paris: Société des anciens textes français, 1970–73.

Wahlgren, Lena. *The Letter Collections of Peter of Blois: Studies in the Manuscript Tradition*. Studia Graeca et Latina Gothoburgensia, 58. [Göteborg, Sweden:] Acta Universitatis Gothoburgensis, 1993.

Waitz, Georg. [Transcription of BL, Add. MS 8167, fols. 88r–90v.] *Neues Archiv*, 4 (1879), 339–43.

Woolgar, Christopher M., ed. *Household Accounts from Medieval England*. 2 vols. British Academy, Records of Social and Economic History, new series, 17–18. Oxford: Oxford University Press, for the British Academy, 1992–93.

Zeumer, Carl, ed. *Formulae Merowingici et Karolini aevi*. Monumenta Germaniae Historica, Legum v. Hanover, 1886.

SECONDARY SOURCES

Adamson, Melitta Weiss. *Medieval Dietetics: Food and Drink in Regimen Sanitatis Literature from 800 to 1400*. German Studies in Canada, 5. Frankfurt am Main: Peter Lang, 1995.

Aird, William. *Robert Curthose, Duke of Normandy*. Woodbridge, Suffolk: Boydell, 2008.

Alexander, Jonathan, and Paul Binski, eds. *Age of Chivalry: Art in Plantagenet England, 1200–1400*. London: Royal Academy of Arts, 1987.

Allen, Martin. *Mints and Money in Medieval England*. Cambridge: Cambridge University Press, 2012.

———. "The English Currency and the Commercialization of England Before the Black Death." In *Medieval Money Matters*. Ed. Diana Wood. Oxford: Oxbow Books, 2004, 31–50.

Almond, Richard. *Medieval Hunting*. Stroud, Gloucestershire: Sutton, 2003.

Armstrong, Lawrin, Ivana Elbl, and Martin M. Elbl, eds. *Money, Markets and Trade in Late Medieval Europe: Essays in Honour of John H. A. Munro*. Leiden: Brill, 2007.

Aston, Michael, ed. *Medieval Fish, Fisheries and Fishponds in England*. 2 vols. B[ritish] A[rchaeological] R[eports] British Series, 182 (1988).

Aurell, Martin. *The Plantagenet Empire, 1154–1224*. Trans. David Crouch. Harlow, Essex: Pearson Longman, 2007.

———, ed. *La Cour Plantagenêt (1154–1204)*. Poitiers: Centre d'Etudes Supérieures de Civilisation Médiévale, 2000.

———. *Le Chevalier lettré: savoir et conduite de l'aristocratie aux XIIe ᵉ et XIIIe siècles*. Paris: Fayard, 2011.

Ayton, Andrew C. *Knights and Warhorses: Military Service and the English Aristocracy Under Edward III*. Woodbridge, Suffolk: Boydell & Brewer, 1994.

Bammesberger, Alfred, ed. *Problems of Old English Lexicography: Studies in Memory of Angus Cameron*. Regensburg: Pustet, 1985.

Barker, Juliet R. V. *The Tournament in England, 1100–1400*. Woodbridge, Suffolk: Boydell & Brewer, 1986.

Barlow, Frank. *William Rufus*. London: Eyre Methuen, 1983.

Barnes, Patricia M. "The Anstey Case." In *A Medieval Miscellany for Doris Mary Stenton*. Ed. Patricia M. Barnes and Cecil F. Slade. Pipe Roll Society, new ser., 36. London, 1962, for 1960, 1–24.

Barrow, Julia. "Grades of Ordination and Clerical Careers, *c.* 900–*c.* 1200." In *Anglo-Norman Studies*, 30. Ed. Christopher P. Lewis. Woodbridge, Suffolk: Boydell, 2008, 41–61.

Bartlett, Robert. *England under the Norman and Angevin Kings, 1075–1225*. Oxford: Clarendon, 2000.

———. "'Mortal Enmities': The Legal Aspect of Hostility in the Middle Ages." In *Feud, Violence and Practice: Essays in Medieval Studies in Honor of Stephen D. White*. Ed. Belle S. Tuten and Tracey L. Billado. Farnham, Surrey: Ashgate, 2010, 197–212.

Batany, Jean. "Un Drôle de métier: le 'Status conjugatorum.'" In *Femmes, mariages-lignages: XIIe–XVIe siècles: mélanges offerts à Georges Duby*. Ed. Jean Dufournet, André Joris, and Pierre Toubert. Bibliothèque du Moyen Âge, 1. Brussels: De Boeck Université, 1992.

Bautier, Anne-Marie. "Contribution à l'histoire du cheval au moyen âge," *Bulletin philologique et historique* (Paris, 1978, for 1976), 209–49.

Bazeley, Margaret. "The Extent of the English Forest in the Thirteenth Century," *Transactions of the Royal Historical Society*, 4th ser., vol. 4 (1921), 140–72.

Bean, John Malcolm William. *From Lord to Patron: Lordship in Late Medieval England*. Manchester: Manchester University Press, 1989.

Bearman, Robert, ed. *Charters of the Redvers Family and the Earldom of Devon, 1090–1217*. Devon and Cornwall Record Society, new ser., 37. Exeter, 1994.

Bellhouse, D. R. "*De Vetula*: A Medieval Manuscript Containing Probability Calculations," *International Statistical Review*, 68, no. 2 (August 2000), 123–36.

Bennett, Adelaide. "The Windmill Psalter: The Historiated Letter E of Psalm One," *Journal of the Warburg and Courtauld Institutes*, 43 (1980), 52–67.

Bennett, Henry Stanley. *Life on the English Manor*. Cambridge: Cambridge University Press, 1937.

Bennett, Matthew. "The Medieval Warhorse Reconsidered." In *Medieval Knighthood V: Papers from the Sixth Strawberry Hill Conference, 1994*. Ed. Ruth E. Harvey and Stephen Church. Woodbridge, Suffolk: Boydell, 1995, 19–40.

Berlow, Rosalind Kent. "Wine and Winemaking." In *Dictionary of the Middle Ages*. Ed. Joseph R. Strayer. Vol. 12. New York: Charles Scribner's Sons, 1982–89, 648–54.

Birrell, Jean. "Who Poached the King's Deer? A Study in Thirteenth-Century Crime," *Midland History*, 7 (1981), 9–25.

Blake, Ernest O., ed. *Liber Eliensis*. Camden Society, 3rd ser., 92. London, 1962.

Blumenfeld-Kosinski, Renate. "Jean le Fèvre's *Livre de Leesce*: Praise or Blame of Women?," *Speculum*, 69 (1994), 705–25.

Bolton, James L. "Inflation, Economics and Politics in Thirteenth-Century England." In *Thirteenth Century England IV: Proceedings of the Newcastle Upon Tyne Conference, 1991*. Ed. Peter R. Coss and Simon D. Lloyd. Woodbridge, Suffolk: Boydell, 1992, 1–14.

Bond, C. J. "Monastic Fisheries." In *Medieval Fish, Fisheries and Fishponds in England*. Vol. 1. B[ritish] A[rchaeological] R[eports] British Series 182 (1988), 69–112.

Bonnier, Charles. "List of English Towns in the Twelfth Century," *EHR*, 16 (1901), 501–3.

Borthwick, E. Kerr. "'The Wise Man and the Bow' in Aristides Quintilianus," *Classical Quarterly*, new series, 41, no. 1 (1991), 275–78.

Boyle, Leonard E., O.P. "Canon Law Before 1380." In *The History of the University of Oxford*, vol. 1, *The Early Oxford Schools*. Ed. Jeremy I. Catto. Oxford: Clarendon, 1984, 531–64.

Braekman, Willy, and Maurits Gysselling. "Het Utrechtse Kalendarium van 1253 met de Noordlimburgse gezondheidsregels," *Verslagen en Mededelingen der Koninklijke Vlaamsche Academie voor Taal- en Letterkunde* (1967), 575–635.

Brand, Paul A. "Aspects of the Law of Debt, 1189–1307." In *Credit and Debt in Medieval England c. 1180–c. 1350*. Ed. Phillipp R. Schofield and Nicholas J. Mayhew. Oxford: Oxbow Books, 2002, 19–41.

———. "Henry II and the Creation of the English Common Law." In *Henry II: New Interpretations*. Ed. Christopher Harper-Bill and Nicholas Vincent. Woodbridge, Suffolk: Boydell & Brewer, 2007, 215–41.

———. "The Age of Bracton." In *The History of English Law: Centenary Essays on "Pollock and Maitland."* Ed. John Hudson. Proceedings of the British Academy, 89. Oxford: Oxford University Press, for the British Academy, 1996, 65–89.

———. *The Origins of the English Legal Profession*. Oxford: Blackwell, 1992.

———. "The Rise and Fall of the Hereditary Steward in English Ecclesiastical Institutions, 1066–1300." In *Warriors and Churchmen in the High Middle Ages: Essays Presented to Karl Leyser*. Ed. Timothy Reuter. London: Hambledon, 1992, 145–62.

Brendler, Silvio. "Hareslade: A Note on Robert Carpenter's Place of Abode," *Notes and Queries* (March 2002), 12–13.

Brett, Martin. *The English Church Under Henry I*. London: Oxford University Press, 1975.

Britnell, Richard. "The Economy of British Towns, 600–1300." In *The Cambridge Urban History of Britain*, vol. 1, *600–1540*. Ed. David M. Palliser. Cambridge: Cambridge University Press, 2000, 105–26.

Britnell, Richard, and Bruce M. S. Campbell, eds. *A Commercialising Economy: England 1086 to c. 1300*. Manchester: Manchester University Press, 1995.

Brooke, Christopher N. L., assisted by Gillian Keir. *London, 800–1216: The Shaping of a City*. London: Secker and Warburg, 1975.

Brown, S. D. B. "Leavetaking: Lordship and Mobility in England and Normandy in the Twelfth Century," *History*, 79, no. 256 (June 1994), 199–215.

Brundage, James A. *Law, Sex and Christian Society in Medieval Europe*. Chicago: University of Chicago Press, 1987.

———. *The Medieval Origins of the Legal Profession: Canonists, Civilians, and Courts*. Chicago: University of Chicago Press, 2008.

———. *The Profession and Practice of Medieval Canon Law*. Aldershot, Hampshire: Ashgate, 2004.

Burger, Michael. "The Date and Authorship of Robert Grosseteste's *Rules for Household and Estate Management*," *Historical Research*, 74 (2001), 206–16.

Burrow, J. A., and Ian P. Wei, eds. *Medieval Futures: Attitudes to the Future in the Middle Ages*. Woodbridge, Suffolk: Boydell, 2000.

Cam, Helen M. *The Hundred and the Hundred Rolls*. London: Methuen, 1930.

Camargo, Martin. "The English Manuscripts of Bernard of Meung's *Flores Dictaminum*," *Viator*, 12 (1981), 197–219.

Cameron, Rondo, ed. *Essays in French Economic History*. Homewood, Ill.: Richard D. Irwin, for the American Economic Association, 1970.

Camille, Michael. "Illustrations in Harley MS 3487 and the Perception of Aristotle's *Libri naturales* in Thirteenth-Century England." In *England in the Thirteenth Century: Proceedings of the 1984 Harlaxton Symposium.* Ed. W. Mark Ormrod Woodbridge, Suffolk: Boydell & Brewer, 1985, 31–44.

Campbell, Bruce M. S. *English Seigneurial Agriculture, 1250–1450.* Cambridge: Cambridge University Press, 2000.

Campbell, James, ed. *The Anglo-Saxons.* London: Penguin, 1982.

Carlin, Martha. "Cheating the Boss: Robert Carpenter's Embezzlement Instructions (1261 × 1268), and Employee Fraud in Medieval England." In *Markets and Entrepreneurs in the Middle Ages: Essays in Honour of Richard Britnell.* Ed. Ben Dodds and Christian Liddy. Woodbridge, Suffolk: Boydell, 2011, 183–97.

———. "Fast Food and Urban Living Standards in Medieval England." In *Food and Eating in Medieval Europe.* Ed. Martha Carlin and Joel T. Rosenthal. London: Hambledon, 1998, 27–51.

———. "Shops and Shopping in the Early Thirteenth Century: Three Texts." In *Money, Markets and Trade in Late Medieval Europe: Essays in Honour of John H. A. Munro.* Ed. Lawrin Armstrong, Ivana Elbl, and Martin M. Elbl. Leiden: Brill, 2007, 491–537.

Carlin, Martha, and Joel T. Rosenthal, eds. *Food and Eating in Medieval Europe.* London: Hambledon, 1998.

Carpenter, David A. *The Minority of Henry III.* London: Methuen, 1990.

———. "What Happened in 1258?" In *War and Government in the Middle Ages: Essays in Honour of J. O. Prestwich.* Ed. John Gillingham and James C. Holt. Woodbridge, Suffolk: Boydell, 1984, 106–19.

Carus-Wilson, Eleanora M. "An Industrial Revolution of the Thirteenth Century," *Economic History Review,* 11, no. 1 (1941). Reprinted with a postscript in eadem, *Medieval Merchant Venturers: Collected Studies.* 2nd ed. London: Methuen, 1967, 183–210.

———. "The English Cloth Industry in the Late Twelfth and Early Thirteenth Centuries," *Economic History Review,* 14 (1944), 32–50. Reprinted in eadem, *Medieval Merchant Venturers: Collected Studies.* 2nd ed. London: Methuen, 1967, 211–38.

Catto, Jeremy I., ed. *The History of the University of Oxford,* vol. 1, *The Early Oxford Schools.* Oxford: Oxford University Press, 1984.

Charles-Edwards, Thomas M. "Kinship, Status and the Origins of the Hide," *Past & Present,* 56 (1972), 3–33.

Cheney, Mary. "The Litigation Between John Marshal and Archbishop Thomas Becket in 1164." In *Law and Social Change in British History.* Ed. John A. Guy and H. G. Beale. Royal Historical Society Studies in History, 40 (London, 1984), 9–26.

Chew, Helena M. *The English Ecclesiastical Tenants-in-Chief and Knight Service.* London: Oxford University Press, 1932.

Chorley, Patrick. "English Cloth Exports During the Thirteenth and Early Fourteenth Centuries: The Continental Evidence," *Historical Research,* 61, no. 144 (February 1988), 1–10.

Church, Stephen D., ed. *King John: New Interpretations.* Woodbridge: Boydell, 1999.

Clanchy, Michael T. *From Memory to Written Record: England, 1066–1307.* 2nd ed. Oxford: Blackwell, 1993.

Clark, D. "The Shop Within?: An Analysis of the Architectural Evidence for Medieval Shops," *Architectural History,* 43 (2000), 58–87.

Cobban, Alan. *English University Life in the Middle Ages.* London: UCL Press, 1999.

Collectanea Topographica et Genealogica, 2 (London, 1835).

Colvin, Howard M. "A Medieval Drawing of a Plough," *Antiquity,* 27, no. 107 (September 1953), 165–67.

Constable, Giles. "The Structure of Medieval Society According to the *Dictatores* of the Twelfth Century." In *Law, Church, and Society: Essays in Honor of Stephan Kuttner.* Ed. Kenneth Pennington and Robert Somerville. Philadelphia: University of Pennsylvania Press, 1977, 253–67.

Coss, Peter R. *The Origins of the English Gentry.* Cambridge: Cambridge University Press, 2003.

Coss, Peter R., and Simon D. Lloyd, eds. *Thirteenth Century England IV: Proceedings of the Newcastle Upon Tyne Conference 1991.* Woodbridge, Suffolk: Boydell, 1992.

Coulton, George Gordon. *Medieval Panorama: The English Scene from Conquest to Reformation.* Cambridge: Cambridge University Press, 1938; rpt. New York: Meridian Books, 1955.

Crawford, Anne. *A History of the Vintners' Company.* London: Constable, 1977.

Critchley, J. S. "Summonses to Military Service Early in the Reign of Henry III," *EHR,* 86 (1971), 79–95.

Crook, David, and Nicholas Vincent, eds. *Records, Administrations and Aristocratic Society in the Anglo-Norman Realm.* Woodbridge, Suffolk: Boydell, 2009.

Crouch, David. "The Administration of the Norman Earldom." In *The Earldom of Chester and Its Charters.* Ed. Alan T. Thacker. *Journal of the Chester Archaeological Society,* 71 (Chester, 1991), 69–95.

———. *The Beaumont Twins: The Roots and Branches of Power in the Twelfth Century.* Cambridge: Cambridge University Press, 1986.

———. "Between Three Realms: The Acts of Waleran II, Count of Meulan and Worcester." In *Records, Administrations and Aristocratic Society in the Anglo-Norman Realm.* Ed. David Crook and Nicholas Vincent. Woodbridge, Suffolk: Boydell, 2009, 75–90.

———. *The Birth of Nobility: Constructing Aristocracy in England and France, 900–1300.* London: Longman, 2005.

———. "The Culture of Death in the Anglo-Norman World." In *Anglo-Norman Political Culture and the Twelfth-Century Renaissance.* Ed. C. Warren Hollister. Woodbridge, Suffolk: Boydell & Brewer, 1997, 157–80.

———. "Death in Medieval Scarborough," *Yorkshire Archaeological Journal,* 72 (2000), 67–72.

———. *The English Aristocracy, 1070–1272: A Social Transformation.* New Haven: Yale University Press, 2011.

———. "From Stenton to McFarlane: Models of Societies of the Twelfth and Thirteenth Centuries." *Transactions of the Royal Historical Society,* 6th ser., 5 (1995), 179–200.

————. "Geoffrey de Clinton and Roger Earl of Warwick," *Bulletin of the Institute of Historical Research*, 55 (1982), 113–24.

————. *The Image of Aristocracy in Britain, 1000–1300*. London: Routledge, 1992.

————. "The March and the Welsh Kings." In *The Anarchy of King Stephen's Reign.* Ed. Edmund King. Oxford: Clarendon, 1994, 255–89.

————. *Tournament*. London: Hambledon, 2005.

————. *William Marshal: Knighthood, War and Chivalry, 1147–1219*. 2nd ed. London: Longman, 2002.

Crowley, D. A., ed. *Victoria History of the Counties of England, Wiltshire*, vol. 13, *South-West Wiltshire: Chalk and Dunworth Hundreds*. Oxford: Oxford University Press, for the Institute of Historical Research, 1987.

Dales, Richard C. *The Problem of the Rational Soul in the Thirteenth Century*. Leiden: E. J. Brill, 1995.

Daniell, Christopher. *Death and Burial in Medieval England, 1066–1550*. London: Routledge, 1997.

David, F. N. *Games, Gods and Gambling: The Origins and History of Probability and Statistical Ideas from the Earliest Times to the Newtonian Era*. New York: Hafner, 1962.

Davies, James Conway. *The Baronial Opposition to Edward II: Its Character and Policy.* Cambridge: Cambridge University Press, 1918.

Davies, Robert Rees. *The Age of Conquest: Wales, 1063–1415*. Oxford: Oxford University Press, 1987.

Davis, Ralph Henry Carless. *The Medieval Warhorse*. London: Thames & Hudson, 1989.

d'Avray, David. *Medieval Marriage: Symbolism and Society*. Oxford: Oxford University Press, 2005.

Denholm-Young, Noël. "Robert Carpenter and the Provisions of Westminster." *English Historical Review*, 50 (1935), 22–35. Reprinted in idem, *Collected Papers on Mediaeval Subjects*. Oxford: Basil Blackwell, 1946, 96–110. Also reprinted in idem, *Collected Papers*. Cardiff: University of Wales Press, 1969, 173–86.

————. *Seignorial Administration in England*. London: Oxford University Press, 1937.

Dent, Anthony Austen. "Chaucer and the Horse," *Proceedings of the Leeds Philosophical and Literary Society*, 9 (1959), 1–12.

Dobson, Barrie. "The Medieval York Jewry Reconsidered." In *Jews in Medieval Britain: Historical, Literary and Archaeological Perspectives*. Ed. Patricia Skinner. Woodbridge, Suffolk: Boydell, 2003, 145–56.

Dodds, Ben, and Christian Liddy. *Markets and Entrepreneurs in the Middle Ages: Essays in Honour of Richard Britnell*. Woodbridge, Suffolk: Boydell, 2011.

Dufournet, Jean, André Joris, and Pierre Toubert, eds. *Femmes, mariages-lignages: XIIe–XVIe siècles: mélanges offerts à Georges Duby*. Bibliothèque du Moyen Âge, 1. Brussels: De Boeck Université, 1992.

Dugdale, Sir William. *Monasticon Anglicanum*. Ed. John Caley, Henry Ellis, and Bulkeley Bandinel. 6 vols. in 8. London: Record Commission, 1817–30.

Dunbabin, Jean. *Captivity and Imprisonment in Medieval Europe, 1000–1300.* Basingstoke, Hampshire: Palgrave, 2002.

Dyer, Christopher. "The Consumption of Fresh-Water Fish in Medieval England." In *Medieval Fish, Fisheries and Fishponds in England.* Ed. Michael Aston. 2 vols. B[ritish] A[rchaeological] R[eports] British Series 182 (1988), 1:27–38.

Eaglen, R. J. "The Evolution of Coinage in Thirteenth Century England." In *Thirteenth Century England IV: Proceedings of the Newcastle Upon Tyne Conference 1991.* Ed. Peter R. Coss and Simon D. Lloyd. Woodbridge, Suffolk: Boydell, 1992, 15–24.

Emmison, Frederick G., and Roy Stevens, eds. *Tribute to an Antiquary: Essays Presented to Marc Fitch by Some of His Friends.* London: Leopard's Head Press, 1976.

English, Barbara. *The Lords of Holderness, 1086–1260.* Oxford: Hull University Press, 1979.

Finucane, Ronald C. "Sacred Corpse, Profane Carrion: Social Ideals and Death Rituals in the Later Middle Ages." In *Mirrors of Mortality: Studies in the Social History of Death.* Ed. Joachim Whaley. London: Europa, 1981, 40–60.

Fleckenstein, Josef, ed. *Das Ritterliche Turnier im Mittelalter: Beiträge zu einer vergleichenden Formen-und Verhaltensgeschichte des Rittertums.* Göttingen: Vandenhoeck & Ruprecht, 1985.

Francis, Alan David. *The Wine Trade.* London: Adam & Charles Black, 1972; rpt. New York: Harper and Row, 1973.

Fryde, Natalie. "How to Get on in England in the Thirteenth Century? Dietrich of Cologne, Burgess of Stamford." In *England and Europe in the Reign of Henry III (1216–1272).* Ed. Bjorn K. U. Weiler, with Ifor W. Rowlands. Aldershot, Hampshire: Ashgate, 2002, 207–13.

Galloway, James A. "Driven by Drink? Ale Consumption and the Agrarian Economy of the London Region, *c.* 1300–1400." In *Food and Eating in Medieval Europe.* Ed. Martha Carlin and Joel T. Rosenthal. London: Hambledon, 1998, 87–100.

García-Ballester, Luis, Roger French, Jon Arrizabalaga, and Andrew Cunningham, eds. *Practical Medicine from Salerno to the Black Death.* Cambridge: Cambridge University Press, 1994.

Gillingham, John. "Conquering the Barbarians: War and Chivalry in Twelfth-Century Britain," *Haskins Society Journal,* 4 (1992), 67–84.

———. "The Context and Purposes of Geoffrey of Monmouth's *History of the Kings of Britain,*" *Anglo-Norman Studies,* 13 (1990), 99–118.

———. "Royal Newsletters, Forgeries and English Historians: Some Links Between Court and History in the Reign of Richard I." In *La Cour Plantagenêt (1154–1204).* Ed. Martin Aurell. Poitiers: Centre d'Etudes Supérieures de Civilisation Médiévale, 2000, 171–86.

Gillingham, John, and James C. Holt, eds. *War and Government in the Middle Ages: Essays in Honour of J. O. Prestwich.* Woodbridge, Suffolk: Boydell, 1984.

Gil-Sotres, Pedro. "Derivation and Revulsion: The Theory and Practice of Medieval Phlebotomy." In *Practical Medicine from Salerno to the Black Death.* Ed. Luis García-Ballester, Roger French, Jon Arrizabalaga, and Andrew Cunningham. Cambridge: Cambridge University Press, 1994, 110–55.

Given, James Buchanon. *Society and Homicide in Thirteenth-Century England*. Stanford: Stanford University Press, 1977.

Given-Wilson, Chris, and Alice Curteis. *The Royal Bastards of Medieval England*. London: Routledge and Kegan Paul, 1984.

Gladitz, Charles. *Horse Breeding in the Medieval World*. Dublin: Four Courts, 1997.

Grant, Lindy, ed. *Medieval Art, Architecture and Archaeology in London*. British Archaeological Association Conference Transactions for the Year 1984 (1990).

Green, Judith A. *The Government of England under Henry I*. Cambridge: Cambridge University Press, 1986.

———. "The Last Century of Danegeld," *EHR*, 96 (1981), 241–58.

Hagger, Mark. "A Pipe Roll for 25 Henry I," *English Historical Review*, 122, no. 495 (2007), 133–40.

Harper-Bill, Christopher, and Nicholas Vincent, eds. *Henry II: New Interpretations*. Woodbridge, Suffolk: Boydell & Brewer, 2007.

Harriss, Gerald L., ed. *England in the Fifteenth Century*. Oxford: Oxford University Press, 1981.

Harte, Negley Boyd, and Kenneth G. Ponting, eds. *Cloth and Clothing in Medieval Europe: Essays in Memory of Professor E. M. Carus-Wilson*. Pasold Studies in Textile History, 2. London: Heinemann Educational Books, The Pasold Research Fund, 1983.

Harvey, Barbara. *Living and Dying in England, 1100–1540: The Monastic Experience*. Oxford: Oxford University Press, 1993.

Harvey, Paul D. A. "Agricultural Treatises and Manorial Accounting in Medieval England," *Agricultural History Review*, 20 (1972), 170–82.

———. "The English Inflation of 1180–1220," *Past and Present*, 61 (November 1973), 3–30; rpt. in Rodney Hilton, ed., *Peasants, Knights and Heretics: Studies in Medieval Social History*, Past and Present Publications (Cambridge: Cambridge University Press, 1976), 57–84.

———. "Manorial Accounts." In Robert Henry Parker and Basil S. Yamey, eds. *Accounting History: Some British Contributions*. Oxford: Clarendon, 1994, Chap. 3.

———. "Personal Seals in Thirteenth-Century England." In *Church and Chronicle in the Middle Ages: Essays Presented to John Taylor*. Ed. Ian Wood and Graham A. Loud. London: Hambledon, 1991, 117–27.

———. "*Rectitudines singularum personarum* and *Gerefa*," *EHR*, 108 (1993), 1–22.

Harvey, Ruth E., and Stephen Church, eds. *Medieval Knighthood V: Papers from the Sixth Strawberry Hill Conference, 1994*. Woodbridge, Suffolk: Boydell, 1995.

Haskins, Charles Homer. *Norman Institutions*. Harvard Historical Studies, 24. Cambridge, Mass.: Harvard University Press, 1918.

———. "The Latin Literature of Sport," *Speculum*, 2 (1927), 235–52.

———. "The Life of Medieval Students as Illustrated by Their Letters," *American Historical Review*, 3, no. 2 (January 1898), 203–29. Revised and expanded in idem, *Studies in Mediaeval Culture*. Oxford: Clarendon, 1929, Chap. 1.

Heiser, Richard R. "Castles, Constables and Politics in Late Twelfth-Century Governance," *Albion*, 32 (2000), 19–36.

Henisch, Bridget Ann. *Fast and Feast: Food in Medieval Society*. University Park: Pennsylvania State University Press, 1976.

Heslop, T. A. [Picture essay on peasant seals.] In Edmund King, *Medieval England, 1066–1485*. Oxford: Phaidon, 1988, 214–15.

Hey, David. "Yorkshire's Southern Boundary," *Northern History*, 37 (2000), 31–48.

Hickling, C. F. "Prior More's Fishponds," *Medieval Archaeology*, 15 (1971), 118–23.

Hicks, Michael. *Bastard Feudalism*. London: Longman, 1995.

Hillaby, Joe. "Jewish Colonisation in the Twelfth Century." In *The Jews in Medieval Britain: Historical, Literary and Archaeological Perspectives*. Ed. Patricia Skinner. Woodbridge, Suffolk: Boydell, 2003, 15–40.

Hilton, Rodney, ed. *Peasants, Knights and Heretics: Studies in Medieval Social History*. Past and Present Publications. Cambridge: Cambridge University Press, 1976.

Hoffmann, Richard C. *Fishers' Craft and Lettered Art: Tracts on Fishing from the End of the Middle Ages*. Toronto Medieval Texts and Translation, 12. Toronto: University of Toronto Press, 1997.

Hollister, C. Warren, ed. *Anglo-Norman Political Culture and the Twelfth-Century Renaissance*. Woodbridge, Suffolk: Boydell & Brewer, 1997.

———. "The Annual Term of Military Service in Medieval England," *Medievalia et Humanistica*, 13 (1960), 40–47.

———. "The Misfortunes of the Mandevilles," *History*, 58 (1973), 315–33.

Holmes, Urban Tigner, Jr. *Daily Living in the Twelfth Century, Based on the Observations of Alexander Neckam in London and Paris*. Madison: University of Wisconsin Press, 1952.

Holt, James C. "Feudal Society and the Family in Early Medieval England: IV. The Heiress and the Alien," *Transactions of the Royal Historical Society*, 5th ser., 35 (1985), 1–28.

———. *Magna Carta*. 2nd ed. Cambridge: Cambridge University Press, 1992.

———. *The Northerners*. Oxford: Clarendon, 1961.

———. *Robin Hood*. London: Thames & Hudson, 1989.

Holt, Richard. *The Mills of Medieval England*. Oxford: Basil Blackwell, 1988.

Homans, George C. *English Villages of the Thirteenth Century*. Cambridge, Mass.: Harvard University Press, 1941; rpt. New York: Norton, 1975.

Howell, Margaret. *Eleanor of Provence: Queenship in Thirteenth-Century England*. Oxford: Blackwell, 1998.

Hudson, John, ed. *The History of English Law: Centenary Essays on "Pollock and Maitland."* Proceedings of the British Academy, 89. Oxford: Oxford University Press, for the British Academy, 1996.

Jenkins, David, ed. *The Cambridge History of Western Textiles*. Cambridge: Cambridge University Press, 2003.

Jewell, Helen M. *English Local Administration in the Middle Ages*. Newton Abbot, Devon: David & Charles, and New York: Barnes and Noble, 1972.

Johns, Susan M. *Noblewomen, Aristocracy and Power in the Twelfth-Century Anglo-Norman Realm*. Manchester: Manchester University Press, 2003.

Jones, Michael, and Simon Walker, eds. *Private Indentures for Life Service in Peace and War, 1278–1476*. In *Camden Miscellany*, 32 (1994), 1–190.

Kealey, Edward J. *Harvesting the Air: Windmill Pioneers in Twelfth-Century England.* Berkeley: University of California Press, 1987.

Keefe, Thomas K. *Feudal Assessments and the Political Community Under Henry II and his Sons.* Berkeley: University of California Press, 1983.

Keene, Derek. "Issues of Water in Medieval London to *c.* 1300," *Urban History*, 28, no. 2 (2001), 161–79.

———. "London from the Post-Roman Period to 1300." In *The Cambridge Urban History of Britain*, vol. 1, *600–1540.* Ed. David M. Palliser. Cambridge: Cambridge University Press, 2000, 187–216.

———. "Shops and Shopping in Medieval London." In *Medieval Art, Architecture and Archaeology in London.* Ed. Lindy Grant. British Archaeological Association Conference Transactions for the Year 1984 (1990), 29–40.

———. "Wardrobes in the City: Houses of Consumption, Finance and Power." In *Thirteenth Century England, VII: Proceedings of the Durham Conference, 1997.* Ed. Michael Prestwich, Richard Britnell, and Robin Frame. Woodbridge, Suffolk: Boydell, 1999, 61–79.

———. *Winchester Studies*, vol. 2, *Survey of Medieval Winchester.* 2 vols. Oxford: Clarendon, 1985.

Kemp, Wolfgang. *The Narratives of Gothic Stained Glass.* Cambridge: Cambridge University Press, 1997.

Kerr, Julie. "The Open Door: Hospitality and Honour in Twelfth/Early Thirteenth-Century England," *History*, 87 (2002), 322–35.

King, Edmund. "Estate Records of the Hotot family." In idem, ed., *A Northamptonshire Miscellany*, Northamptonshire Record Society, 32 (Northampton, 1983), 1–58.

———. *Medieval England, 1066–1485.* Oxford: Phaidon, 1988.

Kleineke, Hannes. "Carleton's Book: William FitzStephen's 'Description of London' in a Late Fourteenth-Century Common-Place Book, *Historical Research*, 74 (2001), 117–26.

Koziol, Geoffrey. *Begging Pardon and Favor: Ritual and Political Order in Early Medieval France.* Ithaca, N.Y.: Cornell University Press, 1992.

Labarge, Margaret Wade. *A Baronial Household of the Thirteenth Century.* London: Eyre and Spottiswoode, 1965; rpt. New York: Barnes and Noble, 1966.

Lachaud, Frédérique. "An Aristocratic Wardrobe of the Late Thirteenth Century: The Confiscation of the Goods of Osbert de Spaldington in 1298," *Historical Research*, 67, no. 162 (February 1994), 91–100.

———. "Liveries of Robes in England, *c.* 1200–1330," *English Historical Review*, 111, no. 441 (April 1996), 279–98.

Langlois, Charles Victor. *La Vie en France au Moyen Âge, de la fin du XIIe au milieu du XIVe siècle, d'après des moralistes du temps.* Nouv. éd. 4 vols. Paris: Hachette, 1924–28.

Lawrence, Clifford Hugh, ed. *The English Church and the Papacy in the Middle Ages.* London: Burns & Oates, 1965.

———. *Medieval Monasticism.* 3rd ed. Harlow, Essex: Longman: 2001.

————. *St. Edmund of Abingdon.* Oxford: Oxford University Press, 1960.

Lewis, Christopher P., ed. *Anglo-Norman Studies*, 30. Woodbridge, Suffolk: Boydell, 2008.

————. "The Earldom of Surrey and the Date of Domesday Book," *Historical Research*, 63 (1990), 329–36.

Liebermann, Max. *The March of Wales, 1067–1300: A Borderland of Medieval Britain.* Cardiff: University of Wales Press, 2008.

Lloyd, Terrence H. *The English Wool Trade in the Middle Ages.* Cambridge: Cambridge University Press, 1977.

————. *The Movement of Wool Prices in Medieval England. Economic History Review Supplements*, 6 (1973).

LoPrete, Kimberly A. *Adela of Blois: Countess and Lord, c. 1067–1137.* Dublin: Four Courts, 2007.

Maddicott, John. *Simon de Montfort.* Cambridge: Cambridge University Press, 1994.

McGovern, John F. "The Hide and Related Land-Tenure Concepts in Anglo-Saxon England, A.D. 700–1100," *Traditio*, 28 (1972), 101–18.

McFarlane, K. Bruce. "Bastard Feudalism." Reprinted in *England in the Fifteenth Century*. Ed. Gerald L. Harriss. Oxford: Oxford University Press, 1981, 23–44.

Meekings, Cecil Anthony Francis. "More About Robert Carpenter of Hareslade," *English Historical Review*, 72 (1957), 260–69.

Michael, M. A. *Stained Glass of Canterbury Cathedral.* London: Scala, 2004.

Mitchell, Sydney Knox. *Studies in Taxation Under John and Henry III.* New Haven: Yale University Press, 1914.

Mokyr, Joel. *The Lever of Riches: Technological Creativity and Economic Progress.* New York : Oxford University Press, 1990.

Moore, Ellen Wedemeyer. *The Fairs of Medieval England: An Introductory Study.* Toronto: Pontifical Institute of Mediaeval Studies, 1985.

Morgan, Nigel. *Early Gothic Manuscripts.* 2 vols. In *A Survey of Manuscripts Illuminated in the British Isles*, 4. London and Oxford: Harvey Miller, 1982–1987.

Morris, Colin. "From Synod to Consistory: The Bishops' Courts in England, 1150–1250," *Journal of Ecclesiastical History*, 22 (1971), 115–23.

Morris, William Alfred. *The Medieval English Sheriff to 1300.* Manchester: Manchester University Press, 1927.

Mundill, Robin R. "Christian and Jewish Lending Patterns and Financial Dealings During the Twelfth and Thirteenth Centuries." In *Credit and Debt in Medieval England c. 1180–c. 1350.* Ed. Phillipp S. Schofield and Nicholas J. Mayhew. Oxford: Oxbow Books, 2002, 42–67.

Munro, John H. A. "The Anti-Red Shift: To the Dark Side: Colour Changes in Flemish Luxury Woollens, 1300–1550." In *Medieval Clothing and Textiles*, vol. 3. Ed. Robin Netherton and Gale R. Owen-Crocker. Woodbridge, Suffolk: Boydell, 2007, 56–66.

————. "Medieval Woollens: Textiles, Textile Technology and Industrial Organisation, *c.* 800–1500." In *The Cambridge History of Western Textiles.* 2 vols. Ed. David Jenkins. Cambridge: Cambridge University Press, 2003, 1:181–227.

Musset, Lucien. "Récherches sur les communautés de clercs seculiers," *Bulletin de la société des Antiquaires de Normandie*, 55 (1961, for 1959–60), 5–38.

Netherton, Robin, and Gale R. Owen-Crocker, eds. *Medieval Clothing and Textiles*, 3. Woodbridge, Suffolk: Boydell, 2007.

Norgate, Kate. *The Minority of Henry the Third*. London: Macmillan, 1912.

Oggins, Robin S. *The Kings and Their Hawks: Falconry in Medieval England*. New Haven: Yale University Press, 2004.

Origo, Iris. *The Merchant of Prato*. London: Jonathan Cape, 1957; rpt. Penguin, 1992.

Ormrod, W. Mark, ed. *England in the Thirteenth Century: Proceedings of the 1984 Harlaxton Symposium*. Woodbridge, Suffolk: Boydell & Brewer, 1985.

Oschinsky, Dorothea. "Medieval Treatises on Estate Accounting," *Economic History Review*, 17: 1 (1947), 52–61.

Page, Raymond Ian. "*Gerefa*: Some Problems of Meaning." In *Problems of Old English Lexicography: Studies in Memory of Angus Cameron*. Ed. Alfred Bammesberger. Regensburg: Pustet, 1985, 211–28.

Painter, Sidney. *Studies in the History of the English Feudal Barony*. Baltimore: The Johns Hopkins Press, 1943.

Palliser, David M., ed. *The Cambridge Urban History of Britain*, vol. 1, *600–1540*. Cambridge: Cambridge University Press, 2000.

Palliser, David M., T. R. Slater, and E. Patricia Dennison. "The Topography of Towns, 600–1300." In *The Cambridge Urban History of Britain*, vol. 1, *600–1540*. Ed. David M. Palliser. Cambridge: Cambridge University Press, 2000, 153–86.

Parker, Robert Henry, and Basil S. Yamey, eds. *Accounting History: Some British Contributions*. Oxford: Clarendon, 1994.

Pennington, Kenneth, and Robert Somerville, eds. *Law, Church, and Society: Essays in Honor of Stephan Kuttner*. Philadelphia: University of Pennsylvania Press, 1977.

Pollock, Sir Frederick, Bart., and Frederic William Maitland. *The History of English Law Before the Time of Edward I*. 2 vols. 2nd ed. Cambridge: Cambridge University Press, 1898.

Postan, Michael M. *Medieval Trade and Finance*. Cambridge: Cambridge University Press, 1973.

Poster, Carol, and Linda C. Mitchell, eds. *Letter-Writing Manuals and Instruction, from Antiquity to the Present: Historical and Bibliographic Studies*. Columbia: University of South Carolina Press, 2007.

Powicke, Sir Maurice. *The Thirteenth Century, 1216–1307*. 2nd ed. Oxford: Clarendon, 1962.

Powicke, Michael R. *Military Obligation in Medieval England*. Oxford: Clarendon, 1962.

Prestwich, Michael. *Armies and Warfare in the Middle Ages: The English Experience*. New Haven: Yale University Press, 1996.

Prestwich, Michael, Richard Britnell, and Robin Frame, eds. *Thirteenth Century England*, VII: *Proceedings of the Durham Conference, 1997*. Woodbridge, Suffolk: Boydell, 1999.

Pryce, Huw. "Negotiating Anglo-Welsh Relations: Llywelyn the Great and Henry III." In *England and Europe in the Reign of Henry III, 1216–1272*. Ed. Björn K. U. Weiler and Ifor W. Rowlands. Aldershot, Hampshire: Ashgate, 2002.

Pugh, Ralph B. *Imprisonment in Medieval England*. London: Cambridge University Press, 1968.

Purdie, Rhiannon. "Dice-Games and the Blasphemy of Prediction." In *Medieval Futures: Attitudes to the Future in the Middle Ages*. Ed. J. A. Burrow and Ian P. Wei. Woodbridge, Suffolk: Boydell, 2000, 167–84.

Rackham, Oliver. *Trees and Woodland in the British Landscape*. London: J. M. Dent, 1976.

Rawcliffe, Carole. *Medicine and Society in Late Medieval England*. Stroud, Gloucestershire: Sutton, 1995; rpt. London: Sandpiper, 1999.

Renouard, Yves. "The Wine Trade of Gascony in the Middle Ages." In *Essays in French Economic History*. Ed. Rondo Cameron. Homewood, Ill.: Richard D. Irwin, for the American Economic Association, 1970, 64–90. Originally published as "Le Grand commerce des vins de Gascogne au Moyen Age," *Revue historique*, 221 (1959), 261–304.

Reuter, Timothy, ed. *Warriors and Churchmen in the High Middle Ages: Essays Presented to Karl Leyser*. London: Hambledon, 1992.

Richardson, Henry Gerald. "An Oxford Teacher of the Fifteenth Century," *Bulletin of the John Rylands Library*, 23, no. 2 (1939), 436–57.

———. *The English Jewry Under Angevin Kings*. London: Methuen, 1960.

———. "Gervase of Blois, Abbot of Westminster." In idem, *The Governance of Medieval England*. Edinburgh: Edinburgh University Press, 1963, 413–21.

———. "The Oxford Law School Under John," *Law Quarterly Review*, 57 (1941), 319–38.

———. "The Schools of Northampton in the Twelfth Century," *EHR*, 56 (1941), 595–605.

Richardson, Henry Gerald, and George Osborne Sayles. "Early Coronation Records [Part I]," *Bulletin of the Institute of Historical Research*, 13 (1935–36), 129–45.

Richardson, Malcolm. "The *Ars dictaminis*, the Formulary, and Medieval Epistolary Practice." In *Letter-Writing Manuals and Instruction, from Antiquity to the Present: Historical and Bibliographic Studies*. Ed. Carol Poster and Linda C. Mitchell. Columbia: University of South Carolina Press, 2007, 52–66.

Rio, Alice. "Freedom and Unfreedom in Early Medieval Francia: The Evidence of Legal Formulae," *Past and Present*, 193 (2006), 7–40.

———. *The Formularies of Angers and Marculf: Two Merovingian Legal Handbooks*. Liverpool: Liverpool University Press, 2008.

———. *Legal Practice and the Written Word in the Early Middle Ages: Frankish Formulae, c. 500–1000*. Cambridge: Cambridge University Press, 2009.

Round, John Horace. *Feudal England*. London: Allen & Unwin, 1964.

———. "The Introduction of Knight Service into England." In idem, *Feudal England: Historical Studies on the XIth and XIIth Centuries*. London: Swan Sonnenschein, 1895, 225–314; rpt. London: Allen & Unwin, 1964, 182–245.

Rowlands, Ifor W. "King John and Wales." In *King John: New Interpretations*. Ed. Stephen D. Church. Woodbridge: Boydell, 1999, 273–87.

Salzman, Louis F. *Building in England Down to 1540*. Oxford: Clarendon, 1952; rpt. with corrections and additions, 1967.

Sanders, Ivor J. *English Baronies: A Study of Their Origin and Descent, 1086–1327*. Oxford: Clarendon, 1960.

———. *Feudal Military Service in England: A Study of the Constitutional and Military Powers of the* Barones *in Medieval England*. London: Oxford University Press, 1956.

Sayers, Jane E. *Papal Government and England During the Pontificate of Honorius III, 1216–1227*. Cambridge: Cambridge University Press, 1983.

———. *Papal Judges Delegate in the Province of Canterbury, 1198–1254: A Study in Ecclesiastical Jurisdiction and Administration*. London: Oxford University Press, 1971.

Scammell, Jean. "The Rural Chapter in England from the Eleventh to the Fourteenth Century," *EHR*, 86 (1971), 1–21.

Schofield, Phillipp R., and Nicholas J. Mayhew, eds. *Credit and Debt in Medieval England, c. 1180–c. 1350*. Oxford: Oxbow Books, 2002.

Skinner, Patricia, ed. *Jews in Medieval Britain: Historical, Literary and Archaeological Perspectives*. Woodbridge, Suffolk: Boydell, 2003.

Smith, D. Vance. *Arts of Possession: The Medieval Household Imaginary*. Minneapolis: University of Minnesota Press, 2003.

Southern, Richard W. "From Schools to University." In *The History of the University of Oxford*, vol. 1, *The Early Oxford Schools*. Ed. Jeremy I. Catto. Oxford: Oxford University Press, 1984, 1–36.

———. *Robert Grosseteste*. Oxford: Oxford University Press, 1986.

Spufford, Peter. *Money and Its Use in Medieval Europe*. Cambridge: Cambridge University Press, 1988.

Stacey, Robert C. "Jewish Lending and the Medieval English Economy." In *A Commercialising Economy: England 1086 to c. 1300*. Ed. Richard H. Britnell and Bruce M. S. Campbell. Manchester: Manchester University Press, 1995, 78–101.

———. *Politics, Policy and Finance Under Henry III, 1216–1245*. Oxford: Oxford University Press, 1987.

Staniland, Kay. "Provision and the Great Wardrobe in the Mid-Thirteenth Century," *Textile History*, 22, no. 2 (Autumn 1991), 239–52.

Steane, John M. *The Archaeology of Medieval England and Wales*. Athens: University of Georgia Press, 1985.

Steiner, Arpad. "The Vernacular Proverb in Mediaeval Latin Prose." *American Journal of Philology*, 65, no. 1 (1944), 37–68.

Stenton, Frank M. *The First Century of English Feudalism, 1066–1166*. 2nd ed. Oxford: Clarendon, 1961.

———. *The Free Peasantry of the Northern Danelaw*. Oxford: Clarendon, 1969.

Stephenson, David. *The Governance of Gwynedd*. Cardiff: University of Wales Press, 1984.

Stephenson, M. J. "Wool Yields in the Medieval Economy," *Economic History Review*, 2nd ser., 41, no. 3 (1988), 368–91.

Stones, Jeanne, and Lionel Stones. "Bishop Ralph Neville, Chancellor to King Henry III, and His Correspondence: A Reappraisal," *Archives*, 16, no. 71 (April 1984), 227–57.

Stringer, Keith J. *Earl David of Huntingdon: A Study in Anglo-Scottish History.* Edinburgh: Edinburgh University Press, 1985.

Summerson, Henry T., ed. *Crown Pleas of the Devon Eyre of 1238.* Devon and Cornwall Record Society, new ser., 28 (1985).

Taylor, Arnold. "Royal Alms and Oblations in the Later 13th Century: An Analysis of the Alms Roll of Edward I (1283–4)." In *Tribute to an Antiquary: Essays Presented to Marc Fitch by Some of His Friends.* Ed. Frederick G. Emmison and Roy Stevens. London: Leopard's Head Press, 1976, 93–125.

Thacker, Alan T., ed. *The Earldom of Chester and Its Charters. Journal of the Chester Archaeological Society*, 71 (1991).

Tout, Thomas Frederick. *Chapters in the Administrative History of Mediaeval England: The Wardrobe, the Chamber and the Small Seals.* 6 vols. Manchester: Manchester University Press, and London: Longman, 1920–33.

Townley, Simon. "Unbeneficed Clergy in the Thirteenth Century: Two English Dioceses." In *Studies in Clergy and Ministry in Medieval England*, Borthwick Studies in History, 1 (1991), 38–64.

Turcan-Verkerk, Anne-Marie. "Le *Liber artis omnigenum dictaminum* de Maître Bernard (vers 1145): états successifs et problèmes d'attribution," *Revue d'Histoire des Textes*, nouvelle série 5 (2010), 99–158 (Part 1); 6 (2011), 261–328 (Part 2).

Turner, Ralph V. "The *Miles Literatus* in Twelfth- and Thirteenth-Century England: How Rare a Phenomenon?" *American Historical Review*, 83 (1978), 928–65. Reprinted in idem, *Judges, Administrators and the Common Law in Angevin England.* London: Hambledon, 1994, 119–36.

Tuten, Belle S., and Billado, Tracey L., eds. *Feud, Violence and Practice: Essays in Medieval Studies in Honor of Stephen D. White.* Farnham, Surrey: Ashgate, 2010.

Uytven, Raymond van. "Cloth in Medieval Literature of Western Europe." In *Cloth and Clothing in Medieval Europe: Essays in Memory of Professor E. M. Carus-Wilson.* Ed. Negley Boyd Harte and Kenneth G. Ponting. Pasold Studies in Textile History, 2. London: Heinemann Educational Books, The Pasold Research Fund, 1983, 151–83.

Veale, Elspeth M. *The English Fur Trade in the Later Middle Ages.* 2nd ed. London Record Society, 38 (2003).

Vincent, Nicholas. "Hugh de Neville and His Prisoners," *Archives*, 20 (1992), 190–97.

———. *Peter des Roches.* Cambridge: Cambridge University Press, 1996.

———. "William Marshal, King Henry II and the Honour of Châteauroux," *Archives*, 25 (2000), 1–15.

Voigts, Linda E., and Michael R. McVaugh. "A Latin Technical Phlebotomy and Its Middle English Translation," *Transactions of the American Philosophical Society*, 74, part 2 (1984), 1–69.

Walker, Ron F. "Hubert de Burgh and Wales, 1218–32," *EHR*, 87 (1972), 465–94.

Walker, Sue Sheridan. "Free Consent and Marriage of Feudal Wards in Medieval England," *Journal of Medieval History*, 8 (1982), 123–34.

Waugh, Scott L. "Marriage, Class and Royal Lordship in England Under Henry III," *Viator*, 16 (1985), 181–208.

———. *The Lordship of England: Royal Wardships and Marriages in English Society and Politics, 1217–1327*. Princeton, N.J.: Princeton University Press, 1988.

Weiler, Bjorn K. U., ed., with Ifor W. Rowlands. *England and Europe in the Reign of Henry III (1216–1272)*. Aldershot, Hampshire: Ashgate, 2002.

Whaley, Joachim, ed. *Mirrors of Mortality: Studies in the Social History of Death*. London: Europa, 1981.

Wightman, William E. *The Lacy Family in England and Normandy, 1066–1194*. Oxford: Clarendon, 1966.

Wood, Diana, ed. *Medieval Money Matters*. Oxford: Oxbow Books, 2004.

Wood, Ian, and Graham A. Loud, eds. *Church and Chronicle in the Middle Ages: Essays Presented to John Taylor*. London: Hambledon, 1991.

Woolgar, Christopher M. *The Great Household in Late Medieval England*. New Haven: Yale University Press, 1999.

Worstbrock, Franz Josef. "Die Anfänge der mittelalterlichen Ars dictandi," *Frühmittelalterliche Studien*, 23 (1989), 1–42.

Young, Charles. *The Royal Forests of Medieval England*. Philadelphia: University of Pennsylvania Press, 1979.

Zimmermann, Michel. *Ecrire et lire en Catalogne: ixe–xiie siècle*. 2 vols. Madrid: Casa de Velázquez, Madrid, 2003.

GENERAL INDEX

Hugh of Avalon (St.), bishop of Lincoln, 7, 65, 176, 177
Hugh of Wells, bishop of Lincoln, 176
Hull, Yorkshire, 34
Huntingdon, 189–90; earl of, *see* David II, John le Scot; prior of St. Mary, 67
Huntingdonshire, 185, 189

Innocent III, pope, 5, 11, 12, 163, 178
Inquest of Sheriffs (1170), 230
Ireland, 126
Isaac Judeus, 76
Isabel of England, daughter of King John, empress, 6, 11, 125–26, 127, 130
Isabel of Angoulême, queen of England, 238
Isabel de Warenne, countess of Surrey, 211
Isabel, countess of Pembroke, 201, 234
Isabel, daughter of Thomas of Woodstock, 224
Italy, 3, 61

Jacques de Vitry, bishop of Acre, 50, 263
Jakemes, 215
Jean Bodel of Arras, 263
Jean de Joinville, 234
Joan, daughter of King John, princess of Gwynedd, 118
Joanna de Cornhill, 201
John, bishop of Bath, 234
John, king of England, xxiv, 9, 11, 12, 29, 30, 32, 36, 37, 45, 50, 65, 100, 107, 112, 114, 115, 118, 122, 123–24, 128, 132, 133, 138, 141, 154, 159, 227, 232, 238
John de Kirkby, bishop of Ely and treasurer of England, 67, 244
John, priest of Kirkby Lonsdale, 80
John de Lacy, constable of Chester and earl of Lincoln, 208
John de Warenne, earl of Surrey, 190
John de Lascelles, 146
John le Scot, earl of Huntingdon and Chester, 190
John Mansel, treasurer of York, 73
John Marshal I (fitz Gilbert), 106, 110
John Marshal II, 109–10, 227,
John of Garlande, 222
John of Marbury, 88
John of Salisbury, 195
Jordan Fantosme, 162
Joseph, Biblical patriarch, 79, 220, 221

Kenilworth, Warwickshire, 192
King's Lynn, Norfolk, 37, 60, 65

La Rochelle, Saintonge, 36
Labarge, Margaret Wade, xvii
Lancelot, 215
Languedoc, 203
Lateran Council (1215), 178–79, 196
Lawrence del Brok, king's attorney, 155
Leicester, 60, 65; castle of, 86; earls of, *see* Robert I, Robert II, Robert III
Leighton Buzzard, 139
Lewes, Sussex, 190
Lincoln, 43, 146; bishops of, 180, 232, *see also* Hugh of Avalon, Hugh of Wells, Robert Grosseteste; countess of, *see* Margaret de Lacy; dean and chapter of, 260; diocese of, 171; earls of, *see* Edmund de Lacy, John de Lacy
Lincolnshire, 136, 169
Llywelyn ab Iorwerth (the Great), prince of Gwynedd, 8, 117–18, 122
Loire Valley, France, 4
London, 9, 34, 38, 42, 50, 55–56, 59, 60, 65, 89, 108, 149, 151, 174; archdeacon of, *see* Peter of Blois; archdeaconry of, 227; cathedral church of St. Paul, 151, 270; Cheapside, 55; Clerkenwell priory, 56; conflagrations in, 55; council of (1237), 80; mint of, xxiv, 39; Skinners' Company, 52
Loos, count of, 162
Louis VIII, king of France, 9–10, 240
Louis IX, king of France, 266
Luffield, priory of St. Mary, 141

Mabel, daughter of Earl William of Gloucester, 37
Mabel de Francheville, 153
Magna Carta (1215), 9, 76, 114, 123–24, 125, 132, 133–34, 135–36, 185
Magna Carta (1217), 10, 136
Magna Carta (1225), 10–11, 124, 136
Magna Carta of Cheshire, 133, 135
March of Wales, 8, 118, 121–22; barons of, 102, 120, 121–22,
Margaret de Lacy, countess of Lincoln, 166–67, 170, 208
Margaret Plantagenet, countess of Norfolk, 89
Marlborough, Wiltshire, 39, 47, 65, 109
Mathieu de Boulogne, 239
Matilda de Auberville, 20
Matthew Paris, xxiv, 130, 135, 231
Mauger monk of Luffield, 142
Mauger of Ripon, priest, 181
McFarlane, K. Bruce, 163
Mercia, 116

SUBJECT INDEX

abbot (*abbas*), 175
account (*compotum*), xvi, 6, 85–98, 167;
    dietary, xvi; household, 92; specimen,
    90–91; travel, 92
acre (*acra*), 27
address, 14; formal, 15–16; plural, 15–16
administration, estate, 158–60
adultery (*adulterium*), 222–32
affinity, 69, 163, 209, 217
agent (*cliens*), 15, 160
agreement (*conventio*), 27
aid (*auxilium*), 125, 129
ale (*cervisia, servisia*), 73, 92–93, 286
aliens, foreigners, 135
allegiance (*ligancia*), 127
alms (*elemosina*), 95
amercement, 114
annuities, 67
Annunciation of the Virgin, feast of (25
    March), 29
archbishop (*archiepiscopus*), 150
archdeacon (*archidiaconus*), 79, 150, 177–79,
    184, 225, 229, 230
archdeaconry (*archidiaconatus*) 225
arms (*arma*), 99, 105, 120
army service (*exercitus*), 106
arrears (*reragium*), 32
assize, grand, 157
attorney (*attornatus*), 155, 156

bacon (*baco*), 96–97
badger, 193
bailiff (*ballivus, famulus*), 2, 90, 137, 144, 165–
    66, 172
banner (*vexillum*), 201–2
barbel (*barbellus*), 92–93
barn (*horreus*), 172, 266, 286, 289

baron (*baro*), 119, 124, 128, 191, 196, 197, 201,
    216, 218
barony. *See* honor
barrel, cask (*cadus*), 73
basin (*pelvis*), 92–93
beadle (*bedellus*), 90
beam (*trabs*), 257–58
bed (*thalamus*), 222, 224
bedlinen, 242–43
beef (*bos*), 96–97
Bible, 2
bird dogs, 194
bishop (*episcopus, pontifex*), 79, 82, 128, 150,
    230
blood-letting. *See* phlebotomy
boar, 193
board (*tigna*), 257–58
bond-trading, 65
boon-works (*precature*), 27
brachet (*brachius*), 191
broadcloth. *See* cloth
building materials, 55
burel cloth, 60
buttery, 94

calendar, Roman, 30
campaign (*expeditio*), 106, 121
carpenter (*carpentarius*), 23, 280, 283–84, 288
cauldron (*cacabus*), 92–93
celibacy, 232
chamber (*camera*), 92–93, 288–89
chaplain, junior cleric (*capellanus*), 177–80,
    182–83, 230, 231
charge, mounted (*estor*), 202
cheese, (*caseus*), 169
chivalry, knightliness (*militia*), 201, 205
Christmas (*natale*), 27, 31, 193
clergy of England, 128–30

fulling, 47; mill, 31
funeral (*exequie*), 108
fur, 45, 48–50, 54, 269. *See also* vair, miniver

gamester, gambler, dice-player (*aliator*), 182–83, 262–63
geld, (*geldum*), 157
girdle (*zona*), 222, 223, 224
Glanvill, legal tract, 109, 156, 157
God's penny (token sum), 58
gold, xxiii
goose (*auca*), 286–87
goshawk (*hostorius*), 191, 196–98
gout (*gutta*), 213–14
grain (*bladum*), 77–79, 123, 105, 168, 266
grange (*grangia*), 286, 289
gray cloth, 60
grayhound (*leporarius*), 191, 194
gridiron (*craticulus*), 92–93
gyrfalcon, 194–95, 196–97

halfpenny (*obolum*), xxiii
hare, 193
harvest (*messis*), 77–79, 266–68
harvest-time, 28, 124
hauberk, mail coat, 47
hawker, 198
hawking, 194–95, 197–201
hay (*fenum*), 92–93
hayward, 170
health regimen, 74–76
herring (*alleca*), 92–93, 269
hide, land assessment, 157
holidays, per annum, 64
homicide, 138–39
honor (appreciation), 41, 147, 201, 204, 221, 259
honor (baronial estate), 103, 104, 106, 207
horse (*equus*), 68, 99, 105, 120, 159, 289. *See also* cob, destrier, palfrey, sumpter
horse trappings (*cooperte*), 216–17
hospitality, 80–81, 83
hostage, pledge (*obses*), 113
house (*domus*), 172, 173, 261, 270
house fire, 54–55
housebreaking, 270–73
household, aristocratic or military (*familia*), 117–18, 286; size of, 80–81
household department (*officinum*), 92–93
household officers, 14, 138, 168
household servant (*famulus*), 105
humors. *See* elements

hundred (*hundredum*), 115–16, 144–45, 147, 150
hunting, 185–88, 191–201

illegitimacy, 180–81
impetration, 151
incumbent of ecclesiastical benefice (*persona*), 79, 82, 175
inflation, monetary, 167
innumeracy, 96–97

jail (*carcer*) 184; jail breaks, 113–15
Jewry (*judaismus*), 64, 65
Jews, 58, 63–68, 71; expulsion of (1290) 67
Jews, Exchequer of, 66
joust, 202
judges delegate, papal, 151, 152
jurisdiction, bailiwick (*balliva*), 137, 189
justices, justices in eyre, 139, 156

King's Bench, court of, 154, 155
kinsman (*cognatus*), 261, 262
kitchen (*coquina*), 92–93
knife (*cultellus*), 92–93
knight (*miles, eques*), 14, 52, 99, 106, 119, 128, 130–31, 135–36, 172, 197, 207, 210, 215, 219, 241, 271–73, 274, 278, 280, 286, 288, 289; daily wage of, 107; fee of, 126–27; fellow-knight (*commilito*) 135, 201–2, 218
knighthood (*militia*), 201–2
knightliness. *See* chivalry

laborer, workman (*operarius*), 64, 283, 288
Lady Day. *See* Annunciation
lamb (*agnus*), 96–97
lambskin (*agnelinus*), 48
lanner falcon (*lannarius*), 191, 195
largesse, generosity, liberality, 3, 41
law, canon 12; Roman, 12. *See also* common law
lawsuit (*causa, lis*), 153, 175
lawyers, canon, 151
layperson (*laicus*), 177
legacy, 150
legitimacy, 150, 180
Lent, 78
letters (*littere, petitorie*) 1, 14, 15–17, 38, 53, 54, 92–93, 101, 135, 149, 173, 183, 254, 272, 278. *See also* dictamen
letters of orders, 179–80, 182–84
letter-writing, art of. *See* dictamen
liberality. *See* largesse
liberties, baronial, 191

ACKNOWLEDGMENTS

We are grateful to the British Library for permission to publish this material from Add. 8167; to the Bodleian Library, University of Oxford, for permission to publish extracts from Fairfax 27; to the Master and Fellows of Corpus Christi College, Cambridge, for permission to publish extracts from MS 297; to the Master and Fellows of Gonville and Caius College, Cambridge, for permission to publish extracts from MS 205/111; and to the Walters Art Museum, Baltimore, Maryland, for permission to publish extracts from MS W. 15.

We are also grateful to the following for permission to reproduce images: The Bodleian Library, Oxford (Frontispiece); The British Library, London (Fig. 9); Cambridge University Library (Fig. 16); Canterbury Cathedral (Fig. 8); The Fitzwilliam Museum, Cambridge (Fig. 1); The Master and Fellows of Corpus Christi College, Cambridge (Fig. 10); The Morgan Library and Museum, New York (Figs. 13, 15); The National Archives, London (Fig. 6); Dr. Stuart Whatling, www.medievalart.org.uk (Figs. 2, 3, 4, 5, 7, 11, 12, 14).

We offer grateful acknowledgments to the University of Wisconsin–Milwaukee, the University of Hull, the British Academy, and the American Philosophical Society for generous financial assistance for this project.

We owe special thanks to Caroline Barron, who kindly read and commented on a substantial portion of this book in draft. We also gratefully acknowledge the generous assistance and advice of many friends and colleagues, including Martin Allen, Andrew Ayton, the late John Barron, Paul Brand, David Carpenter, David d'Avray, Faye Getz Cook, Anne DeWindt, Barbara Harvey, Julian Haseldine, Paul Hyams, Maryanne Kowaleski, Richard Leson, Richard Monti, Susan Reynolds, Richard Sharpe, Robert Stacey, Nicholas Vincent, Linda Ehrsam Voigts, and Stuart Whatling. We are also grateful for the comments and suggestions of the anonymous readers for the University of Pennsylvania Press of the draft proposal and manuscript of this volume. Any errors that remain in the text are ours alone.